principles of management

a decision-making approach

principles of
management

a decision-making approach

Robert C. Ford

Cherrill P. Heaton

University of North Florida

Reston Publishing Company, Inc., Reston, Virginia
A Prentice-Hall Company

Library of Congress Cataloging in Publication Data

Ford, Robert Clayton.
  Principles of management.

  Includes bibliographical references and index.
  1. Management—Decision making. I. Heaton,
Cherrill P., joint author. II. Title.
HD30.23.F67   658.4   79-25127
ISBN 0-8359-5593-1

© **1980 by**
Reston Publishing Company, Inc.
A Prentice-Hall Company
Reston, Virginia 22090

10 9 8 7 6 5 4 3 2 1

Printed in the United States of America

to

Barbara and Loren Ford

and

Paul N. Heaton
Administrative Officer, Retired
U.S. National Park Service

contents

preface

This book is designed for use in the first undergraduate management course. The student does not need any special background to use the book successfully.

The book should also be useful in management training courses offered to industry personnel, governmental agencies, health care organizations, and other groups outside the academic setting. The book's decision-making approach, its coverage, and its wide variety of examples and cases will be relevant for organizations of many kinds.

The book is divided into five parts. Part One reviews the historical background of the managerial task and explains the importance of goals to organizational success. Parts Two and Three are about making and implementing decisions. Using the problem-solving process as its organizational framework, Part Two deals with problem identification, evaluating alternative solutions, making the decision, and then implementing it. Part Three expands on the implementation phase of the decision-making process.

Part Four takes the general decision-making principles developed in the first three parts and relates them to the five functional areas comprising the managerial task: planning, organizing, staffing, directing, and controlling. Part Five covers three evolving topics in management: organizational development, social responsibility, and international management.

We think the book has two primary advantages. First, its decision-making approach gives it a focus that most principles of management books do not have. Second, we have tried to make the book as readable and interesting as possible.

For his comments on an early draft, we would like to thank John Newstrom. We also appreciate the comments of our University of North Florida colleagues in the Management Department. The management students who critiqued a preliminary draft offered many good suggestions. Tom McWhirter provided valuable special support services.

Robert C. Ford
Cherrill P. Heaton

part one

an introduction to management

Part One contains two chapters. Chapter 1 offers a chronological view of the management field from prehistoric times to the present. Chapter 2 discusses the importance of goals to the organization's success.

management:
the historical background

What is management? Many answers to that question are available. For example:

Management is decision making.

Management is responsibility for results.

Management is effective communications.

Management is getting work done through people.

Management is the process of planning, organizing, staffing, directing, and controlling to reach organizational goals.

Management is coordinating the accomplishment of organizational goals with individual and group goals.

Most of these definitions are general enough to include the broad range of activities, tasks, and responsibilities associated with the managerial task. However, their very generality may frustrate the student seeking to pin down the scope and domain of "management."

This introductory chapter will review the historical development of the management field. The logic underlying various definitions of management will be explained. The review will be chronological—from prehistoric times to the present—to show how technological, social, economic, and political changes have influenced the development of management concepts.

After showing how management concepts have evolved over the course of time, the chapter concludes with a specific, simple model that binds together the broad and diverse definitions of the management field and the managerial task. This model provides the framework on which the book is organized.

PERVASIVENESS OF MANAGEMENT IN HISTORY

Prehistoric Examples

Even cave dwellers needed a process for securing and enforcing cooperation to reach commonly shared goals. So basic an activity as having the children necessary to carry on a family unit required some elements of management. Initial cooperation was followed by a division of labor between the person giving birth and caring for the young cave dweller and the person supplying the family's wants.

For primitive social groups to coexist and survive, more complex patterns of cooperation, division of labor, and authority relationships somehow had to be established. Hunting, growing food, and defending against attack were group efforts. Someone had to develop a management structure, interpret and specify the collective goal, make decisions, organize the group's skills, plan, direct, and review the group's results. Primitive managerial concepts evolved over time, and those social groups survived that were effectively managed.

Early Historical Example: The Pyramids

History continually demonstrates the ability of people to develop new concepts in response to new social needs and technological advances. The early Egyptians displayed incredible construction skills in their building of the pyramids. For example, the Great Pyramid of Cheops covers 13 acres and contains 2,300,000 stone blocks weighing an average of 2.5 tons apiece. Over 100,000 men worked for 20 years to build the pyramid.

In addition to construction skills, pyramid building required sophisticated managerial concepts. Great quantities of stone had to be quarried, shaped, moved, and placed properly. Managers had to plan, organize work teams, coordinate the men and the material, provision and support this vast work force, and keep everyone heading toward the common goal. How many modern-day construction firms would have enough confidence in their managerial expertise to bid on such a project?

Pre-1900 Developments

The Arsenal of Venice. The modern assembly-line, mass-production technique commonly credited to Henry Ford's process for building the Model T can be seen as far back as the mid-1400s. The city-state of Venice developed a shipbuilding facility covering 60 acres and employing between 1000 and 2000 workers. Although the ships were rather small by present-day warship standards—approximately 100 feet long—they were the standard fighting ships of the day.

These vessels were produced in an assembly-line fashion. An unfinished and unprovisioned vessel was towed past a series of warehouses stocked with the equipment necessary to complete and outfit a battle-ready vessel. As the ship passed by the long warehouse area, the arms and equipment were placed on board in the proper outfitting sequence. At one point, the Arsenal prepared 100 ships for battle in about 75 days. In a demonstration for Henry III of France in 1574, the Arsenal assembled, launched, and completely armed a warship in one hour.

To produce at such incredible levels, the Arsenal needed superb management skills to match its assembly-line techniques. Inventory procedures kept the necessary number and kind of ship parts on hand and accessible. Personnel practices were needed to hire, train, supervise, evaluate, and pay all levels of personnel. Standardization of parts allowed the assembly-line procedures to flow smoothly, without the delays of hand-fitting parts to a particular ship. Finally, cost-accounting techniques kept control over the thousands of parts and people required to build the ships. The Arsenal displayed amazing management skill in a time without courses or textbooks on the topic.

EMERGENCE OF MANAGEMENT AS A SEPARATE DISCIPLINE

Adam Smith's *The Wealth of Nations*

In 1776 Adam Smith (1723–1790) wrote *The Wealth of Nations.* Although this book focused primarily on economic and political matters, it also contributed to management theory by graphically describing the effects on production that division of labor (or specialization) could have. Specialization had long been recognized as a useful concept, but never had it been written about so forcefully. Here is Smith's famous pin-making illustration:

> A workman not educated to this business (which the division of labor has rendered a distinct trade), nor acquainted with the use of the machinery employed in it (to the invention of which the same division of labor has probably given occasion), could scarce, perhaps, with his utmost industry, make one pin in a day, and certainly could not make twenty. But in the way in which this business is now carried on, not only the whole work is a peculiar trade, but it is divided into a number of branches, of which the greater part are likewise peculiar trades. One man draws out the wire, another straights it, a third cuts it, a fourth points it, a fifth grinds it at the top for receiving the head; to make the head requires two or three distinct operations; to put it on is a peculiar business, to whiten the pins is another; it is even a trade by itself to put them into the paper; and the important business of making a pin is, in this manner, divided into about eighteen distinct operations, which, in some manufactories, are all performed by distinct hands, though in others the same man will sometimes perform two or three of them. I have seen a small manufactory of this kind where ten men only were employed, and where some of them consequently performed two or three dis-

tinct operations. But though they were very poor, and therefore but indifferently accommodated with the necessary machinery, they could, when they exerted themselves, make among them about twelve pounds of pins in a day.[1]

Philosophical and Technological Developments

This line of thinking emerged simultaneously with several other developments. Machine-based production factories grew out of the industrial revolution, and a new independence arose out of the American Revolution. All of these ideas came together to create an acceptance of the notion that productive efficiency should be sought through the application of managerial effectiveness. The social system was ripe for accepting the concept of productive enterprise and readily endorsed any idea for increasing the efficiency of industry in transforming raw materials into finished products.

The unique dovetailing of social and religious philosophy with technical capability led to eager acceptance and application of Adam Smith's notion of "comparative advantage." Everyone was encouraged to maximize their own gains, which would lead in turn to everyone's gain. Through the market mechanism of capitalism, the impersonal forces of the market directed economic rewards and punishments, ensuring that, while everyone acted to maximize their own welfare, they would be automatically maximizing society's welfare.

Market Impersonality. The impersonality of the market regulated man's natural greedy tendencies. This notion marked an important break from the pre-industrial revolution era. Formerly, the craftsman worked independently. Knowing more about production than marketing, he humbly accepted small monetary tokens of appreciation for products of skilled craftsmanship. Once the impersonal forces of supply and demand began to set the price, skilled craftsmen became more highly rewarded than the less skilled. With the surplus monies earned, they could hire other men and buy equipment to produce more, to obtain more revenues, and consequently to grow.

Effect on Management

The expansion of the market system and the change in societal norms and values represented in Smith's book were instrumental in the development of management as a discipline. Before the industrial revolution, the technical skills of independent craftsmen were sufficient. As enterprises grew in size, the need for productive efficiency also grew, and managerial skills became required. Necessity is so often the mother of invention, and much of today's

[1]Adam Smith, *The Wealth of Nations*, Book I (Chicago: Henry Regnery Company, 1953), pp. 8–9.

management theory grew out of the problems and opportunities associated with the industrial revolution and the market system.

The Soho Foundry.   As time went on and organizations grew, other manager-ial concepts evolved. Early industrialists experimented with various produc-tion concepts and supervisory ideas in the quest for efficiency. The Soho Engineering Foundry in England, originally founded to build James Watt's steam engine, is an example. This 1800 foundry used forecasting, production planning, machine layout studies, site location planning, standardized com-ponents, cost-accounting systems, work-incentive programs, and training programs.

New Lanark.   At about the same time, a second progressive industrial organi-zation appeared in Scotland. The New Lanark Mills are frequently cited in history books and sociology texts as an early example of a socially responsible company. New Lanark represented an experimental test of Robert Owen's (1771–1858) social beliefs and managerial philosophy that a worker's output was influenced by the work environment. That notion, commonplace to us, was radical at the time. In this New Lanark experiment, workers were pro-vided with good housing, schooling for children, and recreation centers. By creating this positive environment for the worker, New Lanark became highly profitable.

   Although it attracted some attention and eventually influenced the di-rection of factory reform legislation, New Lanark was rarely imitated. Most employers continued to ignore the human factor and to treat their workers as animate machines. Soho and New Lanark were ahead of their time.

Eli Whitney.   Other production and management illustrations show the si-multaneous evolution of managerial practice and social philosophy. A famous example is Eli Whitney (1765–1825) and his successful development of an interchangeable-parts production procedure for his patented invention, the cotton gin. At first, Whitney was frequently frustrated by people sneaking into his plant and stealing parts from partially completed machines. Since every machine was hand crafted, he had to take precious time to go back and refit the missing part into the machine. After some time, Whitney started making his parts to standardized dimensions so that he could easily replace lost, broken, or stolen parts.

   This development, although not unique to him, allowed Whitney in 1798 to get a government contract for supplying muskets. His assembly-line, interchangeable-parts technique enabled him to produce musketry more effi-ciently than anyone else. Interchangeable parts were an important develop-ment in warfare. A weapon could be repaired instantly on the battlefield, eliminating the need to have a blacksmith available for custom fitting of bro-ken musket parts. Standardized musket parts greatly increased the efficiency of soldiers.

The Scientific School

The Whitney example represents the evolution of management as a reflection of developing social norms and values. The age of reason had dawned. Statistics and the scientific method had been accepted. All areas of knowledge saw explosive growth in the discovery and verification of scientific principles. Results achieved by studying physical phenomena in a controlled environment while holding external factors constant were the pride of the sciences and the envy of people seeking universal truths in other disciplines. So much could apparently be learned by rigid application of the scientific method that all persons wishing to sound seriously concerned with advancing knowledge had to include the scientific mystique in their writings and speeches.

Frederick Taylor.   Frederick Winslow Taylor (1856–1915) represents this trend. Taylor, frequently called the father of scientific management, best articulated the cumulative thinking about management at a time when industrial organizations needed a codified body of knowledge developed through scientific methods. Many of Taylor's ideas can be traced back to the writings of Charles Babbage, W. S. Jevons, and other nineteenth-century thinkers. But by virtue of his experiences and training, Taylor was able to make a forceful and complete argument for using scientific procedures in solving the management problems of the evolving mass production industries.

The young Taylor showed the inquisitive mind that would later be reflected in his career. Taylor played baseball and tennis. At that time, baseball was a relatively new sport played with underhand pitching. Taylor felt that this pitching style was a poor use of the human body. He studied the physiological mechanics involved and pioneered overhand pitching for the game. In a similar effort to "find a better way," a phrase that has come to be associated with him, Taylor also developed a curved tennis racket to improve player control of the ball. To Taylor, hitting a round object with a flat surface was obviously inefficient and ineffective. Taylor's tennis innovation has not stood the test of time.

Although admitted to Harvard, Taylor chose not to go because his eyes had started to fail and he needed glasses. At that time, people requiring glasses were thought to be incapable of finishing a rigorous college program. Taylor was advised to do something else. Taylor's desire to find a better way carried over into his career with Midvale Steel. Beginning in 1879 he rose quickly from laborer to chief engineer in 1884 at the age of 28. He published his first work on management in 1895.

In 1898, Taylor went to work for the Bethlehem Steel Works. In 1899, he convinced Bethlehem Steel to allow him to experiment with men loading pig iron onto freight cars. Each pig of iron weighed 92 pounds, and the men were loading an average of 12.5 long tons per day (2240 pounds to the long ton). Taylor specially selected and trained a worker who he called "Schmidt."

Through scientific investigation and analysis of the job, Taylor decided that if Schmidt worked 43 percent of the time and rested 57 percent of the time, he should be able to load 47 long tons a day. On the first day, Schmidt loaded 47.5 long tons. The Bethlehem Steel management quickly became enthusiastic about Taylor's ideas.

Taylor's Principles.   Taylor is famous for a number of innovative managerial developments, including functional foremanship, standardization of tools, differential pay incentive programs, and management by exception. However, his major contribution was the popularization and packaging of *scientific management.* By 1911, Taylor had formalized the principles of scientific management into four simple categories:

1. "Develop a science for each element of a man's work, which replaces the old rule-of-thumb method." Primarily by means of scientific study, analyze the job to find the best way of doing it.
2. "Scientifically select and then train, teach, and develop the workman, whereas in the past he chose his own work and trained himself as best he could." Find the best man for the job, then use the best methods for training him.
3. "Heartily cooperate with the men so as to insure all of the work being done in accordance with the principles of the science which has been developed." One form of cooperation should be an incentive system of production. The right worker in the right job should be able to make more money than ever before.
4. "There is an almost equal division of the work and the responsibility between the management and the workmen. The management take over all work for which they are better fitted than the workmen, while in the past almost all of the work and the greater part of the responsibility were thrown upon the men." Workers work and managers manage. Such a division of labor should result in the greater good of both.[2]

Frank Gilbreth.   An inquisitive spirit equal to Taylor's was found in Frank Gilbreth (1868–1924). He also achieved impressive production gains by applying scientific management principles.

Turning down a chance to go to the Massachusetts Institute of Technology, Gilbreth entered the contracting business by apprenticing as a bricklayer. He was surprised that such an ancient craft was carried on in so many different ways. Showing the same concern with finding a better way that Taylor brought to the steel industry, Gilbreth noted the variations in bricklaying style and wondered how the activity might be improved. Gilbreth

---

[2]Frederick W. Taylor, *Principles of Scientific Management* (New York: Harper & Brothers, 1911), pp. 36–37.

focused on the motions used by the bricklayers as they performed the various aspects of their jobs, from mixing mortar, to carrying brick, to the actual brick placement.

By scientific observation and investigation, Gilbreth reduced the required motions for laying interior brick from 18 to 2. He increased the average productivity from 120 to 350 bricks per man-hour. He also designed an improved scaffolding, developed an optimum mixture for mortar, and offered other innovations to simplify the bricklaying process. By standing back, observing the job, thinking about it scientifically, and then planning and implementing the best way to do it, Gilbreth quickly improved a craft that had been done inefficiently for hundreds of years.

Gilbreth married psychologist Lillian Moller (1878–1972) in 1904. Together they developed methods for increasing industrial production efficiency. They studied time and motion by taking moving pictures of people working with a clock in the background to measure the time required for each motion. In their later work, they attached a light bulb to a worker's hand to determine the acceleration, deceleration, and direction of the worker's movement. They categorized worker movements into 17 basic motions, modestly called *therbligs* (Gilbreth spelled backward with the "th" reversed).

Two of the Gilbreth children wrote a best-selling novel entitled *Cheaper by the Dozen* about the Gilbreths' large family. The book was made into a successful movie starring Clifton Webb, Myrna Loy, and Jean Crain.

Influence of Taylor and the Gilbreths.   Taylor and the Gilbreths achieved impressive results. Disciples applied scientific principles and time and motion studies to a wide variety of manufacturing operations. These disciples easily understood the benefits and logic of Taylor's first two principles of scientific management (find the best way, then train the best worker), but they never really saw the benefits of cooperating and sharing with the work force. Most organizations obtained large productivity gains by merely redesigning and standardizing work methods. Why go farther down Taylor's list? Besides, the idea of cooperating closely was not easily accepted by most employers or workers of this era. Indeed, Taylor's later work reflects his own discouragement at his inability to instill a feeling of cooperation and shared responsibility within his workers:

> I was a young man in years, but I give you my word I was a great deal older than I am now, what with the worry, meanness and contemptibleness of the whole damn thing. It is a horrid life for any man to live, not to be able to look any workman in the face all day long without seeing hostility there, and feeling that every man around you is your virtual enemy. These men were a nice lot of fellows, and many of them were my friends outside the works. This life was a miserable one, and I made up my mind to either get out of the business entirely and go into some other line of work, or to find some remedy for this unbearable condition.[3]

[3]In F. B. Copley, *Frederick W. Taylor: Father of Scientific Management*, Vol. I (New York: Harper & Brothers, 1923), p.5.

Worker Reaction.   Workers were not enthusiastic supporters of Taylor and the Gilbreths. Fear and hatred, not cooperation and responsibility, were the normal reactions when workers discovered that analyzing jobs scientifically could eliminate two out of every three jobs. However, the scientific management movement was born and grew quickly. Its assumptions about workers fit neatly with those of owners and managers during this historical period.

Nineteenth-Century Managerial Attitudes

Protestant Ethic.   The emerging class of industrialists held assumptions about workers based on a combination of the Protestant Ethic and Social Darwinism. The Protestant Ethic is the belief that earthly effort and hard work will lead to both earthly and heavenly rewards. God allowed those predestined for heavenly rewards to know about their future eternal good fortune through the degree of their success in the material state of existence. The richer you were on earth, the more favored you were to be hereafter.

Social Darwinism.   Social Darwinism was equally supportive of the emerging industrial class. Intellectuals accepted the evolutionary theory of Charles Darwin (1809–1882) as expressed in his book *The Origin of Species* (1859). Darwin showed that through a natural selection process those species best adapted to survive in the struggle for existence did so. Social scientists sought to apply the evolutionary idea to societies as well as species. Herbert Spencer (1820–1903) made a social application of Darwinism in his book *Man Versus the State* (1884). Darwin argued that the fittest species survive and prosper in the natural course of evolution because they are best adapted to the natural environment. Spencer argued that the same is true about individuals within a species. Consequently, the rich and powerful get that way by being best adapted to the social norms as a result of natural processes.

For those on top of the social ladder—the Rockefellers, Carnegies, Morgans, and other wealthy industrialists of the era—this theory was very reassuring. Their rightful position in society was the result of natural evolutionary laws. They deserved to be at the top, and their workers deserved to be at the bottom, because that was the natural order of things. Workers on the shop floor found this philosophical stance less than reassuring.

Social Philosophy of Management.   For our purposes, the point is that scientific management was enthusiastically accepted and implemented by owners and managers in such a climate. If employees are indeed basically stupid, machinelike creatures who must be closely supervised to keep them from loafing, stealing, or making mistakes, then the principles of scientific management (at least the first two) make great sense. Today we may look back with horror at the "robber barons" and "ruthless industrialists" of the early twentieth century. However, they were only products of their era's social philosophy and beliefs, as we are of ours. In the context of Social Darwinism and early scientific management, Andrew Carnegie could refuse to spend money on safety equipment that would keep men from falling into his steel mill blast furnaces, while at the same time spending millions for public libraries.

Social Philosophy and Scientific Investigation.   These widely held assumptions about the working class carried over into the new science of industrial psychology. Although psychology was a relatively new field of inquiry at the turn of the century, interest in it grew quickly as scholars sought to further their knowledge about how the mind works.

A pioneer of industrial psychology was Hugo Munsterberg (1863–1916). In his *Psychology and Industrial Efficiency* (1913), he proposed that the science of psychology could complement Taylor's science of management through rigorous investigation. Taylor and the Gilbreths studied the *job* and emphasized *physical* skills. Munsterberg studied the *people* and emphasized *mental* skills, psychological traits, and states of mind. Psychological tests and experiments could be used to help find the best potential employee for a job and to investigate the impact of the physical environment (temperature, lighting, and so forth) on employee productivity and physiological condition. The areas of concern to the early industrial psychologists clearly reflect their belief in the machinelike character of the workingman—a belief shared by the early scientific management thinkers.

Scientific School: Summary.   The scientific school of management was the first major school of management thought. It reflected the era's scientific orientation, with its emphasis on numerical measurement to prove or disprove any issue. It also reflected the era's social philosophy. Workers were stupid, lazy, incompetent, untrustworthy, machinelike creatures. They could not be otherwise because of the natural selection process and predestination. Industry leaders seeking even greater measurable earthly signs of heavenly favor had to get these human machines to work more efficiently—to lay more brick, to load more pig iron. The scientific management movement and industrial psychology provided ways to accomplish these goals and thereby became dominant forces in managerial thinking for at least the next 30 years. Their influence still exists in many industrial situations.

The Human Relations School

The Hawthorne Studies.   Industrial psychologists and scientific managers studied the spectrum of physical factors influencing the man on the shop floor. One such study, carried out at the Western Electric Company's Hawthorne Works, accidentally led to the second major school of management thought.

The 1924–1927 work was sponsored by the National Research Council. The 1927–1932 work, sponsored by the Rockefeller Foundation, was done by a group of investigators from Harvard University led by Elton Mayo (1880–1949). Experimenters began by studying attitudes and reactions of Western Electric employees under varying physical conditions. Their surprising results led them in new directions.

Illumination Experiment.   The first experiment was designed to test the effect of lighting on productivity. Since much work at Western Electric depended on eye–hand coordination, the researchers felt that how well the work area was lit should affect the amount of work produced.

For the control group, illumination remained the same throughout the experiment. For the experimental group, light was gradually increased. The result? Production increased for *both* groups. When lighting level was decreased for the experimental group, production for both groups *continued* to increase. As the lights were turned down one step at a time, productivity kept rising. When a lighting level approximating moonlight was reached, productivity in the experimental group finally leveled off and began to drop.

These results did not match the expectations of scientific management at all. The workers did not react as machines would have reacted. Apparently, influences other than lighting level were present. Further experiments in the relay assembly test room, along with an extensive interview program, confirmed that *social and emotional factors*—not physiological factors—caused the variations in output.

The Hawthorne Effect.   The Hawthorne experimenters were informative, courteous, and considerate to the workers. In the relay room experiment, they made a point of being friendly and personally interested in the workers. During their industrial experience, the workers had never known such treatment. The workers were willing to cooperate and were eager to produce *in spite of* the lighting levels. The positive response of experimental subjects to a new and interesting situation in which they are the focus of attention has come to be called, appropriately, the Hawthorne effect.

The Bank Wiring Room Study.   To explore these findings more systematically, the investigators undertook the last major part of the Hawthorne experiments: the bank wiring room study. The workers in the bank wiring department were an existing, functioning team already somewhat isolated from the rest of the work force. The experimenters placed an observer in the work room to record group influences on productivity.

The observer confirmed that social factors affected productivity. Workers did not work up to their capacity for various reasons. The group seemed to establish an output level that was satisfactory for its purposes. If a man varied from a group code—for example, by producing too much or too little—he was punished by "bopping" or "binging": another employee hit him as hard as possible on the upper arm. In such a way, the social patterns of the job were created and enforced.

Conclusions.   In their major review of the Hawthorne studies, F. J. Roethlisberger and W. J. Dickson drew these conclusions about the way people work:[4]

1. Work is a social activity as well as a physical activity.
2. People in business and industrial organizations tend to develop informal social organizations.
3. The informal social organization within the work environment creates and enforces its own norms and codes of behavior.
4. The informal social organization helps define the status of its members and determine their behavior.
5. The informal social organization helps fulfill the needs of members for recognition, a sense of belonging, and security. These needs are *more important* in determining worker morale and productivity than the physical conditions in the job environment.

Scientific Management and Human Relations.   All these conclusions had significant implications for prevailing management practices, based as they were on "scientific" management assumptions. The last point was especially troubling for the leaders of the scientific management school. To increase productivity, managers had to practice good human relations and consider employee feelings and emotions. Unconvinced, many scientific managers labeled human relations investigators the "moo cow" school, since they were clearly saying the same thing that Carnation said about its milk: contented workers give contented (and more and better) work.

Workers as People.   Although many scholars and managers received the Hawthorne conclusions coolly, the argument that *workers are people too* was difficult to refute. Some earlier writers on management had put forth this idea but had not been able to prove it. The Hawthorne results scientifically supported the humanistic approach to management to such an extent that the human relations point of view could never again be ignored. The Hawthorne studies also helped shift the focus of industrial psychology from worker physiology to worker attitudes.

The Process School

Henri Fayol.   The next major school of management thought was the *process school* or *principles school.* Attributed to the Frenchman Henri Fayol (1841–

[4]F. J. Roethlisberger and W. J. Dickson, *Management and the Worker* (Cambridge, Mass.: Harvard University Press, 1949), Part V.

1925), this school is difficult to place in chronological sequence. Fayol wrote his classic work *General and Industrial Management* in 1916, but it was not widely known in the United States until a translation appeared in 1949.

According to this school, management is a five-component process involving 14 universal principles. The processes and principles are essentially the same, regardless of whether the manager is managing in church, government, business, or at home. Therefore, learning and using the process and principles will lead to managerial excellence.

Taylor's scientific management stressed the immediate gains in productivity resulting from scientifically investigating the *workman's* task. Fayol's broader, long-term approach focused on the *manager's* task. As general manager and director of a large mining corporation, Fayol observed and analyzed the managerial tasks required to make an organization run effectively. Taylor quadrupled Schmidt's output in one day. The gains that would be achieved by looking at the overall operation were less immediate than those obtainable from Taylor's principles, so some time elapsed before Fayol was widely recognized even in France.

In America, individualistic entrepreneurs strongly resisted consideration of their own possible managerial limitations. Everyone knew that an owner, almost by definition, could manage. Getting the worker to work was still seen as the problem.

Need for Management Theory.   At this point, the forces of historical development once again played an important role in the development of management thought. Natural economic growth plus the explosive growth associated with World War I resulted in an increasing demand for managerial expertise. Needed was a theory of general management, rather than merely some methods for supervising workers. A managerial class was rapidly evolving. This group needed training in the managerial point of view, so universities began offering business management courses.

Fayol's Great Contribution.   Fayol provided the first important theory of general management. He offered a logical, well-organized perspective on both the tasks and functions of management. He viewed "management" as a teachable body of knowledge organized around the manager's five functions:

1. *Planning* the organization's tasks.
2. *Organizing* the people, money, and material necessary to perform these tasks.
3. *Commanding* the people assigned to the tasks.
4. *Coordinating* their activities to ensure proper direction.
5. *Controlling* the processes, procedures, and people involved.

Fayol's Principles of Management.   Based on his extensive observation of people and organizations, Fayol derived 14 universal management principles.

They provided the basis for organizing management knowledge. Here are Fayol's principles of administration:[5]

1. *Division of work.* Adam Smith saw specialization as appropriate and necessary for pin making. Fayol saw that specialization could improve managerial efficiency as well.

2. *Authority and responsibility.* The manager has the power of authority. He has the equal responsibility for the use he makes of that power.

3. *Discipline.* Effective managers produce or induce good discipline. They encourage obedience and diligence, and they punish insubordination.

4. *Unity of command.* Each person has only one boss and reports only to that boss.

5. *Unity of direction.* A group of activities having the same objective must have only one boss and only one plan for achieving that objective. Plans must be coordinated, rather than overlapping.

6. *Subordination of individual interest to the general interest.* Managers must promote this principle by example and by counteracting violations.

7. *Remuneration.* Fair and reasonable payment plans are necessary (but they are not a substitute for good management).

8. *Centralization.* Centralization refers to the organization's tendency to keep decision-making authority near the top. Under decentralization, the organization delegates decision-making authority down through the organization. The manager must determine how much centralization or decentralization the organization needs.

9. *Scalar chain.* All employees should be aware of the organizational hierarchy, the different levels in the chain of command. Communications should generally flow through the formal chain of command. Persons on the same level may communicate directly across the chain, to avoid the necessity of sending a message up through the chain of one person's superiors and then down through the chain of the other's superiors.

10. *Order.* All people and things have their place and should be in that place.

11. *Equity.* The manager must be fair and firm, but friendly.

12. *Stability of personnel.* For best results, organizations should encourage the long-term stability of both managers and workers. Rapid turnover is destructive of organizational goals.

13. *Initiative.* Managers must be able to originate projects and complete them.

14. *Spirit.* Managers must work together harmoniously and must encourage harmony and unity within their people.

[5]H. Fayol, *General and Industrial Management* (London: Sir Isaac Pitman & Sons Ltd., 1949), pp. 19–20.

Fayol's logic and comprehensiveness have made the principles approach one of the most commonly used in teaching management to this day. Because it neatly arranges and categorizes so much information, many teachers see it as the most appropriate way to discuss the management field. Part Four of this book is organized according to the principles approach.

The Operations Research School

The next development in the historical evolution of management knowledge was the *operations research school*. Although many earlier management writers had included quantitative techniques, the *OR* movement stressed the mathematically oriented approach.

Origins of Operations Research.   During World War II, a major problem for Great Britain was defending the coastline. To solve the problem, experts from various academic and professional disciplines were brought together. They pooled their knowledge, created and tested hypotheses, used quantitative techniques, and investigated with scientific rigor. They came up with patrolling patterns for locating enemy submarines, more effective radar systems, and better uses for military equipment.

In the United States.   After its British success, operations research was adapted into the United States war effort, where it led to major advances in naval mining techniques and antisubmarine warfare.

After the war, Ford Motor Company hired ten of these armed services OR men as a group. They helped to reestablish Ford as a solid competitor in the automotive industry. By 1955, they had succeeded so well that Ford finally outsold Chevrolet. Six OR group members eventually became Ford vice-presidents and two became presidents. The names of three group members may be familiar. Charles B. "Tex" Thornton left Ford and later bought a small California electronics company, which eventually became Litton Industries. Robert S. McNamara became Secretary of Defense under President John F. Kennedy and later the director of the World Bank. Arjay R. Miller became dean of the Stanford University College of Business Administration.

Contributions of Operations Research.   The OR movement has provided many useful techniques for analyzing and solving managerial problems. The work of the OR school led to managerial applications of such techniques as decision trees, linear programming, inventory models, queueing theory, game theory, and other mathematical, statistical, and economic concepts. The OR notion that the "one best way" can be determined by manipulating mathematical models of managerial problems has been highly influential.

The Decision Theory School

Management as Decision Making.   Shortly after World War II, another school of management thought was developed under the leadership of Herbert A. Simon (1916–   ). This *decision theory school* held that the basis of management is decision making. Therefore, managerial research ought to focus on the process and techniques of making decisions. This approach fits nicely with the conceptual foundations of the operations research school. Over time, the two approaches have for all practical purposes become one. This merger has led to an emphasis on mathematical representations of the decision process.

Since expressing the human aspects of the decision process mathematically is so very difficult, most mathematical models express relationships among more predictable, more easily described factors, such as amount of inventory available to sell, the optimal trade-off between a product's storage costs and its susceptibility to perishing, and so on.

The Decision Process.   This school's major contribution has been to focus attention on the fact that managers are decision makers. How they make decisions can differentiate good managers from bad managers. In addition, this school suggests that researchers should study the steps in decision making as they relate to making managerial decisions. Here are the steps:

1. Find the problem.
2. Identify the alternative solutions.
3. Evaluate the alternative solutions in terms of their advantages and disadvantages.
4. Choose and implement the best solution.

Although this process sounds simple, it soon becomes complicated when the manager considers the conflicting needs of individuals, groups, and the organization itself. Good decisions must take into account numerous personal, social, and organizational variables.

The Systems School

The most modern school of thought is the *systems school.* Impressed by the explanatory power of "systems" in the physical sciences, social scientists led by Kenneth Boulding (1910–   ) sought to apply this idea to the managerial aspects of social systems.

Interrelationships.   The systems approach states that all things are interrelated. Therefore, investigating anything in isolation from its larger context is useless. Individuals do not exist in isolation. They are influenced by all things and people with whom they interact. The behavior of the individual worker must therefore be studied within the context of the worker's organization. Likewise, the organization must be investigated with reference to its social system, governmental pressures, market forces, historical trends, and employee expectations.

Theory Unsupportable But Influential.   On the one hand, the obvious truth and comprehensiveness of the systems approach make the other schools seem incomplete. At the same time, research and precise scientific investigation become almost impossible because the investigator cannot hold the rest of the system constant while studying any one of its components. Consequently, systems scholars are left with a satisfying theory that cannot be supported (or rejected) through investigation. Even so, the systems approach has greatly influenced ideas about the role and scope of management.

AN INTEGRATING MODEL

These numerous and diverse schools of management thought confuse many students and professionals. Management scholars spend much time trying to sort out conflicting approaches and claims. To illustrate, about 15 years ago, the leading management scholars representing all schools and approaches got together to seek agreement. They wound up agreeing not to agree on a common definition of the term "management."

However, if we are to make effective use of the information and ideas that each school has made available to the management student, we need to arrange and integrate these concepts somehow. The following model incorporates the essential ideas from the various schools into an integrated description of the act and art of management (see Figure 1-1). Much of this book is devoted to explaining the different parts of this management model.

Process.   The center of the model represents the manager's primary and recurring task: making decisions. The manager makes decisions in five areas, represented by the five outer circles. Each circle is one of Fayol's five management functions: planning, organizing, staffing, directing, and controlling. Together they make up the management process. The five circles are tied together by the organizational communication process. Information flows within each circle and from circle to circle. The circular arrangement makes it possible to place Fayol's fifth function (controlling) next to the first function (planning), to reinforce the fact that planning should be based on information derived from controls, as part of a continuing cycle.

Decision Making.   The outer circle surrounding each of the five process functions represents the decision-making process loop. The five managerial func-

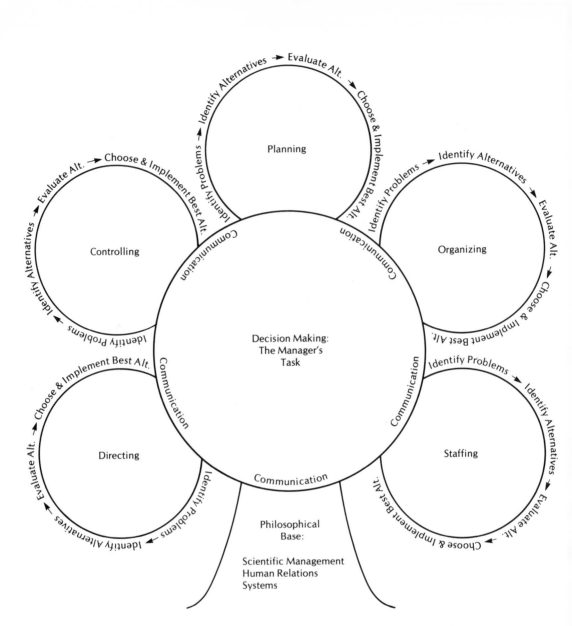

FIG 1-1 A management model.

tions all require decision activity: problem identification, alternative search, alternative evaluation, and decision choice and implementation. The decision process is presented as five loops because each function will require continuing decision activity.

The Manager's Philosophical Approach.   The base of the model represents the manager's philosophical approach to management. Although that approach may vary somewhat from time to time, depending on situations and people, it represents the manager's basic beliefs about how decisions should be made. Some managers are humanistically or behaviorally oriented as they make their decisions about planning, organizing, staffing, directing, and controlling. Others are more task oriented, so they use a more scientific management approach. Still others see their managerial decision situations in terms of the total system involved.

Goals and Objectives.   All organizations (and all people within organizations) have goals, purposes, and objectives—some written, some unwritten. These goals are the standard against which performance is based. If a goal is not being achieved, the manager responsible for achieving it has a problem. At that point, decision activity begins.

Although the management model does not specifically mention goals and objectives, they underlie all decision activity. Without goals, managers have no standards for deciding. Without goals, managers do not even know whether decisions are called for. For example, if managers have no goals for the staffing function, then they have no basis for making staffing decisions or even for recognizing that staffing decisions should be made.

Since goals are critical to good decision making, Chapter 2 is devoted to identifying and defining goals.

Plan of the Book

The management model serves as the organizational plan of the book. Part Two investigates the decision process in detail. Part Three covers how to implement decisions once they are made. Part Four then investigates the specific managerial functions that managers make decisions about. Part Five covers three subjects of current interest: organizational development, social responsibility, and international management.

SUMMARY

This chapter has offered the historical background of the management process. After presenting such early examples requiring management skill as primitive families, the pyramids, the Arsenal of Venice, the Soho Foundry, the New Lanark Mills, and the cotton gin, the chapter discussed the major schools of management thought.

The *scientific school* of Frederick Taylor and the Gilbreths brought scientific principles to the study of the workplace. The Protestant Ethic and Social Darwinism provided theoretical underpinnings for the scientific approach.

In contrast, the *human relations* school emphasized that workers are people, not machines to be "scientifically" manipulated. The Hawthorne studies provided empirical data that good human relations are important to productivity.

The *process school* of Henri Fayol focused on the manager's (rather than the worker's) task in terms of the manager's five functions: planning, organizing, staffing, directing, and controlling. Fayol's 14 management principles continue to have much validity.

The *operations research school* brought mathematical modeling to the study of management. The *decision theory school* of Herb Simon considers the manager to be primarily a decision maker. The *systems school* emphasizes the interrelationships of workers, managers, and all influences affecting the organization.

The chapter concluded by offering a management model. The model integrates management philosophy, the manager's decision-making tasks, and the functions making up the management process.

DISCUSSION QUESTIONS

1. Which school of management seems best to explain the field of management? Why?
2. How does a manager's philosophy influence the manner in which the manager supervises?
3. What are the differences and similarities between the scientific school and the operations research school?
4. What supervisory lessons can be learned from understanding the Hawthorne effect?
5. "The need for a 'science' of management arose from the circumstances of the times." Defend or attack this statement.
6. Management represents the difference between a mob and an organization. True?
7. What would you propose as a complete definition of the term "management"?
8. What was the influence of Social Darwinism and the Protestant Ethic on early management style?
9. Why was it so hard to get people to accept the conclusions of the Hawthorne studies?
10. What do you think the next school of management thought will be like? Why?

2

goals

Organizations are goal-seeking devices. This chapter begins by offering several traditional definitions of goals. Then the goals of business organizations are divided into operational (measurable or specific) and nonoperational (nonmeasurable or general) goals. Most organizations have both goal types. Since all organizations (and all levels within an organization) have more than one goal, the problems that can result from multiple goals are then discussed.

Finally, goals are considered in terms of inducements (offered by organizations) and contributions (supplied by members). One function of managers is to translate the organization's general goals into specific tasks. The chapter shows that the successful manager considers the personal goals of members and offers them the combination of inducements that will encourage them to contribute their best efforts in completing tasks necessary to organizational goal achievement.

GOAL DEFINITIONS

Profit Maximization

Organizational goals have been defined in many ways. For profit-making firms, the most familiar definition is probably the classical economic concept of *profit maximization*. Under this definition, the firm aims all its efforts toward making as much profit as possible.

This definition seems sensible and clear cut, but actually it is not. For example, profit-maximizing behavior this year may hurt profits in the long run. This year the firm might maximize profits by emphasizing quantity at the expense of quality, but that approach may endanger long-run profits. This year the firm might try to maximize profits by taking extreme risks. The better long-term approach might be to encourage steady profit growth by being more conservative. In short, even if management establishes profit maximization as a goal, it is almost impossible to decide what behavior will lead to that goal.

An example will point up some of the difficulties. Assume that you run a hog ranch and that you want to process hogs in such a way as to maximize your profits. You must decide what combination of bacon, pigs feet, pork, and footballs to produce, which is to be the primary product and which the by-products, what price to put on each item, and how to allocate your firm's financial and marketing resources among products. Only by making perfect decisions in all these respects can you hope to maximize your profits.

Since profit maximization as a goal has practical difficulties, top management often establishes some arbitrary target in the form of profit levels that seem desirable (rather than maximum).

Creating a Customer

Another goal definition is that of Peter Drucker. He believes that the only valid goal of a business is *to create a customer*. According to Drucker, "The customer is the foundation of a business and keeps it in existence. He alone gives employment. To supply the wants and needs of a consumer, society entrusts wealth-producing resources to the business enterprise."[1] Although this definition shifts emphasis away from profits, it is not altogether different from profit maximization, since focusing on the customer's wants and needs will presumably lead to solid profits.

The Organization as a Natural System

Organizations are founded in order to achieve goals. However, according to the natural system model, the organization soon takes on the characteristics of an organism with needs and goals of its own. These goals may be quite different from those envisioned by the organization's founders. Like any other organism, the business organization has self-preservation as its primary goal. Once its survival is no longer in question, the overall organization and each of its parts generate further goals and needs. Although top management can affect the behavior of this growing natural system, the organization and its parts have taken on purposes of their own—which may or may not include management's stated goals.

Who Benefits?

Organizations can be categorized according to who benefits most from their activities. A bowling club pursues the benefits of its *members*. A school attempts to benefit the *public*. A mental health clinic may have as its goal the

[1]Peter F. Drucker, *Management: Tasks, Responsibilities, Practices* (New York: Harper & Row, 1974), p. 61.

benefit of its *clients*. A business firm exists to benefit its *owners*. Although a business may benefit its members or employees, its clients or customers, and the general public, the goal of its owners is to make a profit.

The stated goals of an organization are not always its actual goals. Keeping the prime beneficiary in mind often helps avoid confusion by pinpointing true goals.

Profit, Growth, and Survival

A popular modern definition combines three interrelated goals: *profit, growth,* and *survival*. In a capitalistic and competitive economic environment, profit is obviously necessary. Without profit, there can be no growth or survival. However, business organizations often choose to give up maximum profits this year in order to encourage future growth or survival, or both.

For example, consider a company that has a near monopoly in a product that society needs. The organization may choose to keep the price down (and give up maximum profits) to avoid the antitrust suit that could endanger its survival. Consider another example. Corporations are owned by their shareholders. Many corporations are called "growth companies" simply because the shareholders are willing to plow profits back into the business rather than take them as dividends, which would be the way to maximize each owner's returns in a given year.

OPERATIONAL AND NONOPERATIONAL GOALS

Here is yet another way of looking at organizational goals. The goals of most organizations can be divided into two general categories: operational and nonoperational. Two independent observers can look at an operational goal and agree about how to measure its accomplishment. Their opinions might vary widely about how to measure accomplishment of a nonoperational goal.

Nonoperational Goals

An example of a nonoperational goal would be a New Year's resolution to "be a better student." By definition, every person but one can be a better student than someone else, and even this year's worst student can satisfy the goal by being a better student than a tin can or by being better next year than this year.

In the business world, many well-intended goal statements are nonoperational. As you consider the following goals, ask yourself whether you would like to be evaluated on how well you accomplished them.

Jim Walter Corporation. The development and operating success of Jim Walter Corporation is an outgrowth of a continuing two-fold long-range objective.

The first is to become the lowest cost producer of the widest range of building material products in the nation while continuing to expand opportunities in natural resources and industrial markets . . . .

The second continuing objective is to maintain prudent management of the company's assets and operations so as to provide fair and consistent returns to stockholders on their investment . . . .[2]

3M Company. The objective of 3M Company is to produce quality goods and services that are useful and needed by the public, acceptable to the public, and in the best interests of the global economy—and thereby to earn a profit, which is essential to perpetuation of the useful role of the Company. 3M profit is not an abstraction. It is the wherewithal to support individuals, government and social institutions through salaries, taxes, dividends, purchases of goods and services, contributions, and to provide growth and additional job opportunities . . . .[3]

Eastman Kodak Company. We must be dedicated to fulfilling the needs of the customer and doing it better than anyone else. We need not be absorbed with the activities of competitors as such. Our concern is with the *customer* and the *products* and *services* offered to him by others and available to him from others. Our simple dedication is to offer the customer the best possible products and services. How well we satisfy this compelling purpose will determine how well shareowners and Kodak men and women will fare, and how well we meet and satisfy our responsibility to the public interest.[4]

Westinghouse Electric Corporation The basic purpose of Westinghouse, in all its decisions and actions, is:

1) To attain a continuous high level of profit which places it in the top ranks of industry in its rate of return on invested capital, recognizing that Westinghouse can serve society only if it is financially viable.

2) To operate all elements of the Corporation throughout the world in a manner which contributes to the improvement of society and which is sensitive to the natural and human environment.

3) To achieve steady growth in profits, sales volume and highly productive investment at rates exceeding those of the national economy as a whole.

4) To be responsive at all times to the needs of customers and of people by providing quality products and services, by improving them continuously and by creating new products and services which increase user satisfaction.

5) To distribute equitably among owners, employees and customers the fruits of improved productivity and efficient use of management, labor and capital.

6) To maintain a dynamic business structure by continuously shifting investment from areas which have lost their profit vitality into new business fields where potential for growth is high.

7) To create an environment in which, without discrimination, all employees are enabled, encouraged and stimulated to perform at their highest potential of

---

[2]Jim Walter Corporation, *Annual Report*, 1974.

[3]3M Company Board of Directors, "Corporate Position on Social Responsibility," Committee on Corporate Responsibility Memo, 1974.

[4]Ira C. Werle, "'SPICE' Concept Guides Kodak Business Practices," Eastman Kodak Pamphlet, 1974.

output and creativity and to attain the greatest possible level of job satisfaction in the spirit of the Westinghouse Creed.

8) To conduct all affairs of the Corporation in conformance with the highest ethical and legal standards.

These eight points are indivisible. Together, as a unit, they express the basic purpose and fundamental management philosophy of the Westinghouse Electric Corporation.[5]

These goal statements are high-minded and worthy. Yet they are almost uniformly nonoperational.

Operational Goals

Achievement of operational goals can be measured fairly objectively. The goal itself may or may not be appropriate or worthwhile, but at least the organization knows whether the goal has been reached. Organizations need to break down such nonoperational goals as profit, growth, and survival into operational goals. The organization can then recognize whether these operational goals are being accomplished.

As an example, DuPont has translated the traditional—yet nonoperational—goal of profit maximization directly into a specific measure of return on investment for every product. If a product cannot achieve the targeted return, it is dropped. Although the required return is somewhat arbitrary, it is at least a measurable, commonly understood goal that permits problem areas to be identified rapidly.

Problem Identification.   Identifying problems quickly and accurately is a major reason for establishing operational goals and making them known. If goals could be stated operationally throughout the organization, problem identification would become nearly automatic. If you are assigned the task of selling 15 elephants (assuming that this is a "reasonable" goal) and you sell 15, there is no problem. If you sell 12 elephants, your sales manager sees an automatic red flag that indicates a problem. (Selling 30 elephants also signals a problem. It suggests that something is wrong with the goal.)

Ideally, then, we would like to have measurable targets, rather than the generalized goal statements found in company annual reports to stockholders. The problem is that such precision is rarely possible. Our expectations of ourselves, our economic organizations, and our social institutions continually change. Therefore, operational goals that can serve as automatic problem identifiers for everyone in a business organization are not very common. All too often, management's only choice is to express a general goal and hope that people in the organization will read it, understand it, and try to implement it.

[5]"The Westinghouse Purpose," Westinghouse Electric Corporation Pamphlet, 1974.

Managers can play an important part in converting nonoperational company goals into more specific, understandable goals for their subordinates. Chapter 16 will discuss how managers can motivate their subordinates to work toward accomplishing the organization's goals.

Means–End Chains

Jim Walter Corporation wants to become "the lowest cost producer of the widest range of building material products in the nation." Somehow the specific work activity of every Jim Walter employee must contribute to the achievement of that goal. One way to envision how specific job activities relate to company goals is in terms of *means–end chains*.

General goals are transmitted down from the top throughout the organization. As managers on each level are given goals, they translate them into more specific, more operational terms for their subordinates. As lower-level goals or ends are met, they become the means for meeting succeeding higher level goals. The worker becomes the means whereby the supervisor achieves his ends; the supervisor becomes the means whereby the manager achieves his ends. And so the means–end chains move back up through the organization to the board of directors, which established the organization's goals in the first place.

MULTIPLE GOALS

Multiple Operational Goals

Even if goals can be made operational, the multiplicity of goals in the modern business organization adds complications. Organizations cannot often exert maximum effort in favor of all goals at once. Which should receive priority?

For example, the personnel department may be told to design programs for reducing product defects by 15 percent and for reducing industrial accidents by 10 percent. What follows may well be an example of the "cycle of emphasis" problem. In one month the department publicizes a quality-control program. The desired quality increase is achieved, but the accident rate rises. In the next month the department focuses successfully on safety, but quality slips. Failure to achieve an operational goal causes it to become the interest of the month, limited personnel prevents equal emphasis on the multiplicity of goals, and so the cycle continues.

This example points up some of the difficulties managers may face when trying to rank multiple operational goals. Managers are held accountable for reaching several goals. Which is most important? On which should emphasis be placed? Managers may well decide not on the basis of what is best for the company but in light of their own personal goals and their perceptions of what their own managers want or expect.

Departmental Versus Overall Goals

Another problem with multiple operational goals is that focusing on their own goals may cause units of the organization to lose sight of overall goals. For example, in many organizations the sales personnel and the credit department maintain a running argument. The sales force argues that they could perform much better if credit restrictions were not so "unrealistically tight." The credit personnel argue that sales wants to endanger the firm's assets by extending credit "to every warm body."

In trying to meet or exceed its own goals, each department may be undercutting the firm's total effectiveness. The general principle to keep in mind would be this: The more operational goals that an organization establishes, the more its managers will be tempted to maximize those operational goals *at the expense of* overall organizational goals. Operational goals are in a sense ends in themselves; but, more importantly, they are a means of achieving the goals of the organization itself.

Multiple Nonoperational Goals

Over a period of time, managers may use simple trial and error to resolve this balancing problem for multiple operational goals. The balancing problem for multiple nonoperational goals is much more difficult. For example, all companies must translate the multiple nonoperational goals of profit, growth, and survival into more meaningful, operational terms. In particular, these general goals must be made specific within such major areas as market standing, productivity, research and development, social responsibility, and the like.

Market Standing.   Defining operational goals within such areas is not easy. Establishing specific goals that are consistent with all three general goals—profit, growth, and survival—is even more difficult. Let us use market standing as an example.

Before establishing a goal (such as "to increase our market share by 10 percent next year"), the company must determine where the market is (geographically), what it consists of, and who makes up the competition. Here is an illustration of the difficulties that can arise when trying to answer those questions. Some time ago, American Can Corporation was accused by the federal government of having a monopoly, because the company possessed 90 percent of the tin can market. American Can convinced the judge that the relevant market for determining monopolization was not tin cans but "all kinds of containers." In that market, American Can had only a small percentage of total sales, so the government's antitrust suit was defeated.

Social Responsibility.   Another major area within which nonoperational goals must be made operational is social responsibility. Just what responsibility does a business organization have to society? The Westinghouse Electric Corporation purpose statement presented earlier expresses the company's interest in serving and improving society in a manner that is sensitive to the natural and human environment. Does this translate into political gifts for favored candidates, closing down plants rather than pollute the air, and donating money to colleges? Or is it perhaps enough just to provide people with jobs?

If social responsibility includes all these activities, should Westinghouse engage in all of them or only some of them? To what extent, if any, should Westinghouse sacrifice its desire for "a continuous high level of profit" to satisfy its social goals? Which social responsibility should be met first and to what extent? Can the answers to these questions be made consistent with profit, growth, *and* survival? Difficult as these questions are, they must be answered if a company is to know what it is doing in the area of social responsibility, and why.

THE INDUCEMENTS–CONTRIBUTIONS THEORY OF GOALS

Benefits of Organizational Membership

Organizational goals are *those aims to which a group of affected people collectively agree at a point in time.* These affected people are willing to give up some freedom and to engage in some cooperative activity that it is hoped will further the best interests of all. If the organization fails to satisfy expectations, members will leave and join another.

Consider marriage as an organization. Two people give up considerable discretion over their behavior in order to pursue common goals that both agree are in their best interests. These goals may vary from marriage to marriage, but both partners in any marriage agree at the outset to exchange complete individual freedom for the opportunity to achieve common goals. If either partner later feels that these best interests are not being met by pursuing common goals, the marriage falls apart.

In a similar sense, we join social and economic organizations to secure benefits that we could not have as totally free individuals. Primitive man found it easier to secure food by joining groups to kill dinosaurs. Modern man may find it in his best interests to work for an automobile manufacturing company rather than making a car by himself.

Balancing Inducements and Contributions

To encourage and maintain continuing involvement in organizational activities, organizations offer members *inducements.* In exchange, members are expected to make *contributions* to organizational goals. Just as primitive man expected only a share of the slain dinosaur, modern man expects only a share of the automobile factory's returns. The member and the organization have expectations about what constitutes "a fair day's contributions for a fair day's inducements." When these expectations fail to match up, corrections will occur. In the extreme case, a dissatisfied member will leave the organization. In a less extreme case, the member may reconsider and accept the inducements presently offered, request more or different inducements, reduce contributions, offer to increase contributions if inducements are also increased, and so on.

Every organizational member goes through this very personal and dynamic process of balancing inducements with contributions. The inducements that members demand depend on their estimates of what their contributions are worth to the accomplishment of the organization's goals. The inducements that organizations offer to members are similarly determined. If the member and the organization agree on the worth of the member's contribution, the best interests of both are met.

In addition, the values that members place on inducements depend upon how well those inducements will enable members to fulfill their personal goals. If inducements do that, the quality and quantity of contributions will be enhanced.

Example: An Assembly-Line Worker

Here is a statement by an automobile assembly-line worker. He likes his job, but he would prefer to be the "utility man" who can handle any job in the department. The statement provides insight into the kinds and amounts of inducements that one member seeks from his business organization.

> I know I could find better places to work. But where could I get the money I'm making? Let's face it, $4.32 an hour. That's real good money now. Funny thing is, I don't mind working at body construction. To a great degree, I enjoy it. I love using my hands—more than I do my mind. I love to be able to put things together and see something in the long run. I'll be the first to admit I've got the easiest job on the line. But I'm against this thing where I'm being held back. I'll work like a dog until I get what I want. The job I really want is utility.
>
> It's where I can stand and say I can do any job in this department, and nobody has to worry about me. As it is now, out of, say, sixty jobs, I can do almost half of 'em. I want to get away from standing in one spot. Utility can do a different job every day. Instead of working right there for eight hours I could work over there for eight, I could work the other place for eight. Every day it would change. I would be around more people. I go out on my lunch break and work on the fork truck for a half-hour—to get the experience. As soon as I got it down pretty good, the foreman in charge says he'll take me. I don't want the other guys to see me. When I hit that fork lift, you just stop your thinking and you concentrate. Something right there in front of you, not in the past, not in the future. This is real healthy.[6]

[6]Studs Terkel, *Working* (New York: Avon Books, 1974), pp. 224–225.

The man indicates what inducements are meaningful to him. Besides pay, he wants job-related growth, responsibility, challenge, and the opportunity to achieve. The organization may provide him with these inducements as a reasonable trade for his contributions. However, this combination of inducements is valuable only for this one member at one point in his life. The next worker on the assembly line may value an entirely different set of inducements.

Such a balancing of inducements with contributions occurs at all levels of all organizations. If managers believe that the only thing workers want from the job is a paycheck, they are likely to become confused when workers ask for more variety, responsibility, or participation in decision making. Some autocratic managers in business who become chairpersons of voluntary organizations experience the same confusion. They cannot understand why volunteers don't do exactly as they are told to do. The successful volunteer chairperson finds out what inducements volunteers consider to be a worthwhile trade for their contributions.

The Changing Values of Inducements

By offering inducements, organizations elicit contributions that will help to accomplish group goals. Members (or organizations) determine what contributions they will give (or demand) in return for inducements. The values and expectations attached to both inducements and contributions are constantly changing.

For example, as a reasonable contribution in exchange for the inducement "opportunity for advancement," many organizations once demanded that new junior executives travel from one plant location to another every few months. Such training programs may create emotional turmoil for potential executives and their families. Organizations now find that "opportunity for advancement" is often not a sufficient inducement to encourage this particular contribution. So more and more organizations are offering training programs in one location, appealing to potential managers who consider rapidly rotating assignments as disrupting other important aspects of their lives.

As the beliefs, values, and customs of organization members change, so will their attitudes toward inducements and contributions. The ability of decision makers to recognize and respond to these changes will have considerable impact on the organization's performance.

External Influences on Internal Goals

Organizational goal setters must keep an eye out for changes in the values that inducements have for persons within the organization. They must also remain aware that external interests affect the organization's actions. Even if it were possible to establish goals with which all organization members could agree and to offer inducements that would encourage all members to work toward those goals, other influences might cause a shift in organizational goals and inducements. The interests of suppliers, distributors, customers, stockholders, governmental subdivisions, and the general public will affect management's freedom to establish goals and incentives.

In addition to conscious consideration of external groups, management also considers their interests through culturally derived and commonly held codes of behavior. For example, a fiercely competitive small retail firm may proclaim that its only goal is profit maximization. Yet the firm will give money to the Little League, United Fund, and other worthy causes even though these gifts reduce profitability. Managers at all levels of organizations are similarly influenced by cultural factors of which they may often be unaware.

Categories of Inducements

Managers responsible for achieving organizational goals must determine (1) what inducements satisfy the personal goals of members and (2) what contributions members should make in return for these inducements. Two basic personal goals of all organizational members are *self-preservation* and *self-satisfaction*. What kinds of inducements help employees to achieve these personal goals?

Material Inducements.   The value of some inducements is primarily monetary: wages and salaries, retirement benefits, stock-option plans, bonuses, company cars, discounts on purchases, and so forth. Part of an employee's monetary compensation goes toward achieving the goal of self-preservation, but most employees are able to use some financial compensation to help achieve their goals of self-satisfaction.

Social Inducements.   People derive benefits from getting together with other people. No monetary inducements may be involved, and the benefits of social association may have nothing directly to do with the organization's purpose. Some social benefits result from the one-to-one exchanges that take place throughout the typical work day. Other benefits result from membership in groups—ranging from the work group to the organization itself.

Organization Purpose.   A third set of inducements arises out of the organization's purpose. People join many organizations not for material gain or to associate with other people but because they believe in what the organization stands for and want to help the organization achieve its goals. Members of a group opposed to capital punishment will not receive any direct, tangible benefits if capital punishment is abolished, nor do they belong to the group for reasons relating to sociability.

The Inducements Package.   Organizations make the foregoing three categories of inducements available to members as a total package. As compensation for giving up some personal freedom and contributing to the common organizational goals, each member may select from the offered benefits. Some members may select only the material, tangible rewards—content to trade their time and effort for the organizationally derived financial rewards. Other members may be seeking companionship, a challenging job, a worthy cause, or some combination of tangible and intangible returns. Current research indicates that members of our culture value inducements related to sociability and organizational purpose more than they do material inducements—once enough material rewards are gained to assure self-preservation.

Herzberg's Variables.   Frederick Herzberg has identified a number of inducements that encourage organization members to make contributions. Table 2-1 categorizes these inducements in terms of whether they are material, social, or related to the organization's purpose.

TABLE 2-1   Inducements offered by organizations and contributions expected

Inducements Offered	*Contributions Expected*
	Time
Material	Effort
Pay	Cooperativeness
Fringe benefits	Loyalty
Vacation time	Identification with
Working conditions	group goals
Security	Commitment
	Effective performance
Social	
Interpersonal relationships	
Supervisory relations	
Job status	
Recognition	
Chance for advancement	
Organization Purpose	
Work itself	
Achievement of organizational goal	

Goals and Inducements.   In Chapter 16, we will discuss these inducements in greater depth. For the moment, it is sufficient to say that from these three broad categories of inducements successful managers in successful organizations provide combinations or packages of inducements that cause desirable contributors to remain. The more diverse the membership, the greater will be the need for management to define (1) general goals with which all can agree and (2) specific, multiple inducements that will attract diverse worthwhile contributors.

For example, the president of the United States will have far more difficulty in expressing his organization's goals in a meaningful, operational way than will the captain of a five-man bowling team. After considering the nation's diversity of ethnic backgrounds, regional customs, religious beliefs, and cultural norms, the president must come up with goals that the entire nation can accept as being reasonable inducements for membership in the nation's social structure. Since the bowling team members probably share similar beliefs, values, and attitudes about bowling, the team captain can be quite precise in stating the team's goals and in offering inducements.

The Manager's Responsibility: Providing the Link

Earlier we presented the goal statements of four corporations. The reason for the extreme generality of those statements should now be clear. The membership of large organizations represents great diversity in beliefs, values, needs, and goals. To keep the organization's goals consonant with that diversity, goal statements must express goals in a very general way.

Individual managers provide the link between the organization's general goals and the specific goals of organization members. Managers do this by being aware of inducements that the organization can offer, discovering the personal goals of group members, and then offering those inducements that will encourage members to make their most worthwhile contributions. Individual and organizational goals will rarely mesh perfectly. However, if supervisors are trained to recognize the needs and aspirations of group members, and if they have some latitude in combining and offering specific types of inducements that different members prefer, then members should be willing to make the contributions necessary to accomplish organizational goals.

Inducements and Contributions Affect Goal Definition.   In the process of making organizational goals operational, managers actually help to shape and define these goals. The way in which they do so is affected by their own inducements–contributions combinations. Like other employees, managers have their own reasons for joining organizations, staying with them, and exerting effort in the organization's behalf. These reasons affect and become part of goals as managers define them for subordinates.

The president of AT&T and the president of Pat's Pizza Palace both put their personal stamp on the goals of the organizations they lead. As goals are passed down through the organization in the means–end chain process, succeeding members redefine these goals in terms of their own goals, inducements, and contributions.

Each person's definition of the inducements–contributions balance influences the way in which that person makes (or does not make) organizational goals operational. The company president or the department manager may try to define goals. Subordinates can then moderate, modify, or otherwise act to constrain the goal setter's ability to impose goals. Whether the goal *as stated* becomes the goal *in fact* depends on how well it fits in with the inducements–contributions mix of employees.

SUMMARY

This chapter first covered several traditional approaches to defining goals: profit maximization, creating a customer, the natural system model, the prime beneficiary, and the profit–growth–survival combination. Organizational goals were then discussed in terms of their operational or nonoperational nature. Several corporate statements of purpose were seen to include mainly nonoperational goals. The chapter explained some advantages (and some difficulties) of making nonoperational goals operational, particularly with regard to problem identification. Goals were also analyzed in terms of means–end chains. The achievement by each organizational level of its goals (ends) becomes the means whereby the next-higher level achieves its goals.

Multiple goals, whether operational or nonoperational, can create multiple problems for organizations. This chapter offered several examples of such problems: quality control versus safety, sales versus credit, and determination of market standing and social responsibility.

The chapter's last major section dealt with inducements and contributions as they relate to the achievement of organizational goals.

DISCUSSION QUESTIONS

1. The inducements–contributions theory of goals states that people are willing to give up something to get something back from an organization. What do you think of this idea?
2. What kinds of inducements do people look for in their associations with groups? Do they seek the same inducements from each group they join?
3. List some examples of nonoperational goals that you have either set for yourself or that have been given to you. How would you make them operational?
4. How useful is the concept of means–end chains?
5. If you managed a company, which of these goal definitions would you favor: profit maximization, creating a customer, or profit–growth–survival?
6. What is the goal of a hospital? Is it operational or nonoperational?

7. How do people's inducements change over time?
8. How do organizations balance many goals at the same time? How do people balance a number of goals at the same time?
9. What factors change an organization's goals?
10. A hardware store has the only supply of snow shovels in town. A blizzard strikes. According to classical economics, what should the store owner do to the existing price of shovels in order to maximize profits?

The Cases

Two short cases follow each of the book's remaining chapters. In addition, Parts Two to Four are each followed by three longer cases. The cases enable the reader to apply the steps in the decision-making process to different areas of managerial responsibility.

The appropriate questions to ask of most case situations are these:

1. What is the problem in this case?
2. What are the possible alternative solutions?
3. Which alternative solution is best?
4. How can that solution best be implemented?

STATE MENTAL HEALTH AGENCY

Sally Johnson is a supervisor in a state agency offering mental health services. Once a year, she must evaluate each of her 12 case workers. After a recent evaluation session with Judy Adams, Johnson realized that the agency had a problem.

Judy Adams has been with the agency for two years. She is bright and dedicated, always willing to help co-workers when they get behind. She has mastered her job and performs it with confidence. In the evaluation conference, supervisor Johnson told Adams that her work was outstanding, her attitude excellent, and her leadership skills widely recognized. Johnson said that she was giving Adams the highest appraisal rating in the department.

Then Adams asked her supervisor two tough questions: "What rewards do I get for doing a good job? And where do I go from here?" Adams mentioned the unfairness of the state compensation system and said that the distinctions between state salaries were too small to reward outstanding performance. While she had not been pushed to the desperation point, she was very troubled by the state's unwillingness to recognize economic realities.

She went on to say that, although she really liked her work and received much personal satisfaction from it, she thought she might be ready for something different—possibly a supervisor's job. Because of her desire for fair pay and more responsibility, she said frankly that she was about to investigate other job opportunities.

After the interview, supervisor Johnson thought about what she might do. She did not want to lose Adams and wondered what inducements she could offer that would keep Adams with the agency.

THE BOYS HOME ASSOCIATION

Over 50 years ago, a group of concerned citizens founded the Boys Home Association, a nonprofit organization. They wanted to establish a home to care for boys not eligible for either legal adoption or foster home placement. The average stay of a Home resident is 3 years, although some boys have remained there for as long as 14 years.

The Boys Home Association is supported entirely by private contributions, acquired principally through an annual membership campaign.

Fred Jones, executive director of the association, is in charge of the Home. He states that the Home's goal is "to make every possible effort to produce good citizens. Our measure of success is how many good citizens we produce." Jones also believes that every boy must be taught the importance of hard work, must have an opportunity to develop a skill, and must be given academic and physical training to suit his needs.

What are the goals of the Boys Home Association? How would you make these goals operational?

---

the decision maker's task

Part Two contains four chapters, each covering one step in the problem-solving process. Chapter 3 relates the goal setting of Chapter 2 to problem solving. Problems are seen as failures to achieve organizational goals. Chapter 4 shows that generating alternatives is a creative activity; much of the chapter discusses the creative process, barriers to creativity, and techniques for stimulating creativity. Also covered are primary and secondary research methods for generating alternatives.

Chapter 5 explains some quantitative methods for deciding which alternative solution to a problem is best. Once the alternatives have been evaluated, the manager must choose the best one. Making the choice is the subject of Chapter 6.

The end product of the process described in Part Two is a good decision. Part Three will show how to implement good decisions.

identifying the problem

This chapter first relates goal setting (the subject of the previous chapter) to problem solving. Problems are seen as a failure to achieve organizational goals. The chapter describes four methods for discovering problems and determines that the management-by-exception strategy is best.

Specific problem signals are then covered. Individual, group, and cultural factors are shown to influence the employee's ability and willingness to see and interpret these signals.

The chapter concludes with some suggestions for ensuring that the employee's perspective and the organization's perspective on problem solving are as similar as possible.

GOALS AND PROBLEMS

Organizational goals are critical for problem identification. Unless the organization can tell its members what it is trying to do, no one will know whether problems exist, because no one will know whether the organization is succeeding or not. Throughout every successive management level, the organization has the responsibility to translate its broad goals into operational terms for the next level down. When managers have performed this function successfully, they have established a set of norms or targets for their subordinates. These targets can then serve as automatic problem signals for subordinates, in the sense that they specify clearly what the organizational superior expects. Setting specific targets for subordinates has obvious motivational aspects. In addition, this process gives the manager an objective measure for overseeing the subordinate's activities.

Goals as Problems

Specified operational goals can be an effective managerial tool. They can make the organization's members more effective by focusing their attention on problems. Goals can also be a human relations problem. They can destroy employee effort by providing overly restrictive controls that discourage original thought and new ideas. An important management skill is knowing *how precisely* to specify goals for a particular subordinate in order (1) to maximize the human potential and time effectiveness of both manager and subordinate, and (2) to minimize the missing of important problems.

In some bureaucratic organizations, employees complain that human potential and time are used ineffectively because goals are *too precise.* Such organizations have so many rules and regulations (highly precise specifications of organizational goals) that the employee has no opportunity to grow and develop in the job. In some other organizations, people are given so little direction that they spend many frustrating hours trying to decide exactly what they are expected to do—how they fit in with the organization's goals. Effective managers realize what people expect in the job, what the organization expects from the people, and then provide the degree of structure that will serve both their subordinates and the organization.

How Much Structure?

The Job Structure Continuum.   The degree of structure will fall somewhere along a continuum such as that seen in Figure 3-1. Extreme job structure situations appear at either end. At the left end, the worker (probably self-employed) totally defines the job content, its success measurement, and its structure. These definitions are internal to the worker. At the right end, someone external to the worker defines every aspect of the job for the worker. Most managerial and nonmanagerial jobs are in between; the employee has some opportunity to structure organizational tasks and responsibilities. In some aspects of the job, the employee may have total discretion. In other areas of responsibility, the employee may have no discretion at all.

The organization and the employee are often in conflict about what degree of structure is desirable. The organization wants its employees to focus

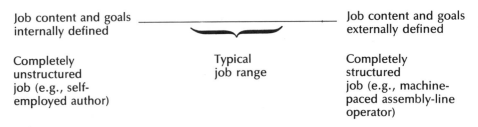

| Job content and goals internally defined | Typical job range | Job content and goals externally defined |

Completely unstructured job (e.g., self-employed author) — Typical job range — Completely structured job (e.g., machine-paced assembly-line operator)

FIG 3-1   A continuum of job structures.

their attention on problems that the organization thinks are important. So the organization may seek to move the job structure toward the "externally defined" end of the spectrum. On the other hand, the normal employee wants to grow and develop on the job. Therefore, the employee may seek to move the job definition toward the "internally defined" end of the continuum.

Job Content and Job Goals.   The human relations point of view and much research on goal-directed behavior suggest that two continuums might describe the job situation more accurately. One continuum would represent job goals, and the other would represent job content. The job goals should be structured and precisely defined by the person *assigning* the job, and the job content should be defined largely by the person *doing* the job.

This arrangement would be the best of both worlds in the sense that the organization could encourage its members in specific directions and provide the tools for immediate and accurate problem identification, that is, deviation from the specific goals. At the same time, ample opportunity for personal growth and development would be built into the job by allowing the organization's members to decide *how* to accomplish the goals. If the goals are appropriate, measurable, and objective, the organization can ensure that its members are all going in the same direction. At the same time, the goals provide a tool for measuring and evaluating the effectiveness of organization members—identifying strengths to build on and weaknesses to overcome through training.

From the employee's point of view, this approach has great benefits. The employee has the latitude to establish the means whereby the organization's ends will be achieved. Therefore, the employee has room to experiment, learn, and grow.

Why Ends and Means Get Confused.   Most managers have difficulty in mastering this separation of job content from job goals. Several factors cause this mixing up of ends with means:

1. The managers themselves have an incomplete understanding of their own goals because no one has specified the organization's goals.
2. The job of setting specific goals is hard to do and easy to avoid.
3. Most managers have had no training in setting job goals because most of their experiences have been concerned with the *process* of the job, rather than with end results.
4. Many organizations reward structured conformity of job process, rather than creative and new ways of reaching job goals.
5. Many organizations penalize failures so heavily that the risk taking involved in the personal growth process is discouraged.

MANAGEMENT BY EXCEPTION

A good manager wants to ensure proper attention to the organization's problems and potential problems. The best way to do that would be to oversee personally all the information relevant to the organization, whether the information comes up through the organization itself or from outside sources. In an organization of any size, no one person can attend to all this information. Therefore, most managers in this situation have three choices:

1. They can try to handle all the information anyway. Everyone has met the frantically busy manager who won't delegate any decision-making capability, works 10 to 12 hours a day, takes home a bulging briefcase, and so forth.
2. They can hire people who closely resemble themselves. Such managers operate by crisis. They focus on today's crisis, do what must or can be done, then move on to the next crisis, hoping that their subordinate managers are doing likewise.
3. They can set organizational goals for subordinates and then manage by exception.

Management by Exception and Specific Goals

Although the first two choices are commonly found, they are not very effective. Management by exception (MBE) can be effective. This classic principle goes back to Frederick Taylor and his scientific management approach. Under MBE, measurable targets are established for as many aspects of the organization's operations as possible. Standards are based on averages of past performance or projections of future performance. When the standards are being met (within reasonable limits), the manager does not need to oversee the job process. Instead, managerial time can be spent in future planning or researching new ways of doing the job. When a deviation (or exception) from the standards occurs, the manager then has an immediate signal that managerial attention is needed. Since an exception is defined as a deviation from the goal or standard, management by exception can obviously occur only if goals have been developed and made known.

MBE and Problem Recognition.   Management by exception is widely used by people in all types of problem-solving situations. In its broadest definition, the MBE principle is the key to any problem recognition, because problems are deviations from norms, whether the norms are precise and definite (like numbers) or imprecise and vague (like a "gut feeling" that something is wrong). In either case an exception to some preestablished norm—or expectation or goal—indicates the existence of a problem.

MBE and Numerical Targets. In a formal sense, however, management by exception is generally applied only to those areas in which numerical targets or goals can be set. For example, statistical quality-control models are based on a defect rate that can be permitted to fluctuate within a normal range. By plotting quality-control measurements, the manager can manage by exception. When defects rise beyond the normal range, the problem is signaled and the manager starts the problem-solving process. Other common applications of MBE include financial ratios for monitoring the organization's financial health, break-even charts for monitoring operating costs, and budgets for monitoring the organization's ongoing revenues and expenses. If a norm can be established, management by exception can be used.

Management by Exception: Advantages

Here is a summary of MBE's advantages.

1. MBE helps the manager avoid spending time in unimportant ways. Details and trivial problems are attended to by subordinates.
2. MBE helps the manager concentrate on the problems that really need attention, rather than on so many problems—big and little—that none are handled properly.
3. MBE avoids the need for constant decision making. If operational goals have been established and are being met, the operation runs itself.
4. MBE passes along only the complex problems to the highly paid executives. They earn their pay in solving those problems, not in making routine minor decisions.
5. MBE forces the manager to consider the important influences on the organization's operations, because reasonable targets can be established only in light of those influences.
6. MBE helps avoid truly critical problems. Variations from established standards flag difficulties before they become critical.

RECOGNIZING PROBLEMS

Managers become aware of problems through several means other than by recognizing deviations from targets, standards, or norms. Three of these ways are head-on confrontation, external discovery, and random wandering.

Head-On Confrontation

A car swerves across your path as you drive to work. A power failure shuts down your department's equipment. The government orders you to recall a product to correct a defect. Your product's market share slips from 10 to 5 percent. These examples all represent head-on collisions with the unexpected. The Arab oil embargo illustrates a head-on confrontation that all industries using oil had to face.

External Discovery

When organizational problems are discovered by an outsider, the method is called external discovery. Sometimes management realizes that something is wrong but "can't see the forest for the trees." An outside consultant may be hired to define the exact nature and scope of the problem.

For example, a construction company having employee relations difficulties may not understand the impact that the *variability* in construction employment has upon employee life styles and mortgage payments. Although construction wages are good while they last, they are inconsistent. Employees usually need a constant income expectation pattern to avoid the depressing and demoralizing effects of the construction industry's boom-and-bust cycle.

If you were raised in the construction trade, you might recognize that employee relations were not satisfactory, but you might not recognize the problem as one of job insecurity. An outside consultant might be able to identify the problem quickly and suggest new ways for smoothing out the cycle's impact on employees.

Random Wandering

In a head-on confrontation, the problem looks for you. In random wandering, you go out looking for problems. Such a search assumes that things cannot be perfect, even if organizational goals are being met.

Most organizations have some problem finders. The problem-finding group may be called a methods department, a value analysis group, efficiency experts, troubleshooters, or systems analysts. Whatever the name, they specialize in preventive treatment by spotting and diagnosing problems before they become critical. The danger in this process is that sometimes these groups tend to create problems in order to justify their own existence.

Management by Exception Works Best

Head-on confrontations are problems that the organization, group, or person experiences as a result of what some other organization, group, or person does *unexpectedly*. When the external source creates the problem, the organization begins the problem-solving process. Sometimes the organization perceives that something is wrong but cannot pinpoint the problem. External discovery in the form of a consultant may be used to zero in on the specific difficulty. For those periods in between acute problems, randomly wandering investigators provide a useful precautionary mechanism.

These three methods have their place. However, *the organization can derive the greatest payoff from the MBE strategy for problem recognition.* The organization can make its managers sensitive to most potential problem areas and can provide them with a method for distinguishing what is normal from what is not. Once the organization does so, it has made great progress toward avoiding unforeseen crises, poor direction of employees, lost time, and wasted money.

PROBLEM SIGNALS

The organizational membership needs problem signals that are clear, precise, and unambiguous—signals that all managers perceive and interpret in exactly the same way. Unfortunately, even if problem signals appear to be flawless, different employees are going to perceive the same situation differently. A theoretically perfect problem signal will not help the employee who *cannot* see the problem (because of a perceptual failure) or *will not* see the problem (because of a motivational failure).

Furthermore, examining a difficult *situation* to define the *problem* accurately is a skill not easily taught or learned. And it is an important skill, because not seeing the problem at all or seeing the wrong problem both involve so much waste. If you do not notice an inconsistency between your checkbook and your bank statement, you have missed a problem signal. If you do notice the inconsistency, how you define the problem will greatly influence how—and how hard—you search for alternative solutions.

We are now going to survey two kinds of problem signals: external and internal. External signals are those outside the employee. They are norms or targets established by the organization. When performance varies from the norm or when the target is not reached, a problem is identified almost automatically. Internal signals are those inside the employee. They are flashed when an internal standard or expectation is not met. The discussion of internal signals will explore the differences in the way people perceive things, because perceptual differences, resulting from individual, group, and cultural influences, directly affect how we see problems (or whether we see them at all).

External Signals

We would all like for our subordinates to see the same problems we see, in the same way that we see them. If that situation existed, we would not have to tell people what to look out for. Since managers and their subordinates are rarely so similar, most managers establish goals that subordinates can use as norms for problem identification. If a shipment is due on June 1, or if the third-quarter sales quota is $1,000,000, both manager and subordinate have a standard for problem definition. If the shipment does not arrive on June 1, or if third-quarter sales are $800,000 (or $1,200,000), a problem is signaled automatically.

Budgets.   One common external signal is the budget. Once the budget is established, whether it be a time, cash, sales, or travel budget, it can serve to identify problems. The person managing the budget can note overspending or underspending by merely comparing the budget with reality. Problem solving to close the gap can then begin.

Other external signals include cost-accounting standards, policy manuals, and every device and procedure discussed in Chapter 17. The biggest advantage of these identifying signals is that they do not require personal interpretation.

Internal Signals

When setting up objective problem signals is impractical or impossible, managers must rely on internal signals. When a manager refers to a "gut feeling" or says something "just doesn't look right," an internal signal has flashed a warning.

Sometimes the organization may have difficulty in determining when a normal situation has become abnormal. Here is an analogy to demonstrate that point.

Turtles.   If a common turtle walks across your path, you probably do not view it as a problem. If you round a bend in the path and bump into a turtle 20 feet long and 10 feet high, you would probably start problem solving. At what point does the small no-problem turtle become large enough to represent a problem? On the continuum of turtles from large to small, many different opinions would exist as to when a turtle is too big to be ignored.

If the organization hardly ever bumps into turtles, it has probably not established a problem signal. Managers who bump into turtles are on their own. If the organization begins bumping into more and more turtles of varying sizes, top managers may get together and determine that (1) turtles smaller than 1.5 by 1 foot will be ignored, (2) turtles larger than 1.5 by 1 foot but smaller than 4.5 by 3 feet will be watched closely, but (3) turtles larger than 4.5 by 3 feet require attention by the Turtle Removal Department.

The analogy applies to many organizational tasks. When is the job "too big"? When is the paperwork "too backed up"? When has the number of subordinates become "too large" or "too small"? The answers will vary from manager to manager, because *managers* vary from manager to manager. To see why different managers perceive different situations differently, we need to examine three categories of influences on perception: individual, group, and cultural.

INFLUENCES ON PERCEPTION

Individual Influences

Psychologists continue to debate the causes of perceptual differences. Still, enough information is available to describe how physiological and psychological factors interrelate to cause perceptual differences in seeing problems.

Optical Illusions. We can be tricked into seeing that which is not there. Much of what we "see" is a function of how we have developed our ability to see. Through experience, we have learned to arrange the images coming through our eyes to our brains. The common optical illusions seen in Figure 3-2 use our learning against us, to trick us.

Artists have long known how to use the biases of our training against us. To show a road stretching out in the distance is impossible in a two-dimensional painting unless the artist can make us think we see "depth." Painting shadows behind trees and depicting images in different sizes can create this illusion.

Organizing the Environment. How we organize the environment is another individually based influence on how we see the reality in a situation. The marks in Figure 3-3 could be described as a bunch of dots or as a circle, depending on whether or not the perceiver's mind closes in the gaps between the dots to form a circle. Images on television and photographs in the newspaper are similar; they are nothing but a series of dots. These dots are so close together that viewers hardly ever see dots rather than pictures.

What we *usually* see influences what we *actually* see. Look at the drawing in Figure 3-4. Since we tend to organize information into familiar patterns, most people would describe the drawing as "a square in a circle." A geometrician noticing the drawing might perceive and describe "the region of a disc which is complementary to an inscribed square." Since most of us live in a world of circles and squares, we would probably use the former description.

The Way We See Things. The secret of the optical illusions in Figure 3-2 is that they force us to look at things in new, unfamiliar ways, and we find that very hard. Much of comedy is based on forcing people to see things from an unexpected perspective. The magic of the classic W. C. Fields movies rests on this idea. In a typical example, Fields goes to deal with a banker. The audience knows that Fields is a fraud, even though he is dressed in the clothing of the

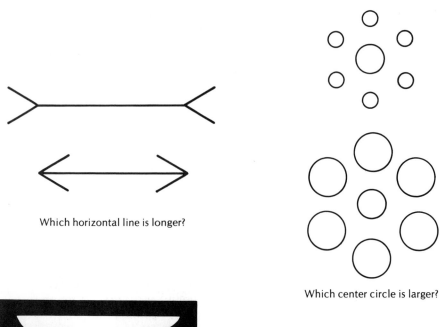

Which horizontal line is longer?

Which center circle is larger?

Vase or faces?

What's the hidden word?

FIG 3-2 Some common optical illusions.

FIG 3-3 A bunch of dots, or a circle?

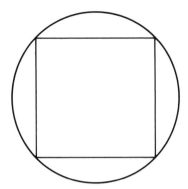

FIG 3-4 A square in a circle?

rich and acts arrogantly successful. The banker confuses Fields' appearance with reality and deals very respectfully with him. The audience sees the incongruity between reality and appearance, but the banker does not. We are reminded in an exaggerated way of the times when we also confused appearance with reality.

The Screening Process.   Experience teaches us to filter out useless information. You may use a certain staircase for 20 years and not know how many steps it has. You may drive the same route to work every day and not know how many billboards you pass. As we lead our daily lives, we are surrounded by vastly overwhelming quantities of information. If we tried to take it all in, we would be totally confused.

To avoid confusion, we screen and organize new information. Based on our experience, we try to notice or retain the relevant and ignore or forget the irrelevant. The number of stairs in the staircase and the number of billboards alongside the road are irrelevant pieces of data for most of us, so we ignore them.

Although this screening process is necessary, it may hinder our ability to see problems. We may filter incoming information so thoroughly that important data cannot get through. The quality of our ability to screen is directly related to the quality of our problem identification skills. The most highly refined of screens are found in the great fictional detectives like Sherlock Holmes and Hercule Poirot. They are nearly infallible at perceiving the useful and screening out the useless.

Physiological Limitations.   Although the preceding influences on a person's perceptions are affected by physiology, some purely physiological aspects of the human information-processing skill affect the problem identification process. Some obvious reasons for literally not seeing problems are loss of eyesight, neural blockages, mental breakdowns, faulty depth perception, fatigue, stress, color blindness, and so on. In addition, all of us have some information processing limitations. The mind can receive and categorize information only so fast. The limits are approximately seven bits of single-dimension data at one time, with an increasing (but not proportionate) capacity for multidimensional data.

For example, most people cannot say their social security numbers without pausing for the hyphens. What they do is to take nine random bits of information and categorize them into three "words," which they are then able to memorize as a numerical "sentence." If you are asked for the third "word," you will probably need to go through the entire "sentence" to remember it. You have put nine random bits into three units, and then have put the three units together into a further refined organizational grouping. You have then filed the entire sequence in your mind as a single chunk of information, rather than as three isolated words.

The Need to Organize.   To compensate for its limited processing ability, the mind organizes incoming information. The need to organize further limits our ability to see the parts of an entire situation. Rather, we see the organized whole and not the individual pieces. We see and then remember a person's *face*, consisting of eyes, nose, hair, mouth, chin, teeth, and so on. (Of course, we may remember an especially prominent feature such as Bob Hope's nose.) People proficient at remembering names merely take the organization scheme that we all use to remember faces, then build the name into this scheme. They not only see a person and remember the face, but the learned association also permits recall of the name. So far as the mind's information-processing procedures are concerned, little difference exists between a nose and a name. The difference is really based on what some people force their minds to do *beyond* the usual association of independent data into "sentence" groupings.

Personal Needs.   Beyond limitations based on psychological and physiological perceptual factors are the needs of the particular person. These needs will be more thoroughly discussed in Chapter 16. For the moment, let us just say that the needs of the moment may influence a person's ability to see problems. At certain times, the need for drugs may make an addict oblivious to any other problems in the environment. Less extreme needs, such as mild hunger, may have similar but less drastic effects.

Group Influences

Friends and Associates.   The second major class of influences upon the manager's ability to see problems is those influences derived from association with other people. All groups with whom we associate—family, friends, and fellow workers—can influence our behaviors and, thereby, our ability to see problems.

For example, consider a social worker whose friends and associates are social workers. All share a similar set of values that they apply when dealing with people. If a woman perceives herself to be a "social worker" rather than a "manager," training her to be a manager may be almost impossible unless she can be convinced that the behaviors of a good social worker and of a good manager are quite different—and in some cases mutually exclusive.

The Pressure to Conform.   Even more impressive is what a group can do to influence a person's ability to see problems. A classic experiment used from seven to nine confederates and one unaware subject to assess this influence. All participants were shown one line (the standard) plus three other comparison lines (see Figure 3-5) and were asked to indicate which of the three comparison lines was exactly as long as the standard line. The confederates made an incorrect choice, leaving the unaware subjects in the position of questioning their ability to see what they thought was there. One-third of the time the subjects would *agree* with the incorrect answer given by the group, denying their own ability to see.

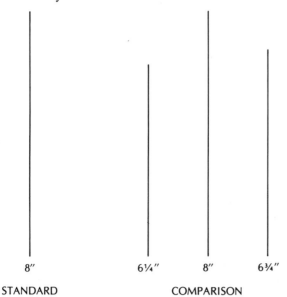

8″   6¼″   8″   6¾″

STANDARD   COMPARISON

FIG 3-5   Match the lines of equal length.

Not all subjects in the preceding experiment were influenced to respond incorrectly, because they had reference points in the form of the other two lines. Without reference points, subjects can be made to doubt their own senses even more easily. In another experiment, a dot of light on the wall of a pitch black room was shown to one unaware subject and a cooperating group. The inaccurate group responses consistently influenced the unaware subject's answers. The subject could be made to report movement when there was none and direction opposite to that which existed merely through group pressure.

In *All the President's Men*, Bob Woodward and Carl Bernstein discussed their effort to expose the Watergate scandal during the Nixon administration. The "length of lines" experiment shows that people will change their perceptions even when they have known points of reference. How difficult it must have been for Woodward and Bernstein not to change their perception of a situation in which the force and power of the entire federal administrative government was pressuring them to see something different from what they thought they were seeing. Having the CIA, FBI, and the Justice Department say you were on the wrong track would probably convince most people that they were indeed on the wrong track.

Cultural Influences

The final category of influence upon a person's ability to see problems is cultural. Some obvious cultural influences are educational major, national or regional identity, religious belief, and career interest. In fact, almost any learned value or belief based on association with culturally similar people can affect the ability to see and define problems. To offer an extreme illustration, consider a black, northern, Catholic industrial engineer trying to explain a problem to a white, southern Baptist market research expert. If they are to perceive the problem in the same way, they must overcome or ignore many culturally based attitudes, beliefs, and values.

Cultural Training.   Here is an example of how cultural training can affect problem definition. Managers in social welfare agencies sometimes tend to manage on the basis of their training in social services rather than their training in management. They consider it a negative comment on their ability to help people if they cannot handle unsatisfactory employees. Instead of defining the problem as "How can I get that job done most effectively?" they see the problem as "How can I rehabilitate that employee?" Some employees are ill-suited to their jobs and should be fired rather than counseled, treated, or rehabilitated. If they are retained, organization will eventually pay for that inappropriate social welfare approach to management by having an ill-suited employee who is nearly impossible to get rid of after the initial trial period.

Cultural Differences and Problems.   Cultural differences are influential in all problem-identification situations. What appears as a problem to one person may be a common occurrence for another. For example, some firms have had real conflict over drugs. The older mid-level and upper-level managers classify use of any drugs as a serious problem. Young gang bosses growing up in a more aware drug climate tend to view drug-involved employees in the same way that they view drinkers, loafers, or skirt or pants chasers.

A recent cultural change has caused organizations to shift their attitudes toward maritally unattached employees. The divorced or single executive used to be considered "a problem." The happily married senior executive type was long sought in the business management world. Now that more persons in our culture are divorcing or choosing not to marry, the stigma against the unmarried executive has virtually disappeared. In fact, the single executive without family distractions and with great mobility is often viewed as an asset.

THE EMPLOYEE'S ORGANIZATIONAL PERSPECTIVE

Inducements, Contributions, and Effort.   As shown in the upper-left section of Figure 3-6, three kinds of psychosocial influences on perception—individual, group, and cultural—have an eventual effect on how much effort the individual is willing to make in order to identify and solve the organization's problems. The psychosocial and physiological aspects in combination influence what inducements (pay, working conditions, and so on) each member (and the membership collectively) requires from the organization.

The bottom of the figure reflects the organization's general goals of profit, growth, and survival. To reach its specific goals, it requires certain contributions (effective performance, commitment, and so on) from its members. To get those contributions, the organization is willing to offer the membership certain inducements.

The degree to which the collective organizational inducements match the collective member contributions will determine the collective effort expended on organizational problem solving. For example, if the membership feels that the organization expects excessive contributions for the inducements offered, the membership will not make a full problem-solving effort. Statements such as "they can't expect me to do that for what I'm paid" reflect this unbalanced situation. When imbalance exists, managers and subordinates do not put their total effort into identifying and solving organizational problems.

The Right Problem.   The key to problem solving is not only recognizing problems but recognizing the *right* problem. A beautiful job of solving the wrong problem or a problem that someone else has already solved wastes time and money. Upper-level managers must recognize individual, group, and cultural influences that affect each subordinate manager's perception of the environment. The organization must continually do its best to ensure that each manager's organizational perspective is correct. Only then will the right problems be identified and solved.

Most managers have a difficult time understanding how much variation their subordinate managers can bring to the problem-identification stage. Managers continually complain about two subordinates: the subordinate who

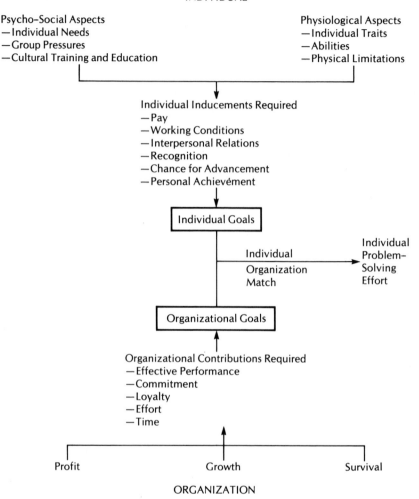

INDIVIDUAL

Psycho–Social Aspects
—Individual Needs
—Group Pressures
—Cultural Training and Education

Physiological Aspects
—Individual Traits
—Abilities
—Physical Limitations

Individual Inducements Required
—Pay
—Working Conditions
—Interpersonal Relations
—Recognition
—Chance for Advancement
—Personal Achievement

Individual Goals

Individual
Organization
Match

Individual
Problem–
Solving
Effort

Organizational Goals

Organizational Contributions Required
—Effective Performance
—Commitment
—Loyalty
—Effort
—Time

Profit   Growth   Survival

ORGANIZATION

FIG 3-6 Inducements, contributions, and problem-solving effort.

did not tell them about a critical problem because the subordinate did not understand how important the problem was, and the subordinate who continually magnifies insignificant difficulties into major problems. Staffing the organization with employees who resemble each other personally and culturally will minimize these differences in problem definition. But variations will still occur.

For example, assume a small work organization comprised of childhood friends who grew up together in the same neighborhood, went to the same schools and churches, had similar experiences, and now have similar interests. Misinterpretations, hurt feelings, and misunderstandings will arise even among this closely knit group of people. However, the group has many com-

56

mon attitudes and characteristics. These qualities in common will encourage them all to recognize and resolve problems in similar ways. Delegating decision making will be simple, because the group members will perceive and interpret situations in roughly the same way.

The diversity of employees in any modern organization makes perceptual differences more likely than similarities. Indeed, from this perspective, it is truly remarkable that anyone ever understands enough about someone else's instructions to get any organizational task done.

SUMMARY

This chapter first showed the relationship between the organization's goals and its problems. This section of the chapter dealt with such questions as how specific should the organization's goals be, and how specific should the employee's assignment be. The suggestion was made that the employee should be given specific goals but should be allowed considerable latitude in terms of deciding how to achieve those goals. In that way, goals can be met, problems can be identified, and employees can grow.

Four methods were then covered for recognizing problems: head-on confrontation, external discovery, random wandering, and management by exception. Although the first three methods have value, management by exception is the best all-purpose approach to problem identification.

Problem signals were divided into those external to the employee (such as budgets and quotas) and those internal to the employee. Employees differ greatly in their ability and willingness to perceive problem signals. One group of influences on problem perception was classified as *individual*. These influences arise out of past experience, the need to screen and organize information, the characteristics of the screening process, physiological limitations, and individual needs. Other influences were categorized as *group*. Our memberships in groups help us to define our experience, but they also pressure us to see things as the rest of the group sees them.

The final influence on perception is *cultural* influence. Group and cultural influences blend together, because our culture is yet another group— one of the largest with which we identify.

The importance of these influences is that *they affect the way in which we perceive situations and define problems.* The organization's task is to encourage its employees to have similar perspectives on organizational problems, despite these many influences that encourage different perspectives.

In a sense, the organization encourages a paradox. *Similar* perspectives seem desirable for identifying problems. But, as we shall see in the next chapter, *different* perspectives seem desirable for creative generation of alternative solutions to problems. For a manager to hold these conflicting attitudes is difficult, but nobody ever said management was easy.

DISCUSSION QUESTIONS

1. How do operational goals aid in problem identification?
2. In your "job" as a student, where do you fall on the job continuum in Figure 3-1?
3. What human problems can arise when goals are too tightly specified?
4. What is management by exception? What are its advantages?
5. How do managers become aware of problems?
6. When external signals are not available to identify problems, how are they identified?
7. How does perception influence the way we see problems?
8. Do groups cause people to see things differently from the way things "really are"? How so?
9. What factors comprise the employee's organizational perspective?
10. Is it possible for two people to see the same situation in exactly the same way? Why or why not?

HARTSELL MANUFACTURING COMPANY

While he was still a college student, Bill Hartsell decided that printed circuit board modules with integrated-circuit chips could be used in many devices, ranging from computers to washing machines. When he graduated, he borrowed some money, rented an old garage, bought surplus equipment from the government, and started Hartsell Manufacturing Company.

He began production with three college classmates, who worked without pay for several months. As orders began to trickle in, Bill found it possible to pay his three employees just enough to get by. The garage was cold in the winter and hot in the summer, but Bill and his friends were highly motivated and worked 12 to 16 hours a day, 6 or 7 days a week.

The hard work paid off. Bill added an assembly line to install components on the circuit boards and increased his staff to 20. He made a determined effort to hire young people, old people, women, minorities, and the handicapped, and he paid them as well as he could. Bill felt a genuine sense of responsibility to his employees and to the community.

His employees did good work, but they had no technical background. To them, a printed circuit board was just a piece of green plastic with copper-etched lines on it. A resistor was just a fat wire with colored bands, to be stuck in holes X-13 and Y-50.

After 5 years, Bill had 300 employees working two shifts. As the business had grown, he had appointed his most senior employees as supervisors of the different product lines and manufacturing steps. Some employees felt that going strictly by seniority did not provide the best leadership.

Bill poured almost all the profits back into the business—into new equipment or facilities or to increase employee pay. He purchased health insurance for his employees, provided generous vacation plans, sponsored an annual company picnic, gave the employees tickets to the university's football games, and so on.

No one worked harder than Bill. He was always the first to arrive and the last to leave. He was all over the plant, attending to every detail, offering advice and suggestions. Everyone knew Bill by sight, and he would stop and listen to the complaints or suggestions of anyone who buttonholed him on the plant grounds. He decided many grievances on the spot and changed work procedures whenever necessary. Not all the supervisors were pleased that employees could take their troubles directly to Bill.

After 5 years of hard work, Bill had a big, new, well-lighted, well-equipped, air-conditioned factory and 300 employees. He was mystified to find that he also had falling production, increased employee turnover and absenteeism, and much talk about "going union." Bill did not dislike the idea of unions, but he was deeply hurt and puzzled about why his employees would want one.

Bill redoubled his efforts to be everywhere at once and to be available to everyone. Matters got worse. Production dropped even more, several key supervisors quit, and union organizing activity stepped up. Bill thought back to the small, close-knit group of friends he had started out with, reflected on his 5 years of hard work, looked around at his beautiful factory with its dissatisfied workers, and wondered what had gone wrong. He realized that he did not even know what his problem was, much less what to do about it.

WILDER'S DEPARTMENT STORE

Since Christmas is approaching and since people are trying to save on gasoline, Wilder's Department Store is selling hundreds of bicycles. Department manager George Nolan realizes that the bicycle department is behind in its record keeping and that the bicycles on display are not always kept neat and clean. Nevertheless, he figures that he and his sales staff can get caught up on such details after Christmas. Meanwhile, they are devoting all their energies to selling bicycles—for cash and on layaway.

If people want boxed bicycles, they can take them home on the day of purchase. If they want assembled bicycles, they are charged $5, are told that they must wait at least 2 weeks, and are told to check periodically by phone to see if the assembled bike is ready. As Christmas nears, the boy assembling bikes is already 100 bikes behind, and every day the bicycle department is selling more bikes than the boy can assemble in a day.

The bicycle department has recently been moved next to toys and sporting goods. Sales of those items are also increasing, and bicycle salespersons have been told to help out with sporting goods and toy sales. The sales for these three departments are all written up at the same cashier's desk and are recorded in the same notebook. Clerks place all sales tickets and layaway stubs in the back of the notebook. As October continues on, the congestion at that desk increasingly gets on the nerves of sales personnel and customers.

Since several department stores obtain bicycles from the same warehouse, clerks in Wilder's bicycle department must call the warehouse several times a day to keep track of which bicycles are in stock. Wilder's cannot sell a particular bicycle if the warehouse has less than 20 of that model left.

The department has a storage problem. It is rapidly running out of space for storing the unsold boxed bicycles, the assembled bicycles, and the bicycles on layaway.

In the middle of October, store manager Mildred Green stops by the bicycle department to commend department manager Nolan on the excellent bicycle sales. Through mid-October, sales are higher than they were through Christmas last year. Green looks around a bit, asks a few questions, and then realizes that if matters continue as they have been going, the bicycle department will be in total confusion during November and December. Bicycles will not be assembled in time for Christmas, the department will have no storage space, the clerks will soon not have time to keep calling the warehouse to check on bicycle availability, congestion at the cashier's desk will increase as clerks fight to record orders in the notebook and to insert or retrieve layaway stubs, customers will be calling constantly to ask if their bicycles are ready, and so on.

Green remembers the bad public relations experiences of last Christmas, when a few children did not get the bicycles that their parents had promised them because the parents did not get the bicycles that Wilder's had promised them. She envisions dozens or hundreds of similar instances this Christmas if she does not get the department squared away.

What is the problem in the bicycle department? What should Green do about it?

4

searching for alternatives

Once the problem has been defined, the search for alternative solutions begins. Since generating alternatives is a creative activity, much of this chapter deals with the creative process.

The chapter begins with an overview of the creative process. The next major section deals with preparing for the alternative search through primary and secondary research. Organizational barriers to creativity are then covered. Finally, the chapter offers several techniques for stimulating creativity.

THE CREATIVE PROCESS

In order for managers to use their own creative talents and to encourage the creativity of their subordinates, they need to understand some fundamentals of the creative process.

Personal Characteristics

Donald MacKinnon says that the characteristics of the creative person include

> His high level of effective intelligence, his openness to experience, his freedom from crippling restraints and impoverishing inhibitions, his aesthetic sensitivity, his cognitive flexibility, his independence of thought and action, his high level of creative energy, his unquestioning commitment to creative endeavor, and his unceasing striving for solutions to the ever more difficult problems that he constantly sets for himself.[1]

Creativity helps in both the problem-identification and the alternative-search phases of the decision-making process. Some organizations may hesitate to encourage creative problem identification, preferring to create automa-

[1]Donald W. MacKinnon, "What Makes a Person Creative?" *Saturday Review*, February 10, 1962, p. 69.

tic problem signals for their members. However, most organizations would welcome greater creativity in the generation of alternatives. Managers would do well to develop in themselves as many as possible of the characteristics MacKinnon mentions.

Steps in the Creative Process

Understanding the stages in creative thinking can help the manager to enhance the organization's creative output. Here is an explanation of the four stages as they apply to problem solving.

Preparation.   Thomas A. Edison said that genius is 1 percent inspiration and 99 percent perspiration. *Preparation* is the perspiration period that must come before inspiration. During the preparation stage, research is conducted, skills are learned, the problem is studied in all its aspects, and the other preliminaries to "creativity" are accomplished.

The problem solver must understand the specific problem and the general situation of which it is a part. When called upon for advice to future managers, many chief executives say something like, "Go learn all you can about the situations you will face in your jobs, because you who are fully prepared to present and defend your point of view will succeed much more often than the people who have not done their homework." This advice means that you cannot do your job without knowing what you're talking about. It also means that the persons who have saturated themselves with the pertinent factors of a problem are most likely to come up with creative alternative solutions.

Incubation.   Incubation refers to the idea of "sleeping on the problem." The problem solver lets the results of stage 1 simmer. No activity toward solving the problem may be apparent. Incubation is largely at the subconscious level, and so it cannot be hurried. Psychologists still do not know why, but this period of incubation is often necessary before a difficult or confusing situation can be seen clearly. Problems with no apparent solutions sometimes become clear after a period of inactivity.

Inspiration.   If preparation has been thorough and incubation has not been rushed, the best alternative for solving the problem may pop out when least expected, without further effort. The humorist James Thurber wanted to write a poem about fish. He did his preparation, then he went to sleep on the problem. He suddenly awoke during the night to find that his subconscious had produced a fish poem. He quickly jotted it down and went back to sleep.

The inspiration occurring during this stage has three qualities. It is sudden, the thinker feels elated, and the inspiration seems to come spontaneously from a mysterious independent source. Most students have had this experience. They study a complex idea in mathematics or physics to the point of exhaustion, become frustrated because nothing seems to make sense, and then all of a sudden the pieces fall together—sometimes after the exam.

Evaluation. Like the preparation period, the evaluation stage involves the hard work of concentrated mental effort. The alternatives generated during the inspiration phase must be viewed with cold objectivity to see whether they are as inspired as they first seemed to be.

The inspired nature of the Thurber poem was not verified in the cold light of the following day. He had written, "The little fish bark / All around the park."

Some Conclusions. Anyone can be creative. Great thinkers and lesser thinkers are different in degree, not in kind. Creativity combines knowledge, imagination, and evaluation. High intelligence helps, but a wide range of personality traits seems related to creativity, including intellectual flexibility, persistence, independence, self-discipline, and even anxiety.

Two general statements seem true of creative problem solving. First, success in solving a difficult problem results from a tremendous preoccupation with that problem. Almost all important discoveries have resulted from long, hard work by the discoverers who have saturated themselves with knowledge about the problem. Second, the problem solver must have a deep tolerance for ambiguity. F. Scott Fitzgerald said, "The test of a first-rate intelligence is the ability to hold two opposed ideas in the mind at the same time, and still retain the ability to function." The same is true of the first-rate problem solver, who must be able to live with the frustrations and anxieties stemming from an unsolved problem.

HOW TO PREPARE FOR GENERATING ALTERNATIVES

This section will offer some suggestions relevant to the preparation stage in the creative process.

The Environment of Search

The search for alternative solutions takes place in an environment of *risk*. That is so because we are never completely certain or completely uncertain about the consequences of any chosen alternative.

The Risk Continuum. On a continuum with certainty and uncertainty as its extremes, the alternatives we choose will have varying degrees of certainty.

Risk

Certainty ⟵ ⟶ Uncertainty

A situation is described as risky when the alternatives of which we are aware fall near the uncertainty end of the continuum. The situation becomes less risky as the consequences of the reasonable alternatives become more predictable.

Open Versus Closed Systems.   Any model attempting to consider various alternative solutions to a problem must somehow take account of risk. The open-system model is open to the many risks of the problem-solving environment. It considers risk rationally. The closed-system model takes into account a certain degree of risk, but *assumes the rest of the risk away* and pretends that it does not exist. The closed-system model includes the important risks, but closes out those risks that are considered unimportant enough to be ignored.

Closed-system computer models or closed-system mathematical expressions are often used in making organizational decisions. They simplify reality in order to simplify the search for alternatives. As an example, consider a manager wanting to determine the "best" inventory level. The manager uses the *usual* influences on inventory in a mathematical expression to find the best solution. The manager *assumes* that *all* forces determining the optimum inventory level are represented in the equation's terms, even though the manager knows that some influences are being ignored. The "best" answer *is* best in terms of the closed model. The manager assumes that this best answer would be the best even if the model were open to the numerous other, minor influences on inventory.

Quantitatively oriented management scholars have contributed many mathematical tools to management. These tools are useful because they incorporate the important alternatives—and the important influences on those alternatives—that must be considered when trying to solve typical organizational problems. Although not all alternatives will be considered, these models ensure that the important ones will be. Expanding the range of possible alternatives would probably cost more than it would be worth.

TYPES OF RESEARCH

Not all problems can be solved by plugging data into a model and punching a button to see what solution comes out. Sometimes the search for alternatives must consist of basic research, both primary and secondary.

Primary Research

Primary research tries to find answers to previously *unanswered* questions. You try to find your answers to your questions. Secondary research tries to find somebody else's answers to somebody else's questions (which have now become your questions, too). In most primary research, (1) a problem is stated, (2) a hypothesis or possible explanation is expressed, (3) data are collected, and (4) the hypothesis is tested by statistically manipulating the data. Three methods for conducting primary research are the survey, simulation, and trial and error.

The Survey.   Primary research is usually the most expensive way to find alternative solutions, but it is sometimes the only way. For example, lack of consumer acceptance can often be explained only through primary research. If Dingle potato chip sales are lagging, the only way to find out why people are not eating Dingles may be to go out and ask them. Different hypotheses and different alternatives could be proposed back at the office, but a primary research investigation in the form of a survey is probably going to be the best way of generating sound alternative solutions.

Morale surveys and attitudinal surveys within the organization also illustrate how this type of primary research can be used to identify alternatives. These surveys may uncover new alternatives that, upon evaluation, might provide the best solution to the problem.

Simulation.   Simulation represents another method for conducting primary research. The researcher constructs a model of the system in which the problem exists. The model can be actual (either scale or full-sized), mathematical, or computerized.

Some situations lend themselves to computer simulation. One complex type is the econometric models that permit computerized simulation of the entire economy. The impact on the country of various economic policies can be simulated by computer. In a simpler instance, computers are used to simulate waiting lines at grocery store check-out counters. Different alternatives for speeding up service are generated by computer simulation.

Other models can be tested without computers. A full-sized model of an airplane wing can be tested in a wind tunnel. A scale model of a city permits generation and exploration of different alternative solutions to a zoning problem. A complete simulation of the Chevrolet Vega assembly operation allowed General Motors to head off a problem before the first Vega was produced. The simulation showed that every so often the dashboard would not meet the surrounding parts smoothly. On the basis of the simulated assembly, the part was redesigned to avoid the poor fit.

Trial and Error.   A less rigorous but widely used method of primary research is "try it and see if it works." This trial-and-error method is similar to simulation except that, instead of experimenting on a model, the researcher experiments directly on the situation itself.

Secondary Research

The most common, least expensive way to search for alternatives is secondary research. It is "secondary" because it involves deriving information from someone else's primary research. To take a simple example, if you have a problem and you ask three other people how they solved the same problem, you are engaging in secondary research. If you read every item in the New York City Public Library concerning your problem, you have also engaged in secondary research. Many possibilities obviously exist between these extremes. The following discussion describes three secondary research methods available to the manager searching for alternative solutions to a problem.

Professional Organizations.   For a practicing manager, an excellent secondary source of information is the trade or professional organization. These groups provide an opportunity to interact with people facing similar problems. The sharing of alternatives and information sources can lead to better solutions for everybody. Many professional organizations, such as the American Society for Personnel Administration, the Financial Executives Institute, the American Business Communications Association, and the American Institute of Certified Public Accountants, publish journals that contain articles on problems and solutions common to the profession.

The Library.   A wealth of no-cost information is available at the nearest library. Numerous indexes, available in the library and listed in the Information Resource Guide at the end of this book, can help the manager find countless alternative solutions to almost any organizational problem. In addition, the library staff can help in deriving information from a vast variety of sources.

The ability to use a library efficiently is important for the manager. A library search takes time, so it should not be used for minor problems. For major problems, the library should often be used because reasonable alternative solutions to all but the most unusual problems can be found *somewhere* in a good library—if the manager knows how and where to look. Since that information is free, why hire a consultant to conduct primary research on a problem that a little secondary research would show has already been solved?

Colleges and Universities.   A third important source of secondary research information is colleges and universities. Many of these institutions have a research and data collection unit, often housed in the College of Business Administration. This office, usually called something like the Bureau of Business Research, collects and analyzes business and economic data relevant to the region served by the school. These bureaus frequently publish their findings in periodical form, which are often available at no charge.

In addition, these research units can frequently serve as a contact point between those seeking and those having expertise. This linkup may lead to a consulting arrangement with a faculty member. Or perhaps a student group may research the problem as an interesting, real-life class assignment.

Never Enough Information. The preparation stage of the creative process must end at some point. Managers hardly ever have all the information they would like to have. Time and money limitations on information acquisition place limits on the number of alternative solutions generated. The manager must be able to assess the costs of finding further information against the benefits (in the form of feasible alternatives) to be derived from that information.

Important problems, complex problems, and risky problems all require time spent in information gathering. Sometimes a problem is complex, risky, *and* important. At other times, the problem may be complex and/or risky but *not* important. Obtaining a well-researched solution to a simple but important organizational problem is far more desirable than obtaining an elegant, complete answer to a complex but trivial problem. Managers must know how to balance these trade-offs and must teach their subordinates how to do so.

Information Costs and Benefits. The ability to know *where* and *how long* to look for alternatives is a critical determinant of an effective manager. The costs and benefits involved in obtaining additional information are shown in Figure 4-1.

The value and cost of additional information appear on the vertical axis. The quality of information appears on the horizontal axis. Information can never be 100 percent perfect, but the more perfect the manager's information, the better the alternatives generated.

The cost-of-information curve (A) will always rise, because getting

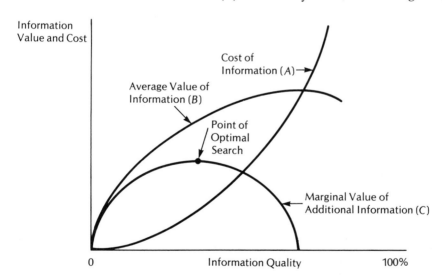

FIG 4-1 The cost, value, and quality of information. (Adapted from *The Managerial Decision-Making Process* by E. Frank Harrison. Copyright © 1975 by Houghton Mifflin Company. Reprinted with permission of the publisher.)

additional information is always going to cost more. In the early stages of investigation, helpful information is often easy to get, so the cost curve rises slowly. Later on, helpful information is harder to find. It becomes increasingly more costly to get, so the curve rises more sharply.

The average-value-of-information curve (B) rises fast at first. It does not take much information to generate some decent alternatives, so the first information units are relatively valuable. The average-value curve levels off as the cost of obtaining information begins to affect the information's value. However, the curve does not turn down for some time because the first information units were obtained so cheaply. Their low cost keeps the average cost down.

Eventually, the average-value curve begins to turn down, as cumulative cost outweighs cumulative value (at the intersection of the cost and value curves in the upper-right part of the figure).

The marginal-value-of-additional-information curve (C) indicates how much the *next additional* piece of information will cost. The curve shows a point of optimal search. Beyond that point, additional information is not worth what it costs. Before that point, additional information is worth what it costs.

This discussion has been largely theoretical. Finding a dependable point of optimality is almost impossible in real life, although closed-system computer models can determine one. The important points for the manager are (1) to remember that early information is cheaper and more valuable than later information, (2) to try not to let average information cost exceed average information value, and (3) to remember that at some point additional units of information are not going to be worth what it costs to get them.

BARRIERS TO CREATIVITY

During and after the preparation stage, barriers of two kinds—organizational and personal—can adversely affect creativity. After describing these barriers in this section, we shall offer some ways of overcoming them in the next section.

Organizational Barriers

Inadequate Incubation.   If an organization does not understand the creative process, it may not realize the need for the incubation stage. For example, at many meetings the facts are laid out and the problem defined; then, in the interests of "efficiency," possible solutions are called for on the spot. The pressures of day-to-day organizational operation may make speed essential. However, managers should recognize that the *quality* of alternatives must suffer if they demand a speedy decision.

Organizational Stability.   Another important influence on organizational creativity is the stability of the environment within which decisions are made. Stable organizations do not feel a need for creative alternatives. They all face similar, recurring problems in regard to technology, markets, and government regulation. These problems have already been resolved with some success many times in the past, so new and creative solutions are not strongly desired.

As an example, the problem-solving atmosphere in a salt mine is probably not as creative as the atmosphere in an organization designing offshore nuclear power plants. Yet, Frederick Taylor's approach to pig iron loading and Frank Gilbreth's approach to bricklaying show that creativity is perhaps needed even more within stable organizational environments. Bethlehem Steel and the bricklayers did not even know they had problems until they were shown the solutions.

Managerial Style.   Managerial style can influence the organization's attitude toward the creative process. People must have time to acquire and incubate the facts, without being under the constant pressure of crises, deadlines, and quotas. The managerial style must be openly supportive of creativity. Yet what do we find in many organizations?

1. Such rigid control over subordinates, jobs, and activities that no possibility of stimulus for creativity exists.
2. A punitive atmosphere that strongly penalizes failure.
3. A lack of involvement by subordinates in decision making.

A harsh, strict managerial style may get today's job done, but the organization will pay a penalty in the long run for its failure to encourage creativity.

Centrism and Organizational Staffing.   Centrism is the tendency to draw toward the middle, rather than expanding out toward the extremes. We exhibit personal centrism in our tendency to associate with people who have interests, backgrounds, training, attitudes, and knowledge like ours. Some organizations do the same thing. Particularly in their staffing, managers hire people like themselves. These similar people may exhibit teamwork and cooperation, but the tendency for the organization to become more like itself is damaging to organizational creativity.

Here is how staffing is affected by the organization's outlook on generating alternatives. All organizations have many recurring problems. Imagine that all the possible alternative solutions to one problem float about in the universe of solutions depicted in Figure 4-2. These alternative solutions are not randomly scattered. They are more dense in certain parts of the universe

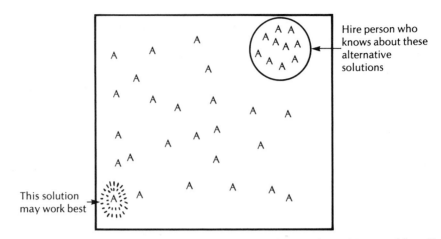

FIG 4-2 The universe of possible alternative solutions for solving problem X.

than in others. Through their staffing practices, most organizations try to hire people who are highly aware of the densely clustered alternatives.

For example, all organizations have personnel problems. So they hire persons with training and experience in the personnel field. Those persons are aware of the most common, most densely packed alternatives for solving personnel problems. The alternatives within the awareness of the personnel expert may all be "good enough" to solve the problem in Figure 4-2. But the very best solution may be in the lower-left corner.

Personal Barriers

Mental Habits.   Even if the organization is relatively free of barriers to creativity, certain personal characteristics can block creativity. In general, persons who are "set in their ways" have blocked their creative impulses. Just as we acquire physical habits of behaving in certain ways, we acquire mental habits of thinking in certain ways. Habits save us from the labor of thinking, but they block an imaginative variety of solutions to a problem.

Sometimes managers get into the habit of pigeonholing things and people. If you find yourself thinking that a product can be used in only one way, or that an employee can perform only certain functions, then you have limited your creative employment of the objects and people around you.

This book is based on a decision-making approach to management. With all its advantages, that approach does tend to emphasize *judgment* rather than creativity. Judgment is often used to preserve or restore the status quo rather than improve on it. Management by exception views a variation from the status quo or norm as a "problem." The manager's goal in solving a problem is to restore the status quo. The manager seeks a practical, high-certainty, low-risk solution, rather than a creative solution. That approach is under-standable and it works, but such an orientation to problem solving does not always help to form a more creative manager.

Personal Centrism.   We tend to associate with people like ourselves. We get our ideas from our associates and give them our ideas. To whatever extent this natural human interaction tendency causes us to reject or be unaware of unfamiliar ideas, we are hampering our creativity.

Several paragraphs ago, a personnel expert reached into the densest part of the alternatives universe for a solution to a personnel problem. That is the way most people, in and out of organizations, go about solving problems. Once the problem is defined and the search for alternatives begins, we reach into the "densest" part of our minds and grab several alternatives that our experience, training, and association with other people have shown to be useful. Our minds rapidly scan the grabbed alternatives. Some may be re-jected immediately. Some may be retained and carried on to the "evaluation of alternatives" stage. The manager in a hurry, or with long experience in solving a particular type of problem, may draw out the *same* solution every time. If the team is doing poorly, fire the coach. If children misbehave, punish them. The more creative solutions might be to fire the team and punish the parents.

A simple illustration will clarify how personal centrism limits the genera-tion of creative alternatives. If your problem is how to get your car from one side of a lake to the other, you will probably grab for the solution you have always used: find a road and drive around. Ideally, though, you should generate and then evaluate all possible alternatives—such as build a raft and float the car across, drain the lake, hire a helicopter, construct a large catapult, disassemble the car and teach some pigeons to carry the pieces across, and so on. While most of these possibilities are silly, they *are* alternatives for solving the problem. In real life, the possibility of training pigeons is not going to occur to the problem solver because of the way in which individuals—and organizations as collections of individuals—actually search for alternatives.

In fact, as a problem solver you have an insoluble dilemma. You cannot know which alternative is best until you have evaluated all the alternatives, and you do not have the time, money, and experience even to *find* all the alternatives, much less evaluate them. Therefore, it is practically impossible to determine what the absolute "best" solution to a problem is.

One way to avoid personal centrism is to force yourself to choose alter-natives at either reasonable extreme of the alternatives continuum. That way you will not always pick alternatives from the cluster most familiar to you. For example, if the team is losing, the reasonable extremes might be "fire the coach" and "fire the team." Then pick a resonable alternative or two some-where between those extremes, like "warn the coach" or "trade some players." As long as time and money last, continue to pick alternatives at different points along the continuum. By choosing and evaluating alternatives in this fashion, you may not hit on the theoretically ideal solution, but you should come reasonably close.

STIMULATING CREATIVITY

The barriers to creativity can be overcome, to an extent. Three groups of techniques for stimulating creativity will now be covered: analytical techniques, free association, and forced relationships. Most of these techniques can be used by individuals, but they can be made even more useful by the application of the synergy principle.

The Synergy Principle

Everybody knows that two heads are better than one. The synergy principle means that two heads are more than twice as good as one—the whole is greater than the sum of its parts. Acting independently, two people can each come up with alternative solutions to a problem. Acting in cooperation, their combined effort will result in more alternatives than the sum of the alternatives they can generate independently. Person 1's contributions trigger new ideas and responses in person 2, which trigger further ideas and responses in person 1, and so on.

Analytical Techniques

Analytical techniques seek to apply the rigors of the scientific method to the creative process. These techniques attempt to ensure that the creativity available to solve a problem *is* focused on the problem. They force problem solvers to consider the problem's various aspects systematically.

The Checklist. A simple, commonly used analytical technique is the checklist. It forces analytical consideration of areas that might otherwise be neglected. Alex Osborne of Batten, Barten, Durstine, and Osborne Advertising Agency urged advertising account executives to apply the following checklist to products:

1. Put it to other uses
2. Adapt it
3. Modify it
4. Magnify it
5. Minify it
6. Substitute it
7. Rearrange it

8. Reverse it

9. Combine it

Checklists have two weaknesses. First, are enough items on the checklist? If some items are left off, not all relevant categories will be explored. Second, are too many items on the checklist? If so, time may be wasted by forced consideration of irrelevant categories.

Attribute Listing.   A second analytical spur to creativity is attribute listing. All attributes, elements, or qualities of an object (or problem, or situation, or person) are listed, and then analyzed one by one. For example, to determine alternative ways of improving a pencil, we would first list its attributes: casing (wooden), color (yellow), lettering (gold), length (7½ inches), width (5/16 inch), lead (no. 2), eraser (red rubber), sides (6). Each attribute would be considered in turn to see whether it could be improved. The attribute list could be used together with Osborne's checklist. Can the wooden casing be put to other uses? Adjusted? Modified? Magnified? And so on. Each attribute could be run through the checklist in this way.

The same process can be used in breaking down a problem into its parts. Most organizational problems are too complex to grasp all at once. Therefore, they are often easier to analyze if they are broken up into attributes or elements. For example, if a company is trying to decide whether to build a nuclear weapons plant out in the country or in the city, it might break the problem down into these elements:

Cost: Yearly operating costs and initial investment in land and plant are cheaper in the country.

Company policy: Company has had success by decentralizing away from the city.

Government requirements: The government wants plants doing nuclear weapons work to locate in isolated areas when possible.

Labor: Skilled and unskilled labor are more readily available in the city, but are more expensive and unionized.

If the problem solvers grapple with the problem as a whole rather than with its elements, they might conclude that locating in the country has many advantages. However, a close look at the "labor" element might reveal that the rural advantages do no good if people cannot be found to work in the plant.

Free Association

The second category of techniques for stimulating creativity is free association. Psychologists often use free-association tests. The human subject is given a word (like *cat*) and is asked for an immediate associative response (like *dog, rat,* or *Siamese*). The pattern of responses enables the psychologist to learn more about the subject. A response of *Hodge* to the test word *cat* would be more revealing (if the psychologist could interpret it) than would be an ordinary response like *dog.* In the organizational setting, free association is used to encourage organization members to build on each other's ideas, rather than to diagnose deep mental states.

Two types of free association will now be discussed: brainstorming and the Gordon technique. These techniques depend on two principles:

1. *Positive attitude* among the participants. These sessions are designed to *generate* ideas, not evaluate ideas. Therefore, no one is permitted to criticize anyone else's ideas. Fear of criticism is a strong personal barrier to creativity. These free-association techniques try to remove that fear by banning criticism.
2. *All types of ideas* are wanted. To keep the creative, synergistic juices flowing, people must be encouraged to generate even strange and impractical ideas, because the most useful idea is often to be found among the most useless. Only after an open exchange of ideas does their critical evaluation occur.

Once these two principles are made known and are understood, the group can let its collective creativity run wild.

Brainstorming. In medieval times, the attackers would storm the castle. In a similar sense, modern brainstorming group members storm their own brains. Alex Osborne's brainstorming technique employs the principles stated above. People come together without a leader to generate a high *quantity* of alternatives. A recorder jots down *all* suggestions for later evaluation. Group members say whatever comes into their heads. Criticism of ideas is prohibited. Members build on each other's ideas. In medium-sized groups of six to eight, synergistic effects can occur, and everyone also gets a chance to offer many ideas.

Disadvantages of Brainstorming. People enjoy brainstorming sessions because they encourage a contagious enthusiasm and an uninhibited atmosphere for producing and building on ideas. However, three disadvantages sometimes occur.

1. *Boredom.* The novelty of brainstorming is exciting at first. People get a thrill out of dropping their inhibitions at the office. After a while, they tire of the "game," lose interest, and stop generating ideas.
2. *Ego involvement.* Group members sometimes have difficulty in maintaining a positive, nonevaluative attitude once their egos get involved. When we hear an idea that we think is absurd, our tendency is to

criticize it. Even if everyone follows the "no criticism" rule literally, group members suspect that other members are being silently critical. Also, people get attached to their own ideas, rather than trying to help the group come up with the *group's* best idea.

3. *Aimlessness.* Since a wide variety of ideas is encouraged—from the practical to the wildly bizarre—the group tends to wander randomly through the universe of ideas. For 2 hours the group may free associate along a train of thought that a moment's critical reflection would demonstrate to be useless or harmful.

The Gordon Technique.   William Gordon tried to remedy some of these problems in brainstorming. One main change he made was to introduce a discussion leader into the leaderless brainstorming format. The leader presents the target topic and then encourages the group to explore its different aspects.

Another change from brainstorming is that the leader uses a key word or concept as a stimulus to group discussion, but the group does not really know *why* they are discussing the key concept. For example, assume that the organization is trying to develop a new kind of toy. Instead of discussing new toys, the Gordon-type group would be encouraged to discuss "play" or "childhood enjoyment." Since group members free associate without limiting their thoughts to "new kind of toy," they may come up with new approaches to conceiving, building, or using toys.

The Gordon technique minimizes ego involvement and aimlessness. Ego involvement is minimal because group members do not know how their ideas are going to be used. Consequently, they do not know whose ideas are outrageous and whose ideas are conservative. Aimless discussion is discouraged by the group leader, who permits "free" association but only along certain lines.

The strengths of brainstorming (anything goes, say whatever you want, no criticism, spontaneity, no leader or boss, creativity) result naturally in its weaknesses (lack of control, aimless discussion, wasted time). For the Gordon method to achieve its advantages (some control, no aimless discussion, little wasted time), some spontaneity and creativity must be sacrificed. However, *if* the leader can provide enough control to avoid aimlessness but not so much as to stifle creativity, the Gordon technique can blend creativity with efficiency.

Forced Relationships

Under this next method for stimulating creativity, the user is forced to detect a useful relationship between two objects or concepts. One type of forced relationship uses a random listing of items. The point is to perceive a useful relationship between each item on the list and every other item on the list. A variation is to pick two random items in a mail-order catalog and then perceive a useful relationship between them.

Although cartoonists use this technique to create new humorous ideas, its applications in the organizational environment are limited. Still it can help stimulate individual creativity in people who know they have barriers to overcome. This technique is worth working on because it embodies one interpretation of just what creativity is: the ability to perceive *new* relationships between familiar items.

SUMMARY

This chapter has related the creative process to the search-for-alternatives phase of decision making. In essence, the messages of the chapter are (1) prepare well, (2) avoid the organizational and personal barriers to creativity, and (3) use the suggested techniques for stimulating creativity.

Floating somewhere in the universe of solutions is the ideal solution to every managerial problem. The manager who knows how to search, properly and creatively, for alternative solutions has a much better chance of approaching the ideal solution than the manager who picks alternatives by using the seat of the pants.

DISCUSSION QUESTIONS

1. What are the steps in the creative process? Is creativity common?
2. Why does an environment of risk characterize search situations?
3. What is the difference between primary and secondary research? Which is more commonly used? Which is less expensive and why?
4. If you were going to conduct primary research, when would you use a survey? Simulation? Trial and error?
5. What is the relationship between the cost of information and its value? How do you know when you have searched for information long enough?
6. What organizational barriers to creativity exist? How might a manager overcome them?
7. What is centrism? How is it related to the searching out of alternatives?
8. What techniques are available for stimulating creativity?
9. What are the differences between the Gordon technique and brainstorming?
10. Assume that you have just been assigned to write a term paper on "Legal Issues in Personnel Management." How would you start your search for information?

AJAX MANUFACTURING CORPORATION

John Hay, founder and president of Ajax Manufacturing Corporation, sat in his office and reflected on the need to find a replacement for himself as president. He had no children and he had neglected to develop a successor to replace himself. The problems of the moment had always seemed too pressing to permit thinking that far ahead. Now medical reasons forced his retirement within the year. Since he was the majority stockholder in Ajax Manufacturing, he could really do anything he wanted to do.

Hay got out a pencil and a piece of paper. He began to jot down some alternative ways of choosing a successor.

What alternatives might John Hay jot down? After he has written down all the alternatives that occur to him upon reflection, what other steps could Hay take to decide on a successor?

JOHNSON POWER TOOLS COMPANY

Edwina Bole, assistant to the president, left a meeting of the Johnson Power Tools Company executive committee with a problem. During the meeting, company president Johnson had told this story: "I was out on the golf course with Billy Dear last weekend, and he told me about a very serious discrimination problem they had over at Dear Electronics. That problem cost them a great deal in terms of money and lost good will. We don't have an affirmative action plan at Johnson Power Tools, and the time has come for us to develop one."

Johnson turned to Edwina Bole. "Ms. Bole, I want you to draft an affirmative action plan for my consideration within two weeks. We can't waste time or we'll be hit with a discrimination suit. Drop everything and get to it. Can you come through on this for me?"

Bole said confidently, "J.B., you'll have your plan in two weeks." However, as she left the meeting, Bole regretted her flat promise, reflecting that she knew very little about affirmative action plans and certainly did not know how to build one. What alternatives might Bole pursue?

evaluating alternatives

Once the problem has been defined and the relevant alternatives uncovered, the next step is to evaluate the alternatives in order to reach a decision. Ideally, *all* alternatives for solving the problem are available to the decision maker during the evaluation stage. In real life, of course, they are not. Consequently, the decision maker always has the option of further exploration to uncover more alternatives, or the option of not making a decision at all—doing nothing.

This chapter explains some quantitative methods for deciding which alternative solution to a problem is best. Mathematical models are first described and are then illustrated by use of the economic order quantity model. A major section of the chapter deals with a popular method for solving certain kinds of resource allocation problems—linear programming.

The preceding models ignore the fact that the future is uncertain. They assume that decisions are made in an atmosphere of certainty. The remaining sections of the chapter explain models that try to account for the risky environment in which decisions are actually made.

QUANTITATIVE MODELS

Closed Models

Many quantitative models are available for evaluating alternative solutions to problems. One type is the *closed* model. The model is constructed so as to represent the relationships among the *important* variables in the problem. Other variables are "assumed away" (ignored); the decision environment becomes closed to them. The model then compares the available solutions and chooses the best one.

Driving to Chicago.   Here is a simple example of how closed models work. If a driver's problem is how to minimize the driving time between Minneapolis and Chicago, the alternative solutions (driving routes) can be determined on a closed model (the road map). The driver can use the model to make reasonably accurate time estimates for driving from Minneapolis to Chicago. On the basis of distances and driving time estimates, the best route can be selected.

However, the "best" route according to the closed model may not turn out to be the best route in actuality. The closed model has ignored Winona, Minnesota's annual Steamboat Days, the traffic jams caused by University of Wisconsin students leaving Madison, Wisconsin, at the end of the school year, and other such predictable events. In addition, the model does not (and cannot) take account of such unforeseen events as detours, traffic accidents, or bad weather. Instead, the closed model merely provides the driving routes with some indication as to the kind of road—two lane, four lane, interstate, and so forth. On the basis of this essential but limited information, the decision maker selects the "best" driving route.

While foreseen and unforeseen difficulties might affect the solution to the route problem, the decision maker would probably consider the time and effort involved in "opening up" the closed decision model not worth the cost. Since experience indicates that the quickest route can usually be perceived on a road map, automobile drivers seldom feel the need to evaluate other variables. On the other hand, the driver of a truck with an oversized load would need information about bridge clearances, overhead wires, local laws, and so on, before choosing a route. The truck driver would have to open up the closed decision model that the auto driver found satisfactory.

Economic Order Quantity Model

In a similar sense, many models used to evaluate organizational alternatives are derived from a mathematical description of the important relationships existing in a problem situation. Consider these questions that each manufacturing firm must answer with regard to its inventory: (1) At what point should we replenish our widget inventory by producing more widgets? (2) When we start producing more widgets, how many should we produce? To help answer the latter question, the economic order quantity (EOQ) model represents the important variables mathematically.

Figure 5-1 shows a typical inventory cycle as it responds to stock depletion and rebuilding over time. Starting at point A, the line between A and B represents the inventory building stage. During this period, product is being both manufactured and shipped to purchasers. Since product is manufactured faster than it is shipped, a stock of product is built. A predetermined maximum stock level is reached at point B, and production is stopped. The continuing demand begins to drain the stock supply, so the line turns down at point B. Inventory runs out at point C, and so the manufacturer accepts back orders until they reach a maximum back-order level at point D. At that

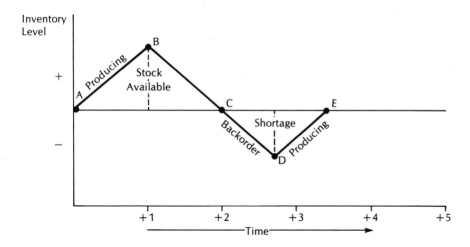

FIG 5-1 A typical inventory cycle.

point production begins again, and the back orders are filled from new production until point E is reached. Points E and A are the same; they mark the completion of one cycle and the beginning of a new cycle. To decide where to start and stop producing, the manufacturer can use the EOQ model.

EOQ Model Components. By using the EOQ model, the producer can mathematically express the important influences on inventory and then use the model to minimize costs. The following factors are important:

1. *Demand rate* (represented by r). How many units of the product will be needed over the coming period? If the manufacturer overestimates demand, too much product will sit in the warehouse or on shelves for too long. If the manufacturer underestimates demand, customers who cannot buy product may go elsewhere.
2. *Production rate* (represented by k). How fast can product be manufactured?
3. *Holding cost per unit over the coming period* (represented by c_1). Carrying unsold product costs money. The manufacturer does not want to hold too much.
4. *Shortage cost per unit over the coming period* (represented by c_2). Carrying insufficient inventory means lost sales. The manufacturer does not want to hold too little.
5. *Setup cost each time production is started* (represented by c_3). To stop manufacturing one product and start manufacturing the product in short supply costs money. If the EOQ formula is being used by a firm that buys its inventory rather than manufacturing it, c_3 would be the firm's *ordering* cost.

81

6. *Quantity produced per production run* (represented by q). When the predetermined low inventory point D has been reached, an automatic "problem signal" is flashed. Given factors 1 through 5, how much new product should be manufactured at point D?

EOQ Formula. The relevant factors are combined in equation (5-1) to solve the manufacturer's problem:

(5-1)

$$q = \sqrt{\frac{2rc_3}{c_1} \quad \frac{1}{1-(r/k)} \quad \frac{c_1+c_2}{c_2}}$$

The model is often simplified by assuming instantaneous production and by assuming that inventory never drops below zero. Those assumptions do away with the seond and third parts of equation (5-1). That operation leaves this simplified, useful EOQ formula:

$$EOQ = \sqrt{\frac{2\pi c_3}{c_1}} \qquad (5\text{-}2)$$

Note the assumptions built into the model as represented in equation (5-2):

1. Demand is known with certainty; the model is closed to the possibility of fluctuations in demand.
2. Inventory will drop at a known, constant rate; the model ignores the fact that inventory depletion is actually irregular because sales are irregular.
3. Inventory never runs out.
4. All needed new inventory can be produced instantly.
5. *When* production should resume is known with certainty.

Under those assumptions, the EOQ model will tell the manufacturer how much to produce during each production run. The model involves unrealistic assumptions, but it does include the important influences on the inventory cycle, and it does encourage a sounder basis for making production decisions than trial and error or intuition.

An Example. Here is an example of how the EOQ model might be used. Rodney Trent, owner of Rodney's Cycle Shop, has decided to sell mopeds. Rodney figures that he will sell 20 mopeds per week at $400 each.

Rodney knows from past experience that he has two basic inventory costs: *ordering* costs and *carrying* costs. He estimates that costs for placing each order (mailing costs, typing costs, and so on) will be $5. He knows that his weekly interest cost on the money he borrows to finance the inventory will be $1.75 per moped. In addition, he must add in a small amount for minor damage that mopeds in the shop will incur, bringing the total weekly holding cost to $2 per moped.

Rodney uses ordering cost as his equivalent of the manufacturing term "setup cost" (c_3 in the EOQ formula). He considers "the coming period" to be one week. Using the EOQ formula, Rodney can determine how many orders he should place each week and how many mopeds he should order at a time.

$$EOQ = \sqrt{\frac{2(20)(\$5)}{\$2}}$$

$$= \sqrt{100}$$

$$= 10 \text{ mopeds per order}$$

Rodney expects to sell 20 mopeds per week. The EOQ formula tells him that he should order 10 mopeds at a time. Therefore, he must place 2 orders per week.

If his holding costs (c_1) increase (or decrease) and all other factors remain the same, he will order more (or less) frequently. If his order costs (c_3) increase (or decrease) and all other factors stay the same, he will order less (or more) frequently.

Now that we have seen a fairly simple quantitative model in action, let us examine a more complex model: linear programming.

LINEAR PROGRAMMING

Allocating Scarce Resources

If a firm makes only one product (antons, let us say), all equipment and labor go toward making antons. The firm's only production decision is whether or not to operate at capacity or at a level short of capacity. If plant capacity is 1000 antons a day, the firm must decide whether to make 1000 antons or to make less than 1000 antons. However, if the firm produces two products (antons and banyons, let us say), the firm must decide how to balance the use of its scarce resources optimally between them—to maximize profit (or perhaps to minimize loss or cost).

Antons and Banyons.   Linear programming is typically used to analyze alternatives when resources are scarce. Consider this production problem. The Deaton Company manufactures two products: antons and banyons. They must both be molded and polished. The molding department has 160 available hours per month, and the polishing department has 240 available hours per month. Each anton is processed for 2 hours in the molding department and for 6 hours in the polishing department. Each banyon is processed for 4 hours in the molding department and for 4 hours in the polishing department. The profit on each anton is $7, and on each banyon it is $10. *Problem:* How many antons and how many banyons should the Deaton Company produce per month? No answer is intuitively obvious.

Profit on Antons or Banyons.   Deaton might approach the problem this way. How many antons can be produced if no banyons are produced? Since the molding department has 160 available hours and each anton requires 2 hours of processing in that department, 80 antons can be molded. The polishing department can process 40 antons (240 available hours ÷ 6 hours per anton). Antons must be both molded and polished. Therefore, only 40 antons can be produced per month since the most severe constraint (polishing capacity) dictates the level of production. Profit to the Deaton Company will be $280 ($7 per anton × 40 antons) if only antons are produced.

How many banyons can be produced if no antons are produced? The molding department has 160 available hours. Each banyon must be processed for 4 hours. Therefore, molding can process 40 banyons. The polishing department can process 60 banyons (240 hours ÷ 4 hours per banyon). Since banyons must be both molded and polished, only 40 banyons can be processed by both departments for a profit of $400 (40 banyons × $10 profit per banyon). If the Deaton Company must decide between manufacturing antons *or* banyons, they will choose banyons since they can make $120 more per month that way.

We are assuming that the company's primary object is to make as much money as possible—to maximize profit. If other influences are at work, the approach we have outlined may not serve the company's purposes. For example, if the Deaton family owns 100 percent of the company's stock and is determined to keep making antons because the firm has made antons for several generations, then the Deaton Company is going to keep making antons.

Profit on Antons and Banyons.   The Deaton Company knows what the profit would be if one *or* the other product—antons or banyons—were produced. But perhaps profit would be even greater if the company manufactured a *combination* of the two. For example, if the company can produce 50 antons ($7 × 50 antons = $350 profit) and 10 banyons ($10 × 10 banyons = $100 profit), total profit will be $450. Linear programming is a quantitative method that allows the Deaton Company to determine the most profitable mixture of antons and banyons to produce, given the limited capacity of Deaton's polishing and molding machines.

Linear Programming Defined.   *Programming* is a mathematical model designed to maximize results (such as profits) or minimize losses when resources (such as molding and polishing capacity) are scarce. *Linear* means that the relationships among the programming model's variables are proportionate. That is, one anton requires 8 hours of processing (molding and polishing) and results in a $7 profit. Five antons require 40 hours of processing and result in a $35 profit. Relationships other than proportionate ones are called *curvilinear*, because a curved line results if they are plotted on a graph.

Plotting the Constraints.   To solve the Deaton Company's anton–banyon problem graphically, the two limitations on production, limited molding and polishing capacity, must be graphed. In management problems, such limitations are called *constraints*. Figure 5-2 pictures the constraints placed on production by the molding department. That department has 160 available hours, so Figure 5-2 graphs the maximum number of antons (80) and banyons (40) that can be molded in 160 hours. Any point within the shaded area or on line *DC* might be the most profitable solution. If a point on the line is selected, all 160 available molding hours will be used. If a point within the shaded area is chosen, only a portion of the available hours will be used, leaving *slack* (unused) time. Any point outside the shaded area would not be feasible because more than 160 hours would be required.

Figure 5-3 plots the situation in the polishing department. The maximum numbers of antons (40) and banyons (60) that can be polished, along with all feasible anton–banyon combinations, appear in that figure.

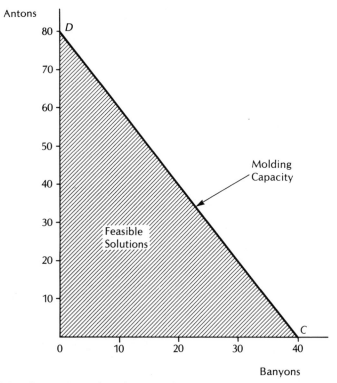

FIG 5-2 Constraints placed on production by the molding department.

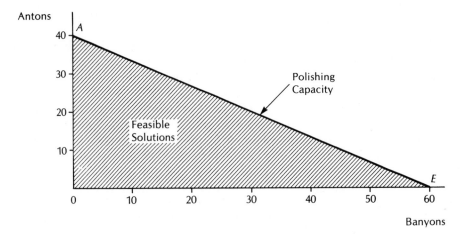

FIG 5-3 Constraints placed on production by the polishing department.

Combining the Constraints. Figure 5-4 combines both constraints. The area bounded by line *OABC* contains all potential anton–banyon manufacturing alternatives. This area is called by various names. *Area of feasible solutions,*

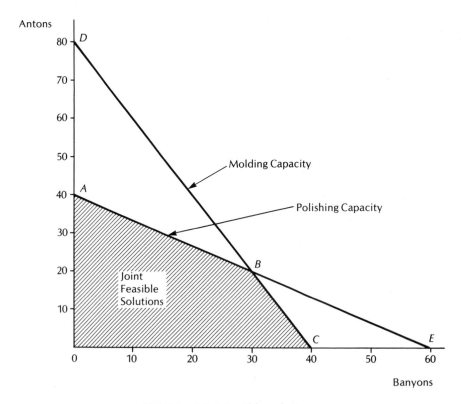

FIG 5-4 Joint feasible solutions.

feasible region, feasibility area, feasibility polygon, solution space, and strategy space are some of them.

Profit at the Corners.   The most profitable manufacturing combination will be found at one of the four corner points O, A, B, or C in Figure 5-4. If point O turns out to be best (with a zero profit), the Deaton Company should probably quit making both antons and banyons. If point A (all antons, no banyons) shows the most profit, the company should probably get out of the banyon business. If point C (all banyons, no antons) shows the most profit, the company should probably stop making antons.

The profit at point O is zero. The profit at point A is $280. The profit at point C is $400. What is the profit at point B? Figure 5-5 shows that point B reflects the manufacture of 30 banyons ($10 × 30 banyons = $300 profit) and 20 antons ($7 × 20 antons = $140 profit), for a total profit of $300 + $140 = $440.

Isoprofit Lines.   Here is another way of describing why point B represents the best anton–banyon combination. Consider Figure 5-6. Any amount of total profit must be made up of the combined profits on some number of antons (at $7 profit each) and some number of banyons (at $10 profit each). For example,

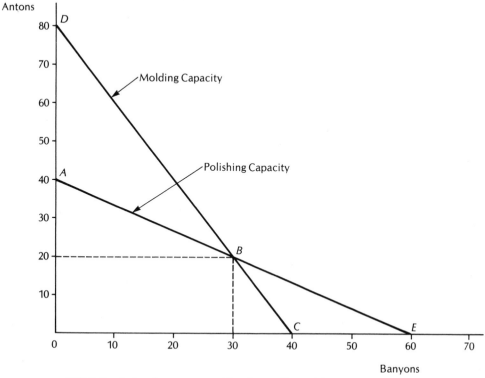

FIG 5-5   Anton-banyon combination reflected by point B.

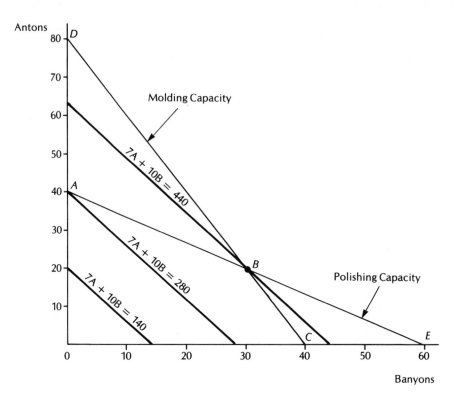

FIG 5-6 Anton-banyon isoprofit lines.

a profit of $140 can be made at any point on the "$140 profit" line, from 20 antons at $7 profit each to 14 banyons at $10 profit each. Similarly, a $280 profit can be made at any point on the "$280 profit" line. If we keep drawing these parallel lines (called *isoprofit* lines), we will find that a line indicating a $440 profit will just touch point B. The $440 profit will consist of a $140 profit on antons (20 antons at $7 profit each) and a $300 profit on banyons (30 banyons at $10 profit each). Because of time constraints in the polishing and molding departments, Deaton cannot make (1) more than 30 banyons while also making 20 antons, or (2) more than 20 antons while also making 30 banyons. So a profit of $440 is the most that Deaton can make on any anton–banyon combination.

To look at the problem in another way, the $440 isoprofit line shows that Deaton could make a $440 profit by manufacturing 44 banyons (at $10 profit each) or 62.86 antons (at $7 profit each). Unfortunately, the molding department has capacity to mold only 40 banyons (not 44), and the polishing department has capacity to polish only 40 antons (not 62.86). However, the combination of 20 antons and 30 banyons is possible and will bring a profit of $440.

Limitations of the Graphic Method. In a linear programming problem, any number of constraints can be graphed. For example, assume that the antons and banyons must be heated, molded, sanded, and polished. The area of feasible solutions might look like the area bounded by line *OABCDE* in Figure 5-7. The manager would have to calculate profit at six points to see which manufacturing alternative should be chosen, or draw isoprofit lines to see which corner is barely "nicked."

Although unlimited constraints can be graphed, only two products can be graphed—one on each axis. Since real-life situations usually involve more than two products, the graphic method has few actual applications, although it is the clearest way to describe how linear programming works.

In actual practice, computers usually do the work. The computerized linear programming model can handle thousands of products and constraints. The computer identifies the most promising production combinations and then specifies the most profitable combination.

More Sophisticated Programs

One disadvantage of the usual linear programming model is that it assumes certain knowledge about an uncertain future. Most organizations do not have complete control over demand for their products and services, reactions by

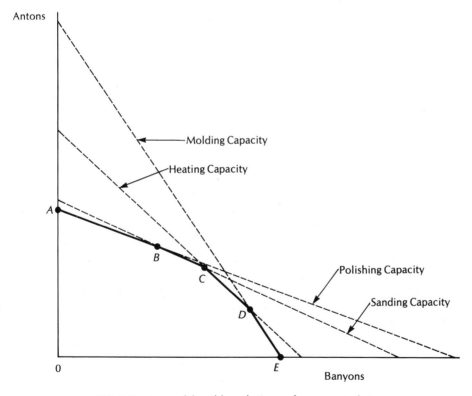

FIG 5-7 Area of feasible solutions: four constraints.

competitors, availability of resources, governmental regulations, and many other external influences on organizational performance. So when any model, quantitative or otherwise, is developed for solving a problem, management must remember that the solution is "best" only until conditions change. And change is often sudden and unexpected.

Sensitivity Analysis.   One method for determining how changing conditions will affect the "best" solution is sensitivity analysis. It answers such "what if" questions as the following:

1. What if a new constraint emerges or a present constraint disappears? (What if the molding department suddenly has more hours in which to process antons and banyons?)
2. What if cost or profit contribution estimates change? (What if the contribution on an anton becomes $8 instead of $7 at present?)
3. What if technology improves? (What if the productivity of Deaton's molding and polishing equipment increases?)

Sensitivity analysis gives answers to these questions after the model is constructed but before it is used. In essence, different extremes are used in the constructed model to see whether they might affect the "best" solution. Since an infinite number of recalculations is possible and they all cost money, the manager is once again in the position of determining at what point additional information costs more than it is worth.

Goal Programming.   Another disadvantage of the usual linear programming model is that it can handle only one goal (like "maximize profit") at a time. Actually, organizations have many goals, and they often conflict. For example, the manufacturing organization may want to maximize profit, but it may also want to increase employee wages. Unnecessary wage increases are incompatible with profit maximization. A quantitative tool called *goal programming* can handle conflicting goals.

Consider Pinball, Inc., a company that leases pinball machines. To use goal programming, Pinball, Inc. must decide what its goals are and must then rank them in importance. Pinball, Inc. comes up with this list:

1. Achieve a return on investment of at least 15 percent.
2. Maintain employee pay at present levels.
3. Maintain the current level of 1200 leased pinball machines.
4. Maintain advertising and promotional expenditures at present levels.
5. Maintain the current growth rate of 50 additional leased machines per year.
6. Achieve a target return on investment of 20 percent.

7. Raise employee pay 5 percent.
8. Increase advertising and promotional expenditures by $3000.
9. Lease 100 more pinball machines via a special sales campaign. The goal-programming procedure will tell Pinball, Inc. whether and under what conditions these goals can be attained.

Criteria for Using Linear Programming

The anton–banyon problem illustrates the kind of situation to which linear programming is applicable:

1. The organization must have a *goal* that it wants to maximize (like profits) or minimize (like costs or losses). Linear programmers call this goal the *objective function*.
2. The goal must be expressed in mathematical terms.
3. The organization must have alternative ways of achieving the goal (like producing all antons, or all banyons, or an anton–banyon combination).
4. Resources (like manpower or raw materials) must be limited.
5. Relationships in the problem must be linear. If sales double, profits must also double. (Nonlinear programming methods are available. However, they are much more mathematically complex.)

Linear programming is one of the most widely applied quantitative techniques. It is often applicable whenever scarce resources must be allocated to different uses—allocation of raw material to products, people to machines, finished goods to warehouses, executives to committees, funds to investment opportunities, and so on. Some areas of application include production, plant location, finance, accounting, marketing, and ecology.

Production.   Linear programming can solve many basic production problems. A classic example occurs in the manufacturing of animal feeds. Since the profit margin is very low, the feed manufacturer must be especially efficient. The problem is to produce animal food at lowest cost while providing at least the minimum nutritional requirements. The linear programming model considers the cost and nutritional value of each ingredient and then indicates the least costly combination that fulfills nutritional requirements.

Other well-known models have been developed for the production of oil, chemicals, blast furnaces, transistors, food, plywood, and so on. Descriptions of these models appear in such journals as *Operational Research Quarterly*, *Operations Research*, *Management Science*, and *Journal of Systems Management*.

Some production problems are quite complex. A firm may use several locations to process numerous raw materials into dozens of finished products. The problem becomes: How many units of each product should be manufactured in order to maximize profit? To solve problems like that, Shell Oil Company began using quantitative methods in the late 1950s. Their linear programming model had to determine how to allocate various crude oil types to refineries, how the oil should be processed and blended, and how to distribute the finished product to numerous markets most efficiently. When a model must consider a dozen grades of 25 products being processed at 75 to 100 refineries and finally distributed to several hundred markets, the problem becomes large. In fact, it may involve hundreds of variables and several thousand equations. The advantages of linear programming over seat-of-the-pants or trial-and-error methods are obvious.

Plant Locations.   Another common linear programming problem is where to locate a new plant. Consider this example. The Deaton Company now has anton plants in Milwaukee and St. Louis. Antons are shipped to warehouses in Miami, Atlanta, Denver, and Chicago. Where should a new anton plant be located so that transportation costs of plant-to-warehouse shipments are minimized? A new plant will affect the total plant–warehouse transportation system, so linear programming might be used to compare all the possible new transportation alternatives.

Finance and Accounting.   Several financial and accounting problems can be effectively framed in a linear programming model, among them capital budgeting, portfolio selection, and bank asset management. Most business firms have limited capital and numerous potential investment alternatives. Firms can analyze the risk and return of each alternative separately, but *combined* packages of investments often have risk–return characteristics that differ from those of the individual assets making up the package. Linear programming considers the *joint* effect of various combinations in light of how high a yield the investing firm requires and how much risk it can accept on its investments.

Marketing.   Although many marketing problems are difficult to quantify, two linear programming applications have gained some support: media selection and retailing decisions.

Organizations want as many potential consumers as possible exposed to their advertisements. How should advertising dollars be allocated among different advertising media? The firm with such a problem has *limited resources* to spend on advertising and has *alternative uses* for those resources—the combination of characteristics for which linear programming is best suited. The alternative solutions to the problem would be the various media combinations. The constraints would be such limitations as funds available for advertising; numbers and types of people exposed to various media; desired minimum and maximum number of advertisements in each medium; desired full-page, half-page, and prime time advertisements; and so on. Just as in the antons–banyons problem, the computer checks the corner points of the feasibility region and identifies the combination of advertising media that will maximize exposure to potential consumers.

Linear programming can be used by retail organizations that are buying items for several price lines. The problem is how to maximize profit. The alternative solutions are the quantities of items to be purchased for each price line. The linear programmer must consider such constraints as cost of the items in each price line to the firm, sale price of these items to the customer, sales per square foot of store floor space, customer age and income, average sales per period, and turnover of merchandise. The computer considers these influences and then concludes, let us say, that 10 percent of available funds should be used to purchase items for the Ritz line, 30 percent for the Standard line, and 60 percent for the bargain basement.

In terms of the problem and constraints as stated, 10–30–60 percent *is* the "best" solution. However, recall that we are describing a *closed* model in operation. Many predictions about the future are incorporated into the retailing linear program model—two large uncertainties being how consumers and the general economy are going to behave over the coming period. If the economy booms or if styles suddenly become more dressy, the proper proportion might turn out to be 60 percent Ritz, 30 percent Standard, 10 percent bargain basement. The model assumes perfect forecasting, and retail forecasting methods are far from perfect.

Ecology.   We need the products that advanced manufacturing technology has made possible. Unfortunately, this technology often affects the ecological balance adversely.

The hundreds of pollutants that thousands of business and governmental organizations emit must be kept below legally allowable limits. The polluting organization's problem becomes how to find the least costly way to use an available combination of pollution-control methods to keep pollutants within legally accepted limits. For example, the computer might explore the options available to a public utility, then recommend converting three boilers to low-sulfur coal and seven to natural gas.

Advantages of Linear Programming

For several reasons, linear programming is one of the most powerful, effective, widely used mathematical tools for solving operational problems.

Alternative Uses of Resources.   Linear programming shows the firm how much each alternative use of scarce resources will contribute to organizational objectives. If a firm uses dozens of raw materials to manufacture hundreds of products, using seat-of-the-pants methods or a gut feeling to determine the best number of each product to manufacture is not very accurate. Once each product's profitability has been calculated and each constraint has been identified, the linear programming model will suggest how resources may be optimally allocated.

Understanding the Problem.   Linear programming provides management with a better understanding of the problem facing the organization. The most difficult aspect of linear programming is *setting up the problem.* To do so, the firm must calculate each product's profitability and must identify each constraint. In the process, the firm may find that some products are not contributing to profit, others are being produced inefficiently, and some resources are not being used to best advantage.

Objectivity.   Another advantage of linear programming is its objective evaluation of alternatives. The linear programming model has no attitudes, values, or psychological limitations. Based on facts and estimates, the model offers management the optimal solution.

Limitations of Linear Programming

Linear Relationships.   Linear programming does have its limitations. First, the model requires the assumption that relationships are at least approximately linear. In a profit-maximization problem, linearity means that doubling the sales volume will double the revenue. In real life, an increase in productivity and sales usually means a decrease in cost per unit and an increase in profit per unit.

Quantification.   Second, like other quantitative techniques, linear programming assumes that all important constraints can be identified and requires that they be quantified. This identification and quantification are hardly ever easy to do. The Deaton Company's linear programming model assumes that the molding department can process an anton in 2 hours. For numerous noneconomic reasons, anton processing time might be well below or above that level. Even more difficult than quantifying constraints is quantifying profit per item. A firm that produces hundreds of items may know what its total costs and profits are, but estimating how much each item contributes to profit may be almost impossible. Yet linear programming models demand the numbers. Furthermore, once the numbers have been estimated, they create a false sense of security. Model users tend to forget that the numbers are often no more than rough guesses.

Lack of Management Understanding.   A third limitation of linear programming sometimes arises because of a limitation within managers. Some of them do not understand linear programming or other quantitative techniques and do not want to broadcast their ignorance. So they may not use all the helpful techniques that are available to them, and they may misunderstand or misinterpret the results of the techniques they do use.

Cost.   Finally, linear programming may be costly. Firms using it must maintain extensive, timely, and accurate information about all resources, products, and services. The organization must employ capable operations research personnel to build models and interpret their output.

Although some simple linear programming applications can be calculated by hand, most of them require access to computer systems. In the future, as more and more firms use computers, the cost of computer time will decrease and the processing capacity of computers will increase. These developments will diminish actual computer costs. However, the human costs of getting managers to sit down and define problems clearly will remain.

METHODS USING PROBABILITIES

Closed decision models like the EOQ inventory model and linear programming imply a level of awareness and certainty on the part of decision makers that simply does not exist in the real world. Therefore, other decision theory techniques use more open models in an attempt to account for the riskiness of different alternatives in some fashion. For example, instead of assuming with certainty that sales next year will be $1,000,000, as a linear programming model might require, a firm might establish a probability of 0.60 for $1,000,000+ in sales next year, 0.30 for $800,000 to $1,000,000 in sales, and 0.10 for less than $800,000 in sales. These probabilities would be one of two kinds: objective or subjective.

Objective Probability

Objective probabilities are based on how often real past events occurred. They assume that the future will repeat the past. If over the past 10 years ABC Company has had 6 years of sales in the $1,000,000+ range, 3 years of sales in the $800,000 to $1,000,000 range, and 1 year of sales below $800,000, then the frequency of these past occurrences can be used to predict that there is a 60 percent chance of $1,000,000 in sales next year. If, instead of 10 years, ABC Company has 100 years of data, the probability estimates might be even more reliable, thanks to the *law of large numbers*. This law states that, given the frequency with which different events have taken place in the past, a stated probability becomes more reliable as the total number of events is increased. That is why an opinion survey based on 1,000,000 responses is more reliable than a survey based on 1000 responses.

Of course, if present circumstances are very different from past circumstances, the decision maker may not believe that the future will repeat the past. The manager trying to forecast ABC Company's sales next year may use the 10-year sales figures rather than the 100-year sales figures, because what happened in the nineteenth and early twentieth centuries is probably irrelevant to the coming year.

Applications.   Accurate frequency-of-occurrence information is available for many decision situations. Based on equipment breakdown histories, electric power companies can produce maintenance schedules. Airline companies overhaul airplane engines on the basis of historical stress and breakdown data. A traffic-flow history can be used to decide how many toll booths on a turnpike should be kept open, and during which hours.

Subjective Probability

In recent years, interest in using statistics to evaluate *nonrecurring* problems has grown. One way of evaluating the alternative solutions to such problems is through *subjective* probability. Even though managers frequently face new problems, they seldom confront complete uncertainty (or certainty) about what the future holds or what the results of different alternative solutions may be. Instead, based on their experience, training, information, and judgment, they can assign probabilities to various outcomes. Certain quantitative models demand that such probabilities be assigned.

Constructing the Matrix.   Managers often have to evaluate alternatives when a long history of information is unavailable or useless. In these situations, they can express whatever information they do have in the form of probability estimates about future events.

For example, suppose that the ABC Company is going to build a new plant. To simplify the situation, assume that ABC has two alternatives: a *big* plant or a *small* plant. Assume that demand for ABC's products next year will be either *big* or *small*. Based upon what the firm knows about its costs and revenues, ABC can construct a *payoff matrix* showing the alternatives, the two possible demand conditions (called *states of nature*), and the possible outcomes or *payoffs*:

	Big Demand	Small Demand
Build Big Plant	$6,000,000 net profit	$1,000,000 net profit
Build Small Plant	$4,000,000 net profit	$3,000,000 net profit

Assigning Probabilities.   If demand next year is going to be big, ABC should build a big plant. If demand is going to be small, ABC should build a small plant. ABC must now assign probabilities to the outcomes "big demand" and "small demand." ABC has historical information, experience, intuition, expert forecasts, and the advice of consultants. Putting these items together, assume that ABC assigns a probability of 60 percent to "big demand" and 40 percent to "small demand." But ABC still does not know whether to build big or small. One more step is needed: the calculation of the *expected value* for each alternative to see which expected value is higher.

Expected Value.   To determine the expected values, each possible payoff for a given alternative must be multiplied by its probability of occurrence, and the results must be summed. In the big plant–small plant example, the equations will look like this:

Expected value, big plant	= $6,000,000(0.60) + $1,000,000(0.40)
	= $3,600,000 + $400,000
	= $4,000,000
Expected value, small plant	= $4,000,000(0.60) + $3,000,000(0.40)
	= $2,400,000 + $1,200,000
	= $3,600,000

On the basis of this analysis, ABC Company would build a big plant because that alternative has the highest expected value.

ABC had better not actually expect to achieve that "expected" value, which is simply a statistical term. If projections are correct, ABC will receive one of the four payoffs in the matrix: $6,000,000, $1,000,000, $4,000,000, or $3,000,000. Expected-value analysis is just a way of comparing alternatives, not a way of arriving at what results can actually be "expected."

Expected-value analysis is not always the most appropriate method for evaluating alternatives. For example, a solid municipal bond portfolio and a portfolio of uranium stocks may both have an expected value (called *expected return* in the investments context) of 5 percent. However, the two portfolios are obviously not equivalent. Some other shortcomings of expected-value analysis will be described in the next chapter.

Decision Trees

For complex problems involving a series of events over time, a manager can combine the expected value approach with another useful tool for evaluating alternatives: the decision tree. Decision trees permit managers to examine the outcomes that a *sequence* of decisions may have. The alternatives and influential events are laid out so as to resemble a tree set on its side.

Like many other decision-making methods, decision trees force the user to specify the important *present* alternative solutions to a problem. In addition, decision trees force the user to specify the important *future* events and *future* decision options that may affect the desirability of present options. An example will make these general statements clear.

A New Dune Buggy.   Assume that Bill Terry owns a dune buggy that he uses to take customers for rides across the Cape Cod dunes. At the beginning of the dune buggy season, he is considering two alternatives: keeping his old dune buggy (the "do-nothing" alternative) or buying a new one. The season can either be a good one (with lots of bright sunny days and many customers) or a poor one (with overcast skies, chilly weather, and few customers). Bill figures that the chances are 0.70 for a good year and 0.30 for a bad year. With its attractive appearance and large seating capacity, a new buggy would generate higher revenues. At the same time, it would increase Bill Terry's investment in rolling stock.

Constructing the Tree.   In Figure 5-8 the two alternatives, the possible states of nature (good dune buggy year, bad dune buggy year), the probabilities, and the payoffs (in terms of profit to Bill Terry) are portrayed in a tree-like format. The small box at the left represents a decision point, and the small circles represent states of nature. The first fork in the tree indicates the actions that Bill Terry can take now, and the next set of forks represents relevant events that may occur in the future. Looking at a decision tree from left to right, the decision and event forks alternate—decisions, events, decisions, events, and so on. Bill can control his actions, but he has no control over future events.

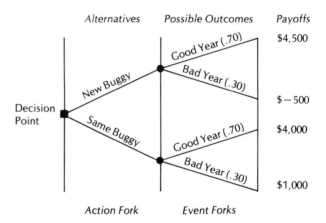

FIG 5-8   One-year decision tree.

The Payoffs.   In a good dune buggy year, Bill estimates that a new buggy will result in a $4,500 profit or payoff. If a bad year occurs, Bill will lose $500. If Bill keeps his present dune buggy and a good year occurs, he will make $4000. In a bad year with the same buggy, he will still make $1000.

The Decision.   The decision tree can be evaluated by expected-value analysis. Here are the expected values of the two alternatives:

Expected value, new buggy   = $4500(0.70) - $500(0.30)
                             = $3150 - $150
                             = $3000

Expected value, same buggy   = $4000(0.70) + $1000(0.30)
                                       = $2800 + $300
                                       = $3100

Unless the probabilities or payoffs change, the best decision is to keep the same dune buggy.

Characteristics of Decision Trees.   A decision tree, made up of decision alternatives and events, must adhere to these conditions.

1. At every fork, only *one* of the events or choices at the fork may occur. Bill Terry must either buy a new buggy or not buy a new buggy. He cannot do both. He will experience either a good dune buggy year or a bad year. He cannot experience both.
2. At every fork, one of the events or choices *must* occur. This is easy to say but sometimes hard to set up. Predicting the likely events and important decision alternatives may be easy or impossible, but a thorough analysis demands that the attempt be made. If an important event or alternative is omitted, the analysis will be faulty.

Decision theorists describe these two conditions by saying that the events or choices at the forks must be *mutually exclusive* (both *cannot* occur) and *collectively exhaustive* (one *must* occur).

Decision Sequences.   The real advantage of decision trees is their ability to link several decisions together. The manager can evaluate the impact of the decision sequence over time. For example, a second year could be added to the dune buggy problem. At the beginning of year 1, Bill Terry would have to project the results of two years' decisions. The year 1 decision is whether to buy a new buggy or not. The year 2 decisions are (1) if I *don't* buy a new buggy at the beginning of the first year, should I buy one at the beginning of the second year? (2) If I *do* buy a new buggy at the beginning of the first year, should I buy *another* new buggy at the beginning of the second year? However, at the end of year 1, Bill Terry might have to adjust the year 2 probabilities and payoffs, based on his first year's experience.

Extending the Decision Tree.   A second year is added to the dune buggy decision tree in Figure 5-9. Bill Terry decides that *if* he buys a new buggy now, and *if* he has a good dune buggy year, he then will have two alternatives: (1) buy another new buggy, or (2) keep the same buggy and not buy a new one. *If* he buys that second new buggy, and *if* he has a second good dune buggy year in a row (he estimates that probability at 0.5), then his two-year payoff will be $9500. We have just put the section of the tree shown in Figure 5-10 into words. The rest of the Figure 5-9 tree can be analyzed in the same way.

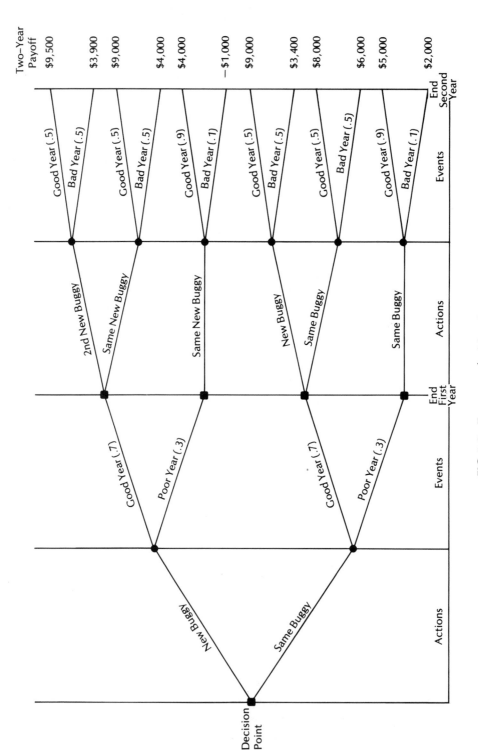

FIG 5-9 Two-year decision tree.

Two-Year Payoff	Events	Actions	Events	Actions
$9,500	Good Year (.5)			
$3,900	Bad Year (.5)	2nd New Buggy		
$9,000	Good Year (.5)			
$4,000	Bad Year (.5)	Same New Buggy		
$4,000	Good Year (.9)			
−$1,000	Bad Year (.1)	Same New Buggy	Good Year (.7)	New Buggy
$9,000	Good Year (.5)			
$3,400	Bad Year (.5)	New Buggy	Poor Year (.3)	
$8,000	Good Year (.5)			
$6,000	Bad Year (.5)	Same Buggy	Good Year (.7)	Same Buggy
$5,000	Good Year (.9)			
$2,000	Bad Year (.1)	Same Buggy	Poor Year (.3)	

End Second Year

End First Year

Decision Point

100

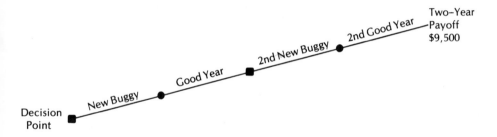

FIG 5-10   One branch of two-year decision tree.

Bill has made two interesting decisions–predictions. If year 1 is a poor dune buggy year, he will not consider buying a new buggy at the beginning of year 2. If year 1 is a poor dune buggy year, he sees a 0.9 probability that it will be followed by a good year. Apparently, his experience suggests that two bad dune buggy years in a row are highly unlikely.

Calculating Two-Year Expected Values.   Decision trees are constructed from left to right, but they are solved by expected-value analysis from right to left. Bill Terry must first find the expected value of all six possible outcomes, as of the beginning of year 2, like this.

Expected value, second new buggy following good first year	= $9500(0.50) × $3900(0.50) = $4750 + $1950 = $6700
Expected value, same new buggy following good first year	= $9000(0.50) + $4000(0.50) = $4500 + $2000 = $6500
Expected value, same new buggy following poor first year	= $4000(0.90) − $1000(0.10) = $3600 − $100 = $3500
Expected value, new buggy following good first year	= $9000(0.50) + $3400(0.50) = $4500 + $1700 = $6200
Expected value, same buggy following good first year	= $8000(0.50 + $6000(0.50) = $4000 + $3000 = $7000

Expected value, same buggy   = $5000(0.90) + $2000(0.10)
following poor first year   = $4500+ $200
                              = $4700

Figure 5-11 shows the 2-year decision possibilities and their expected values. At each decision fork to the far right, Bill Terry can eliminate the decision alternative with the lower expected value. Figure 5-12 shows the result of this operation.

Bill must now multiply the four expected values by the first-year probabilities:

2-year expected value,   = $6700(0.70) + $3500(0.30)
new buggy first year   = $4690 +$1050
                            = $5740

2-year expected value,   = $7000(0.70) + $4700(0.30)
same buggy first year   = $4900 +$1410
                            = $6310

The analysis shows that Bill Terry should take no action. He should keep his same dune buggy for 2 years, because the 2-year expected value of that alternative is $6310.

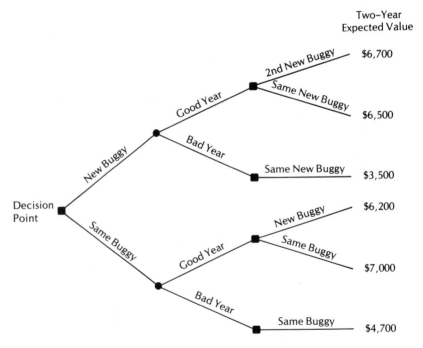

Two–Year
Expected Value

2nd New Buggy — $6,700

Same New Buggy — $6,500

Good Year

Bad Year

Same New Buggy — $3,500

New Buggy

Decision Point

Same Buggy

Good Year

New Buggy — $6,200

Same Buggy — $7,000

Bad Year

Same Buggy — $4,700

FIG 5-11   Two-year decision possibilities and expected values.

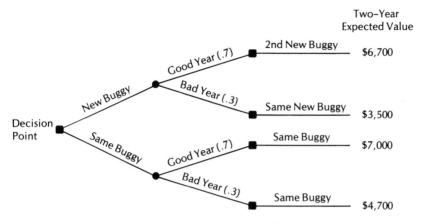

FIG 5-12   Reduced decision tree: higher expected value at each decision fork.

Advantages of Decision Trees

Decision trees offer decision makers several important advantages.

Problem Clarification.   A manager cannot construct a good decision tree without understanding exactly what the problem is. If the manager's understanding of the problem is vague, the process of constructing the tree will force the development and clarification of the problem statement.

Uncovering Alternatives.   While developing the tree, the manager may uncover alternatives not noticed previously. Overlooking reasonable alternatives is less likely if the manager uses a decision tree to solve problems because of the careful thought stimulated by the act of constructing the tree.

Considering the Future.   Calculating the expected values requires a subjective estimate of the probability that each outcome will occur. The decision tree therefore forces the manager to consider the future carefully.

Evaluating the Logic of the Decision.   Once the tree is drawn, the manager can step back and review the specifics of the decision process. The tree permits an objective reassessment of the assumptions and the reasoning that led to the decision.

Communication of Decision Analysis.   A decision tree enables the manager to communicate the problem, the alternatives, future expectations, the decision, and the entire decision process to other people. The tree gives decision makers and their associates something specific to talk about.

Queueing Theory and the Monte Carlo Method

Another mathematical technique that managers can use to make decisions in certain situations is queueing theory, sometimes called waiting-line theory. A queue is a line, as when people queue up outside a theater box office. The basic situation for which queueing theory might be used is the check-out lanes in supermarkets. People do not like to stand in line. Whenever people line up in a supermarket, costs to the store are involved because some dissatisfied customers may take their business elsewhere.

To reduce the length of waiting lines, the supermarket must open up more check-out lanes. But opening more lanes costs money. The supermarket would like to know the point at which opening up another lane costs more money than it saves. Queueing theory uses mathematical equations to handle such problems.

Here are examples of questions that queueing theory can answer. Should a restaurant hire more help and enlarge its seating capacity to avoid customer waiting lines? Should a factory hire more maintenance workers to handle machines waiting to be repaired? How many loading docks should a company build to keep delivery truck waiting time down to an acceptable level? Does a clinic have enough patients to justify hiring another doctor? Does a certain intersection really need another lane for traffic? How many toll booths should the Florida Turnpike keep open on Memorial Day?

Whenever people or things might become congested as they pass through a service area, queueing theory may be an appropriate tool to use.

If the queueing situation is too complex to be solved by mathematical analysis, the Monte Carlo method may be helpful. This method is a *simulation* technique. It can be used whenever taking an actual sample of people or things passing through a service area is difficult or impossible, either because of practical measurement problems or because people or things arrive within the service area at random intervals. The main advantage of the Monte Carlo method is that, by using a random numbers table or by generating random numbers with a computer, the method can simulate random arrivals at the service area. The manager can use the results to maintain service at the most practical level.

EVALUATING DAY-TO-DAY PROBLEMS

For solving day-to-day problems, the manager may not have the time, money, and expertise to use a mathematical model. One common method for evaluating alternatives is simply to analyze them in terms of their advantages and disadvantages, and then to choose the alternative having the greatest net advantage or the least net disadvantage. Here is an example.

An Unjust Firing

Nancy Martin is the president of a small manufacturing company. Supervisor Smith, a long-time personal friend of Martin's, has unjustly fired an apprentice worker, Joe Jones. The union is very upset. What should president Martin do?

Alternative Solutions.   Martin decides that her two alternatives are to rehire Jones or to do nothing. She might set up the main advantages and disadvantages of the two alternatives this way.

Rehire Jones
   Advantages:

   1. Avoids union trouble.
   2. Corrects an injustice.
   3. Makes Jones happy.
   4. No need to hire and train a new apprentice.

Disadvantages:

   1. Makes Smith mad.
   2. Undermines Smith's authority.
   3. Gives union too much power.
   4. Jeopardizes Martin–Smith friendship.

Do Nothing—Leave Jones Fired
   Advantages:

   1. Makes Smith happy.
   2. Upholds Smith's authority.
   3. Keeps union in its place.
   4. Gets Martin back to work on her own job.

Disadvantages:

   1. Encourages trouble with the union.
   2. Perpetuates (perhaps encourages) injustice.
   3. Makes other apprentices mad.
   4. Fails to develop Smith's leadership, which needs it.

Dollar Values.   Martin might be able to make her decision by simply looking over these important advantages and disadvantages. If she cannot, she may find it helpful (but difficult) to *place a dollar value on every advantage and disadvantage.* For example, Martin may decide that the first advantage of rehiring Jones, "avoids union trouble," is worth $5000 (in terms of time and aggravation saved).

The evaluation could further be quantified by estimating the probability that each advantage or disadvantage will actually occur. For example, Martin *thinks* that rehiring Jones will avoid union trouble, but the union may protest Smith's action even if it is overturned. So the probability that rehiring Jones will avoid union trouble might be estimated at 0.80. Multiplying the value of the advantage times its probability of occurrence ($5000 × 0.80) gives a payoff of $4000.

The same procedure would be used for each advantage and disadvantage. Sum the adjusted values, compare the sums, and choose the alternative with the greatest net dollar advantage or smallest net dollar disadvantage.

Many managers object to placing dollar values on such considerations as "corrects an injustice." But if you as a manager are not basing your decisions on dollars and cents, what are you basing them on? If you are basing them on some other criterion, and you work for a profit-making organization, what criterion are you using, and why?

SUMMARY

This chapter has described several models for evaluating alternative solutions to managerial problems. Closed mathematical models were discussed, and the EOQ model and linear programming were used to illustrate that type of model.

Recent years have seen an increasing use of models that require subjective probability estimates about the future. Many of these models use expected value as the decision criterion, so expected-value analysis was explored in some detail.

The chapter then moved to the construction and analysis of decision trees, queueing theory, and the Monte Carlo method. The chapter concluded by describing a method for analyzing alternatives in terms of their advantages and disadvantages. That method can be applied in either a nonquantitative or a quantitative way.

DISCUSSION QUESTIONS

1. What is the difference between a closed model and an open model?

2. For what kinds of situations is linear programming most appropriate?

Why can't the graphical solution be used for problems with more than two variables?

3. What is the meaning and usefulness of the area of feasible solutions?

4. What is the difference between objective and subjective probabilities?

5. What are the advantages of decision trees to a problem solver? What problems do they best aid in solving?

6. Can alternatives be evaluated even when number values cannot be assigned to them? How do people evaluate their alternative choices for a spouse?

7. Shupp's Trophy Shop uses 100 marble trophy bases per week, on the average. Every order for bases that Shupp sends in costs him $10. His carrying costs for bases on hand run him approximately 20 percent of the value of the bases on hand. Each base costs Shupp $5. In what quantity should he order bases?

8. As a supermarket manager, your problem is that you are losing too many customers to long check-out lines. What technique would be helpful in solving this problem? How would you set it up? What kind of information would you need? How would you get it? What are you going to do with it once you get it? What strengths and weaknesses do you see in this technique?

9. A company has two products to sell: white wine and red wine. The products must both be processed through the same equipment: a presser and a bottler. The presser can handle 10 tons of red grapes or 8 tons of white grapes per hour. The bottler can handle 12 tons of red grapes or 6 tons of white grapes in an hour. If the company makes a profit of $100 per ton of red and $200 per ton of white, what quantities of each should be produced? What will the profit be?

10. You are rapidly reaching the end of your college career and must decide what to do next. You can go to work right now, earning $8000 to start, with a $1000 yearly raise. Or you can go into an MBA program that will take 2 years if you don't flunk out and then start to work at $12,000 per year with a $1000 yearly raise. Or you can enter a 4-year doctoral program and earn $14,000 per year upon graduation (if you don't flunk out) with a $1000 yearly raise. You estimate that your chances of flunking out during any one school year are 50–50. Make a decision that will maximize your income at the end of a 5-year period and show how you came to your decision. Discuss the merits and demerits of the approach you used.

THE FARMER'S DILEMMA

Hal Sands, owner of a 1000-acre farm in a southern state, must decide what crops to plant for the next two seasons. He wants to sequence his crops so as to maximize his profits. He knows that planting certain crops consecutively will use up the soil's nutrients, and he wants to protect his land from that sort of harm.

Sands knows that if he plants tobacco in the first year, he must plant soybeans in the second. If he plants soybeans first, he can then plant either corn or more soybeans in the second year. If he plants corn first, he can follow with soybeans, tobacco, or more corn. Whatever crop he chooses will be planted on the full 1000 acres. That is, he will not plant 500 acres of soybeans and 500 acres of corn.

Sands next estimates market prices for the various crops over the next two seasons. He knows that when the weather is bad, crop yields fall and crop prices rise. When the weather is good, crop yields increase and the larger supply causes prices to fall.

Based on his past experience, he estimates (1) the probabilities of good and bad weather in the next 2 years, and (2) gross profits on each possible crop under good and bad weather conditions. The following table contains these estimates. What crops should Sands plant?

Gross Profits Expected by Crop

	Year 1		Year 2	
Crop	Good Year Probability 70%	Bad Year Probability 30%	Good Year Probability 50%	Bad Year Probability 50%
Corn	$400,000	$375,000	$525,000	$400,000
Tobacco	$300,000	$250,000	$450,000	$375,000
Soybeans	$320,000	$270,000	$280,000	$240,000

COUNTY HOSPITAL X-RAY DEPARTMENT

Jane Gianini, chief administrator at County Hospital, is becoming increasingly concerned about the situation in the x-ray department. On several occasions during the past week, she walked by the department and saw a line of waiting patients. Several other times she walked by and saw no patients at all.

The dramatic rise in malpractice suits has caused doctors to request more x-rays than ever before. Gianini thought she had controlled the situation by implementing a new staffing procedure and a new patient scheduling plan. The department is now using all three machines for 8 hours a day. The patient scheduling plan requires the doctors to send patients at regular intervals over the entire day.

According to her earlier calculations, running all three machines for 8 hours a day and staggering patient visits should have eliminated all patient waiting. Nevertheless, she had seen patients lined up several times. When she first analyzed the data, she had computed simple averages. To construct her present schedule, she had found out how many patients were x-rayed each day and had divided that number by the number of working hours in a day, to arrive at average patient load per hour. She pulled the following data from her files to check on whether she had analyzed it correctly when she had set up her present system.

What was wrong with Gianini's original analysis? How should she have analyzed this problem?

Patient Classification and Percent of Patient Load

Type	Average Service Time in minutes	Percent
Type I: Multiple	20	40
Type II: Diagnostic	10	10
Type III: Routine	5	50
		100

Frequency of Patient Arrivals for 8-Hour Shift

Average Time Between Arrivals in Minutes	Percent
0	30
5	35
10	20
15	10
20	5
	100

6

making the choice

Once the alternative solutions have been thoroughly evaluated, the manager must make a choice. The evaluation stage may end abruptly, with the solution to the problem popping out of the analysis. For example, if a closed mathematical model is used to analyze alternatives, that model will offer a "best" choice. However, decisions are made by *people*, and human managers always have the last word. Even if a mathematical model produces a "best " decision, the human manager must still decide whether to do what the model proposes.

This chapter begins by explaining why decision making cannot be left to models. The rest of the chapter shows how people actually make decisions. Human managers bring to the decision stage different assumptions, orientations, aspiration levels, and attitudes toward risk. These and other factors join with the outcome of the alternatives-evaluation stage to produce the manager's choice.

Although we shall consider making the choice separately from implementing the choice, these steps are related. A satisfactory choice that can be implemented is obviously better than an ideal choice that cannot.

WHY MODELS CANNOT MANAGE

The efforts of decision scientists have resulted in many powerful models, such as queueing theory, linear programming, the EOQ model, and expected-value analysis. These tools provide a highly rational way for reaching a decision. And they do reach decisions; they do give answers. Models do not hesitate. The model analyzes the alternatives and specifies the decision that is best in terms of the information that the model has to work with.

For example, consider a firm seeking to allocate funds to various of the firm's units. The firm can use a capital-budgeting model to evaluate the return on investment yielded by each alternative use and give the funds to those units with the highest projected yields.

The Unpredictable Future

The capital-budgeting model assumes that the future can be forecast. That is one major problem with all quantitative methods. Crystal balls and fortune tellers to the contrary, forecasting future events is very difficult. Since all quantitative models assume that the future will to some extent resemble the past, model users must remember that any model's output may be useless in a very short time due to changing conditions.

As an example, for many years the philosophy of the automobile industry and the automobile-buying public was "bigger is better." People bought the biggest cars they could afford. Then came the energy crisis. Almost overnight the attitudes of both buyer and seller had to change direction. As another example of quick change, a warehouse allocation model designed to place the optimum number of cases at the optimum distribution points may become obsolete overnight if a product recall occurs.

In short, one reason why models cannot manage is that models cannot take changed conditions into account until managers and their model builders incorporate change into the models.

Limited Perspective

Models have a limited perspective. They do not understand or care about the dynamics of the entire organization. For example, a simple investment-maximizing model may determine that making washers is unprofitable and so may allocate 100 percent of production time to nuts and bolts. The model's limited perspective has kept it from realizing that nuts and bolts are not a complete, salable product without washers attached.

So another reason prohibiting management by models is that they are too narrow in outlook. They are incapable of the broad perspective required of the top-level manager.

An Immature Science

This limited perspective is in a sense surprising, because one basic insight underlying all management science is that organizations are *systems* whose parts depend on each other. Success or failure is determined not by how well or poorly any part performs but by how well the entire system performs.

And yet, perhaps because management science is a new, relatively immature discipline, quantitative models have not done much to improve total system performance. True, quantitative models have enabled managers to perform certain traditional functions, such as product mix and inventory control, more efficiently and rapidly. As a result of the quantitative revolution, some parts of some organizations operate better than they did before. But the operation of organizations as productive wholes has progressed little as a result of quantitative modeling.

At present, management science emphasizes tools and techniques rather than principles and philosophy. As time goes by, perhaps quantitative models can enhance the performance of the whole rather than the part.

Further Limitations of Quantification

Many models try to account for future uncertainty by using some kind of expected-value analysis. Influential future states of nature are determined, their probabilities of occurrence are estimated, and the effects of these uncertainties are brought together into one number: expected value. The alternative with the highest expected value is the "best."

Effect of Initial Wealth.   However, expected-value analysis often seems to ignore factors that may be very important in a given situation. Consider a gamble in which you have a 95 percent chance of winning $10,000 and a 5 percent chance of losing $10,000. Offhand, the gamble looks good. Under expected-value analysis, it still looks good:

$$\text{Expected value} \;=\; (0.95)(\$10,000) + (0.05)(-\$10,000)$$
$$= \$9500 - \$500$$
$$= \$9000$$

But who would be more apt to take the bet, a millionaire or a 65-year-old retired person with $10,000 in savings? In other words, expected-value analysis ignores the gambler's starting wealth and assumes that the gain or loss of $10,000 would mean as much to a rich person as to a poor person.

Attitude Toward Risk.   Furthermore, expected-value analysis ignores the participant's attitude toward *risk*. Consider this example. A cattle rustler is caught in the act, tried, and sentenced to hang. The judge tells the rustler that if he can come up with the value of the cattle plus court costs, totaling $10,000, he can go free. The rustler has exactly that amount in his cabin. The sheriff agrees to escort him to the cabin.

As they are returning to town, a gambler steps out on the trail, sees the $10,000 in the rustler's hands, and says, "I'll offer you a bet in which you will have a 95 percent chance of winning another $10,000 and a 5 percent chance of losing your present $10,000. Will you take it?"

If he loves life, the rustler will probably not take the bet. Even though the odds are greatly in his favor, he will probably not be willing to accept the small risk that he may have to forfeit his life.

Here is a problem called the Petersburg paradox. How much should a player pay to enter a game of coin flipping in which the payoff doubles with each flip of the coin until heads is thrown? In other words, for each successive tails thrown, the initial prize doubles. The game ends when heads is thrown. The paradox arises because the expected value of the game is infinitely large; the coin flipper could theoretically flip tails throughout eternity. Yet if a dollar were the initial prize, hardly anyone would pay more than a few dollars to play.

In all three of the preceding examples, the expected-value criterion suggested a "best" solution that was unacceptable to the decision maker. The point is that quantitative techniques cannot always take all relevant factors into account.

HOW PEOPLE MAKE DECISIONS

The previous chapter showed how models analyze alternatives to arrive at decisions. The past several examples have shown that people do not make decisions in the same way that models do. The rest of this chapter will explore how people actually make decisions.

The Prisoner's Dilemma

Consider a classic decision situation called the prisoner's dilemma. A man and a woman have been arrested and charged with a crime. The police are questioning them separately. The pair are told that if they both confess the court will be lenient and will give them each a 1- to 2-year sentence. If one confesses (turns state's evidence) and the other does not, the confessor will be set free for cooperating but the other will get 5 years. If neither confesses, the state will have insufficient evidence, and both will be set free.

Would you confess? Your potential gains from cooperating are attractive (being set free), but your potential losses if you do not confess and your partner does confess are great (a 5-year sentence).

The payoff matrix for the prisoner's dilemma would look like this:

	Partner confesses	Partner does not confess
You confess	1-2 year sentence	Set free
You don't confess	5-year sentence	Set free

Each crook realizes that the optimum outcome is for both to remain silent. If there is honor among thieves, that will happen. But "don't confess" entails the danger of the 5-year term. The name "dilemma" is fitting.

Assumptions About Nature

The prisoners in the prisoner's dilemma must make their decisions based on their assumptions about each other. In other problems, decision makers must make decisions based on assumptions about how mother or father nature is going to treat them in the future.

Neutral Expectations. Some decision makers operate as if nature were neutral. They are following the neutral *principle of insufficient reason,* which says that a particular event is not going to happen if there is no reason for it to happen. Consider Buridan's ass, a beast created in the imagination of Jean Buridan in the fourteenth century. Imagine the ass placed exactly at the midpoint of the distance between two bales of hay. According to Buridan, the ass must surely starve because insufficient reason exists for it to go to one bale of hay rather than the other.

The decision of the ass to do nothing is in keeping with the hypothesis of the eighteenth-century clergyman and mathematician Thomas Bayes: if we have no reason to believe two probabilities to be different from one another, we should assume them to be equal to each other. With .50/.50 probabilities, the ass has no reason to move toward either hay bale.

Many modern-day decision makers join with Bayes and Buridan in assuming that nature is neutral. They may therefore feel justified in assigning equal probabilities to all outcomes in a particular decision problem. If something can go wrong, it may or may not. These decision makers either have not heard of or disagree with Murphy's Law: if something can go wrong, it will.

Pessimistic Expectations. Murphy's Law assumes the worst. Decision makers in many fields have added such corollaries to the basic Murphy's Law as:

> Left to themselves, things always go from bad to worse.
>
> If everything seems to be going well, you have overlooked something.
>
> If you explain something so clearly that no one can possibly misunderstand, somebody will.
>
> The accessibility, during recovery, of parts which fall from the work bench varies directly with the size of the part and inversely with its importance to the completion of the work underway.
>
> Interchangeable parts won't.

Four Game Theory Rules

Expectations about nature affect decision strategies. Here are four game theory rules, often used to analyze organizational problems, that are based on assumptions about nature: maximin, maximax, minimax, and minimax regret.

Maximin. Maximin means *maxi*mize the chances of gaining the *min*imum gain available in the situation. Choose the alternative that at least offers *some* gain. The decision maker believing in Murphy's Law would tend to follow a maximin decision strategy.

Consider the payoff matrix in Figure 6-1. The decision maker can select either alternative 1 (A_1) or alternative 2 (A_2). The forces of nature will result in either outcome 1 (O_1) or outcome 2 (O_2). These outcomes have different values or payoffs, depending on which strategy is selected. The decision maker does not know which outcome will occur. If the decision maker were Thomas Bayes, he would assign a 0.5 probability to each outcome because he would have no reason to predict one outcome over the other. Our present decision maker is of another opinion: if you have no reason to predict one outcome over the other, ignore the concepts of "probability" and base your decision strictly on the payoffs.

	O_1	O_2
A_1	1	5
A_2	2	3

FIG 6-1   Payoff matrix to illustrate maximin strategy.

Susie Smith, a maximin manager, looks at these payoffs. She seeks to maximize her chances of at least gaining something. She wants to come out ahead, however slightly. If she chooses A_1, her minimum gain will be 1 unit. If she chooses A_2, her minimum gain will be 2 units. Therefore, she selects A_2. To be sure of gaining 2 units, she gives up the chance to gain 5 units. Although she has refused to assign probabilities, she is acting just as if she had assigned a higher probability to O_1 than to O_2.

Maximax.   The maximax decision strategy—maximize the maximum gain— optimistically assumes that nature usually smiles. Or perhaps the decision maker just feels lucky on a given day and assumes that Murphy's Law will be suspended for a change. The maximax decision strategy—assume the best and go for broke—is frequently observed in operation at horse tracks and at the Las Vegas and Atlantic City casinos. The decision maker chooses the alternative that, if things work out well, will result in the largest gain.

Look again at Figure 6-1. The pessimistic maximin decision maker chose alternative 2 to ensure the largest minimum gain. The maximaxer would choose alternative 1 with its opportunity for a 5-unit gain. The habitual maximaxer can lose a lot of units in a hurry. If the maximaxer is a manager and the units are money, the organization had better do something to temper the manager's boundless optimism.

Minimax.   The minimax strategy—minimize the maximum loss—is similar to the maximin strategy. If the decision situation contains the possibility of an actual loss, assume the worst and choose the alternative that will minimize loss. In Figure 6-2, the minimaxer would choose A_1.

	O_1	O_2
A_1	-1	2
A_2	-2	4

FIG 6-2 Payoff matrix to illustrate minimax strategy.

Minimax Regret.   The final decision strategy reflecting how people actually make decisions is *minimax regret*. This strategy reflects a very human situation: the manager makes the decision, the wrong outcome occurs, and the manager feels regret: "Oh, if only I had made some other decision." The minimax regret strategy is designed to keep the manager's maximum regret as small as possible.

Consider the payoff matrixes in Figure 6-3. Decision makers who want to minimize their maximum regret must construct the ordinary matrix plus another matrix, called a *regret table*. In that table, R for regret takes the place of O for outcome in the left-hand table. All numbers in a regret table are expressed in absolute terms (without minus signs). The right-hand regret table is based on the left-hand payoff matrix.

	O_1	O_2
A_1	-1	3
A_2	-2	5

Ordinary Matrix

	R_1	R_2
A_1	0	2
A_2	1	0

Regret Table

FIG 6-3 Constructing the regret table.

Here is how the regret table is filled in. If the decision maker picks A_1 and then O_1 occurs, there is no regret at picking A_1 because that was the best decision that could have been made under the circumstances. Therefore, the decision maker puts a zero in the A_1/R_1 square of the regret table. If the decision maker picks A_1 and then O_2 occurs, the decision maker will regret picking A_1 instead of A_2 by 2 units, the difference between the A_1/O_1 payoff and the A_2/O_2 payoff. So the decision maker puts a 2 in the A_1/R_2 square.

If A_2 is picked and then O_1 occurs, 1 unit of regret results. If A_2 is picked and then O_2 occurs, zero regret results from the 5-unit payoff, the largest payoff possible in this decision situation.

The numbers inserted in the regret table represent the cost or penalty of not selecting the best alternative for a particular outcome. The decision maker would use the regret table to select the alternative that minimizes maximum regret. By choosing A_2 the decision maker ensures that 1 unit of regret is the maximum that will be experienced, no matter how badly things turn out.

Like maximin, minimax regret is a pessimistic, conservative strategy that seeks to cushion the blow. In the payoff matrix for the prisoner's dilemma, shown earlier, "confess" maximizes the minimum regret.

Oversimplification. The maximin, minimax, maximax, and minimax regret models are quantitative oversimplifications of what actually goes on in the minds of decision makers. Since they are designed merely to help us conceptualize what goes into the act of deciding, the models should not be taken too literally. For example, in the following matrix, the manager slavishly bound to the maximin strategy would choose A_1 since either outcome under that strategy will result in a positive return. However, most open-minded decision makers not wed to a particular strategy would view A_2, with its opportunity for $10,000 matched against a possible $100 loss, as too good to pass up.

	O_1	O_2
A_1	+$100	+$100
A_2	−$100	+$10,000

The main intent of this discussion is to show that, when it comes down to the moment of decision, the manager's human characteristics and inclinations affect the choice. Some people tend to make those choices that ensure them a gain, however small. Other people choose alternatives that have a chance of both big success and big failure. Still others are guided in their choices not so much by a desire to make gains as to avoid large losses. Decisions are best made by fully informed managers who recognize, as part of their information, their own tendencies toward maximin, maximax, minimax, or minimax regret decision behavior.

FURTHER CONSTRAINTS ON IDEAL DECISION MAKING

Throughout our discussions of decision making, we have been assuming a completely rational manager trying hard to make decisions that are in the organization's best interests. This noble manager formulates each problem precisely, gathers and evaluates the full range of alternatives, makes the choice most likely to achieve the organization's goals, and then implements the choice with a firm, sure hand.

But people being people, decisions are not always made that way. We have just seen that one important influence on decision behavior is the decision maker's predisposition to believe that nature will smile or frown. Four other constraints on ideal decision making are the *atmosphere of crisis* in which many people work, the *lack of authority* to implement ideal decisions, the manager's *level of aspiration*, and the manager's *attitude toward risk*.

The Atmosphere of Crisis

One reason for the failure of many managers to make good decisions is that their workdays consist of a mad scramble from one crisis to another. The superficial difficulty must be resolved; the fire must be put out. If we are stuck in a swamp full of alligators, we must concentrate today on not being eaten alive. Maybe we can solve the basic swamp drainage problem tomorrow.

Consider manager Jane Brown, ordered to submit a report by tomorrow noon—just another crisis in the crisis atmosphere within which she works. Brown may recognize the organization's basic problem as a lack of planning coupled with a poor communication system. But she does not have the luxury of being able to define and solve the problem in those terms. The report must come first.

Implementation Authority

The preceding illustration also points up a second major difficulty with the ideal problem-solving model: the manager may lack the *authority* to implement the best solution. Jane Brown's position on the organization chart may prohibit her from solving the problem. If a problem is accurately defined as "lack of top management direction" or "poor planning by the regional vice-president," then a mid-level manager will only become frustrated by trying to follow the ideal decision-making process.

Level of Aspiration

Three Managers. Imagine that a decision is to be made. Three managers all have access to the same information: an exact formulation of the problem and a thorough analysis of many alternatives. These are the three managers: (1) Jane Doe doesn't like her job and is planning to quit tomorrow; (2) John Smith desperately wants to keep his present job until he retires next year; (3) Polly Johnson hopes someday to be president of the company. In light of their different aspirations, these three managers may make three different decisions, none of which may be ideal from the organization's point of view.

Generalizations About Aspiration.   Aspiration levels affect behavior. Furthermore, aspiration levels are constantly changing. For example, the manager who is successfully proceeding along a chosen career path continues to have high aspirations. The manager who fails or who gets stuck in a dead-end job experiences declining aspirations. The manager with high aspirations may search widely in an attempt to find relevant alternative solutions to a problem and may make the maximaxing choice. The manager with lower aspirations may survey a few readily available alternatives and then choose the maximin strategy.

   To sum up, then, level of aspiration helps explain how widely a manager will search for alternatives, how thoroughly they will be analyzed, and, to an extent, whether the choice will be creative or ordinary, daring or conservative.

Attitudes Toward Risk

Related to aspiration level is the manager's attitude toward risk. The extent to which a manager avoids, accepts, or seeks risk will affect the manager's decisions.

   Figure 6-4 displays lines that describe the attitudes of the manager who avoids risk, the manager who seeks risk, and the manager who is neutral to risk. Risk-neutral managers want fair odds, no more and no less. They will accept one additional unit of risk for the opportunity of gaining one additional unit of return. Risk-averting managers want the opportunity of gaining *more than* one additional unit of return per additional unit of risk. If that opportunity is not present, they take no action. The risk seeker will accept risk when the odds are not even fair.

   Two influences on risk taking are the amount of information present and the manager's personal characteristics.

Amount of Information.   The more information the manager has, the less risky will be the decision situation. Yet, as reflected in Figure 4-1, information costs time and money to obtain. Managers hardly ever have all the information they would like to have, but decisions must still be made. The conservative manager will try to reduce risk by acquiring as much information as possible—even beyond the point of optimality in Figure 4-1 on page 67. The less conservative manager will gather the necessary information, make the decision, and then go ahead to the next problem.

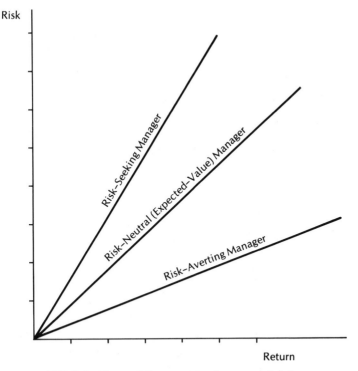

FIG 6-4   Three different attitudes toward risk.

Personal Characteristics.   Researchers have studied the relationship between certain personal characteristics and the willingness to accept risk. For example, rigid and dogmatic persons tend to be overconfident, to take more chances than perhaps they should.

As one might expect, age is apparently related to risk taking. Even if older persons are quite sure of themselves, they are not as willing to take risks as younger persons are, particularly where money is concerned.

Many decisions can be made without regard for a manager's risk preferences. For example, if the EOQ model says "resume production," the manager's attitude toward risk is irrelevant. But when quantitative analysis is impossible or inappropriate, the manager's view of risk becomes an important influence on the decision process.

The Risky Shift.   An interesting effect sometimes occurs when a group (rather than an individual) makes a decision. This effect is called the *risky shift*—the tendency for decisions made in groups to be less conservative than the decision of the average group member. For example, crowds and mobs often take extreme actions that the group members would not take if they were acting alone.

In the organizational setting, people in groups may tend toward riskier decisions because responsibility for risk taking can be spread among the group members rather than falling on one decision maker. Or perhaps our society values risk takers. Group members may want to enhance their status by being perceived as daring and courageous.

Opinions and research findings differ as to whether the risky shift does actually occur. If group decisions really do tend to be riskier than individual decisions, the implications for organizations are enormous. More and more organizations are using committees, study groups, and task forces to formulate problems, generate and study alternatives, and make recommendations. If group decisions are in fact riskier, then decision-making groups should be used sparingly, particularly if the penalty for taking risk unsuccessfully is high.

Groupthink.   Another characteristic of group problem solving may affect the quality of decisions. *Groupthink* has been called "the psychological drive for consensus at any cost." Because disagreement is uncomfortable, the group wants to agree on *any* decision as soon as possible. Therefore, dissent is minimized, controversial topics are avoided, safe alternatives are superficially explored, and so on. Group discussion can be highly productive if members are able to think and speak independently and critically. If the group emphasizes friendliness in a cozy atmosphere, rather than discussing the problem frankly and openly, groupthink may result.

The group indulging in groupthink has several characteristics.

1. Limited discussion of limited alternatives. The group ignores the range of possible alternative solutions and discusses only a few—often only two.
2. Unwillingness to vary from first tentative choice. If at the outset the group tends toward one alternative, the group will stick with that choice even if drawbacks and risks are later brought up.
3. Unwillingness to reexamine early tentative rejections. If at the outset the group tentatively rejects an alternative, the group will continue to reject it even if it is later discovered to have many advantages.
4. Prejudicial attitude toward information. The group does not seek outside advice and reacts to any factual information in terms of tentative judgments already made. "I've made up my mind—don't confuse me with facts" is truly the groupthink attitude.

Groupthink may not usually be very harmful. However, Irving L. Janis[1] attributes four of our nation's greatest fiascoes to groupthink at the top poli-

---

[1]Irving L. Janis, *Victims of Groupthink* (Boston: Houghton Mifflin Co., 1972).

cymaking level. These four "hardheaded actions by softheaded groups" were our unpreparedness at Pearl Harbor, the invasion of North Korea, the Bay of Pigs invasion, and the escalation of the Viet Nam war.

THE TEST–OPERATE–TEST–EXIT UNIT

The preceding paragraphs have described how personal attitudes and inclinations can affect decision makers. To conclude this chapter, here is a model that attempts to describe actual rather than ideal decision behavior.[2]

The ideal decision model described over the past four chapters makes some unrealistic assumptions about decision makers. First, the model assumes that managers *try* to find and solve problems, that managers have enough organizational commitment to expend effort on problems. The truth is that managers sometimes are not motivated to get involved in decision activity, so they ignore problems or define them superficially so they can be solved easily. Furthermore, the ideal model makes the unrealistic assumption that managers who make the attempt *will* be able to define problems adequately. Actually, identifying problems accurately is often more difficult than solving them.

The ideal model further assumes that managers will systematically and rationally search out the relevant alternatives in the way that best trades off the cost of search with the value of new alternatives found. The model then assumes a thorough analysis of all relevant alternatives and finally a rational choice of the best alternative.

The ideal model does not often resemble real-life decision making very closely. Consider Ron Perry, a maintenance supervisor who has just lost an employee in his department. To do his job of maintaining the organization's equipment, Perry must hire a new worker. If Perry is an ideal decision maker, he will carefully construct an exact job description, advertise the job in many places for several days or weeks, screen all applicants, make his choice, and then train the new worker. But Perry is under the gun to get the work out in a hurry. Furthermore, he remembers that once, while he was spending several days writing the perfect job description, another department asked for his department's vacant position and got it.

What Perry does in this situation is what most managers do when they face a problem. He makes a decision that may not be ideal but that is "good enough." TOTE unit analysis describes the usual decision process of making adequate but not ideal decisions.

Test. TOTE stands for test–operate–test–exit, the four phases of any be-

[2]For a complete description of the model, see George D. Miller, Eugene Galanter, and Karl H. Pribram, *Plans and the Structure of Behavior* (New York: Holt, Rinehart and Winston, Inc., 1960), pp. 26–39.

havior, not just decision behavior. During the first test phase, the manager makes constant comparisons or tests between what is going on in the environment and what the manager (using some subjective or objective standard) *thinks* should be going on. If an incongruity exists between what is and what should be, the manager enters the next TOTE phase.

Operate. The manager perceiving an incongruity during the test phase then "operates" on the environment in order to get it back to normal. If Ron Perry is hungry, he eats. If a cat runs in front of his car, he swerves. If coffee cans are coming down the production line with no coffee in them, he checks the machinery. The point is that he performs an operation; he does something.

Test. The third step is to test the situation again, after performing an operation, to see if normalcy has returned. If Perry's adjustment of the equipment gets coffee into the cans, he has accomplished what he set out to do. If he finds during this second test phase that the coffee cans are still coming down the line empty, he will try further operations.

    As another example, what do you do if you misplace your car keys? The incongruity during the first test phase is "no car keys." You then perform various operations (retrace your steps, look through the pockets of the clothes in your closet, look under the papers on your desk) until you locate your keys. Then you enter the last TOTE phase.

Exit. Once the environment returns to normal, you get out of your current TOTE unit of behavior and start testing the environment again for abnormalities.

Personal Perception. An important point is that personal perception determines what is normal and what is not. So personal perception determines whether the manager sees a problem during the first test phase and whether the problem has been solved during the second test phase. If Ron Perry is in a hurry, does not understand the problem's importance, or does not care, his final decision may be far from ideal.

    Organizational and departmental goals should serve as yardsticks for problem definition. However, as Chapter 2 explained, many goals that should help managers define problems as they scan the job environment are of no help because they are largely nonoperational. Consequently, the decision maker's subjective standards—influenced by all the psychosocial and physiological factors shown in Figure 3-6—come into play during the two test phases of the TOTE unit.

    According to the originators of the TOTE concept, *all* behavior is broken up into TOTE units. Life is a series of decisions to be made, some within the organizational context, but most outside of it. The TOTE unit is the lowest common denominator of all behavior. It symbolizes in miniature how we make all our decisions.

SUMMARY

This chapter first described some shortcomings of mathematical models as decision makers. The unpredictability of the future coupled with the immaturity of management science means that decisions will be made by human managers for a long time to come.

The rest of the chapter discussed certain characteristics of human managers that may keep them from making ideal decisions. The prisoner's dilemma illustrated the human aspects of many decisions; we often decide what to do based on our predictions concerning what other people are going to do (and, as in the prisoner's dilemma, those other people may simultaneously be trying to decide what to do based on their predictions of what *we* are going to do).

The chapter then moved to a discussion of assumptions about nature that decision makers may hold. Murphy's Law and the strategies of maximin, maximax, minimax, and minimax regret exemplified these different assumptions.

Two further influences on decisions were seen to be the manager's level of aspiration and the manager's attitude toward risk. Two phenomena sometimes seen in decision groups were then described and discussed—the risky shift and groupthink. The chapter concluded by presenting the TOTE unit as a model for symbolizing decision behavior.

The chapter stressed how people *do* make decisions. Most management students want to know how people *should* make decisions. Unfortunately, no simple guidelines exist. Although this chapter is devoted specifically to the decision step, every chapter in the book is designed to improve the manager's decision-making ability. No one person can embody all the ideal decision maker's characteristics. But studying the basic principles of management within a decision-making framework should do much to improve the quality of every manager's decisions.

DISCUSSION QUESTIONS

1. In light of the great power to evaluate alternatives that mathematical models have, why does the decision maker have to make a choice at all? Couldn't the decision maker simply take the optimal mathematical answer and implement it?

2. How does nature influence the decision maker's choices?

3. What is the difference between the maximax, maximin, minimax, and minimax regret decision criteria? Are these criteria reflective of how managers actually make choices?

4. How does a manager's level of aspiration affect the manager's choices?

5. How does the manager's attitude toward risk affect the manager's choices?

6. What is the difference between the risky shift and groupthink?

7. What is a TOTE unit? In your opinion, how accurately does it describe decision behavior?

8. The decision model of problem identification, alternatives generation, evaluation, and choice is a fairly simple representation of decision making. How closely do you think it actually represents the decision-making behavior of real managers?

9. In the payoff table below, what are the minimax, maximax, minimax regret, and expected-value decisions? Which of these decision rules do you believe is most rational? Why?

	Outcome 1	Outcome 2
Alternative 1	-10	15
Alternative 2	-4	10
Alternative 3	-3	6
Alternative 4	-1	5

10. You have just been offered a job by both the American Snuff Corporation and IBM. The salaries, training programs, opportunities for advancement, and fringe benefits are approximately the same. Which job will you choose and why?

CHATHAM THRIFT SHOP

The Service League of Chatham has operated the Thrift Shop in downtown Chatham for 26 years. The shop sells donated clothing and household articles at bargain prices to low-income Chatham residents and distributes the profits to worthy community projects.

Service League members are young women dedicated to improving the community. They are each required to work 10 hours a week at the Thrift Shop—marking and selling merchandise, arranging storage, and so on.

On June 1 the League members chose Joan Ferguson to be Thrift Shop Committee chairperson. She has worked on different shop committees for 4 years, so she is aware of shop problems.

Numerous discount stores are springing up in Chatham. They offer new clothing at prices only slightly higher than the Thrift Shop's. As a result, the shop is barely making enough money to cover the League's financial commitments.

The quality of donated goods is declining. Because costs of new clothing are rising rapidly, donors are keeping their clothing longer. Also, the newer permanent-press fabrics do not hold up as well as cotton, linen, and silk. So by the time clothing arrives at the shop, it is in poorer condition than clothing donated several years ago used to be.

Joan Ferguson also perceives a staffing problem. The current shop manager is satisfactory, but Ferguson knows she is thinking about quitting because of low pay, too much responsibility, and having to put up with volunteer help. All work other than that done by the shop manager is done by Service League members. Many of them find the work boring. Consequently, they come in late, take long lunch hours, and do not show much initiative in helping the customers.

Just after Joan Ferguson's election in June, the landlord announced that the League could not renew the lease in December. The building is going to be demolished and replaced by a parking lot. Joan Ferguson has 6 months in which to come up with some alternatives and make a decision.

COLEN JOHNSON: FOOTBALL COACH

Colen Johnson, 27 years old, wants to be the youngest head football coach in University of Michigan history. To do so, he must get the job before he is 33.

Johnson is now head coach at Milow University in Franklin, Ohio. Before he arrived 4 years ago, Milow football teams usually lost more games than they won. Under Johnson's coaching, the team has won the Middle Valley Conference championship for the past 2 years and last year won the national division II championship. Milow is an excellent football team in a small-college conference. But Johnson wants to coach at the University of Michigan, a division I school. Michigan officials do not think his 4 years of success at Milow qualify him for their head coaching job.

Football players attend Milow University to play football, not to get an education. Johnson imposes strict discipline on the players. Here are some of his rules:

1. No smoking or drinking during the season.
2. No drugs, ever.
3. Curfew at 10:30 during the season.
4. No women in the rooms after 7 P.M.

All rules are strictly enforced. Penalties for breaking the rules range from a one-game suspension to expulsion from the team.

Earlier this year, Johnson and Milow University agreed to a new 2-year contract. Both parties realize that this is the best contract Milow will be able to offer for some years, even if Johnson keeps winning. Some contract provisions are:

1. Salary: $40,000.
2. Television contract: $7500.

3. The university makes Johnson's house payments.
4. The university provides Johnson and his wife with cars.
5. The university makes payments on a $100,000 life insurance policy in Johnson's name.

Johnson has recently received an offer to become head coach at Hubbard University, a division I school located in Hubbard, Illinois. Hubbard is one of the nation's finest schools academically, but its football record is poor. Hubbard usually beats teams outside its Small Ten Conference but for the past 10 years has finished either ninth or tenth in the conference. In short, Hubbard is a mediocre team in a very good conference.

Hubbard athletes are comparable in size and ability to other athletes in the conference. However, their attitude is different. They attend Hubbard on football scholarships not primarily to play football but to get a good education. Of course, they would rather win than lose, but losing does not bother them a great deal.

Hubbard has had five coaches in the past 10 years. Most football people view Hubbard as a "graveyard for promising young coaches." At Hubbard, good coaches usually take good athletes and get bad results. Consequently, after their Hubbard experience, coaches are no longer viewed as promising. However, Johnson knows that if he could turn Hubbard into a winner, he would probably be viewed very favorably by the University of Michigan.

The contract offered by Hubbard University includes these provisions:

1. Salary: $51,500.
2. Television contract: $15,000.
3. A home.
4. Free schooling for children.
5. Use of two cars.
6. Payments on a $120,000 insurance policy.

Since the cost of living in Hubbard is higher than the cost of living where he is now, Johnson views these financial arrangements as only slightly better than his present arrangements. However, the offered contract is for 4 years, not 2.

Hubbard football players have experienced few restrictions. They have never had to observe a curfew, no rules have existed concerning smoking or drinking, they may see women whenever and wherever they please, and discipline for drug use has not been particularly harsh. Johnson wants the following provisions to be written into the Hubbard contract:

1. Johnson would have complete control over hiring and firing assistant coaches.
2. Johnson would have absolute control over player discipline.
3. The football budget would be increased by 20 percent.

Hubbard officials have agreed to provisions 1 and 3, but the Hubbard president reserves the right to approve or disapprove each disciplinary condition separately.

Johnson knows the Hubbard fans and alumni want a winning team. He can expect their support, at least initially. He likes the challenge Hubbard presents, and he knows that success in division I will do much for his reputation.

Should he take the job, or stay where he is?

Part Two: Comprehensive Cases

ACME FOOD SERVICE COMPANY

Acme Food Service Company is having some trouble in handling success. Acme has been in business for 25 years. Starting as a small family operation, Acme has enjoyed a growth in sales every year. The facilities have been expanded several times. The company was incorporated several years ago. Mr. Acme and his family own a controlling interest.

Even though business has increased annually, the organizational structure and operating procedures are basically the same as they were when the firm was started. The company has developed a few key personnel but does not really have any depth in first-line supervisors. As sales volume continues to increase, the supervisors are stretched to their limits.

The Acme family and other members of operating management have always been personally involved in supervision. However, in recent years the Acmes have moved farther away from direct supervision, although still participating in the business. As a result, other members of operating management have had to take on additional supervisory responsibilities.

To handle the steady annual improvements in sales, Acme has increased the number of operating personnel and has improved production methods. Yet the organizational structure continues to be strained as managers and supervisors are responsible for larger numbers of employees.

By most standards, Acme is a successful business. The company has achieved what all companies want: steady annual increases in sales and profits. Yet the company's personnel and facilities are barely able to handle each year's volume of business. The management group feels that staying the same means losing ground to the competition, and that dropping back would be inconceivable. But by going ahead, continuing to hire more people and to expand facilities, Acme might be overextending itself.

Acme has never taken the time to do any long-range planning. The business has regularly faced the problem of handling increased sales efficiently and has never looked far beyond that immediate necessity.

The management group got together recently and decided that Acme Food Service Company was at a crossroads. They had to evaluate their present situation and plan for the future. The group decided on a series of meetings. The first meeting would attempt to establish the plan for the series itself.

As the group came together for the first meeting, they showed some anxiety and awkwardness. No one seemed quite sure what was going to happen, what to say, or what to do. Finally, Mr. Acme got the group settled down, and the open discussion began.

How would you analyze the Acme situation? What would you recommend?

PAGLIARA TRUCKING COMPANY

Pagliara Trucking Company (PTC) of St. Louis was founded in 1925 by Louis M. Pagliara, Sr. The current owner–president is his only son, Louis Jr. The company hauls bulk commodities (sand, gravel, cement, salt, and oil) in dump trucks and tanks within a 100-mile radius of St. Louis. Thanks to hard work, close family cooperation, and sound business associations, PTC has continued to expand over the years.

When Louis Sr. retired in the mid-1960s, his son took over full control of the business. An intelligent and highly dedicated man, Louis Jr. was raised in the trucking company and understood all aspects of the operation. Upon taking control, Louis launched an ambitious expansion program. He bought 20 new tractors in 1967 and 20 more in 1969. He also acquired Carlson Cartage Company, a small firm owning important interstate operating rights to haul salt and other commodities throughout Missouri and parts of adjoining states. By January 1, 1974, Louis Pagliara owned and operated 140 tractor-trailers, making PTC the largest privately owned bulk material hauler in the Midwest.

If ever a company's structure was set up around one person, Pagliara Trucking is that company. Louis Pagliara runs the main terminal. He lives, eats, and sleeps with his trucks. Louis, his wife, and their three small children live in an apartment directly above the office at the main terminal. This location enables Louis to keep a constant eye on the terminal. He even has all company phone calls directed upstairs after work.

Louis has employed many relatives over the years, and two have become permanent PTC members. Brother-in-law Bert has been employed for 15 years and is now the figurehead president of Carlson Cartage Company. Cousin Don runs the stock room and orders supplies. The remaining management staff consists of the bookkeeper and treasurer (Jim Jones), the manager of the branch terminal about 30 miles away (Bill Rogers), two radio dispatchers (Joe Saunders and Harry Mitchell), a computer specialist, a rate clerk, and a keypunch operator–office boy. The office staff is very streamlined, considering that PTC's total revenue exceeded $5,000,000 in 1978.

The drivers are all union-scale Teamsters. Union pressures have steadily driven wage costs up so that in mid-1978 the drivers were making over $9 an hour. Each driver operates a Mack tractor pulling either a dump or tank trailer. The drivers are responsible for keeping the tractors reasonably clean and performing minor maintenance (checking oil, adding water, changing light bulbs, making minor on-the-road repairs, and so on). Each driver's main concerns are to drive safely and legally and to operate the equipment effectively in off-the-road activity (dump trailers are notorious for turning over while dumping). The garage performs all other functions for the drivers.

Several other facts of the PTC situation are important.

1. The cement fleet is much more profitable than the dump fleet. Daily revenue from a cement truck is about $50 more than daily revenue from a dump truck.
2. The branch terminal handles 60 dump trucks. Their drivers are in a different Teamsters local, and they have a seniority list separate from the main terminal's seniority list. All 50 of the cement trucks and 30 of the dump trucks are based at the main terminal.

3. PTC's business is highly seasonal. On a clear July day, all 140 units may be on the street. In January, only 20 units may be out. Resources, people, and equipment are stretched to the limit for half the year. Then they are often idle during the other half. Seasonal layoffs are a fact of life for all drivers except those with highest seniority.

4. Management is salaried and has never been laid off, so that expense is constant. Branch terminal manager Bill Rogers makes $500 a week. Both dispatchers earn $400 a week. Brother-in-law Bert ($375 a week), cousin Don ($300 a week), the computer specialist ($300 a week), the rate clerk ($250 a week), and the office boy ($150 a week) are active year round. When things are slow in their own areas, they work on something else. For example, if office work is slow, the office boy fuels the trucks or works on tire records.

The year 1978 was a very good one for the company. However, by the fall of 1979, Louis Pagliara saw that St. Louis building contractors were not starting new projects after completing their current projects. In years past, PTC had always experienced a rush at year end, as contractors hurried to complete projects and get a head start on new ones before winter set in. In 1979, the rush did not happen. Pagliara had to park his trucks and lay off his drivers much earlier than ever before.

It is now November of 1979. In view of the long winter ahead, Louis Pagliara faces financial difficulties. He writes down a list of money-saving possibilities as he sees them.

1. Simply do some belt-tightening and achieve greater economy by cutting down on wage expense and increasing production by supervising the drivers more closely.
2. For the first time, lay off some management people.
3. Sell some tractors (and possibly same trailers) to the drivers, allowing them to share the profits as owner–operators, rather than receive hourly wages.
4. Sell the company.

What should Louis Pagliara do?

MORRISVILLE HOSPITAL

Morrisville Hospital is a not-for-profit corporation with 200 beds. The hospital has been serving the Morrisville area for 60 years and has an outstanding reputation. The hospital has always kept up with new medical developments and has frequently been the first hospital in the area to introduce new medical techniques and technologies.

The hospital introduces these medical advances mainly because of its close relationship with the Morrisville Clinic group of medical specialists. That group is highly trained and respected. About 80 percent of Morrisville Hospital's admissions come through the clinic group.

Morrisville Hospital has been able to keep up to date without much use of federal or state funds. New medical technology has been financed through normal hospital activities.

A few months ago the hospital executive committee asked for a feasbility study on the possibility of forming a renal dialysis center at the hospital. Renal dialysis is a process of cleansing impurities from the blood of persons with kidney disorders. The procedure takes about 7 hours. Acute cases must have hospital care. However, once past the acute stage, most patients can be treated at home. The patient buys a dialysis machine, and the renal dialysis center trains family members in how to administer the procedure.

The following facts were included in the feasibility study.

1. Approximately 30,000 Americans die from kidney failure each year. Many die because dialysis machines are not available for them.
2. The state's three other hospitals with dialysis centers lost money on them last year.
3. Collecting full payment for dialysis is often difficult because most hospital insurance plans do not fully cover dialysis.
4. The machine costs $6000. The average treatment costs $125.
5. Several hospitals in the state started dialysis centers but discontinued the service due to financial problems and difficulty in finding trained personnel.
6. Three of the 12 renal dialysis specialists in the state are connected with the Morrisville Clinic.

The feasibility study presented these comments from hospitals in other cities across the country.

City 1. We find that the expense of treatment cannot usually be borne by the patient.
City 2. We estimate our cost per patient per year at $12,000. For the most part, we must obtain these funds from private sources.
City 3. The average patient cannot afford this treatment, so we must look to county, state, and federal sources of funds.
City 4. We use dialysis only on acute patients awaiting kidney transplants.
City 5. Our renal dialysis program is largely financed by the federal government, through the Public Health Service.
City 6. Our dialysis costs are paid this way: hospital contributions, 20 percent; grant income, 60 percent; general contributions, 10 percent; patient payments, 10 percent.

As the feasibility study proceeded, pressure mounted for the rapid installation of dialysis machines at Morrisville Hospital. Community sentiment throughout the state favored making dialysis machines more readily available, especially since a law suit had been filed against one of the state's three dialysis centers for allegedly "turning a patient away." The three kidney specialists at Morrisville Clinic of course want the dialysis center. One member of the hospital's board of directors has expressed great interest, since she has only one kidney and anticipates needing the machine some day.

On the other hand, Morrisville Hospital is not large and is limited in its financial resources, since it is not subsidized by government sources.

In light of these problems and pressures, what should the Morrisville Hospital board of directors do?

part three

implementing decisions

Once good decisions are made, they must be implemented. The manager's ability to implement decisions depends first of all upon communication, the subject of Chapter 7. Decisions must be quickly and easily communicated to those affected by them or responsible for implementing them. Chapters 8 and 9 discuss the individual factors and group factors affecting the implementation of decisions. Whenever decisions are implemented, individuals are affected. Chapter 8 presents several models that attempt to describe why individuals behave as they do. The chapter also discusses authority and power, because those elements may enter into the implementation of decisions. Chapter 9 shows how group processes influence the organization member's acceptance of decisions. The manager who wants to implement decisions successfully must consider the dynamics of group behavior.

Chapter 10 covers organizational change. The chapter discusses the forces causing change and the forces resisting change. Different methods for bringing about change are explained, and the participative method is recommended.

7

communication

All the steps in the decision-making process require effective communication. The ability to recognize the existence of problems, to discover and evaluate appropriate alternatives, and to choose the best alternative all depend on the manager's skill in acquiring and using appropriate information. The good manager knows how to get accurate and timely information about the internal and external environmenal factors relevant to problem identification and solution.

Many managers believe that they are decision makers—period. They make the choice, and then—by some mystical process—it is implemented. But making good decisions is not enough. The art of management lies in implementing good decisions after they are made. The manager's ability to implement decisions depends upon communication skills. The best decision is useless unless it can be quickly and easily communicated to those affected by it or responsible for implementing it. Communication is the glue that holds the organization together. It enables the separate members of the organization to act in unison.

The ability to monitor the environment for problem situations and to change the organization through implementing decisions both rest on the ability to communicate. Therefore, this chapter focuses on the process of communication, the barriers that impede effective communication, and the design and use of systematic procedures for making information available to decision makers.

THE COMMUNICATION PROCESS

Humans differ from other animals in their ability to represent their experience symbolically, primarily through language. We can discover facts and develop ideas, theories, concepts, and opinions, and then pass this information to other people, present and future. Similarly, organizations develop procedures for conducting their affairs and making decisions. Contemporaries and

135

successors can use these procedures to avoid the inefficiencies of trial and error.

Although communication is the most pervasive and important of human activities, it is also one of the most difficult and neglected. This section will review the elements of the communication process. It will also serve as a reminder of how difficult it is to meet our responsibilities as both senders and receivers.

The communication process has been symbolized in many ways. Figure 7-1 presents a communication model or picture that should help to clarify the process. It will enable us to understand each part of the process and to grasp how the parts fit together. Communication begins with *ideation*: a sender has an idea to transmit to a receiver. The idea can be a fact, a command, an observation, or anything else that the sender wants to communicate. The idea is developed by the sender into a symbolic representation, transmitted through an appropriate channel, and interpreted by the receiver. Finally, the receiver responds to the message, and this response may stimulate further communication from the original sender. Although the model may seem simple, communication problems can occur at each of its phases.

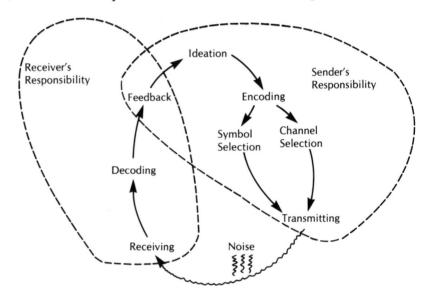

FIG 7-1 The communication process.

Source

Interpersonal Communication. In interpersonal communication, the communication source or sender is someone with a reason for communicating. The source could be a sales representative with an idea for a prospective buyer or an executive with an idea that could improve the productive efficiency of a plant.

To communicate effectively, the first requirement for the communicator is to *empathize*. In other words, before the message can be formulated, the source must consider the receiver's position and look at the situation from the receiver's perspective. For example, the executive must consider any proposed change from the viewpoint of all employees affected by the change. Although top management may view the change as an improvement in efficiency, middle management may see it as a threat to their jobs, responsibility, or authority. When executives communicate changes to subordinates, they must therefore carefully explain why, when, and how the changes will take place. In fact, many executives solicit input from employees before making a decision in order to understand employee reactions and feelings. Information obtained in this way may affect the nature of the subsequent communication.

Here is an example of communication inefficiency caused by the sender's failure to empathize with the receiver's experiences, attitudes, and values. As part of an international promotional strategy, Exxon Oil Company publicized the phrase "Put a tiger in your tank" in a small country that did not consider tigers to be superior beasts. As a result, the people could not decode Exxon's intended meaning since their frame of reference was not consistent with that of Exxon management.

Mass Communication.   In mass communication, the communication source is normally an industrial, governmental, service, educational, or trade organization with an informative or persuasive message. However, the source may also be an individual like an editor, college professor, or reporter who is communicating not to another individual but to a large group of people.

Although the model for mass communication is essentially the same as for interpersonal communication, mass communication does present some unique problems for the source. In the first place, empathy is difficult because so many people are involved. They have various attitudes and values, so the sender often has difficulty in arriving at a common denominator. Another problem involves the speed of communication. Since individuals may be formulating the message for reception by numerous other individuals, mass communication may be much slower than interpersonal communication.

Encoding

The sender cannot send the idea itself. Encoding involves converting the sender's original idea into a symbolic form or code that will be meaningful to the receiver. The important point about encoding is that the symbolic form must have a common meaning for both the sender and the receiver. The meanings that senders and receivers attach to words and other symbols are a product of their environments. Since no two environments are exactly alike, many communication symbols have more than one meaning (as any diction-ary will illustrate). For example, "computerization" may suggest "efficiency" to top managers but "threat" to clerical workers. In fact, all of a firm's em-ployees have a different meaning for "computerization," depending upon their positions and their past experiences.

In interpersonal communication, the encoding apparatus consists of our vocal and muscle systems. Our vocal mechanisms encode ideas into symbolic words or other meaningful sounds. The muscle mechanisms of the hand produce writing, drawing, and other meaningful visual symbols. Other mus-cle groups encode ideas into such nonverbal forms as gestures or facial ex-pressions.

Filters.   Another problem at the encoding stage is *filtering*: the intentional distortion or holding back of information. In a competitive business environ-ment, communicators are often tempted to place their personal goals above organizational goals. Filtering—leaving out, changing, or adding informa-tion— is one way to do that. Filtering is discussed at greater length in a later section of this chapter on barriers to effective communication.

Message

The product of the encoding process is the message, a set of symbols de-signed to transfer meaning from the sender to the receiver. The message is the end result of vocal or muscular effort. The effectiveness of communication depends upon the sender's ability to build verbal or nonverbal messages. These messages are often made up of written or spoken words, but they may also take the form of a sensuous look, a laugh, a mode of dress, a gesture, and so on.

Channel

The channel is the medium through which the message travels. It carries the message. It may be a sound wave, a touch, or a written note. Although the channel has a simple function, carrying the message from the source to the receiver, it has been given much attention in studies of communication. For example, Marshall McLuhan suggests that the channel *is* the message. He says that the communications medium itself determines how a receiver envi-sions the sender's idea. Even if the language is the same, the message be-comes changed from one medium to another because people apparently as-sociate different meanings with different channels.

A communication barrier that we will talk more about later is *noise*: any unplanned interruption of the communication process. Noise is usually an external physical barrier to communication (like an explosion or loud music), although it can also be internal (like anxiety or stress). The sender's responsibility is to select the communication channel that minimizes the chance of noise. The sender can also use techniques designed to keep the receiver's attention in the presence of distracting noise, such as unusual phrases and short, concise messages.

Receiving

The sender encodes a message and transmits it along a communication channel. At the other end of the channel, the physical stimuli that make up the message (such as sounds or words on a page) must be received by the receiver's sensory apparatus. Receivers have a difficult responsibility. They must accumulate information by listening, watching, feeling, reading, or other appropriate means.

Decoding

The received message is converted into nervous impulses that are sent to the brain. In a way that we do not fully understand, the central nervous system converts these impulses into ideas that have meaning for the receiver. This process is called decoding.

Decoding effectiveness depends on many factors: the sender's encoding ability; the receiver's need or desire for the message; communication noise affecting the receiver at the time of decoding; and the experiences, attitudes, and values that the receiver brings to the decoding stage.

In many respects, the receiving–decoding process is analogous to computerized data processing. When a message is transmitted through a channel to a human receiver, it is received, decoded, and filed in a short-term memory similar to the core memory of a computer. If the message is considered important, the human receiver may move it from short-term storage and file it in long-term memory. This process is similar to the computer process of moving data from core to a tape for storage. After the message is filed in an appropriate storage location, the human receiver's short-term memory is ready to receive a new message.

Over a given time period, the human mind is capable of receiving much more information than a human sender can send. During those moments between receiving information bits, the receiver should analyze information already received and store it for processing.

Feedback

The last step in the communication process is really the first step in a new communication sequence: physical or verbal reaction to a message. Feedback may be a raised brow, a smile, a positive or negative verbal reply, or some other reaction. Feedback indicates to the source whether the message is understood, as well as the receiver's general reaction to it. If feedback suggests that the message is not understood, the sender can make appropriate changes in the message, the channel, or some other aspect of the process. If the message generates a nonverbal or verbal response suggesting that the message has not been favorably received, the sender can send another message designed to encourage favorable reception or to find out the reason for the receiver's negative feelings.

It can be seen that, in feedback, the receiver becomes the sender (of feedback) and the original sender becomes the new receiver. Therefore, for the communication sequence to be successful, the original receiver must send back a message to confirm that the idea or concept was received and understood, and the original sender must receive that feedback, interpret it correctly, and act accordingly. A frustration for students seems to be the professor who lectures to the chalkboard. The lecturer is sending a message but never knows whether or not it is being received. The communications cycle is incomplete because the sender has not fulfilled an important responsibility: observing feedback from students.

NONVERBAL COMMUNICATION AND LISTENING

Nonverbal Communication

Communication can be nonverbal (without words) as well as verbal. In fact, when we deal with other people face to face, nonverbal messages account for at least half of the total meaning produced. Nonverbal means of communication are of several kinds.

Proxemics. Proxemics has to do with how *space* is used. The arrangement of buildings on a college campus and the arrangement of the rooms within the buildings affect the ways in which communicators interact. Dividing up a large room into small cubicles affects the communication between employees working in the room.

Within a room, different seating patterns influence communication. A conference leader wanting to encourage interaction among participants will place seats in a circle. A group leader who wants to do all the talking will place the chairs in a rectangle of rows. Such aspects of the physical setting as temperature, lighting, drapes, carpeting, and room color also have their effect.

Territoriality is a part of proxemics. We all have an invisible personal space surrounding ourselves, and we allow that space to be entered only under certain conditions. We also consider the space within which we work to be "ours."

Kinesin.   Kinesis is better known as *body language*. We communicate nonverbally by moving our bodies in certain ways. To communicate different ideas you may wave your hand, shake your finger, nod, cross your arms, stamp your foot, point, wipe your forehead, smile, look away, and so on.

Appearance.   Appearance communicates nonverbally. The clothes we wear, the jewelry with which we ornament ourselves, and the way we arrange our hair say something about us. Organizations often have dress and appearance codes (for example, suit, white shirt, solid tie, hat, and no facial hair) designed to convey a certain organizational image. An IBM typewriter salesperson would not make calls wearing a UCLA sweatshirt and Adidas jogging shoes.

By nonverbal means, we display feelings, shades of meaning, confidence, self-control, defensiveness, suspicion, nervousness, and many other aspects of ourselves. From the manager's point of view, nonverbal communication is important for two reasons. First, the manager skilled at interpreting nonverbal cues can be a more effective receiver of communications. The aware manager realizes that, when the verbal and nonverbal messages conflict, the nonverbal message is more apt to be accurate. Second, managers in control of their own nonverbal signals can use nonverbal means to reinforce their verbal communications. If the manager's verbal and nonverbal messages conflict, employees become confused.

Listening

The average manager spends 2 or 3 hours a day in listening to superiors and subordinates. Listening is obviously a significant component of the communication process. The more information the manager has, the better the manager's decisions will be. One of the best ways to gather information is by being a sympathetic listener.

The good listener will try to adopt the speaker's point of view, to see things as the speaker sees them. Furthermore, the good listener will try to grasp both the content of the message (as expressed verbally) and the feeling of the message (often expressed nonverbally).

The manager who is a good listener does much for organizational morale. By listening carefully, the manager communicates to employees that they and their ideas have value.

BARRIERS TO EFFECTIVE COMMUNICATION

Resolving problems and implementing decisions in an organization are certainly made easier by effective, free-flowing communication patterns. When communication is open, management knows where its problems are and whether or not its solutions are working. Management can also head off potential problems by gathering information about difficulties that employees may be having with the job or with other people. However, when communication is restricted, effective decision making must also be restricted to the extent that management awareness of problems and opportunities decreases. The barriers to effective communication fall into three categories: physical, personal, and semantic.

Physical Barriers

Physical barriers (one type of *noise*) are external distractions or limitations that suppress the fidelity of messages. Examples might include a change in temperature, the presence of an attractive person of the opposite sex, a disturbing sound, a competing message, or too many messages coming in at once on one channel (information overload). Some physical barriers are so obvious that most people have learned how to avoid or reduce them. For example, when physical noise is so loud that people cannot speak, they use gestures, signals, or other nonverbal devices. To combat competing messages and other noise, advertisers spend much time and money in transmitting alarming statistics, provocative pictures, captivating dialogue, voluptuous women and handsome men to gain consumer attention for a few seconds.

Personal Barriers

In our discussion of perception, we showed how sociological and psychological factors influence the sending and receiving of messages. Here is a brief review of these influences upon communication effectiveness.

Psychological Barriers. Most of the psychological barriers to communication are *personal filters*. We are all constantly deluged by information. As you read this page, you are taking in information through most of your five senses. However, your personal filtering system is screening out much of this sensory information so that you can focus on the incoming information that is most important—the printed symbols on this page. Our psychological filtering systems may also *add* information, often unintentionally. Communications specialists know that the more links there are in a communication chain, the more the message will be distorted as receivers add to, subtract from, or otherwise change the message before sending it on.

Through training and personal experience, people establish standards for the events that they consider important and unimportant. In management, as in personal experience, people develop ways of focusing on what their preselected standards determine to be important information while ignoring the unimportant. Management by exception is based on such an idea of preestablished norms. The manager takes note only of deviations from the norm. Only those exceptions are "important."

Our parents, peers, employers and other members of our culture teach us some definitions of "important." We learn other definitions by trial and error; we learn to select certain pieces of information and to ignore others. Of the information that we select, we often interpret it to suit ourselves and then embody our interpretation in the information we send along.

Attitudinal Barriers.   While personal filters are very useful in protecting receivers from information overload, they may cause receivers to distort incoming messages. For example, our cultural training produces filters that cause us to *stereotype*—to filter out differences while allowing similarities to come through. The receiver who thinks in stereotypes does not have as efficient a decoding process as the receiver who avoids stereotyping.

Consider the attitudes of three different department managers who are sent the same message about a company effort to reduce inventory. The marketing manager sees a reduction in levels of finished products in inventory as a threat to the department's ability to reach sales, revenue, and customer satisfaction goals as inventory levels fall so low that orders cannot be filled promptly. The production manager perceives the same reduction as a chance to substitute quality for quantity and to avoid wear and tear on equipment. Finally, the finance manager sees inventory as a constant problem; either the production people produce too much or the marketing people sell too little.

The result of such personal filters is distortion and misunderstanding. People filter messages to conform to the attitudes they already hold by virtue of their experience and training. In the preceding example, when top management sends a memorandum indicating an inventory problem, marketing thinks the plant is not producing enough, production believes marketing is not selling, and finance thinks the plant is overproducing and marketing is underselling. These opinions are internalized by the persons involved, and changing their basic beliefs would be difficult. They may take corrective measures if top management tells them to, but they will hesitate to admit failure or responsibility for inventory problems. This phenomenon is referred to as *selective distortion*. Receivers distort incoming messages selectively or unintentionally because of attitudes that they bring to the communication situation.

Intentional Distortion by Sender.   Another barrier is *intentional distortion* or filtering of information by the sender. The sender falsifies or withholds information in order to attain personal objectives. Students manipulate information given to their professors. A President filters information transmitted to the public (or distorts it or withholds it entirely). Lower-level employees filter facts before relaying them to top management. The result is manipulation of information by the sender and, if frequently practiced, skepticism on the part of the receiver concerning the accuracy of the information. The information system becomes inefficient because the receiver may not always get accurate information and may not trust or act on the information even if it happens to be accurate.

Inertia as a Filter.   People often evaluate statements, data, or situations in terms of their long-established habits rather than by using logic or objectivity. The primary cause for biased evaluation is prolonged application of one method or belief that a person or group has used with some success. A company is run in a certain way, a house is cleaned in a particular manner, or a consumer shops at the same store for many years. If the experiences result in profit or satisfaction, the same habitual response will continue—regardless of its appropriateness. The person or organization develops a case of *tunnel vision* and ignores new developments. For example, numerous industrial giants were highly (and successfully) centralized in the late 1800s. Not until the 1960s did they take steps to increase their efficiency by decentralizing, a costly delay resulting from management's bias in favor of centralized operations.

Status.   Another personal barrier to communication arises out of social or organizational status. When the president of a large corporation goes to the production floor to chat with the people on the line, successful communication is not impossible, but it is made difficult by the vast differences in organizational levels. Even when the distance between levels is not so great, the problem exists. When employees are communicating with supervisors who have the power to dispense promotions, pink slips, favorable assignments, and job transfers, they tend to filter out information that may be personally damaging or that supervisors may not want to hear.

Personal Antagonism.   Another personal barrier to open communication is antagonism between the sender and receiver, for whatever reason. Here is an example of the problems that such a barrier can cause. The divisional merchandise manager of a major southwestern retail chain had a personal conflict with a buyer. Therefore, the merchandise manager neglected to inform the buyer about fashions, suppliers, and potential availability of merchandise, and the buyer would not consult with the manager before making buying decisions. The result of the conflict was merchandise that would not sell, followed by one demotion and one termination.

Barriers and Filters in Combination.   The preceding barriers and filters, and many others, affect the everyday communication situations that constantly occur in all organizations. To illustrate how these barriers and filters may affect the fidelity of message sending and receiving, let us consider one person (Sally Johnson), one decision-making situation at XYZ Company ("Should XYZ fire district manager George Smith?"), and one message ("George Smith insulted customer Bob Jones last week").

Consider Johnson as a message receiver. How she processes that message and the weight she gives it can be affected by such factors as the following:

1. How many senders are transmitting messages to Johnson about this situation? Is this the only message, or is it one message out of forty?
2. Is the sender a subordinate, a peer, or a superior? Messages from superiors carry more weight.
3. Is the sender outside or inside XYZ Company? Messages from inside the company generally carry more weight, but perhaps not in this instance.
4. What is Johnson's position in the company? Filing clerks and presidents react differently to identical messages.
5. Is this the first message Johnson has ever received from this sender? If so, she may not weight it very heavily. If not, have the earlier messages contained reliable or unreliable information?
6. How far along is the decision-making process? If deliberations about firing Smith are just beginning, the message may be treated in one way. If deliberations are quite far along, this may be the deciding piece of information, unless it is contrary to most previously acquired information, in which case it will probably be ignored.

Now Johnson has received and evaluated the message. Assume that she is going to transmit it (or her variant of it) to Harry Robinson. The preceding factors may be relevant to the sending process, but others also come into play:

1. What is Johnson's relationship to the original sender? To customer Bob Jones? To district manager George Smith? To Harry Robinson? Are any professional or personal ties, loyalties, or conflicts involved?
2. What is Harry Robinson's relationship to Johnson, Jones, Smith, and the original sender?
3. What are Johnson's hopes for the future? If Robinson is her superior, will the message be good news or bad news for him? Subordinates striving upward tend to avoid sending bad news messages to superiors. Are Johnson and Robinson both filing clerks who are leaving the firm next week? Or is Johnson trying to get President Robinson to support her effort to replace Smith as district manager? The message Johnson sends will be affected by the answers to these questions.

Personal Barriers and the Manager.   Personal communication barriers are a problem that has no quick and easy solution. Being personal, they are subject to the many aspects of interpersonal relationships. The most important point for managers is to realize their existence, understand how they occur, and make the effort to keep personal feelings from affecting business relationships. To overcome these barriers, a sender must carefully observe the receiver's feedback and then respond accordingly. It is the sender's responsibility to ensure that the message is received and decoded accurately. Only by watching and listening for feedback can the sender fulfill that responsibility. The receiver may not like the message or its sender, but at least the message has been understood.

Semantic Barriers

Although language makes learning and communication possible, we must remember that language is simply a symbolic representation of reality and not reality itself. Because people tend to interact with people like themselves, the phrases, mannerisms, and terms common to the group become their verbal symbols of reality. However, outside the group, these symbols lose precision and cause communication problems. The complex, elaborate terminology and jargon of data processing are useful to people within the group but have little meaning to people outside the group. Data-processing managers who want to explain the computer system to production foremen must use verbal symbols that have meaning to the foremen, even if those symbols are not as precise as the terminology of data processing.

One of the most significant semantic barriers is the ambiguity created because the sender assumes (incorrectly) that the receiver will understand. Lack of understanding may be caused by an incomplete memorandum, an ambiguous questionnaire, an unempathetic salesperson, or an overly technical report. Assuming a nonexistent understanding can be particularly devastating in one-way mass communication like a mail survey or advertisement. The receiver, of course, does not respond, and the miscommunication continues until the message is changed because of negative results. In interpersonal communication, the receiver can ask for additional information or can communicate ignorance by a raised brow or blank stare. This feedback can be recognized by the sender, who can then send explanatory messages.

When the sender and the receiver miss each other with their meanings, we say that *bypassing* occurs. Bypassing comes about when both parties use the same word with different meanings or different words with the same meanings. To illustrate the same word–different meaning miscommunication pattern, let us say you need a push to start your car. You tell me that you have an automatic transmission so I must push you at 35 miles an hour to start your car. If I ram into the back of your car at 35 miles per hour, apparently we had different meanings for "push you at 35 miles an hour."

Communication Barriers and Decision Making

Physical, personal, and semantic barriers to communication can create problems in decision making. Decision activity is not even begun unless the decision maker is aware that a problem exists. This problem awareness is directly dependent upon some data or information coming from the environment to signal the need for problem solving. If the communication process that alerts the decision maker is faulty or incomplete, so will be the awareness or definition of the problem. In a similar sense, communication barriers diminish the effectiveness of the search for alternatives, the evaluation of alternatives, and the implementation of the choice.

Most managers are fully aware that effective communication is difficult. They can cite numerous examples of delays, errors, and other organizational problems caused by communication barriers. Although most discussion of barriers focuses on interpersonal oral communication, similar problems can occur in any medium. Indeed, the potential for communication barriers increases when the face-to-face interpersonal process is replaced by some other communication medium.

For example, a primary problem in written communication is getting, recognizing, and acting on feedback. It seems easy to write a memo to someone else. You know what you want to say, and your memo makes sense to you. So it ought to make sense to the receiver. Since a time lag exists between sending the written message and getting a response to it, the sender can easily forget to check for feedback. Although organizations spend considerable amounts of money on programs to train their managers in written communication skills, such communication problems still remain.

MANAGEMENT INFORMATION SYSTEMS

Most organizations have a formal organization chart. It is usually neat and pretty. It shows the lines through which authority and communications should flow. However, the formal lines of communication are often imperfect and limited. Their limitations have two results. One is the informal communication system called the grapevine. It meets the social and emotional needs of employees that the formal communication system does not meet. Another, more recent result—arising out of increasing managerial concern with the communication barriers and gaps in the formal communication system—is the evolution of *management information systems* (or MIS). A management information system can be defined as any *systematic* procedure for providing *information* to a *manager* at the time that information is needed. Although an MIS can be represented by something as simple as a memorandum containing information that helps to facilitate decision making, the term normally refers to a computerized data-retrieval system.

Information that has no bearing on decisions is useless to the manager. Inaccurate information or information that is available at the wrong place or wrong time is equally useless. The goal of a management information system is to provide appropriate information to the right person at the right time.

This goal means that the information provided to the decision maker must be *relevant, timely,* and *understandable.*

As simple as these criteria seem, many management information systems fail to meet all of them. For example, every day managers receive large stacks of timely, relevant computer output without any idea about what it means or how to find what they need. Since they do not want other employees to think them uninformed, they continue making decisions without the aid of the information.

Computer-Based Information Systems

A Utopian System.   Envision a typewriter linked into a computer. Anytime any manager needs information about any problem, the manager simply types out a request for it. Immediately, the typewriter responds by printing out what is requested. The response is accurate, presented in exactly the right format, and completely understandable. This process illustrates what MIS people call an *on-line, real-time, random-access system.* The manager does not have to know anything about the system except how to type the question on the machine.

While this Utopian system does not currently exist, it does represent a goal for MIS designers. More limited applications of the same procedure are now available. Inventory, payroll, and production scheduling are areas in which computer-based management information systems are used successfully. Managers ask the questions. Computers process and manipulate the data, and then generate appropriate reports.

Retail Check-Out.   The check-out system used by many retail operations serves as an excellent example of a specialized MIS. First, a universal product code containing numerous bits of product information was developed. The product code appears as a 1½-inch-wide series of light and dark bars (usually with ten digits underneath) on the package taken off the shelf by the consumer. The first five digits—for example, 21000—signify Kraftco Corporation. The second five digits—65883—specify that the product is Kraftco's 7¼-ounce package of macaroni and cheese dinner. When the consumer reaches the check-out counter, a store clerk passes the code over an optical scanner. A low-energy laser beam reads the code and relays the information to a computer. The macaroni and cheese dinner price, stored in the computer, is then flashed on a display screen in the cash register. The process takes ¼ second, and the scanner does not misread the price as the clerk might. Placing a price tag on the individual product—a costly process for supermarkets—becomes unnecessary (though most stores continue to put prices on items). Instead, the price appears on the shelf holding the product. After all purchases have been scanned, the customer receives a detailed register receipt that lists items, prices, store locations, coupon allowances, food stamp credits, bottle returns, taxes, date, time, check-out lane, and so on.

The same information is retained in the computer for the company's use. In that way, the system gives the store detailed information about each product. The result is accurate inventory-control information that facilitates quantity purchase decisions, planning of special sales, better estimates of personnel needs, and control of spoilage and waste.

Management Information System Design

Such a prearranged series of manipulations and the routing of output to managers (and in some cases to suppliers and customers) are what is commonly involved in MIS design. System designers are specialists who are accountable for placing appropriate data in the system, designing and implementing the programmed instructions and output data channels, integrity and security of the data system, and consistent data flow.

In addition to these functions, systems designers share responsibility with the organization's decision makers to determine what information is needed, how it should be compiled, how often it should be available, and what standards of information quality and quantity should be maintained.

Learning the Language.   Writers in the MIS field have cited these shared responsibilities as the biggest problem in implementing an effective MIS Operation. The newness and special nature of computer technology and language have led many managers to approach MIS with high expectations, followed closely by confusion and frustration.

The first task for managers considering MIS is to learn the specialized systems language. Since most formal MIS operations use computer technology, the specialized vocabulary of computers has become commingled with that of MIS design. Although many of the terms are self-explanatory, others may be foreign to people not trained in computer systems technology. Therefore, managers should review a basic systems or computer book, or take an orientation course.

Problems of Management Information Systems

Since most MIS applications are at the operational level, this is the place where problems have most often occurred. These problems are of four kinds: information overload, numeric myopia, the language barrier, and inadequate cost–benefit analysis.

Information Overload.   Too much information is almost as bad as no information at all, and MIS operations may cause information overload. Most managers have an inadequate idea about exactly what information they need in decision settings. Rather than requesting specific, necessary information, they may ask the systems designer for *all* data that might be relevant. The common assumption is that the more information, the better the decision. Therefore, the systems designer provides a wealth of information in the form of a computer printout. The printout may say so much that it actually tells the manager nothing, because the useful is hidden among the useless.

Humans use psychological filters to prevent information overload. Although it is much easier said than done, organizations must set up similar filters to screen out unimportant information. Furthermore, managers can be taught to reflect more intensely on their information requirements. They can also learn simple techniques for separating the useful from the useless, such as circling important data on computer printouts.

Numeric Myopia.   Myopia is nearsightedness. Numeric myopia refers to the tendency to focus on the numbers close at hand, rather than trying to understand how the numbers came about. Managers have a tendency to believe that the computer output is exact, even though the input information was approximate. Although most managers are familiar with the "garbage in, garbage out" principle, they often have difficulty identifying garbage on the printout.

The only effective way to overcome numeric myopia is to know where the input data comes from and what happens to it in the computer. This is another task that is easier said than done. Most managers learn gradually (usually from their mistakes) how to identify the *quality* of data output. Some give up and disregard all data output.

A partial cure for numeric myopia is to keep firmly in mind that the output is not the decision itself; it is merely the information for decision making.

Language Barrier.   A third problem area is the language barrier between the data-processing and operational people. The operations people tell the systems people what they think they want, and the data-processing equipment is directed to provide what the systems people think the operations people want. However, both groups use terminology peculiar to themselves, and they do not always speak the same language. As a result, anyone involved with computer-based management information systems can tell many tales of forms generated that no one used, information disseminated that no one wanted, and data requested that no one could find.

Cost–Benefit Analysis.   The final problem area is inadequate cost–benefit analysis. When MIS is installed, it is sometimes regarded as a new toy that can be used to play with pet projects. This attitude can hurt any organization, both in selecting equipment and in applying it to operational problems. Management information systems can be expensive. Any MIS project should be carefully analyzed in terms of its costs versus its benefits.

The analysis should not be confined to financial considerations. Other factors, such as effects on morale, must be assessed when determining an MIS operation's costs and benefits.

These problems will be overcome as managers become more aware of the strengths and limitations of electronic equipment and as designers become more oriented toward management applications. At present, managers are not making use of many helpful, inexpensive, and readily available MIS applications because neither group—system designers or managers—properly understands the other's needs and limitations.

Past, Present, and Future of Management Information Systems

Communication barriers are present in all organizations. Increasingly large and complex economic and social systems are accompanied by increasingly large and complex communications difficulties. In very large organizations, information must pass through many people at many levels with corresponding filters, screens, and barriers.

The Potential.   Although managers often recognize these increasing communications complexities, they do not always know how to overcome them. Because of its potential for facilitating communication, the development of MIS in the 1950s was greeted with much enthusiasm. The MIS concept and the speed of the computer seemed to offer solutions to many communications problems.

Over the past two decades, MIS and computers have diminished the effect of barriers at each step in the communication process. And yet, MIS has not brought about Utopia. In theory, the data in an MIS operation would remain unfiltered by any human screening process. Consequently, anyone requesting information would have access to accurate data in the required form. However, the successful application of MIS theory has been moderated by certain realities.

The Reality.   First, *people* supply data for the system. The possibilities for communication distortion at this stage are enormous. People can select the wrong data from the information available, or selectively distort the right data, or encode it incorrectly into the communication system. All these possibilities represent human barriers in the communication process.

Furthermore, *people* design the MIS. The program that processes and stores data and responds to data requests is a human invention, subject to human fallibility. System designers and data users are seldom the same people. Their cultural and educational training is seldom so similar that they see things in the same way. Therefore, as systems people try to respond to requests for information from production people, the intent of the requests may get lost in the semantic gap separating the systems analyst from the person requesting information. The normal result is too much information in the wrong format.

Most managers, like most other people, cannot readily articulate what kinds of information they typically use in making decisions, nor do they always remember the sequence or format in which they seek it out. If production managers are accustomed to taking sales forecasts from the marketing people, subtracting 20 percent, and then adding back a variable "fudge factor," they will have difficulty in asking the systems people to use the MIS operation to provide all this information.

Most people ask for more information than they really need to make a decision, rather than less. Excess data constitutes noise in the communication process. No matter how effectively the information is gathered, encoded, and transmitted, it will be a rare manager who wades through a multiple-page output before making his decisions. The receiver is not receiving what the sender is sending. The receiver is listening or reading, but the noise blocks the communication.

Making MIS Work.   MIS is susceptible to the many problems that people add into the communication process. Nevertheless, the need is so great for more efficient processing of data than the old bureaucratic memo system that computer-based systems must be used more and more. Therefore, we must identify techniques for implementing MIS so as to minimize the people problems and maximize data access and accuracy.

The first step in designing an effective MIS operation must be careful analysis of *how the organization makes decisions.* The following questions must be answered through systematic investigation: What are the major decision types? Who makes them? What information is required? Where does it come from? What could be done to make the information more useful? Who is affected by the outcome, and how? This inquiry process should be undertaken on a decision-by-decision basis. "Make or buy" production decisions, inventory-level decisions, and decisions about resource allocation are excellent starting places because they dovetail with existing mathematical optimizing models already available in most computer applications. Not only would management be shown how to find the necessary input data. The utility of the effort could also be readily demonstrated by means of a quantitative procedure. Solving a few problems in this way would gain enthusiasm and support for the potential of MIS in attacking other organizational problem areas where quantification is less precise.

Once the information requirements for various classes of decisions are known, the information delivery system can be designed. Because analysis has shown the system designer what the manager really needs, the system can be made to provide necessary information in concise, understandable form.

A final step in designing an MIS is convincing the system designers to be sensitive to feedback. Very few people are capable of designing anything exactly right the first time, and MIS operations are especially susceptible to this human failing. Designers must follow through by finding and resolving system-created problems.

MIS and Communication Barriers.   The increasing complexity of modern organizations has brought about a need for rapidly available and accurate information. Management information systems are a necessary response to that need and can provide decision makers in large organizations with the information necessary for responding quickly to a dynamic socioeconomic system. A well-designed MIS can reduce the effects of human filtering, screening, and distorting of information, because the human factors will only influence the communication process at the time when information is placed into the system. Although a faulty computer program may manipulate and distort data if the human designer introduces a fault, the consistency of any barriers created in this way will facilitate their recognition and elimination.

SUMMARY

This chapter began by describing the seven elements in the communication process: the sender or source, encoding, the message, channel selection, receiving, decoding, and action and feedback. Following a discussion of nonverbal communication and listening, three major classes of barriers to effective communication were described: physical, personal, and semantic.

The chapter's concluding major section dealt with the design and use of management information systems. The chapter examined four problems commonly associated with MIS: information overload, numeric myopia, the language barrier between computer and noncomputer people, and the need for careful analysis of the costs and benefits of any MIS program. The potential and the reality of MIS were contrasted, and some suggestions were offered for introducing a successful MIS operation.

DISCUSSION QUESTIONS

1. To ensure effective communication, what responsibilities are specifically the sender's? The receiver's? What responsibilities do they share?
2. What is the significance of filters in the communication process?
3. What are the main barriers to effective communication? What can a manager do to overcome them?
4. Think back to the last communication breakdown in which you were involved. Look at Figure 7-1. Where in the figure did the breakdown occur?

5. What are the characteristics of useful information for decision making?
6. Why is an understanding of communication the first step in implementing a decision?
7. What can an MIS do to aid in overcoming the barriers to effective communication?
8. What are the major problems of MIS? If you were a manager responsible for MIS design, how would you try to overcome these problems?
9. What are the steps in making MIS work?
10. What do you think will be some future applications of MIS? What future problems do you foresee?

STATE FOREST SERVICE

Chief Ranger Ralph Rolf supervises 12 State Forest Service rangers. His job is to oversee their work, coordinate activities, and communicate policies and instructions. Rolf finds that he spends a large part of his time in communicating procedural changes to the rangers.

In an interview, Chief Ranger Rolf said: "It seems to me that just as soon as I get the word out on one regulation, along comes another one from the state office. I'm always pulling the rangers in to headquarters to explain a new way of doing something or to get some information from them.

"As a result, my rangers are unhappy because they think I'm keeping them from their real jobs, my supervisors are unhappy because they don't think I'm getting the word out or responding to information requests fast enough, and I'm unhappy because I don't have time to supervise and coordinate the work properly."

How can Chief Ranger Rolf go about dealing with the constant flow of new procedures and requests for information?

SOUTHERN INSURANCE HOT LINE

Jackie Davitt is a program director for Southern Insurance Company. She receives information, regulation changes, and legal interpretations about the program for which she is responsible. Then she sends the information to the people responsible for implementing the program.

As a staff person, Davitt must be careful not to assume authority within Southern's administrative structure. She must send any changes or new regulations through the service delivery manager, who in turn transmits the information down through two or three more levels. Figure 7-2 is an organization chart that reflects the situation.

Because information must pass through several levels, the process of implementing change in Davitt's program can be quite slow. Furthermore, Davitt must often wait a long time to see if her instructions have been clearly understood or

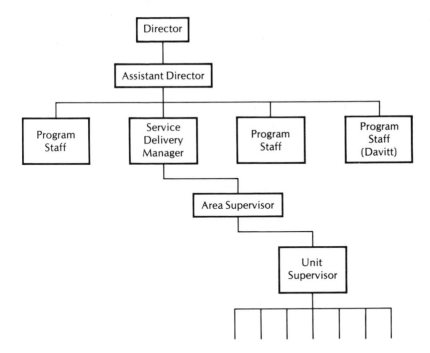

FIG 7-2   Southern Insurance organization chart.

correctly interpreted, because this feedback must come up to Davitt through several organizational levels. The same is true of any information requests addressed to Davitt. Her expertise cannot be obtained directly. Units having a problem must ask for Davitt's help through channels.

One day, while thinking about the problems caused by these delays, Davitt had an idea. Why not a "hot line"? The hot line phone would have no dial, to remind everyone symbolically that the chain of command must be followed if an organization is to run smoothly. Any unit supervisor picking up a hot line phone would be immediately connected to a central switchboard operator. The unit supervisor would state the problem or ask the question, and then the switchboard operator would direct the question to the appropriate program director. That person would handle the problem as quickly as possible by sending a standard reply memo to the inquiring supervisor, with copies to all higher levels of supervisory authority. Davitt thought that this method would encourage fast, easy use of staff expertise without endangering the authority of line supervisors.

What should Davitt do now?

implementation and the individual

Even if good decisions are communicated effectively, they are useless if they are not put into practice. Since decisions must be implemented by people, this chapter looks at *individual* factors affecting decision implementation, and the following chapter looks at *group* factors affecting decision implementation.

We have already seen that different individuals have different organizational perspectives. Members make highly personal, highly individual, self-defined decisions about what they will contribute in exchange for the inducements offered by organizations. At any given moment, most organization members are generally satisfied with the inducements–contributions balance. Although most organizations have some dissatisfied members who will eventually leave, all members are deriving enough from the present situation to make organizational membership worthwhile, or they would not continue as organizational members.

Implementing any decision changes things. Therefore, before trying to implement decisions, managers must understand what benefits the organization's members are deriving from the present situation—soon to be changed. How can managers get supervisors and other subordinates to accept and implement decisions?

To answer this question, the manager needs to understand why people behave as they do. Therefore, this chapter will present several models that attempt to describe individual behavior.

Group members often accept and implement decisions because of the decision maker's *authority* and *power*. The chapter will discuss these concepts as they relate to decision implementation.

WHY PEOPLE BEHAVE AS THEY DO

Role Model

One easy way to build a behavior model is simply to ask people, "Who and what are you?" The answer might be something like, "I'm Thomas Green, and I am the Ajax Food Store manager, a Chamber of Commerce member, a husband, a father, a taxpayer, a Rotarian, a Methodist, a night student at the university, and a veteran." Each of these self-descriptions represents one of Thomas Green's roles, and to some extent each role may serve as a model for describing Thomas Green's behavior.

People closely approximate the behavioral norms of the groups with which they identify. Under the role-model approach, we would have to determine which role Thomas Green is playing at a particular time. If we know the norms of behavior for that role, that is, the ways in which persons playing that role normally behave, then we have a useful model for describing (and possibly predicting) Green's behavior.

Externally Directed.   The role-model approach is essentially *externally* directed. When in his role as a Rotarian, Thomas Green is doing what *other people* expect him to do, for the most part. If he does not match their expectations, they will ask him to leave the club. If the club's expectations do not match the way in which Green wants to behave, he will leave the club.

People adopt roles. Their behavior within these roles is based on the expectations of others. Those two premises are reasonable. Consider going to an organizational meeting (or a party after the meeting) at which you know no one except Thomas Green, who knows everyone else. You would probably stick close to Thomas in order to imitate his role behavior. People new to a group tend simply to imitate, to *do* what is apparently expected of them. Later they try to *understand* what is expected of them and to integrate this understanding into their own personality structures. This period of "feeling out" the situation—trying to find out what the group expects—is typically uncomfortable. Once new members understand their roles and can play them well, they are much more at ease.

Group Influences.   In the organizational setting, the role-model approach implies that a group member's behavior is based almost entirely on the member's understanding of how the group expects the member to behave. Group influences will be discussed more fully in the next chapter. For the moment it is sufficient to point out that behavior in some situations is indeed determined and controlled by group influences. Now and then, if not more often, we all try to "keep up with the Joneses," on and off the job. Managers with decisions to implement should try to keep their decisions and implementation instructions consistent with the role expectations of their subordinates.

Economic Model

Rational, Internally Directed.   A second behavior model is the economic model. It assumes that people are rational, want to maximize their own well-being, weigh the usefulness of different behaviors in terms of their own well-being, and choose the behavior that is most economically satisfying. This approach is sometimes called *utility analysis,* because people are viewed as choosing the behavior having the greatest economic utility or usefulness for them.

Smith and Bentham.   This line of thought is a natural outgrowth of an Adam Smith concept: self-interested people seek to maximize their own self-interest. They behave as they do not because of group influences but because they make *conscious internal* decisions to behave as they do. Jeremy Bentham amplified on this concept of self-interest with his "felicific calculus." According to Bentham, people rationally calculate the pleasure and pain of every contemplated behavior. They derive their greatest utility by choosing alternatives that maximize pleasure and minimize pain. For example, Joan Webb wants the pleasure of having considerable independence in her job. She must realize what other pleasurable job characteristics she will have to give up and what painful job characteristics she will have to accept in order to achieve job independence. Her personal calculus must determine whether the trade-offs are worthwhile.

Marshall.   Classical economist Alfred Marshall elaborated on this type of utility analysis by making *money* the easily measured, objective indicator of utility. Consider Steve Shapiro, a student who loves the field of economics, loves big houses and expensive cars, and has an opportunity to go into his uncle's business at $75,000 a year to start. Shapiro places a money value on his love for economics, balances that against the cost of *not* going into his uncle's business, and then either goes to work for his uncle or chooses to become an economics professor at a much lower salary. All aspects of the decision, including the emotional aspects, are reduced to economic terms.

The Economic Model and the Consumer.   As managers and elsewhere in our daily lives, we often behave in this economic way. If you want a new Buick, you shop around to get the best deal. When you take your $10,000 Buick home, you have bought $4,000 or $5,000 worth of transportation plus $4,000 or $5,000 worth of status and emotional satisfaction.

Other buyers view a car's utility strictly in terms of "a dependable, enclosed mode of transportation." These buyers shop around for the cheapest new car available. The Volkswagen sales curve of the 1950s and 1960s, followed by the explosive growth of Japanese imports in the 1960s and 1970s, was caused by a very large group of people who wanted good, cheap, basic transportation. Such examples show that our normal behavior patterns are often based on economic reasons.

If you usually buy one brand of mushroom soup, but occasionally will buy another brand when it is on sale, you are demonstrating that people also deviate from their normal behavior patterns for economic reasons. We are all living proof that the economic model is frequently descriptive of how people behave.

The Economic Model: Shortcomings.   On the other hand, if the economic model were completely descriptive, people would always take the highest paying job and would accept job transfers or change jobs for very small wage increases. Everyone would drive a stripped-down Chevette. Since such behaviors are not observed very often, managers seeking ways to implement decisions had better not assume that people do what they do for economic reasons alone.

Classical Conditioning Model

Another model that seems to describe how and why some people behave some of the time is the classical conditioning model, or stimulus–response model. When experimenting with dogs, the Russian physiologist Pavlov noticed that if a bell was rung before the dogs were fed, the dogs learned to associate the bell with the food itself. After the food–bell association became fixed (or *conditioned*), the dogs would salivate whenever the bell was rung. One useful modification of the original classical conditioning model contains four central concepts: drive, cue, response, and reinforcement.

Drives.   Drives are the *physiological* drives (such as hunger and thirst) and the *learned* drives (such as cooperation, greed, and fear). They are internal stimuli that impel action or other response.

Cues.   Cues are external stimuli that evoke the drives. A picture of a hamburger might cue the hunger drive. Passing an intersection where you once had an accident could be a cue to fear.

Responses.   Responses are reactions to cues or drives. If the cue (hamburger picture) evokes the hunger drive, the response would be eating to reduce the drive. If the cue (intersection) evokes fear, the response might be to leave the scene immediately and avoid it in the future.

Reinforcement.   Reinforcement is the internal reward (either positive or negative) derived from the response. If eating hamburgers reduces hunger, the experience is viewed as a positive reward (called positive reinforcement) and is likely to be repeated in response to hunger cues. If driving past the dangerous intersection increases the driver's anxiety, the response of driving that route receives negative reinforcement and is not likely to be repeated.

Stimulus–Response.   Environmental cues act as stimuli to responses. We learn behaviors by observing whether or not our responses satisfy our drives. If we are positively reinforced for a behavior, we will repeat that behavior even when it is not always reinforced. A well-trained dog does not need to be given a treat every time it jumps through a hoop. Similarly, employees do not require pay after every unit of acceptable product. A weekly or monthly pay check usually serves as sufficient positive reinforcement.

Classical Conditioning Model: Shortcomings.   As a way of explaining member reactions to organizational decisions, the classical conditioning model has four difficulties.

1. *Which drive is the member trying to satisfy?* Drives motivate different people in roughly, though not exactly, the same ways. Enough differences exist to confuse a manager trying to structure rewards so that they will truly reinforce desired behavior.

For example, the drive primarily affecting Harry Peterson's behavior is social acceptance. When he does not feel accepted, he gets anxious. Harry's work group has decided informally that each man shall produce in the range of 8 to 10 units per hour. Harry's boss sees that Harry has the skill required to produce more than 10 units per hour, so he offers a bonus for each unit per hour over 10 that Harry produces. Money can help Harry to reduce the intensity of his physiological drives, so it is a positive reinforcer. Yet whenever he produces over 10 units per hour, his fellow employees give him the silent treatment. Harry's behavior is being both negatively and positively reinforced. Robert Gunter, Harry's manager, may not realize that Harry has a drive toward social acceptance. Even if he does, he may think that Harry's drives that can be satisfied with money are surely more important to Harry. Not being able to view his dilemma as objectively as Gunter can, Harry may choose to produce 9 units per hour because that behavioral response has the greater drive reduction associated with it.

2. *Which cues trigger the desired behavioral responses?* What the organizational leader needs is cues that will lead to responses that will (1) achieve the organization's objectives and (2) lead to drive reduction in the group member. If cues result in inappropriate responses, confusion will result.

For example, psychologists often use water to reinforce a desired behavior in rats, such as running on a wheel. However, in certain experiments it was found that the rats were reversing the cue and the response. Rather than running to get a drink, the rats were drinking so the experimenter would let them run. This example demonstrates how hard it is to find out what cues rat behavior. Finding out what cues human behavior is even more difficult.

3. *How are the cue and the response linked?* The same cue may not always trigger the same response. The employee may not be paying attention or may have a perceptual block. All drivers have driven through a red light at least once because they did not see the cue designed to elecit the Stop! response. Similarly, people in jobs make mistakes because they do not pick up on cues.

4. *What is a reinforcer?* Some reinforcers work sometimes and not at other times. One hamburger may effectively reinforce a desired behavior. The seventh may be a negative reinforcer to the person who has just eaten six.

Just as people on the job display variations in their drives, so do they display variation in the way they react to reinforcement. One college professor may be positively reinforced by a pay raise, another by a promotion, a third by job security in the form of tenure, and a fourth by the excitement of teaching advanced graduate courses.

The Black Box.   Since managers are not practicing psychologists, employee variations and exceptions to general principles may make the general stimulus–response theory useless on the job. The problem is that this theory, like so many other ideas in psychology, relies on the black-box concept. The mind is like a black box. We can see the input—ideas, information, concepts, cues, sensory data going in—and we can see the behavioral output. But how the input results in the output remains a partially explained mystery, because the processing goes on inside the employee's mind—the black box.

Skinner Model: Behavior Modification

Focus on Response.   B. F. Skinner offers another model for explaining behavior. Ignore the stimulus–response relationship. Do not worry about identifying the exact stimulus that will result in the desired response. Do not worry about what goes on inside the black box. Instead, whenever the desired behavior occurs (no matter what, if anything, caused it), reward it. When the wrong behavior occurs, do not reward it. Modify behavior by giving positive reinforcement to desirable behavior and withholding reward for undesirable behavior.

Chicken in a Basket.   To illustrate this idea, consider Figure 8-1, depicting a chicken in a basket. Imagine an invisible line above the chicken, close enough so that the chicken can lift its head above the line if it wants to but so far away that penetrating the line would be an abnormal response. During its random behaviors, the chicken extends its head above the line. The chicken is immediately fed. Very soon, the chicken will learn to keep its head above the line as long as it wants food.

FIG 8-1   Chicken in a basket.

Managing Through Behavior Modification

Behavior modification is becoming an important idea in many areas requiring the management of people—in education, where children learn desirable behaviors; in industry, where workers learn industrial norms; and in many other situations requiring that a person's behavior be structured. The Skinnerian model has great potential whenever desirable behavior can be defined, explained to the employee, measured, and rewarded.

An Example: Decreasing Tardiness.   Behavior modification can be used to decrease tardiness. The desired behavior (being on time) can be defined. It is different from any other behavior. That is, you are either late or you are not late—like pregnancy, there is no ambiguous middle ground. The desired behavior can be communicated to employees, measured, and rewarded. When Ellen Walters is on time, she gets a point, a token, or some other type of immediate positive reinforcement. When she has accumulated enough tokens, she can exchange them for cash or for a prize.

Immediate Positive Reinforcement.   During its early stages, such a training program provides immediate positive reinforcement every time the desired behavior occurs. Since the desired behavior is so precisely defined and immediately reinforced, it is learned quickly. Its opposite, undesired behavior becomes difficult to maintain. After the desired behavior has been learned well, the time intervals between rewards can be lengthened.

In the Classroom.   In one situation, a teacher learned a new behavior without realizing that she had learned it. The class knew that the teacher enjoyed spirited classroom discussion. So whenever the teacher wandered into one corner of the classroom, the class would discuss the subject with great energy. Whenever the teacher left that corner, discussion stopped. Before long, the teacher was spending the entire class period in the corner, without realizing that the class had modified her behavior.

In the Mental Hospital.   Many mental institutions reward crazy behavior with attention, a positive reinforcer for most sane and insane people. In the mental institution, the way to get attention is to act crazy. The crazier you act, the more attention you get.

Some mental hospitals have been reorganized along behavior modification lines with very good results. At these hospitals, people who act crazy are ignored and people who act sanely are given attention. This approach mirrors the common-sense approach to raising children. Attention is a reinforcer for most children. If the child gets attention only when it acts badly, the only reinforced behavior is bad behavior. Wise parents give children attention when they are behaving appropriately, rather than waiting until the children smash windows.

In the Organization.   The implications of behavior modification for organizational managers are enormous, and rather simple. Managers need not be psychologists in order to encourage desired behavior in subordinates. They merely have to know what behaviors they want to evoke and what kinds of things reinforce different group members—what "turns them on." Good managers have always known that some people require a gentle approach and others a blunt approach; some people respond to the carrot and others to the stick. Some people want to be left alone, and others want constant encouragement. The manager who defines good performance and establishes individually focused reinforcement schedules to reward it can get people to implement decisions—without a psychology degree or formal behavior modification training.

Maslow Model

Our last behavior model is Abraham Maslow's *need-satisfaction model.* This model has been widely used to describe how and why people in organizations do what they do.

The Hierarchy of Needs.   A hierarchy is an order of importance. Maslow's hierarchy of needs appears in Figure 8-2. Needs are of five kinds. Organizations help members to satisfy their needs, while members help organizations to achieve their goals.

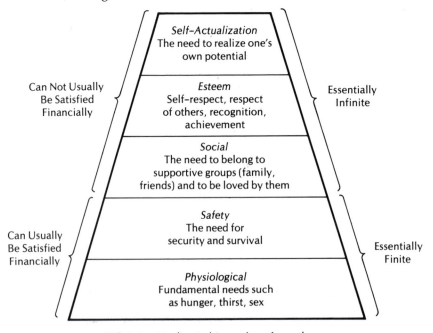

FIG 8-2   Maslow's hierarchy of needs.

The basic needs are *physiological*, the need for food, air, water, and other basic requirements of life. If these needs have not been fulfilled, we can be motivated by them. After our basic physiological needs have been satisfied, we can begin to think about our *safety* and *security* needs. We want to feel safe from harm and want to keep others from taking away what we have.

Once we feel safe and secure, we move upward to a concern for *social* needs. We shift from suspiciously preserving what we have to a guarded interest in being with other people. When social needs have been fulfilled to an extent, we shift our focus upward to the next level in the hierarchy, *status* and *esteem*. At some point during our interactions with other people, we aspire to become leaders or pacesetters and to acquire their respect and esteem.

Finally, we achieve enough status and esteem to satisfy us, though we can always use more. We turn from needs that require external fulfillment to the state of *self-actualization* that can only be found within. This state is difficult to describe, but it is experienced by people who have become all they can become—for a moment or for much longer periods. The inner satisfaction resulting from solving a problem, winning a race, or achieving a meaningful goal all represent brief encounters with self-actualization. Albert Schweitzer and Mahatma Gandhi are often said to represent fully self-actualized persons. They clearly transcended the lower four levels of needs and existed in terms of being all that they could become.

Implications for Management.   The needs hierarchy can help managers understand why their people do (and do not do) things in the organizational setting. Such understanding is particularly vital for managers at the point of implementing decisions. Managers must know whether their decisions will create or destroy a need-satisfying situation for employees.

For example, workers need to feel job security. Their manager wants them to work faster. If the workers are convinced that they are going to be laid off when the present job is finished, the manager will have difficulty in convincing them that a speed-up would be good for them.

Finite Needs.   Here is another important point about the needs hierarchy. In our society, the two lower levels are for the most part satisfied. The physiological needs are finite; they can be filled. After a person has had sufficient food and water, more food and water may actually be harmful. The same is true of safety and security. After a point, more security restricts our freedom and sense of independent action. Consider Howard Hughes, so fanatical in his pursuit of safety and security that he became a virtual prisoner of his own devices.

Infinite Needs.   The three upper-level needs are essentially infinite in capacity. Although you may get some, you can always use more. In advanced societies, employment opportunities and social welfare programs enable people to meet their physiological needs. Social norms and government-provided protection services are usually ample to meet safety and security needs. For these reasons, leaders of organizations in advanced societies must try to meet the higher-level needs of group members. In our society, the lower-level needs have been met. The upper-level ones—being infinite—have not.

The Upper-Level Needs.   Many managers see no reason for trying to fulfill the social needs of employees on the job. However, people spend about one-third of their waking hours on the job, and work is a social, group activity for most workers. Consequently, the manager who helps employees to fulfill their social needs, rather than trying to eliminate social interaction on the job, will have employees more willing to implement managerial decisions.

At the fourth level is the need for esteem and status. We all need to feel that we are worthy and that others think we are worthy. Everyone needs an occasional pat on the back, a positive stroke. Since the lower three needs are partially or fully met in modern industrial societies, the employee's need for esteem and status becomes an important one for managers to understand and try to fulfill.

Last and most difficult to satisfy is the need for self-fulfillment. The manager should help integrate the employee's search for inner satisfaction into the employee's job. Perhaps the manager can structure a particularly challenging, rewarding job for the employee. Or perhaps the manager can help the employee to set and meet ever higher goals.

Economic and Symbolic Rewards.   The final important point about needs and their influence on implementing decisions is that the lower-level needs are satisfied primarily through *economic* rewards, and the upper-level needs are satisfied primarily through *symbolic* rewards. Managers have sometimes felt that they should merely pay good wages and let employees use the wages to satisfy their other needs. Here is an illustration to show that this approach does not always work.

The Expensive Taxi Driver.   Skycloud Airlines has continual difficulty with its pilots. Every time a contract expires, the pilots go on strike, not over wages but over other parts of the job. The difficulty comes about because of the nature of the pilot's job.

Pilots have high status in our society. They have long apprentice programs before they take command, they wear important-looking uniforms, they get a large salary, children are excited over meeting them, they are addressed respectfully as "Captain," and they are in command of lives and expensive equipment. Yet, in many respects, they are expensive taxi drivers. They are told what and when to fly, how high, how fast, where to, and when to land. They have about as much control over their jobs as assembly-line workers do.

The incongruity between the job status and the job actuality creates the difficulty. Pilots have a role conflict because their own role concept of "pilot" does not match management's role concept of "pilot." So the pilots typically negotiate for more decision-making power, and management typically offers more money. The pilots try to fill an unsatisfied need, and management offers further satisfaction of a need that is already satisfied.

What often happens is that pilots wind up settling for more money and *more time off from flying*. In their leisure time, they frequently go into creative or expressive hobbies such as running a flower shop or managing a cattle ranch. Ideally, management should find a way to help the pilots satisfy these creative urges in the job itself. That does not happen, so the pilots seem to be saying, "If you're going to prevent me from having my needs satisfied on the job, then you're really going to pay for it."

AUTHORITY

Authority Acceptance Theory

Managers must understand how people's needs affect the implementation of decisions, once they are made. Also necessary is an understanding of how *authority* and *power* influence decision acceptance. The following discussion of Chester Barnard's *authority acceptance theory* should help to show how and why authority gets decisions implemented.[1]

The manager makes decisions. Someone else in the organization must usually implement them. The manager causes that to happen by giving an order. According to Barnard, authority is the quality of such an order that causes someone else to accept the order and to do as ordered. If someone gives you an order to bring a keg of nails from the storeroom and you do it, that order has authority *for you*. If you do not do it, that order does not have authority *for you*.

So whether an order has authority or not is determined by the order receiver, not the sender or "person in authority." Authority is always *accepted* (though perhaps by force) or there is no authority. Even an army will not advance unless the soldiers give their unanimous consent to the order "Forward, march!"

The factors influencing the acceptance of authority lie in the nature of the sender and receiver, their relationships to the organization and to each other, and in the nature of the communication itself. The manager must understand and pay attention to these factors that influence authority acceptance. Just as many governments must rely on the consent of the governed, so must many organizations. And like so many aspects of organizational mem-

---

[1]See Chester I. Barnard, *The Functions of the Executive* (Cambridge, Mass: Harvard University Press, 1968), Chapter 12.

bership, this one is related to inducements and contributions. If inducements offered are balanced with or outweigh contributions expected, orders asking for further contributions or different contributions will be accepted. If required contributions outweigh inducements, orders will not be carried out.

Conditions for Accepting Authority

Four preconditions must be met before an employee will accept an order that is meant to be authoritative. Even if the preconditions are met, the employee may not accept the order. But if they are not met, the employee either will not or cannot accept the order.

1. *The employee must understand the order.* Otherwise, compliance with the order is impossible. Many employees have listened carefully and then later wondered what the boss was talking about, what the boss wanted done. Many employees have *thought* they understood an order and then found that they did not, because the order was too confusing or too general. Supervisor Jones tells Foreman Smith, "Get rid of the trouble on the number 3 line." Smith removes the troublesome machine, scraps it, and replaces it with a new one, when Jones really wanted the machine repaired. The two men had different meanings for "Get rid of the trouble." Even though they both "understood" the order, their understandings were different.

To sum up, a manager who does not use the principles of good communication to ensure that an order is truly understood has not exercised authority, because those employees who are supposed to comply with the order cannot do what they do not understand.

2. *The employee must believe that the order is consistent with the organization's goals.* A soldier in a blue uniform is sitting in a trench and shooting at soldiers in gray uniforms. The commander orders him to turn around and shoot at a group of soldiers in blue uniforms coming up from the rear. The soldier might shoot the commander instead, unless the commander first explains that the soldiers in blue coming up from the rear are spies and not reinforcements. Without that explanation, the soldier in the trench would not see the order as consistent with the organization's goals. All experienced managers know that employees will not usually follow such orders. So if an order appears to conflict with an organizational goal or with past practice, the manager must explain why this time is different.

A special violation of this precondition is conflicting orders. Both orders are sent down, but they cannot both support the organization's effort. The employee will either accept the authority of one order and reject the authority of the other, or do nothing.

3. *The employee must believe that the order is consistent with the employee's own goals.* This precondition is related to whatever reasons the employee had for affiliating with the organization in the first place. If carrying out the order will result in the organization's becoming less attractive to the employee, the

order will be disobeyed or (more usually) evaded. Such orders are inconsistent with the employee's personal motives, which are the basis for accepting any orders at all. If the order is totally inconsistent with goals or principles that are important to the employee, and the order cannot be disobeyed or avoided, the employee will probably resign.

4. *The employee must be able, physically and mentally, to carry out the order.* This precondition is so obvious that mentioning it seems absurd. Yet we are sometimes asked to do that which is impossible for us. A man with a bad back is told to carry heavy cases of liquor. A saleswoman with a fear of heights is given the top third of the Empire State Building as her territory. The manager who gives orders without knowing each employee's capabilities soon finds out that if it can't be done, it won't.

Securing Compliance

Once the preconditions to the acceptance of authority have been met, how do managers actually secure compliance with orders meeting the preconditions? The compliance necessary for a smoothly functioning organization comes about for three reasons.

1. *Effective managers issue orders that comply with the four preconditions.* The effective executive issues orders that are *accepted.* Orders that do not comply with the preconditions are not obeyed, and the manager who issues them causes big problems. Of such a person it is said, "She abuses her authority" or "He doesn't know how to use his authority."

Poor managers ignore the preconditions primarily for one reason: they think that their formal organizational positions give them the *right* to issue commands of all types. Many managers believe that they have absolute authority over their subordinates. This belief is confirmed by many organizational experiences in which their subordinates do indeed comply with managerial orders.

However, effective managers soon learn that "absolute" authority is absolute only as long as the four preconditions are not violated. If managers meet the preconditions, employees will allow them to be authoritarian and autocratic. Once the manager begins to ignore the preconditions, employees begin to ignore the orders. Instead of realizing the failure as their own, such managers complain that "You just can't get good help any more."

2. *People joining an organization expect to be given commands regarding certain aspects of their behavior in the organization. They obey orders within these "zones of acceptance" without question.* Orders fall into three classes: clearly acceptable, clearly unacceptable, and doubtful.

If Lois Evans tells her secretary Bill Elliot to come into her office and take some dictation, the order would fall within Elliot's zone of acceptance. Elliot knew when he took the job that Evans might tell him to take dictation. On the other hand, if Evans asks Elliot to come over to her apartment for drinks and dictation, Elliot would probably refuse. He would not consider such overtime work to be an acceptable part of the job.

Many orders fall into a third area: the doubtful zone. If Evans asks Elliot to make the coffee, or get a birthday card for Mr. Evans, or some other task that is not really part of the job but is not really outrageous, Elliot may be doubtful about whether to follow the order and would have to think about it.

The width of the acceptance zone depends on the extent to which the organization fulfills the member's needs. For example, the Peoples Temple cult members at Jonestown had a zone of acceptance almost infinitely wide. Their goals so matched the organization's goals that they accepted orders to kill their children and then themselves. On the other hand, the hostile draftees of the Viet Nam war had so little organizational commitment that almost every order fell into the doubtful zone. Since outright refusal to accept an order was a capital offense, draftees often responded to commands—even those given under combat conditions—with such remarks as "Why should we do that, Lieutenant?" or "Let's discuss this a bit first, Captain."

3. *Most group members want "their" organization to run smoothly so they can gain the benefits that they anticipated when they joined. Therefore, group members will bring social pressure to bear on any member unwilling to accept authority.* People joining organizations realize that they cannot achieve their own personal goals if the organization fails. An organization cannot succeed if its members will not accept authority and take orders. Therefore, any member who denies an order or will not cooperate represents a threat to those members who identify with and work toward organizational goals for their own reasons. Accordingly, the group takes an active interest in maintaining every member's compliance with organizational commands.

The *informal* organization plays this important enforcement role in support of the formal organization's authority structure. If the informal organization wants a decision implemented, it is usually implemented. If a decision is not agreeable to the informal organization, they can find many effective ways of holding up implementation and making the manager's life otherwise miserable.

POWER

Authority comes from those over whom the manager exercises it. If group members do not accept it, it does not exist. On the other hand, some types of *power* can influence behavior whether people accept it or not. Power is of three types: physical, material, and symbolic.

Physical Power

In some organizations, the power base for securing cooperation is a loaded gun, a whip, or steel bars. Physical power influences behavior in such organizations as street gangs, concentration camps, prisons, and prisoner of war camps. Group members behave in a manner not so much designed to acquire a physical reward as to avoid physical punishment.

In the public and private organizations that concern us, physical power hardly ever comes into use. Managers do not manage organizations by promising physical rewards or threatening physical punishments. A picket line may physically intimidate or abuse a strike breaker. A football coach may force a defiant player to run up and down the stadium steps 100 times. Other than such rare instances, the exercise of physical power is not often permitted in managed organizations.

Material Power

The base of material power is money, which can be used to buy goods and services. Most incentive systems, including the power to hire, pay, promote, lay off, and fire, are based on material power. It goes without saying that managers should not promise material rewards that they cannot deliver. Nor should they offer material rewards for achievements that employees are not capable of accomplishing.

Material power is very important in the modern world. Without the power that results from their ability to give material rewards, most business, industrial, and governmental organizations would be quite different.

Symbolic Power

Physical power and material power enable the power holder to control the extent to which persons over whom power is wielded fulfill Maslow's two lower-level needs: physiological needs and safety–security needs. Symbolic power is the ability to offer or withhold such symbolic (nonphysical, non-material) rewards as are required to fulfill Maslow's three upper-level needs: the needs for social recognition, esteem, and self-fulfillment. Although symbolic power is exercised in most organizations, it is the sole power available to managers in such organizations as churches, social groups, political clubs, and voluntary associations. Three subtypes of symbolic power are referent power, expert power, and legitimate power.[2]

Referent Power. If boxer Muhammad Ali has influence over Jimmy Johnson because Jimmy admires Ali, identifies with Ali, and wants to be just like Ali, then Muhammad Ali has potential referent power over Jimmy Johnson. This same power relationship can exist between daughter and mother, scout and scoutmaster, subordinate and superior, and in many other relationships.

Groups may also exert referent power over individuals. If a group

---

[2]For further discussion of these power types, see John R. P. French, Jr., and Bertram Raven, "The Bases of Social Power," in Dorwin Cartwright (ed.), *Studies in Social Power* (Ann Arbor, Mich.: Institute for Social Research, 1959), pp. 150–167.

member identifies closely with the group, the group has the power to reward or punish the member symbolically.

Referent power is important for managers. Employees usually figure that the boss *is* the boss for a reason. They are willing to grant referent power to the boss until they perceive that it is not deserved. If managers have referent power, employees give them the benefit of the doubt and implement decisions even if they are not sure about the wisdom of the decisions.

Expert Power.   Expert power comes from the fact that "knowledge is power." Your doctor may be physically more powerful than you are, may be financially powerful enough to give you gold bullion, and may be the kind of person you admire. But you take your green pills regularly because your doctor tells you to. You trust your doctor's expert knowledge.

Organizations are filled with experts, wielding the power of their knowledge. The organization's psychologist says that applicant Robinson has manic depressive tendencies, so Robinson is not hired. The polygraph expert says Brown lied, so Brown is fired. The investments manager says "Sell," so the company liquidates its bond portfolio. In fact, many organization members hold their positions and exercise influence over others because they know more about their specialties than anyone else does.

Legitimate Power.   One final type of symbolic power is known as legitimate power. This notion assumes that some people have an inherent right to power over other people. Children "should" obey their parents, parishioners "should" obey their priest, and second lieutenants "should" obey first lieutenants, because the second member of each pair has legitimate power over the first.

Legitimate power is closely related to authority as that concept was discussed earlier. Employees accept the exercise of legitimate power. They know when they enter an organization that persons above them in the organizational hierarchy have the power to give them orders, and they in turn have the power to give orders to their subordinates simply by virtue of the organizational positions held. Most managerial decisions are implemented readily because employees grant to the decision maker the legitimate power to order their implementation.

Indeed, it may well be argued that, like authority, power must be accepted as legitimate or it is meaningless. When a government loses its power through revolution, all the physical power within its arsenals cannot help. Even naked physical power is accepted only by people who believe they have something to lose. Martyrs are those who refuse to accept physical power as legitimate and are then destroyed by it.

In the organizational environment, manager Barbara Jarvis may use a highly power oriented approach when telling a high-priced computer expert what to do. She may find that she has indeed derived from the organization the power to treat the computer expert that way. She may also soon notice a newly vacant, hard-to-fill job opening in the computer section.

Power and authority must be accepted by the employee. Managers who rely heavily on their power usually learn that the people they wind up having power over are the ones who are stuck in place, who for one reason or another cannot get jobs elsewhere. The better employees move on, to work for managers not so eager to throw their weight around.

SUMMARY

This chapter first offered five models for explaining why people behave as they do: the role model, economic model, classical conditioning, Skinnerian behavior modification, and Maslow's hierarchy of needs. Although each is informative, the Maslow model probably has the greatest usefulness for the modern manager.

The next major section of the chapter dealt with authority, primarily Chester Barnard's authority acceptance theory. Four preconditions for an employee's accepting authority were presented: the order must be understood, congruent with organizational goals and the employee's personal goals, and capable of implementation. Once the preconditions have been met, securing compliance with orders was seen to involve well-trained managers issuing orders falling within employee and group zones of acceptance.

The last major section covered managerial power as a means for implementing decisions, primarily the power to reward and punish. The three power types were physical, material, and symbolic (with its three subtypes: referent, expert, and legitimate power).

Sometimes implementing decisions is easy. Implementing the order "Start World War III" might be as simple as pushing a button. At other times, implementation may be the most difficult stage in the decision process. At such times, knowing why individual employees behave as they do, as well as how and why they react to authority and power, will be very useful for the manager. The next chapter extends the subject of implementing decisions to the ways in which groups react when given orders.

DISCUSSION QUESTIONS

1. In your opinion, which seems more explanatory of the way in which people actually behave: the role model or the economic model?
2. What is the difference between the classical conditioning model and the Skinner model?
3. Would behavior modification work on you?

4. Describe Maslow's need satisfaction model. How well do you think it explains why people behave as they do?

5. Which needs do most workers seem to be trying to satisfy in modern job situations?

6. What preconditions must a manager meet for ensuring authority acceptance?

7. As a student, how wide is your zone of acceptance? Which orders from your teachers do you accept? Which orders would you not accept? Indicate some orders that would fall into your doubtful zone.

8. What types of power can a manager exercise on the job?

9. What can managers do to increase their power and authority? Are they justified in doing so?

10. On the job, do the differences between power and authority really matter?

THE GENERAL ACCOUNTS SECTION

During the last few months, morale in the General Accounts Section has dropped sharply. The group consists of about 100 workers who do simple, highly routine tasks. The group is headed by Ms. Smith. As office manager, she is responsible for the efficient completion of the work.

Ms. Brown seems to be the immediate cause of the morale problem. She has worked in General Accounts for 20 years, is extremely dedicated, and in fact seems "married to her work." She comes in early, stays late, and receives no extra pay for her extra time.

However, she is also pushy and bossy. Although actually on the same level as that of the other workers, she has successfully pushed her way into a position of authority over them.

Recently, she circulated a detailed list of office procedures for the workers to follow. The list described when, where, and how the workers could take coffee breaks. Coffee cups had to be off the desks at the end of the 15-minute coffee break, whether the coffee had been finished or not. The list included a detailed description of what constituted a sandwich. If a certain type of food was classified as a sandwich, then it could be eaten at lunch time only, and not on the coffee break. This rule upset those workers who liked to eat their sandwiches during the coffee break and then use the 45 minutes at lunch time to take care of personal matters.

Ms. Brown also kept a detailed record of each worker's activities—where the worker went, how much company time was used for noncompany matters, and so forth.

Once Ms. Brown had instituted these procedures, office manager Smith approved them and backed Brown completely. Smith viewed the procedures as a healthy tightening up and encouraged Brown to come up with more ideas of the same sort.

An employee group finally visited C. P. Andersen, the vice-president of the Accounting Division, and described the situation. Andersen had heard nothing previously, was taken by surprise, and agreed to look into the complaints.

What is going on in the General Accounts section, and what should Andersen do about it?

ADMINISTRATIVE SERVICES SUPERVISOR

Immediately after she accepted the promotion to administrative services supervisor, Kathy Cohen was called into the office of administrative services manager J. C. Hutchins.

During the interview Hutchins said, "I want you to take the bull by the horns, Kathy. You've been in administrative services for eight years, and you know what needs to be done. Don't be afraid to use your own judgment in supervising the work. As long as you're getting the job done, I won't bother you."

Hutchins concluded by saying, "Of course, my door is always open if you have any problems you can't solve."

Cohen was anxious to look good in her manager's eyes. She wanted to show management that they had made a good choice. So she determined to do everything she could to avoid bothering the boss with problems. She thought taking a problem to Hutchins would reflect weakness on her part.

One frequent problem was that the work was not completed on time. Rather than bother Hutchins or crack down on the person failing to do the work, Cohen found it faster to do the work herself.

Eventually, Cohen found that she could not keep up with all the demands upon her. She finally decided that she could not handle the pressure and was not cut out for supervisor, so she submitted her resignation. Administrative services manager J. C. Hutchins was shocked and amazed.

What happened? What went wrong?

implementation
and the group

The previous chapter showed that a manager's success rests partially on an understanding of what drives *individuals* to accept decisions. This chapter will show how *group* processes influence the employee's acceptance of decisions.

The chapter has five major sections. The first section explains how the informal work group affects employee performance. The second section covers role theory. Which roles do members play within groups, and how do they learn those roles? The third section discusses role conflict—why group members may not play their roles satisfactorily. Next the chapter describes how the group's standards of behavior come about and why group members conform to those standards. The chapter concludes with two examples that show how managerial failure and success in implementing decisions are related to whether group processes are properly considered.

THE INFLUENCE OF THE INFORMAL WORK GROUP

The Informal Group Defined

An informal group is two or more people who associate because they want to, not because they have to. They join together to satisfy their own mutual needs and desires, rather than to satisfy someone else's needs and desires. A group stops being informal whenever the group members feel that they are together not because they want to be but because they have to be.

Examples of informal groups are bowling leagues, bridge clubs, "coffee-break cliques," "water-cooler clubs,"' and the four members of the secretarial pool who have lunch together.

Characteristics of Informal Groups

Most informal groups have several characteristics. First, they have *norms*, standards of behavior that all group members accept. Like formal organizations, informal groups have *goals* and *standard procedures*. Informal groups get together to achieve their goals, and they use standard procedures for handling situations that the group typically faces.

Informal groups are generally *cohesive*. They are bound together by a common attraction. The more cohesive the group is, the more control it has over its members and the less control persons outside the group can exercise. Group norms and group cohesiveness will be discussed at greater length shortly.

Why People Join Informal Groups

People join informal groups, on and off the job, for several reasons. They want to associate with human companions. They want to identify with persons like themselves. They want to keep informed about what is going on, and the informal group is in touch with the organization's grapevine. However, the most important function of informal group membership on the job is that it helps employees to cope with problems and with the formal organization itself. By giving up part of their freedom to make decisions and choices, group members delegate to the group the authority to substitute group values and standards for individual values and standards. When the group member has a problem to solve, the group's standards often determine what the solution will be.

The Study of Informal Groups

Informal groups have been studied for several decades, ever since the Hawthorne studies. Although the primary purpose of the researchers at Western Electric's Hawthorne plant was to examine the effects of different lighting levels on output, they also studied the interactions between workers. In the bank wiring room experiments, the researchers found a status hierarchy among the work group, those sitting near the front of the room having higher status than those sitting at the back. The researchers also saw that the informal group determined its own productivity rate. Group members who produced more or less than the group norm were punished by being "binged" on the upper arm. The Hawthorne researchers concluded that the informal group had a greater influence on employee behavior than the formal organization established by management did.

The Type of Influence Exerted

The type of influence that the informal group has over its members depends on the nature of the group and of the formal organization. Most informal groups arise to fill gaps in the formal organization's policies and procedures. The larger the gap in the formal structure, the more influence on its members the informal group will have. If the formal structure has only small gaps in communication, the informal groups may consist of coffee-break clubs whose members gather to pass along news and gossip. But if the formal structure is inadequate to help employees solve day-to-day problems on the job, informal groups will arise to help employees make decisions. The more help the employee needs and the less help the formal organization is willing to give, the greater will be the informal group's influence on its members.

To understand the group's influence over its members, we need to examine several aspects of the informal group: the leader, the informal communication system (the grapevine), group norms, and group cohesiveness.

The Leader.   The informal group's leader takes charge. The rest of the group imitate that person and ask that person's advice. The informal leader usually embodies most of the group's characteristics, attitudes, and values. The leaders of informal groups are often more influential than their formal counterparts, because informal leaders are quite free to support their groups without having to worry about the formal organization's goals or hierarchy.

Leadership in the informal group does not depend on official organizational position. The leader may become leader because of a strong personality, knowledge of the job, or superior ability at the group's common interest—like fishing or golf.

The Informal Communication Network.   Informal groups use an informal communication network called the grapevine. Despite its reputation for spreading gossip and false rumors, the grapevine is usually remarkably accurate. A grapevine cannot be stamped out. If one communicator is silenced, another takes over. Experienced managers have learned that the grapevine is inevitable, because it is a product of the situation and not of the people. So they have learned to live with it and sometimes to use it to advantage.

Norms and Cohesiveness.   Two important characteristics of the group as a whole are its norms and its cohesiveness. Informal group norms are analogous to the formal organization's standard procedures. The group member who does not adhere to group norms will be physically or verbally "binged" in some way.

Examples of informal group norms are self-established production quotas, sticking up for group members, bans on "shop talk" during lunch breaks, and so on. Through such norms, the group exercises influence over its members. For example, the group may not be able to finish its work by quitting time. Yet the group norm may be not to work overtime. Faced with such a group norm, management is probably going to have to solve its problem in some way other than paying overtime rates.

A final important feature of informal groups is their cohesiveness, their tendency to stick together. Cohesiveness and the presence of a strong set of group norms are interrelated. Norms help make the group cohesive, and cohesiveness helps make the norms acceptable. Management often benefits by having cohesive informal groups. Studies have shown that morale is higher and absenteeism lower among such groups.

Even though many informal groups are cohesive, they are of course less permanent and stable than formal organizational groups. Their leaders and behavior patterns change fairly often. They have no official status, so they are not praised when things go well or blamed when things go poorly. However, despite their informality, they are often quite powerful. Many an informal group has pressured unwanted employees (and managers) into quitting.

ROLE THEORY

The Person and the Group

Inducements and Contributions.   People join a group because of the group's ability to help satisfy certain of each member's basic needs. If the group offers a desirable mixture of inducements, people will join the group and will stay until the inducements disappear or are outweighed by expected contributions.

For example, George Frame likes to bowl so he joins his company's bowling team. At first he enjoys his participation. Then the team names him treasurer and, at about the same time, a man George has never liked joins the team. George's satisfactions are outweighed by two dissatisfactions—the burden of handling the team's finances and the new team member. George quits the bowling team and joins the company hockey team.

Multiple Memberships.   Within organizations larger than a bowling league, a broader perspective is necessary because the member may belong to several groups at the same time. Here are five groups to which the member may belong:

1. The *organizational* group. All people belonging to the organization (the Midwest University faculty, let us say).
2. The *functional* group. All people performing the same function in the organization (all academic department chairpersons at MU).
3. The *departmental* group. All people working in a specific department (the necrology faculty at MU).
4. The *interest* group. All people joined by a particular interest, whether or not the people are in the same department or perform the same function (the Arts Council at MU).

5. The *friendship* group. All people who associate because of an interpersonal attraction (the registrar, auditor, academic vice-president, and volley ball coach at MU, who eat lunch together because they like each other).

Groups and the Manager.   Managers control the membership in the first three groups above. They accept members into the organization and then assign them to functions within departments. Interest groups and friendship groups are pretty much beyond managerial control. Managers may be able to improve the likelihood of friendship groups developing by placing people together into functions and departments. However, personal characteristics and inclinations do more than managerial action to form such groups.

Regardless of how these five groups come about, the important point for managers to realize is that the groups *do* influence the acceptance and implementation of decisions.

Status and Role.   The concepts of status and role are important in understanding how the group influences its members. *Status* refers to the importance of each group member's position within the group's structure. *Role* refers to the way in which persons holding certain positions in the group are expected to behave. In brief, status is where you *are;* role is what you are expected to *do*. Status and role serve to give each person a position in the group setting and to let members know how the group wants them to behave.

When people join a formal organization, they are assigned to roles and they acquire the status that accompanies those roles. Newcomers learn what is expected of them in their roles by reading job descriptions, listening to indoctrination lectures, receiving verbal and nonverbal signals of approval or disapproval from co-workers, and in many other ways. This socialization process by the organization influences and shapes the behavior of all new entrants into the organization. It smoothly integrates new people into the organizational system by helping them to know what to do and how to act.

Learning the Role

Social Roles.   At a very young age, we begin to learn which social roles are played by those around us, as well as what roles we are expected to play. A child soon learns that some people are older and some younger, some people are male and some female, and some people are within the family and some outside. Many organizational roles are extensions of these roles learned within the family. Younger employees honor and respect those with more seniority. Attitudes about the characteristics and capabilities of the two sexes are carried over into the office. For many people the organization takes on the qualities of the family, with the boss receiving parental honor and colleagues receiving the loyalty that might once have been given to brothers and sisters.

The manager wanting to implement decisions should remember that social roles learned outside the organization often have parallels within the organization.

Organization Roles.   Human organizations are essentially role systems. Within these systems, people interact in expected ways. These role expectations are made known to new people over a period of time. Within the functional group and the departmental group, managers play the part (or role) of role senders, and members play the part of role receivers. When a new person enters the organization, the manager evaluates the extent to which the newcomer fits the expectations of the role. In whatever ways the newcomer does not measure up, the manager attempts to change the newcomer's behavior by offering instruction, advice, and information. The newcomer's behavior is further shaped by experienced organization members other than the manager.

Newcomers try to grasp the role training and to blend it with their own conceptions and expectations of their roles. If the manager has been successful in offering information about the role and in influencing the new employee to accept the role, the appropriate role behavior results.

Influences on Role Sending and Receiving.   In addition to the teacher–learner aspects of role sending and receiving, other elements affect the ways in which the new employee accepts an unfamiliar role. First, *organizational influences* are present. The organization has certain expectations of its role players. No matter what kinds of people hold down positions in the organization, certain duties and functions of each position must be performed. Newcomers must learn how their roles fit into the larger organizational structure. They must learn the organization's policies and procedures, in addition to learning their own jobs.

So to an extent the organization's expectations determine the member's behavior in the role. But the *individuality* of members also affects the way in which roles are perceived and played. Since many personal characteristics are not easily changed, good managers hire people whose personalities are compatible with organizational role expectations.

The personalities of group members determine the nature of their *interpersonal* relationships. These relationships affect the ways in which role receivers accept the training of role senders. If the role receiver likes and respects the role sender, the receiver will make a greater effort to meet the sender's expectations. If the receiver has no confidence in a sender who has established a cold, unfriendly work atmosphere, the receiver is less likely to accept the role as sent.

The New Foreman.   Here is an example to show how the preceding influences might affect the way in which Don Scanlon plays his new role as general foreman of manufacturing. The company's idea of how the role should be played appears as a job description in Figure 9-1.

TITLE: General Foreman,
                    Manufacturing

REPORTS TO: Production Superintendent

BASIC FUNCTION:
To ensure that the department's production output meets or exceeds quantity and
quality standards within established time limits, while maintaining standards of
safety, sanitation, and cost.

NATURE AND SCOPE:
This position reports to the Production Superintendent. Three shift foremen report
to this position, which has a 24-hour responsibility for the department. The General
Foreman maintains liaison with the production scheduling area and with the Personnel Department regarding personnel needs, discipline, and labor relations. The
General Foreman receives and acts upon quality-control reports and works with staff
and consulting engineers to develop new processing and packaging techniques and
machinery.

The General Foreman attempts to settle grievances at the first step, holds primary
responsibility for recognition and elimination of unsafe working conditions in the
department, and ensures the smooth flow of information between the Manufacturing Department and other managerial areas of responsibility within the plant. The
General Foreman ensures that proper departmental records are kept, that supervisory and hourly personnel are properly trained, and that production supplies are in
the department when needed.

The General Foreman informs the Production Superintendent whenever production
problems are encountered that can be expected to reduce output below standard or
whenever quality deficiencies cannot be remedied immediately. The General Foreman consults with the Personnel Department whenever new contract interpretation
questions are raised or when a deviation from standard personnel policy may be
advisable.

The position requires several years of experience as a first-line supervisor in the
Manufacturing Department, since the General Foreman is expected to have the most
detailed knowledge of the department's machinery and personnel. In addition, the
position requires administrative ability and the ability to communicate with management and hourly personnel with equally sound effectiveness.

FIG 9-1   Position description: general foreman, manufacturing.

Scanlon reads these organizational expectations, and they are reinforced
in talks with production superintendent George Bauer. The superintendent
explains how the organization expects Scanlon to behave in a wide variety of
organizational role situations. He also gives Scanlon a supervisory handbook,
designed to answer any remaining questions that Scanlon may have.

In addition, Scanlon brings his own personality, traits, and experiences to the foreman's role. He behaves in accordance with his own style. Some foremen like to "mingle with the troops." Others prefer to be more isolated, believing that "familiarity breeds contempt." Scanlon tries to find ways of behaving that are comfortable for him in his new role.

Scanlon's interpersonal relationships with other supervisors will also influence his role behavior, as they react positively or negatively to what he says and does. Even though Scanlon may choose not to follow their advice, he will probably listen to what they have to say.

ROLE CONFLICT

Learning organizational roles is sometimes difficult for employees because most roles have many new, different behaviors attached to them. In addition, six types of role conflict make organizational role playing even more difficult.

Types of Conflict

Conflict Between Role and Self.   Sometimes the requirements of the organizational role conflict with the role player's character, personality, or ability. The mild-mannered person may find managerial assertiveness difficult to learn. The free and independent spirit may find the rigorous discipline of the Marine Corps impossible to accept. Managers should realize that the organizational role players to whom they give orders have personal characteristics that may conflict with role requirements.

Conflict Between Two Roles.   Organization members may find that two or more roles that they are expected to play conflict with each other. For example, a professor of English may also be the English department's union steward. The behaviors expected of those two roles are quite different, and they may conflict.

Same Role, Different Expectations.   A similar conflict may occur when two or more subgroups within the organization each define a role differently. For example, the first-line supervisor is viewed in different lights by management, workers, and fellow supervisors. Each group makes different demands and has different expectations.

On the university campus, academic department chairpersons are pushed and pulled in several directions. Are they primarily faculty colleagues of other department members, serving to keep the departmental paperwork moving? Or are they primarily administrators, who make decisions regarding department matters and who implement the decisions of the deans, the academic vice-president, and the president? Definitions of the chairperson's role may vary widely. Some are elected by the faculty, while others are appointed by the administration. On some campuses the role has high prestige and is played by a respected and powerful department member. On other campuses the respected and powerful members want nothing to do with the nuisances of administering the department, so they give the job to a junior faculty member who gets a title but no power.

Same Role Sender, Different Expectations. If you wish that your superiors would make up their minds, you may be working for people who expect conflicting behaviors from the role you play. One day you are told to improve your department's sales, and the next day you are told to cut your advertising expenditures in half. You are told to spend more time in the field, and then you are criticized because you are never in your office. Employees want consistency from their managers. They want to know what to expect. So managers should try to make their orders and decisions consistent with employee role expectations.

Too Many Expectations. Some roles have so many expectations attached to them that no one group member can handle them all. The result is that the role conflicts with anybody's capacity to fulfill it. One penalty for doing a good job within a role is that people more and more often turn to the good group member for help. Many employees assume so many responsibilities and get stuck with so many others that they feel unsuccessful in fulfilling any of them.

Organizational Position and Role Conflict

The amount of role conflict experienced by an organization member is related to the member's position and function within the organization. Persons who do exactly the same work every day—either because the work is so simple or so specialized—have little role conflict. As the employee rises within the organization and takes on diverse duties, role conflicts start to occur.

At the top levels, managers must learn to live with constant role conflict. For example, presidents of large, publicly owned corporations must somehow meet the expectations of local, state, and national governments, stockholders, the board of directors, managerial and nonmanagerial employees, consumers, and other interest groups. These expectations are changing all the time.

The Bureaucrat. One special type of role conflict often troubles members of large modern bureaucracies—organizations that handle their tasks and achieve their goals by subdividing into a hierarchy of bureaus or departments. When we consider the successful founders of industrial bureaucracies— Henry Ford, Andrew Carnegie, John D. Rockefeller, J. Paul Getty, Howard Hughes—we see models of daring, imagination, and independence. Yet the bureaucracies they founded seem to thrive on efficient implementation of established policies and procedures by unimaginative, dependent conformists. This problem must arise for any thinking organizational role player: "How individualistic and creative can and should I be in this position? Should I do my best to meet the expectations of others? That seems to be the way to get ahead in this outfit. Or should I be true to my own expectations of myself, follow my own inclinations, and let the chips fall where they may?"

Group members who adapt to everyone else's expectations, maintain a level of bare competency, do not make waves, and give the organization an honest 40 hours of work per week are probably not going to fail within the organization. But their successes will probably be limited. Conversely, the interdependency of functions within bureaucracies means that wildly imaginative and eccentric behavior cannot be accepted. Somewhere in between is the organizational member who is both individualistic and loyal to the organization, both creative and dependable, who accepts the organizational role definition and brings creatively individual interpretations to carrying out that role.

DEVELOPMENT OF GROUP NORMS

Implementing decisions usually means changing individual role behaviors in groups. It also means changing the ways in which groups as a whole do things. To introduce changes as smoothly as possible, managers should understand how group norms develop, what conformity means, and how conformity influences behavior.

Characteristics of Norms

A norm is a standard. To get the work done, work groups establish norms of behavior that members are expected to follow. These norms have certain characteristics.

In the first place, they are specific. Abstractions may be tossed around up in the executive suite, but people on the shop floor need specifics if they are to know how to behave.

Although norms must be specific, they may vary from work group to work group, even though all groups are doing the same kind of work. Group A may have established a production norm of 70 to 90 widgets per hour, whereas group B may regularly produce in the 60 to 80 range.

In some work groups, the behavior of members is carefully monitored by other members to see whether norms are being met. In other groups, individual variations from the norm are viewed more casually.

Managers should know their groups and should be aware of each group's self-established norms—both those related to the job and unrelated to the job. Unless they can help it, and they usually can, good managers do not issue orders and implement decisions that disturb group norms.

Conformity to Norms.   People conform to group norms for two reasons. First, the *information* that they take in through their own senses may cause them to see the wisdom of conforming. Second, *group pressure* may cause members to conform. Most people do not want to be different, to stand out in a crowd. If a member values the group, the group can exert conformity pressure on the member.

Informational pressure and group pressure are usually present at the same time. When the member's information conflicts with the group's pressure, the member has to decide which to follow.

Information and Conformity

Task Difficulty.   If a group task is difficult and complex, the typical group member will do the task as everyone else in the group is doing it. Consider a committee revising an organization's bylaws. The committee has just come up with a draft of a particularly complex paragraph, and everyone except David Decker is ready to move to the next paragraph. David does not quite understand the draft paragraph and does not think it says what the committee wants it to say. He nevertheless conforms silently to the committee's wish because he does not have enough information or understanding about this difficult task to take a firm stand against the committee.

Expertise.   Related to task complexity are group and member expertise. If David Decker happens to be the organization's parliamentarian, thoroughly familiar with *Robert's Rules of Order (Newly Revised)*, he will probably not let the committee rush on to the next paragraph. In the instance above, David did not have confidence in his own ability to handle the difficult paragraph. In the second instance, he knew so much that he did not need or want anyone else's judgment.

Standing Alone.   Most people do not want to stand alone against the group. The influence of the opposition group does not seem to increase in direct proportion to its size. That is, a member standing alone against six people is not twice as uncomfortable as a member standing alone against three people. If you are stuck out there on the limb all by yourself, it takes tremendous confidence in your own judgment not to rejoin the group.

A minority of two or more is much stronger than a minority of one. Seeing someone else—anyone else—affirming your position lets you know that your answer may be right, that your information may be valid.

Group Pressure and Conformity

Certain pressures that the group can bring to bear are independent of information.

Group Attraction. If the member is attracted to the other members personally, conformity is more likely. Similarly, if the member is strongly attracted to the group's purpose or goal, conformity will more often occur.

Status. Persons of low or high status are less likely to conform than persons of medium status. The low-status members may conform in an attempt to raise their status. However, they may also refuse to conform if they do not feel like it because group retaliation in the form of status reduction holds no threat for them. High-status members may conform to maintain their status. They may also feel safe enough in their status to deviate from group norms on occasion. Fearing a drop in status and hoping for a rise in status, the group member of average status conforms.

Public Compliance. People conform more in public than in private. If everyone else knows what you do, you are more apt to do what they expect you to do. In fact, your private resolutions may crumble under public pressure.

Public and Private Commitment. Group members do not like to back down from publicly stated positions. Nor do they like to change private commitments they have made to themselves. If a group member has made a sufficient commitment—in public or in private—to an idea, that member cannot be swayed by personal appeals or by promises or threats involving status.

Cognitive Dissonance

Cognitive dissonance is a term that can describe the mental state of a group member who does not conform to the group norm. Cognitive dissonance occurs when we "know" two things, and those two things conflict; they can't both be true. Let us say you have carefully considered the issue of whether casino gambling should be allowed in your state, and you have decided that it should not. You go to lunch with four of your fellow workers—all aware, sensitive, and well-read—and you find that they favor casino gambling. In fact, they are bewildered that someone as aware, sensitive, and well-read as you are does not favor casino gambling. Their cognitions are dissonant with yours; they clash with yours. Since you usually respect them enough to accept their cognitions, your own cognitions are now dissonant. This state is very uncomfortable, and most people want to get out of it as fast as possible. They feel that they must do *something,* even if it is wrong—that any action is better than inaction.

What can you do about your cognitive dissonance concerning casinos? One choice is conformity. The group is right and you are wrong. Another choice is nonconformity—standing against the group and reaffirming your own opinion so strongly that the dissonance disappears. Or you might simply stay away from the dissonant cognitions and eat lunch with four antigambling friends. Finally, you might decide that this is an issue about which there is no right and wrong, strictly a subjective matter about which each person must make a personal decision.

Norms and the Manager

Managers must understand how group norms develop, what their characteristics are, and why people conform to them. Managers must understand how conformity is related to the information at the group member's disposal and to the different pressures exerted by the group. Implementing decisions within this complex and changing environment is not easy, but that is one reason why most managers get paid more than the people they manage.

TWO CLASSIC CASES

So far, we have spoken generally about how group factors affect the implementation of decisions. Two classic cases will now serve as examples of how—and how not—to implement decisions involving group efforts.

British Coal Mines

The Work Group.   Throughout the 1940s, British coal miners worked in teams of six, with two teams to an 8-hour shift. Each miner was trained in all three mining operations: taking the coal from the coal face, loading and transporting it out, and moving the roof supports as the tunnel went deeper. One shift picked up where the previous shift left off. Each member of the work group was paid the same amount, depending on the group's production. The work groups chose their own members, set their own pace, and generally made their own decisions.

New Method.   Then the work group method was changed to the *longwall* method. The teams were broken up, and each miner was given a single job to do. The first shift cut coal, the second shift loaded coal, and the third shift moved tunnel supports. Within each shift, even more detailed specialization was instituted. The result of the changeover to a new method was a series of problems.

Coordination Problems.   Since the workers were separated into three shifts having no personal or social connection with each other, they saw no reason to take any responsibility for a coordinated flow of work. Therefore, management had to create the new position of supervisor to keep the work moving.

Payment Problems.   Once the groups were broken up, each worker became interested mainly in making his own task easier and better paid. Through negotiation, a long list of prices for each coal mining task had to be drawn up. Miners constantly complained that the tasks they were called upon to perform were harder and less well paid than the tasks assigned to others.

Status Problems.   Under the old arrangement, every miner performed every function, so no miner's status was higher than any other miner's status. Under the new arrangement, certain jobs acquired higher status than others. For example, cutting coal was a more skilled job than shoveling the coal once it was cut, so cutters were of higher status than shovelers.

Narrow Task Problems.   Under the old system, the miner's work was varied. Under the new system, the miner performed one narrowly defined task. The miners much preferred the old way, under which they could take pride in the variety of skills they performed.

The Work Team Longwall Method.   In one variation of the longwall system, the miners were allowed to form their own work teams of six men, all paid according to how much the team produced. The new method was more complicated than the old one, so not every man on the team knew every skilled mining function. However, each *team* possessed someone who could perform every skill needed.

Performance Differences.   The existence of the conventional longwall method and the work team longwall method, with both types of miners working under similar mining conditions, permitted some performance comparisons. First, voluntary absenteeism was only one-tenth as great among the work teams. Production for the teams was 5.3 tons per shift, as opposed to 3.5 tons for the conventional system miners. The work teams were judged to be producing at 95 percent of their potential, whereas the conventional system miners were working at 78 percent of theirs. And of course the conventional system required supervisors, while the work teams did not.

Members of the work teams planned ahead to the effects that their work would have on their team members who followed them. Their workmanship was better, they kept their timbers in straight lines, and they maintained their equipment in good condition. In contrast, conventional longwall workers were not concerned about the effects of their sloppy work on the miners who came after them. By stressing technology at the expense of the social system, the decision makers increased absences, accidents, and expenses, and decreased productivity.

The decision makers thought that training each worker to be especially skilled in one task would bring greater efficiency to the mining operation. The decision makers ignored the group aspects of the situation—important in any organization but even more important when the organization's members are doing dangerous work underground.

Indian Calico Mills

A second example occurred in the 1950s at the Ahmedabad calico mills in India. The chairman of the mills invited a research group to offer suggestions about how new technological developments in the weaving industry could best be implemented in the mills. The researchers showed the company how to make technological changes without disrupting the existing social system.

Automatic Looms.   Automatic looms were introduced into the mills, and productivity did not increase as expected. All workers performed one of twelve different tasks. The researchers concluded that productivity did not increase because the workers had no motive to cooperate and had no feeling that they were part of a group effort. They were like the conventional longwall workers in the British coal mines, doing individual tasks without regard for the group's accomplishment.

Work Teams.   The researchers recommended grouping the workers into teams, exactly the reverse of what was done in the coal mines. Management agreed and explained the idea to one group of workers and supervisors, who accepted the idea enthusiastically. They formed themselves into seven teams of four men each. The effects of the change on productivity and morale were amazing.

Productivity.   Before the experimental arrangement was introduced, productivity had averaged 80 percent of potential. During the 27 months after the new arrangement began, productivity averaged 95 percent of potential. The quality of the cloth woven was also much higher than before.

Morale.   Morale rose incredibly. Workers *ran* from task to task. They had to be forced to take lunch breaks. They were now members of a *group* engaged in accomplishing a meaningful task. Their performance and morale rose accordingly.

SUMMARY

This chapter has stressed that managers who understand group processes can implement decisions more smoothly than managers who do not.

The chapter first described the influence of the informal work group on group member performance. The characteristics of informal groups were explained, as were the ways in which the group exerts its influence on individual members. The group's leader, norms, and cohesiveness were seen as especially important influences.

The chapter's second major section described role theory. People join groups and adopt group roles in order to satisfy their needs. Complications arise because each member may play more than one role in the group and may belong to more than one group at a time.

The chapter's third major section concerned role conflict. Several types of conflict were explained. The organization's expectations about the role may conflict with the employee's personal expectations. Within the organization, the employee is probably playing more than one role, and the roles may conflict. Different organizational members may view the employee's role differently, or the same organizational member may view the employee's role differently at different times.

The chapter's next major section showed how group norms develop. Employees conform to organizational norms because of information they acquire that leads them to conform and because of group pressure to conform. Cognitive dissonance was seen as a special type of conflict that employees sometimes face.

The chapter concluded with two examples, the British coal mines and the Indian textile mills, that demonstrated how important it is for managers to understand group effects before they implement change.

DISCUSSION QUESTIONS

1. Do you view the influence of informal groups on organization member performance as a good thing or as a bad thing?
2. What is the concept of role theory? How does it explain the influence of the group on the individual?
3. How do groups influence whether decisions are implemented successfully?
4. How do people learn their appropriate roles in the organizations they join? Give an example from your own experience.
5. What kinds of role conflicts exist? How might they influence decision implementation?
6. What are norms? How are they developed? How do they influence a group member's behavior?
7. What reasons draw people to group membership?
8. What is cognitive dissonance? What does it have to do with managing?

9. What are the lessons of the coal mine and calico mill experiments? How could similar problems be avoided?

10. Does the job description in Figure 9-1 set operational goals for Don Scanlon?

THE TESTING DEPARTMENT

The testing department employs six technicians and one supervisor. The department calibrates gauges and performs preventive maintenance on boilers, turbines, pumps, and electronic equipment.

Roger Maitland became testing department supervisor about 6 months ago. He immediately decentralized decision making in the department, so that now all technicians are pretty much their own bosses.

Until fairly recently, the department members were a strong social group as well as a smoothly functioning work group. Off the job, they and their families were quite close. Then, 3 months ago, technician Dennis Holt was separated from his wife and was soon divorced. At the time of the separation, he had no place to stay, so technician Harry Reutlinger and his girlfriend Nancy Schultz suggested that Dennis stay temporarily in the large house that Nancy's parents had given her to live in. Dennis moved into Nancy's house and, to make a long story short, within 6 weeks Harry and Nancy had broken up, and Nancy and Dennis were engaged to be married.

From that point on, the testing department was not as pleasant a place to work as it used to be. As work orders came in, supervisor Roger Maitland distributed them to the technicians. Dennis continued to work well, but Harry Reutlinger and the other technicians performed poorly. When Roger asked them why their performance was so bad, they said that they refused to do their best work for an organization that permitted one member to stab a good friend in the back.

As a result of their refusal to perform properly, the department and the plant itself started showing signs of neglect. Many analyses were left undone, and plant engineers were not getting the information they needed to maintain proper fuel and air mixtures in the boiler burners.

Roger knew that he had a real problem. Instead of his managing the group, it was beginning to manage him.

THE MANAGEMENT SEMINAR

"I'd like to sum up what we've been talking about during this 4-week management seminar," said Professor Stilwell to Trina Morgan and 19 other participating managers. "Research and practical experience both show that if you give your employees the opportunity, they will get together, discuss problems, analyze alternatives, and then come up with good decisions that they will implement with enthusiasm."

Morgan was persuaded that group discussion and group decision making could work at Hoffman Plastics. Once back at the plant, she called together the 30 employees in her department and spoke to them this way:

"Our current production standards were established 7 years ago. Last year we installed automated equipment to make the work easier, but we have not changed the production standards. I am asking you to discuss the situation thoroughly and then to decide what the new standards should be. I'll be back at 11 o'clock to hear what you have decided."

Morgan thought surely that the employees would set high standards and, because they had made the decision themselves, would try extra hard to achieve them.

When Morgan returned, she listened to supervisor Rollie Morris, spokesman for the group: "Ms. Morgan, we appreciate your faith in us, and we are convinced that we have justified that faith by coming to the right decision. We talked it over and decided that, even with the automated machinery, the production standards are still too high. Therefore, we unanimously agreed to reduce them by 20 percent."

Morgan excused herself from the meeting, went to her office, and placed a call to Professor Stilwell.

organizational change

This chapter on organizational change concludes Part Three. The last two chapters covered the individual and group factors related to the implementation of decisions. We now consider how implementation is related to the organization itself. Since implemented decisions lead to changes, this is a chapter on organizational change.

Minor changes, such as filling out one column on a form rather than another, may not seem to require that the manager understand much about making changes. Yet even small changes are more smoothly implemented if the manager understands the change process and realizes how people react to change.

The first two sections of the chapter deal with forces causing change and forces resisting change. The third section explains the dynamic social equilibrium that all organizations strive to maintain. The rest of the chapter explains different methods for making changes, with emphasis on the participative approach.

FORCES CAUSING CHANGE

Imagine the organization as a balloon, floating within the space of its social system. The organization is surrounded by different forces—social change, population and demographic trends, foreign factors, market forces, government influences, and many others—that can move the organizational balloon this way and that.

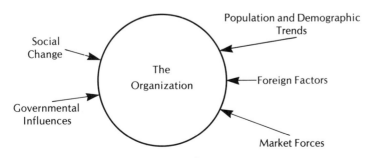

External Control Increasing

One trend over the past decades has been that the influence of these external forces has been increasing. Historically, business organizations have had control over most internal matters: product and pricing decisions, market channel selection, staffing changes, and financial structure. Nonbusiness organizations have also had considerable control over internal matters, although less than business organizations have had.

However, currently both business and nonbusiness organizations are slowly losing control of their traditional power to make decisions about internal matters. The expectations and demands of government and society are limiting the organization's choices. Major changes are occurring, and organizations must be sensitive to the organizational balloon's movements. They must be able to adapt to the organization's new position within its social system.

Equal Employment

Managers used to be able to hire anybody they wanted to hire for whatever reasons. Then along came the minority rights movement and the requirements that employment, promotion, and pay opportunities must be equal for all. An external force has given the organizational balloon a big push, and managers had better realize it. If they do not, they and their organizations may find themselves in legal difficulties.

The Risk of Legal Action.   Organizations these days must be able to justify who they hire, fire, promote, and retire. No longer can managers make capricious personnel decisions without running the risk of legal retaliation. True, some firms do accept the risk. They correctly conclude that most people do not have the time, money, or knowledge to file a discrimination suit. However, the risk is there for all organizations, particularly nonprofit charitable organizations and government agencies. Modern organizations must be prepared to spend much time and energy in keeping track of laws to be sure their practices and procedures are legal and are being followed. They must also monitor changes in social expectations, to get ready for the next attempt by external forces to control internal organizational matters.

Other Social Changes

The Role of Business in Society.   The debate goes on as to the proper role that business organizations should play within their social environment. This debate has been an outgrowth of changes in social expectations and industry structure. Corporations are becoming larger and increasingly visible within the social system. An increasingly literate and socially aware population searches the news media for newsworthy events. Under these conditions, many a television camera winds up pointing at a corporation which is doing something that somebody does not like.

If the company is Nick's Pizzeria, accused of watering the chianti, not many people become concerned. If the company is a large corporation and the accusation is price fixing, we see a flood of national news accounts and letters to the editor, perhaps followed by some legislation. *Size* by itself attracts interest, that interest creates a monitor, and any deviations detected by the monitor often lead to legislative redress.

Enforced Social Norms.   Clearly, legislation in itself is neither bad nor good. The point is simply that the sheer size of many organizations and their impact on society have caused the society to observe the behavior of organizations carefully. Our society has a system of standards (however vaguely defined) as to what is good organizational behavior and what is bad organizational behavior. Whenever an organization violates these norms, the society does to the organization exactly what groups do to nonconforming individuals: society finds ways of enforcing its norms. The enforcement mechanism is typically a mixture of publicity and legislation.

Change Is Continuous

Change, then, is continuous within every organization. Just as you cannot step into exactly the same river twice, so is it impossible to find exactly the same organizational market, personnel, or competition from one day to the next. Somebody quits; somebody new is hired. A new product is introduced; an old customer goes bankrupt. A citizen's group complains that the organization's television commercials are offensive; a government pollution-control restriction is lifted in response to the energy crunch. Years after the low birth rates during the Great Depression, the population of available upper-level managers declines; but the junior-executive population explodes, as the products of the postwar baby boom become old enough to be middle managers. Each of these developments means an organizational change, as the organization seeks to keep heading toward its goals and objectives.

FORCES RESISTING CHANGE

Three major forces resist organizational change: the force of habit, homeostasis, and fear of the unknown.

The Force of Habit

Personal Habits.   Like people, organizations are creatures of habit. We all tend to develop fairly predictable behavior patterns. From morning when we get dressed and ready for work, until night when we get undressed and ready for bed, we follow patterned sequences of activity. These habit patterns save us considerable time.

For example, consider how much time would be consumed if we had to use every stage of the decision-making process for every daily activity. Think of how many decisions would be necessary for so simple an activity as putting on a pair of shoes in the morning. Which shoes shall I wear? Which one shall I put on first? Should I put them on while I'm standing or seated? Which shoelace should I grab first? And so on. The complexity of the process never occurs to us because at one point in our lives we went through the process, made a decision about how to put on shoes, and kept putting on shoes in that same way until it became a habit. In that manner we avoid having to make the same decisions over and over again.

Organizational Habits.   Organizations also develop habitual patterns of doing things. These habits are at least as fixed as individual habits are. In fact, they may be even more firmly fixed because so many organization members share and reinforce the same habit patterns.

One major task of each new organization member is to "learn the ropes," to learn the organization's habits. Each organization has its own unique ways of doing things that new employees must master before they can function effectively within the organization.

For example, a student at Midwest University may perceive vast status differences between students but may perceive all faculty members as being of pretty much the same status. A new faculty member may not perceive status differences between students; they all seem to be pretty much alike. However, the faculty member is well aware that not all faculty members have the same rank, and that different status privileges accompany the different ranks.

Table 10-1 shows the differences in desk and office size, office location, and office equipment at Midwest University. The physical differences are important because they symbolize status differences. Within some companies these symbols are so important that any member trying to bring in a noncompany rug or painting is in trouble.

These symbols of office are part of the organization's socialization process. The organization teaches its habits to new employees and then enforces their maintenance. For the organization to change its habits is at least as difficult as for the organization's president to stop smoking.

A Steady State.   Individuals seek to maintain what systems people call a *steady state*, a position in which the person is in balance with the environment. In

TABLE 10-1   Faculty Status Symbols at Midwest University

	Desk Size in Square Feet	Office Size in Square Feet	Office Location	Office Equipment
Faculty member	18	89.9	No window, first floor	1 file, 2 bookcases, 2 side chairs, 1 swivel chair, 1 waste basket
Department chairperson	20	93	Window, first floor	Same as above, plus credenza
Dean	22, wood trim	116	Window, second floor	Same as above, plus sofa or conference table (dean's choice)
Vice-president	24, solid wood	138	Corner office, window, balcony, second floor	Same as above, plus plant

small and large ways, we try to maintain our positions relative to an ever-changing world. Standing up on a moving subway or bus, you shift your body's position to keep your balance. If your company installs a computer, you sign up for a college night course on computers. You adjust your behavior to cope with change. You seek to maintain your balance in relation to your environment.

Organizations do the same thing. When somebody quits, or a competitor shifts pricing strategy, or a new government form has to be filled out, the organization shifts position slightly to regain its balance.

Minor changes in the environment do not cause much trouble for people or organizations. When major change occurs, another concept comes into play: *homeostasis.*

Homeostasis

Homeostasis is the body's tendency to combat major change, to maintain a relatively stable internal environment. If the outside temperature drops to 40 degrees below zero, the body's homeostatic physiological processes interact to maintain body heat at about 98.6 degrees. A similar psychological tendency toward homeostasis exists. Most of us tend to maintain a relatively stable psychological condition, even though we are beset by contending drives, motivations, and other psychodynamic forces. Groups also have a homeostatic tendency to maintain relatively stable social conditions in the face of competing tendencies and powers.

One result of homeostasis is that people and organizations tend to ignore change and go on as if nothing has happened—at least temporarily. Rather than immediately coping with significant change, we either stick our heads in the sand and ignore the change or try to go back to the balanced way things were before the change.

The End of the Merit System.   Here is an example of how homeostasis works for individuals. Jane Todd is young, bright, and hard-working. Since her company uses merit rather than seniority as the major criterion for promotion, she has advanced rapidly. She likes the promotion system and she likes the company. She is balanced within her organizational environment.

Along comes a pronouncement from top management that future promotions will be based primarily on seniority. At first, Jane has a "You've got to be kidding" reaction. Surely it can't happen here, in this progressive company. Jane refuses to accept the inevitability of the new policy. She thinks it will be reversed shortly. She has the homeostatic tendency to expect that the status quo will soon be restored.

Once she realized that the company is not going back to the old promotion system, she must try to regain her balance in some other way. She may rationalize her new position to her satisfaction: "I got my early promotions on merit. The merit system used to be to my advantage, because it let me advance in a hurry. But now that I am an assistant vice-president, the seniority system is to my advantage because all I have to do is put in my time and I'll be promoted to vice-president. I'm happy and feel in balance with my organizational environment."

The End of the World.   Homeostasis also causes groups to deny that major change has occurred. Groups also try to return to the status quo.

Consider this example, based on fact. Guru Jones, leader of the Maharishi Pentecostalites, convinced his followers that the world was going to end on a certain day at a certain time. Jones told his flock to gather at the temple during the night prior to the day of destruction, so they could be rescued at sunrise by a flying saucer. The group gathered and prayed.

The flying saucer did not appear at sunrise. The group tolerated that change in schedule. By evening the flying saucer had still not appeared and, worse yet, the world had not ended. The group was thrown into confusion, disbelief, and disarray. They had been anticipating and expecting the end of the world, so now the major change they had to face was that the world was apparently not going to end.

Guru Jones went up on the temple roof and prayed for several hours. When he came back down, he provided the group with a homeostatic mechanism: "During my prayerful vigil, I communicated with the forces which were going to cause the end of the world. They were so overwhelmed by the seriousness of our belief and the devoutness of our prayers that they are not going to destroy the world. Because of our efforts, the world is going to be given another chance." Not only was the group brilliantly restored to its status quo before the nonending of the world, but they were now much stronger in their faith because they could see the result of their efforts—the continued existence of the world.

Ignoring Change.   Homeostasis also keeps less eccentric groups from coping effectively with change. The founder of XYZ Corporation refuses to delegate authority because the firm's enormous growth "hasn't really changed the way we operate." Organizations often think that new technological developments are just a flash in the pan. Such technological innovations as computers, subcompact cars, semiconductors, and quartz crystals meant large profits for corporations recognizing their importance and a loss of potential profits for corporations that did not. Organizations can foresee and plan for many major changes that may affect them. However, ignoring change is the more tempting alternative in the short run. Ignore it and maybe it will go away.

Fair Trade Laws.   The fair trade laws passed in the 1950s are another illustration of a homeostatic mechanism. These laws were a direct result of the protests that small retailers made against large merchandisers. As people gained great mobility following World War II, merchandisers found that they could build very large stores, attract many customers, and quickly turn their merchandise over. The discount stores became an important market force, almost wiping out the smaller "Mom and Pop" stores overnight.

The economics of a Zayres or a Kings were hard to beat. These stores could sell hundreds of television sets in a floor space of a few hundred square feet, surrounded by many other types of merchandise whose sales could share in the costs of lights, rent, management, and other expenses. Mom and Pop's little corner television store served a small market, and television sales had to cover all labor, rent, and utilities costs of the owner–manager. Television set prices at Mom and Pop's were obviously going to be much higher than prices at K-Mart or Woolco.

The Mom and Pops offered neighborhood location, highly personalized service, and higher prices. More and more consumers began to prefer discount stores in suburban shopping centers. They were farther away and their service was rather impersonal, but their prices were lower.

In addition, the discounters developed direct channels of supply from manufacturers. They bought in great volume, received quantity discounts, and passed along the savings to customers.

The small retailers persuaded Congress to pass a set of powerful homeostatic mechanisms: the fair trade laws. In essence, these laws prevented mass merchandisers from selling products any cheaper than the Mom and Pop stores could. The status quo was reestablished. With their price disadvantage removed, the Mom and Pops were able to reassert themselves in the marketplace by emphasizing their same old features: neighborhood location and personalized service. The fair trade laws remained an effective barrier to competitive pricing for many years until they were finally eliminated in 1975.

Social groupings and individuals tend to resist major change. Although the *idea* of change is widely endorsed in our society, it seems to be widely endorsed for someone else. We know that we should drive slower to conserve fuel. Even so, many of us buy radar detectors and CB radios to avoid the police, and keep driving at 65 to 70 miles per hour.

Fear of the Unknown

Change is addressed through homeostatic mechanisms partly because habit patterns are difficult to break but also partly because of fear. People fear the unknown. They want to keep their present behavior patterns because they do not really know what to expect from new ones. If Bob Brown wants to try a less autocratic management style, he may be more inhibited by the possibility that his subordinates will not know how to react to his new style than by any philosophical doubts about the style's value. After all, the organization is doing well enough now, and his employees know what to expect from him. Why should he change to a more democratic style?

Fears about three kinds of adjustments—economic, personal, and social—cause resistance to change.

Economic Adjustments. People fear the possibility of economic adjustments. If Jane Adams is transferred from Atlanta to New York, she may not be able to maintain the same standard of living that she presently enjoys. Many people have refused normal job rotation transfers simply to avoid the potential economic hardship of a higher cost of living.

In a similar sense, the organization member might fear that a position or location change may mean less opportunity to work, less base pay, or more work for less pay. Some classic struggles in the railroad and coal industries have dealt with this very issue: the worker's fear of unfavorable economic adjustments.

Personal Adjustments. People fear change for purely personal reasons. When something changes, we immediately want to know how the change will affect our own needs, wants, hopes, and desires. An employee can often view a change in work or working conditions as a demotion, a reduction in status, an increase in monotony, or some other shift in the job's attractiveness. The computer revolution eliminated many white-collar clerical jobs in accounting and payroll departments. Fear was widespread thoughout industry, as white collar workers saw the need to learn a new trade. The hundreds of computer jokes and cartoons appearing during the 1960s indirectly reflected the great fear of personal adjustments that these machines created, as people were forced to shift from one career path to another.

Social Adjustments. People fear social adjustments. Even if they do not particularly like their co-workers, they fear going to a new group. Regardless of the old group's faults, at least the group is predictable and the working relationships are defined, known, and accepted. Going to a new group means new role behavior and different interpersonal relationships. Few people actively seek these tremendous adjustments.

A DYNAMIC SOCIAL EQUILIBRIUM

Because people resist change and fear the unknown, the manager will do well to understand the concept of a *dynamic social equilibrium*. Knowledge of the concept can help the manager to make changes by understanding how social groups react to change.

A dynamic social equilibrium is a *constant* relationship in a *changing* social environment. Here are some characteristics of organizations that lead them toward a state of dynamic social equilibrium.

1. Every organization is a system of interrelated parts.
2. The parts are interdependent, so a change in one part affects all other parts.
3. The parts are forever changing, doing, moving, so a purely static situation is impossible.
4. The organization has a homeostatic tendency to resist major change and to maintain a steady state.

The Size of the Change

A certain amount of friction and conflict between the organization's departments and social groups is normal. Minor changes are accepted and are easily worked into the organization's ongoing routine. Indeed, part of the manager's job in a system of hierarchical control is to deal with minor deviations from the normal. The system recognizes that minor changes are always occurring and builds in adapting mechanisms for coping with them.

If managers keep in mind the organization's dynamic social equilibrium, they can better match the change strategy with the magnitude of the change. What may seem like a major change from one point of view may in fact have only minor impact on the organization's equilibrium. For example, a major change in car design may be important to the new car buyer. If no new personnel, skills, or equipment are required, the change may seem relatively unimportant to assembly-line workers. It does nothing to upset their social equilibrium.

The Doll Factory

On the other hand, seemingly trivial changes in procedure or policy may affect the dynamic social equilibrium dramatically. In the following example, an apparently minor change had major consequences on a doll factory's social equilibrium.

Problems in the Painting Department.   The factory used an assembly line that ran through different departments. The painting department was the last on the line. Six workers lifted dolls off a conveyor belt, painted faces on them, and then placed them on another belt leading to the baking ovens necessary for enamel finishes. The face-painting function had the lowest status in the factory, and turnover was high.

The face painters complained about how hot their work area was because it was so near the ovens. The plant engineer measured the temperature at work stations throughout the factory and found that the painting department temperature was no higher than the temperature anywhere else. The workers still complained and suggested that installing a fan and opening certain windows that had been nailed shut might cool down the area. Management took both of these steps, and complaints about the heat decreased. The face painters then shifted their attention to the speed of the machine-paced assembly line. They complained that the speed was much too fast for them to keep up.

The Consultant's Solution.   A behavioral consultant was sent to talk with the face painters. The consultant and the workers conferred at length about the speed of the assembly line. At the consultant's suggestion, a small inventory holding area was created as a buffer zone between the face painters and the rest of the assembly process. Management then installed a separate three-speed control box. The face painters could regulate the line speed as they wished. Slow speed was much lower than the current speed standard, medium was about the same as standard, and fast was much higher than standard. Management expected the worst—that the workers would leave the control box on slow, and work would pile up in the inventory holding area.

The face painters were delighted and excited about the control box. Before it was installed, they talked constantly about how they would use it. When they got the box, they matched line speed to their biological rhythms. They took some time to get warmed up in the morning and ran the line at slow. Later, as the morning progressed, their alertness, energy, and line speed were in high gear. After lunch they ran at slow speed until they felt energetic enough for the mid-afternoon high-speed run. They then rolled into quitting time at medium.

The face painters were very happy, enjoyed having some control over their jobs, saw that management was responsive to their needs, left the job less tired at night, and exceeded all their previous production rates. Since they were paid by the piece, they not only felt better about their jobs but got paid more besides. This would have been a happy ending, if the story had only ended there.

Equilibrium Destroyed.   The six face painters were happy, but the rest of the doll factory was in an uproar, its social equilibrium completely out of balance.

The face painters used to be in the low-status dependence position of waiting for what others sent them. Now their output had so increased that they were rushing the people up the line, forcing them to catch up. They were also making more money than workers farther up the line, who had previously considered getting out of the painting department to be a promotion with higher pay. The low-status department suddenly became the high-status department. The three-speed control box turned the plant's role and status systems upside down. Workers throughout the plant demanded either that they be given control boxes or that the old order of things be restored.

Equilibrium Regained.   Management was unwilling to cope with the social disequilibrium by installing control boxes throughout the plant. So they pulled out the control box, nailed the windows shut again, and took away the fan. The old order was reestablished, high turnover and complaints within the painting department resumed and were accepted, and the peace of a dynamic social system in equilibrium was regained.

Any organization is a dynamic social system of interconnected parts. Managers must be sensitive to the status systems and role behaviors within the overall organizational system. Otherwise, making a small change—like touching a house of cards—may throw the entire system out of equilibrium.

Methods for Making Changes

Changes are made in four basic ways:

1. Issue a command.
2. Replace something or somebody.
3. Change the structure.
4. Get member participation.

These approaches are not mutually exclusive; they can easily be used in combination. The appropriate change strategy is determined by (1) managerial understanding of the situation to be changed and (2) the time span within which change is to take place.

Change by Command

Under the command approach—sometimes called the *fiat* or *decree* approach—someone with higher formal authority within the organization orders someone in a lower position to change something. The most common of these one-way communications is a memorandum that makes known a new way of doing something:

> To: All department heads
>
> From: Gail Smith, vice-president
>
> Subject: Anton prices
>
> Effective January 1, Antons will be priced at $10.50 each, instead of $10.00 each as at present.
>
> Quantity discounts will no longer be granted on orders smaller than ten cases of antons.
>
> Please inform all personnel.

Appropriate Commands. A command is often an appropriate means for making changes. Some commands reflect routine managerial decisions. Somebody must make decisions about such matters as how much to charge for antons. Other commands reflect the need for changes based on factors beyond managerial control. For example, if a new law requires that certain data be compiled on all employees, a command to that effect will be issued. Other commands are a necessary result of earlier changes. If the company has replaced an old machine with a new one, the new oiling procedure will be sent to the machine operator, who will be "commanded" to follow it.

If changes do not threaten employee economic, personal, or social well-being, or if changes are obviously beyond anyone's control, employees usually accept them without much interest or comment. Assuming good communication channels, this method for making changes works well if employee interest and concern are low.

Commands are also necessary when time is short. Military recruits are taught to accept commands without hesitation or question. Military commanders believe that unquestioning obedience in executing military commands quickly and effectively is a major contributor to battlefield success. Time is often important in the nonmilitary setting also. In some businesses, such as securities and commodities trading, decisions must be implemented in moments.

Inappropriate Commands. Commands are also frequently issued when other change strategies might be more effective. Some managers believe that military and nonmilitary organizations should have a similar authority structure. Many people with military experience wind up applying their command principles as "captains of industry." In inappropriate situations, they expect rapid obedience by merely sending out a memo stating that "henceforth it shall be done as follows."

Such managers do not include the appropriate support material that would generate employee acceptance of their instructions. Nor do they explain the need for change. Except in emergencies or concerning routine matters, commands should be avoided. Employees resent them, and they create an atmosphere of military tension.

However, the command remains the most popular method of implementing decisions. Most managers simply tell employees what they want done and assume that employees will understand the command, accept the change, and happily remodel their behavior.

Change by Replacement

The replacement method assumes that getting rid of the bad apples will keep the rest of the organizational barrel from going bad. Although the best known replacements have occurred at top political and corporate levels, the method is used throughout many organizations. Perhaps a worker and a supervisor have clashing personalities that create dissension, production problems, and group conflicts. Replacing the worker, the supervisor, or both may be necessary to reestablish equilibrium.

At a higher organizational level, if a governmental agency is doing poorly, a hospital is running out of funding, a corporation is losing money, or a team is losing games, the reason may be that the organization's top manager is not providing leadership and direction. Replacing the manager may be the best way to change things. Many corporations have made dramatic turn-arounds in their profitability and market standing after firing their chief executives and replacing them with new ones.

On the other hand, focusing on a *person* rather than on the total situation may mean missing a serious underlying problem. The electorate often thinks that changing presidents is the way to solve major problems, and presidential aspirants encourage that attitude. People are invariably disappointed that the new president seems to have as little success with economic and social problems as the former president did. Many problems must be solved by some change other than replacing people.

Change the Structure

The third approach to change is *structural*. Instead of issuing orders or changing the people, change the *relationships*.

This approach has had some success in organizations that have experienced significant growth, market changes, or technological advances. For example, General Electric's reorganization into profit centers permitted better top management control of the enterprise. In two other industries, former waste products were turned into new salable products. Instead of throwing away berry pulp and skins, the cranberry sauce industry created a new product by combining whole berries into the sauce. Instead of disposing of orange rinds, the orange juice industry converted the rinds into profitable cattle feed. In both instances, the industry's people, management, material, and resources had to be reorganized in order to make the change work.

The structural-change strategy is sometimes used to resolve personality conflicts. It is also used when several capable candidates are available to fill one vacancy. Rather than run the risk of losing valuable employees because promotion opportunities are scarce, the firm may introduce a new layer of management, a new listing of job titles, or a reorganization of job responsibilities. In the book publishing industry, successful executives sometimes cannot be promoted because openings are scarce. These executives may well be given the opportunity to start new publishing subsidiaries. These new companies have tax-loss advantages at first and later may add to the parent company's profit.

Sometimes valuable but aging executives are shifted into positions where their talents can be retained (and their dignity maintained), but where they do not block the advancement of junior executives who are ready to move either up or out. Such organizational restructurings often have merit. At other times, organizational reshuffling is done quickly and carelessly. Observant employees then take sadistic delight in pointing out that the "Peter Principle" still works—capable, useful employees have finally been promoted, transferred, and shifted around until they have attained positions in which they will be incompetent.

THE PARTICIPATIVE APPROACH

The last method for implementing change is the *participative* approach. Participation is more a philosophy than a technique or method. It represents management's sincere attempt to encourage employee participation in decisions about matters that concern employees.

Degrees of Participation

As seen in Figure 10-1, employee participation in decision making can be small or large, from "tell-and-sell" to group problem solving. Under the tell-and-sell approach, the manager tells the employees what the change is going to be, sells them on the benefits of the change, and asks for their suggestions on how to implement the change. At the other end of the spectrum, the employee group identifies problems, evaluates alternatives, and makes choices. The problem-solving group's manager provides advice, moderates group discussions, informs the group about the needs and expectations of other groups within the organization, searches out information, and provides resources. The manager becomes the group's *facilitator* rather than its director by helping the group to make its own decisions.

Some Early Evidence

The Hawthorne Studies. The studies done at Western Electric's Hawthorne Works were described in Chapter 1. Elton Mayo and his associates at first intended to study the relationship between lighting levels and worker pro-

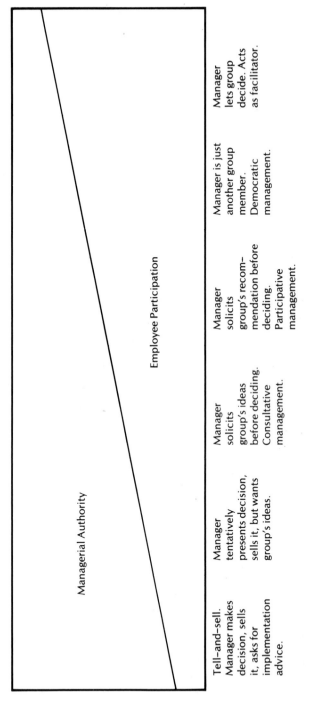

FIG 10-1 Employee participation in decision making.

ductivity. However, because of the Hawthorne effect, productivity *rose* even when lighting level *dropped*. The workers were producing more and their morale was higher, not because lighting levels were increased or decreased, but because their supervisors and the experimenters were listening to them and paying attention to what they said.

Bavelas Studies.   Another early study of participation was conducted by Alex Bavelas. He chose a group of sewing machine operators who were averaging about 74 units per hour and asked them if they would like to set their own standard. They agreed to do so, decided on 84 units per hour, and soon exceeded that standard. After another discussion, they decided to attempt 95 units per hour, but they failed. They finally decided on the more realistic, but still high, standard of 90 units per hour and almost met it over a period of several months. Participation in goal setting resulted in a productivity increase of about 15 percent.

Coch and French Studies.   In the late 1940s, Lester Coch and John French, Jr., compared the output of sewing machine operators under four conditions: no participation, very little participation, some participation, and total participation.

The company wanted to introduce some changes. The control group (no participation) was simply told about the changes. Over a 30-day period, 17 percent quit and the rest complained, held up production, refused to cooperate, filed grievances, and experienced a 20 percent drop in output. The first experimental group was told-and-sold. They slightly outperformed the control group. The some-participation group was told about the change and asked to participate in implementing it by helping management to develop methods and pay rates. After 2 weeks of adjustment, this group began to exceed its output before the changes, and for the next 2 weeks the group's production curve trended upward.

In the total-participation group, workers and managers jointly made all decisions about the changes. This group took a few days to reach its original output level, and then gradually improved so that output at the end of 30 days was 15 percent higher than output before the changes were implemented.

Why Participation Works

Philosophically.   The notion of participation has considerable philosophical appeal. Participation assumes that people want to work, enjoy doing their work well, and are uniquely qualified to participate in decisions about how the work should be done—because they are the ones doing it. The manager who uses a participative approach is sending a message to employees: "I want you to participate in decisions because I value your opinions, your experience, and your desire to do a good job." Managers who discourage employee participation are sending quite a different message to employees.

In Practice. In addition to its philosophical advantages, six other reasons exist for effecting change through participation.

1. *Two heads are better than one.* We have already seen that group discussion is an effective method for generating alternative solutions to problems. This same effectiveness carries over to making changes.
2. *Participants in change understand the change better.* Everybody knows that change is necessary. Many people resist particular changes because they do not see any good reason for them. Participation enables employees to understand the need for changes. When employees participate, managers must clearly understand why changes are necessary so they can explain them to employees. Instead of making changes just to see what will happen, managers are forced to analyze how proposed changes will affect the achievement of the organization's goals and objectives. In short, participation reduces unnecessary changes and increases employee acceptance of necessary changes.
3. *Participation clears the communications channels.* In some cases, changes that employees might view as acceptable and necessary are resisted because communication breaks down somewhere between manager and employees. Since participation ensures a two-way communication channel, any misunderstandings can be cleared up.
4. *Participation reduces employee fears.* Employees fear the unknown. Participation permits a full and frank discussion of the change. Participating employees understand what effects the change will have on their economic, personal, and social concerns.
5. *Participation increases employee morale.* Employees appreciate managerial consideration of employee feelings, opinions, and concerns.
6. *Participation increases the chances of success.* If employees have an opportunity to decide about changes, they will try harder to make the changes work.

When Participation Works

Participation works better in some situations than in others. Sometimes it may not work at all. Here are some factors that determine whether or not the participative approach is appropriate.

Time. Participation takes time. In emergencies, managers must issue commands rather than call employees together for a discussion.

Money.   Participation costs money. Managers must do a cost–benefit analysis of participation possibilities. Workers cannot spend all day in discussion meetings. Managers must be sure to consider the intangible benefits of participation along with the tangible costs of participation.

Ability.   Participants must have the ability to participate. They must be sufficiently intelligent, informed, and articulate to understand and talk about problems and decisions. Also, participants must have the freedom and authority to do something about the situation. A participating employee group cannot make decisions that are against the law, contrary to company policy, or that will negatively affect other employee groups.

Interest.   Participants must have an interest. They must find the potential change relevant and important. If employees simply do not care about which alternative solution to a problem is chosen, they resent the time spent in meetings. If employees have no special interest in a change, the manager should go ahead and make the change by command.

Some managers permit employees to participate in minor matters (such as how to oil a new machine) but shut them out of important matters. Such empty gestures in the direction of participative management probably do more harm than good. Whenever employees of such a manager are asked to participate, they assume that the problem cannot be very important or they would not be asked to offer input.

If employees are *too* interested, participation will probably not work very well. For example, consider a situation in which half of the workers must be laid off. If employees are asked to participate in deciding who should be laid off, they may be too interested in the situation to participate helpfully.

Change by Replacement, Structure, and Participation

Participation cannot be considered in isolation from other aspects of the organizational social system. In particular, participation is related to the organization's personnel and structure.

One way to implement change is by replacing people. Another is by changing the organization's structure. To encourage employee participation in making decisions and implementing changes, the organization may have to make some changes in personnel and structure.

A belief in the value of participation must come from within a manager. The organization cannot superimpose a participative approach on a manager who is basically an authoritarian. If a manager does not have faith in the ability of employees to participate constructively and intelligently, the organization may need to change managers.

The organization's structure must also be conducive to participation. If the structure is rigid, with emphasis on positions and functions rather than on people, participation will not work. Employees participate best when managers and organizational structure are humanistic and flexible.

OVERCOMING RESISTANCE TO CHANGE

Influences within and outside organizations continuously stimulate change. Even so, the forces for change often seem overwhelmed by the forces against change: the force of habit, homeostasis, and fear of the unknown. How can managers overcome these forces? The answer to this question is important, because making changes is what management and the decision-making process are all about.

Wanted: A Problem or an Opportunity

The first requirement for change is dissatisfaction. Someone or something must be thrown out of equilibrium. Perhaps the "manager by exception" perceives an exception. Or perhaps the manager sees a new moneymaking opportunity and is dissatisfied that the organization is not taking advantage of it.

Furthermore, the problem or opportunity must be significant. Managers at all levels have plenty to do all day. As minor problems occur, managers make the adjustments necessary to regain organizational or departmental equilibrium. To draw the manager's attention away from day-to-day matters, a problem must be fairly serious or an opportunity must be quite striking. So the first requirement for change is that there be enough dissatisfaction with the status quo to overcome the force of habit, homeostasis, and fear of the unknown. If everybody is happy, why change anything?

Management Support for Change

If significant change is to take place, top-level personnel must perceive that the problem is serious or that the opportunity is significant. Top managers created the status quo, so they are often interested in preserving it. If top management loudly and firmly supports the status quo, lower-level people are probably going to keep quiet about their dissatisfactions.

We have already said that one way to implement change is to replace people. A new company president has no vested interest in the status quo. In fact, a new president will probably engage in a flurry of change activity, known variously as "housecleaning," "eliminating the dead wood," or "getting rid of the soft spots." Managers often line up outside the new president's door, trying to enlist the president's support for solving problems or grasping opportunities that were of no interest to the former president.

Participation

Major change can occur only if top-level people are dissatisfied. Once the upper-level managers take an interest in effecting change, they must attract the interest of the many people who must make the change work. All points made previously about the benefits of participation are relevant here. Management must supply the time and money for participation. Employees must have the ability and the interest.

During participatory sessions, the manager must be a skillful persuader. Unless resistance to change is overcome, employees will be thrown into disequilibrium by the change. Part of the manager's job is to encourage subordinates to accept the company's point of view about changes. No longer is it possible simply to demand employee compliance, as it was 50 years ago.

Change and the Decision-Making Process

Some steps in the change process parallel steps in the decision-making process.

Problem Identification.   Something occurs that throws the organization into a state of disequilibrium. Somebody important becomes dissatisfied. This dissatisfaction overrides habit, inertia, homeostasis, and fear. Something must be changed. What must be determined now is the solution to the problem, the direction of the change.

Alternative Solutions and Decision.   Someone with expertise and prestige becomes a champion of change. That person leads in the search for alternatives, their evaluation, and in making the choice. The new direction is determined. The problem has been solved, theoretically. Actually, nothing has yet been changed, because the theoretical solution has not yet been implemented.

Implementation.   The manager responsible for change, in cooperation and participation with the organization's members, now needs to convert the solution into subgoals and objectives. Once persons throughout the organization understand the new goals and objectives, they are in a position to work out new tasks, activities, procedures, and methods—the specifics of implementation.

Managers must give positive reinforcement to those new procedures and methods that seem to be achieving the new goals and objectives. Employees need to see that their new behaviors are appropriate and appreciated. Otherwise, the change will not be internalized throughout the organization. It will not stick. The newly achieved equilibrium will not be maintained, and the organization will backslide into its old ways.

SUMMARY

This chapter first covered forces causing change within organizations in our society and forces resisting change. The internal control of their operations that organizations have traditionally enjoyed is decreasing. Equal employment laws and other social developments mean that many organizations will be changing in ways that they cannot completely predict or control.

Among the forces resisting change are the force of habit, homeostasis, and the fear of the unknown. Like people, organizations develop habits. These habits are necessary if the organization is to function regularly and smoothly. Without organizational habits—often written up in the form of policy and procedure statements—organizations would have to make the same decisions over and over again. Although organizational habits are a necessity, they are a force that resists change.

Homeostasis is the tendency of the person or organization to keep its balance and regain balance once it is lost. Two examples of homeostatic mechanisms were offered: the end of the world and the fair trade laws.

A final force resisting change was shown to be human and organizational fear of having to make economic, personal, and social adjustments.

The concept of dynamic social equilibrium was illustrated by showing what happened in the doll factory when an apparently minor change had major negative social impact.

Four methods for making changes were presented: give a command, change the people, change the structure, and change by inviting participation. Although the participative approach is not always appropriate, it has many philosophical and actual advantages.

The last section of the chapter explained the elements necessary for overcoming resistance to change: top-level dissatisfaction, top-level support for change, and a participative approach to making and implementing changes.

DISCUSSION QUESTIONS

1. What is so important about the topic of change?
2. Why is change so difficult to bring about? What forces work against changing an existing situation?
3. What are the three types of adjustments people must make to accommodate change? How do these adjustments affect the change process?
4. What is dynamic social equilibrium? What does this concept have to do with change?
5. What methods are available for securing change? Which work best? Why?
6. What is the participative approach to making changes? Why does it work?

7. What factors may work against the use of participation?
8. How can a manager overcome resistance to change?
9. Does top management need to support a change? Why or why not?
10. Why is an understanding of change so important to the decision-making process?

ALL-AMERICAN CORPORATION

For ten years George Barker had been Northern Region manager of All-American Corporation. And for ten years he had made all the decisions about how to allocate inadequate resources within the region. He felt that only he had the knowledge and administrative perspective necessary to make the tough decisions.

Within the region were six districts, each with a manager. Within each district were from six to ten offices, each with a manager. Every year the office managers complained to the district managers about inadequate budgets, and the district managers passed these complaints (along with many complaints of their own) to George Barker, who felt that he did the best he could with what he had.

Then Barker began working on a masters in business administration degree. In several courses he studied the idea of participatory management. He was intrigued by the thought that participatory management might help him to avoid complaints about his funding decisions. In fact, participatory management might even result in better decisions.

His professors had pointed out several advantages of participation:

1. More participants would mean more knowledge brought to the decision-making process.
2. The participants would understand decisions better and would be more committed to them, if they played a part in making them.
3. Participants would better understand the problems of allocating scarce resources.
4. Participants would get some good training in what it is like to make important management decisions.

Since resource allocation decisions had to be made soon, Barker was tempted to give participatory management a try in his region. He liked the theoretical advantages that his professors had pointed out, but he was not totally convinced that he and the region were ready for participatory management. What should George Baker do?

THE CELLULOSE MILL

Jean Crine works in a mill that produces 500 tons of chemical cellulose per day. She has prime responsibility for the five process waters required for cellulose production. The mill uses 23,000,000 gallons of water a day. Except for Crine and a few other women, the mill's 619 employees are men.

Crine shares an office and laboratory with four chemists and two assistant chemists, all males. The atmosphere in the lab was very relaxed and was more social than professional until Crine was hired. At first, the chemists tended to treat Crine like a little sister—teasing her about her clothing, her hair, mistakes in her work, what she ate for lunch, and her life style. She expressed her annoyance at this patronizing treatment, but her irritation only prompted an increase in the teasing.

On one occasion, Jean noticed an assistant chemist (subordinate in organizational level to her) washing his hands in distilled water reserved solely for making up chemical solutions. She politely asked him not to use the water for that purpose. He responded by sticking a soapy hand into her mouth. She retaliated by throwing a jar of water on him. Some of the water splashed onto a chemist working on the other side of the sink. He grabbed Crine and started shaking her. She told him to remove his hands, and he yelled that no woman would tell him what to do. The assistant chemist was also yelling that no woman would tell him how to wash his hands.

On another occasion, one of the chemists put a suggestive picture of a nude woman on the lab wall. Crine asked him to remove it, but he refused. Crine spoke to the department head, who made the chemist take the picture down. The chemist was furious.

The chemists complain that Crine is outspoken, easily offended, domineering, and rebellious. They claim that she is the cause of all disharmony in the lab and that she is detrimental to morale and production. Her supervisor has spoken severely to her about her tendency to "overreact."

Concerning the incident with the distilled water, Crine maintains that the assistant chemist's sticking a soapy hand in her mouth was inexcusable and that her reaction was normal for any person with self-respect. She insists upon her right to be treated as a professional by her co-workers, despite their apparent feeling that women are not equal in ability to men. She feels that to tolerate treatment as an inferior in the business world would put an end to her career.

Recently, Crine returned to the lab after a two-day absence. She remarked that it was good to see everyone again. One of the chemists replied, "Too bad the feeling isn't mutual. I wish you hadn't come back."

How could the organization have avoided this problem? What now?

Part Three: Comprehensive Cases

GALLAGHER CONSTRUCTION COMPANY

Gallagher Construction Company is a small commercial contractor. The company's yearly volume is around $3,000,000, with an average of six jobs in progress at any one time.

Partners Mike and Paddy Gallagher have recently hired Dick Smith as a project manager. In addition to such activities as keeping job records, writing contracts for subcontractors, selecting suppliers, producing shop drawings, and approving purchase orders, one of Smith's important functions is to serve as the link between the Gallagher brothers and the job superintendents. Before Smith was hired, the superintendents dealt directly with the Gallaghers.

The Gallagher Construction superintendents have a great deal of independence in handling a job. They schedule and coordinate the subcontractors selected by the project manager, keep the job on schedule and according to specifications, hire the general labor, keep time records for payroll purposes, and order supplies. The Gallagher brothers always tried to treat the superintendents as equal partners in charge of field operations, making decisions by consensus instead of direct order. Dick Smith uses this same approach. However, in the event of disagreement, the project manager is supposed to have the final word.

A conflict has developed between Dick Smith and one of the superintendents, Bill Brownell. In his early fifties, Brownell has been a superintendent with Gallagher Construction for 5 years. He has not gladly accepted Smith's authority as project manager and at times takes his problems directly to "the boss," as he refers to senior partner Mike Gallagher. The senior partner has tried to discourage Brownell from jumping the lines of authority, because the most important reason for hiring project manager Smith was to relieve the Gallaghers from the pressures of handling day-to-day problems. However, the relationship between Brownell and Gallagher developed over the years, and Gallagher finds changing it difficult.

Brownell is a competent, cost-conscious superintendent. He can be trusted to keep a job going on schedule without pressure from the office. He is proud of his work crew, and they are extremely loyal to him. Smith has observed that from time to time, when no work on the job is available, Brownell lets the men loaf around or leave for the day, without reporting the fact to the office. This practice is one way of reinforcing their loyalty to him.

Brownell wants to run his crew without any interference from the managerial level. If Smith so much as asks one of Brownell's men a casual question, Brownell objects that Smith is not using the proper line of authority. Brownell's particular quirk is that he clearly sees the line of authority below him but does not see it above him. However, he is always fairly polite to Smith, and he does get results.

Now, Brownell has refused to keep daily reports of labor and material used on the jobs he supervises.

At project manager Smith's recommendation, the Gallaghers have decided to collect daily data from each job, showing the number of hours worked by laborers, mechanics, and foremen, and the specific types and quantities of work completed. These reports are designed to establish unit costs for specific parts of a job so that future bids on jobs will be more accurate. Before requiring these reports, the company had simply relied on experience to make bids. As bidding became more competitive, the Gallaghers recognized the need for cost figures when Smith pointed that need out to them.

Brownell has refused to keep the reports properly. When Smith questioned Brownell about the lack of reports, Brownell did not reply directly. Instead he said, "In order for me to know where I can save the company money, I need to get from you a breakdown of how much you estimated each operation was going to cost when you submitted the bid for a job. That's they only way I can know where we can save some money."

Smith regarded this request as highly unusual. He replied, "Bill, we don't have the data in that form, but I suppose we could do some calculations for the next couple of days and come up with the numbers. But I can't drop everything to do that. Anyway, you've always done a good job of holding down field costs without that information. And you've got to be just as cost-conscious about each operation on the job, no matter what we estimated that operation would cost when we made the bid."

Brownell said, "I don't see that as a very helpful answer, and if I can't get a cost breakdown, you'll get no daily reports from me."

Smith took the problem to Mike Gallagher, who said that the request was unreasonable and that he would get Brownell to produce the reports. Gallagher spoke to Brownell and then got back with Smith: "You will get reports from Brownell, and if you don't, start looking for another superintendent."

Smith did not get the reports, submitted some names of possible replacements for Brownell, waited—and heard nothing. Smith felt that the Gallaghers were not supporting him, so he stopped asking Brownell for reports.

Two months went by. The company began bidding for more and more jobs, and the Gallaghers saw that they simply had to get reports from all superintendents. Paddy Gallagher went to see Brownell and, as a result of their conference, Brownell began submitting reports. They were not in good order. They usually gave about half of the information needed. In addition, Brownell usually penciled in an unpleasant comment or two. One day he included among the penciled notes the fact that his resignation would be effective in 3 months, when the current job ended.

The Gallaghers do not know what to do. Good construction superintendents are scarce, and Brownell is good. Many companies advertise widely in major cities hoping to attract capable superintendents. The Gallagher's do not want to lose Brownell, but they do not want to put up with his insubordination any longer because they see how useful timely reports can be.

202ND MISSILE MAINTENANCE FACILITY

The 202nd Missile Maintenance Facility is located at a remote air base on the coast of South Korea. Its job is the assembly and maintenance of air-to-air guided missiles carried by the supersonic fighter-bombers assigned to the air base.

The maintenance and assembly of these missiles require the handling and check out of highly explosive warheads, moderately explosive solid fuel rocket motors, and complex guidance and control units ranging from radar-guided to heat-seeking types.

Successful performance of maintenance and assembly procedures requires careful handling and much concentration, because a mistake can result in serious injury or death, and damage to thousands of dollars worth of equipment. The men working in this facility have undergone extensive training in the Air Force missile school, have several years of practical experience, and are well above average in intelligence. They know their difficult jobs, and they do them well.

The minimum work schedule at the facility is specified as 10 hours per day, 6 days per week, with a very rare half-day off on Saturday. The long hours and difficult work put great stress upon the workers. In addition, the 13-month tour of duty is designed as "unaccompanied"—that is, no families—and most of the men assigned to the maintenance facility have families back home. The already difficult working conditions are compounded by periodic alerts. These exercises begin with a siren blast at about 4:30 A.M. and last 2 or 3 days. During these alerts, the munitions facilities operate 24 hours a day, with the workers on 12-hour shifts.

Major Parker, the supervisor of the missile maintenance facility, has tried to give the workers as much free time as possible in order to make conditions more bearable. He realistically schedules the day's objectives and, if they are accomplished before the end of the formal workday, he lets most of the workers leave early. Major Parker and the men feel that this time off is an honestly derived benefit of their efficiency in performing their tasks.

The maintenance facility runs smoothly, and the workers are fairly satisfied. They require very little supervision and make most of the decisions concerning routine maintenance. They report these decisions and the resulting status of the missile inventory to Major Parker, who relays the information to the central munitions control section. Being allowed to handle maintenance as they think best indicates to the men that their judgment and experience are respected. The occasional shortening of their working hours indicates to them that Major Parker trusts them to meet their objectives. They feel that as long as they can produce, they can avoid constant 10-hour workdays.

Higher base officials sometimes conduct inspection tours. During one of these tours, on the afternoon of an average workday, the inspecting official (a logistics officer knowing little about munitions) noticed that fewer workers were present than the number listed on the duty roster. When asked about this difference, Major Parker replied that his practice was to let some of the men go if they had completed all their assigned tasks for the day.

Shortly thereafter the squadron commander (who had been to the missile maintenance facility only twice in the previous year) issued a directive stating that all workers would work a full 10-hour day every day unless they were sick or had to attend to a genuine emergency. Major Parker relayed this news to the workers. After some initial expression of discontent, they did not seem to be too upset.

However, in the past 3 or 4 weeks, Major Parker has noticed a significant drop in the unit's performance level. The men are accomplishing less work in a 10-hour day than they had previously accomplished when working only 7, 8, or 9 hours a day. When he confronted the workers with this fact, they asked why they should work at top speed and finish a project early when all they had to look forward to was meaningless work designed to keep them busy until the end of the workday. That work often consists of sweeping, mopping, painting, or cutting grass. On those occasions, their friends never seem to tire of commenting on how far their highly specialized technical training has gotten them.

Other unfortunate signs have also appeared. Workers now go to rather lengthy "emergency" appointments during the workday, and production is decreasing still further. Three or four men often go on an errand that actually requires only one person. And no one seems to think of reordering needed maintenance materials until the facility is completely out of them. The lack of materials occasionally makes it necessary to withdraw missiles from an operationally ready status.

Major Parker understands what is going on. He realizes that the men sincerely disagree with the new policy for good reasons and that they are letting their disagreement be known. They view the new policy as a penalty for their initiative in improving the overall performance of the squadron. They therefore have decided to perform no better than any other unit, even though they know that the squadron's performance and rating will be hurt.

Major Parker has discussed the situation with several of his fellow officers.

They have offered possible solutions ranging from punishment to weekly beer parties for relieving tension. Major Parker does not feel that most of these suggestions would have a definite positive effect. If they did, he thinks the effect would be short-lived. However, something has to be done, or there will soon be serious consequences for all concerned.

RIDGEDALE COMMUNITY COLLEGE

Some colleges can grow gradually. At the directive of the state legislature, Ridgedale Community College had to start out almost full grown. Therefore, President E. V. Traynham saw the need for strong central administration and control. Plans, policies, and procedures had to be established quickly so that campus personnel might have the guidelines necessary to set up their diversified operations. Within 3 years the college had 18,000 students, the maximum that it could handle.

As Ridgedale Community College entered its fourth year of operations, noticeable unrest had developed throughout the staff. Although the board of trustees had known for a while that all was not well, they had done nothing. Once stories about the college's difficulties began to appear in the newspapers, steps had to be taken.

The board instructed Dr. D. T. Garland, recently appointed as vice-president for administrative services, to look into the college's problems. Garland's study reflected dissatisfaction among staff at all levels. Many would resign if they could find jobs elsewhere.

Their complaints seemed to follow a basic pattern: no opportunity to be creative, no recognition of their efforts, no voice in matters affecting them. Although many of them sat on formal committees designed to offer input into how the college was run, their voices were ignored and their recommendations unheeded. Garland found little dissatisfaction with salary, working conditions, or direct supervisor–subordinate relationships.

The report concluded that a communications gap had caused a credibility gap. Information was not properly flowing up and down through the chain of command. Therefore, every act of management was open to misinterpretation.

The discovery of these apparent gaps seemed to satisfy the board, which concluded that the cause of the college's problems was the failure of college president E. V. Traynham to establish meaningful communications within the college. Dr. Traynham was asked to resign and was replaced by Dr. P. J. Ponce.

Immediately upon appointment, Ponce began conferring with different employee groups. At their recommendation, Ponce formed two organizations: a Faculty Senate and a Career Employees Association. These groups were to report directly to Ponce to ensure proper communications.

For a short time, morale and performance rose. However, the unrest soon returned, indicating that Ridgedale Community College's problems had not been caused entirely by past president Traynham's failure to establish meaningful communications.

The new complaints are similar to the earlier complaints. The academic people complain of having no voice in any of the decisions affecting them, program directors complain that the college is a "giant paper mill," and both faculty and professional staff complain that good performance is not properly appreciated. In addition, the criticism that the college administration stifles initiative and creativity has recurred. A new criticism has also surfaced—that responsibility and authority are not adequately balanced within the organization.

New president Ponce realizes that replacing the president and forming a Faculty Senate and Career Employees Association have not solved Ridgedale's problems. Perhaps the study method had been at fault—assigning one vice-president to the task. In any event, Ponce recognizes that Ridgedale will soon have another new president if matters do not quickly improve.

the focus of decisions

Students familiar with the material in Parts One to Three should be well equipped to explore the five areas within which managerial decision activity takes place: planning, organizing, staffing, directing, and controlling. These areas are the subjects of Part Four.

Chapter 11 describes what planning is, explains why many managers fail to plan, and covers such plans as policies, methods, and procedures.

Organizing is the process of establishing and maintaining the structure that will help to achieve organizational goals. The discussion of organizing is divided into two chapters. Chapter 12 shows how the organization divides up its work. Chapter 13 explains how the organization coordinates the units into which it is divided.

A third major decision focus, staffing, is the subject of Chapter 14. Decisions are of two kinds: finding new organizational members and maintaining the existing membership.

The fourth managerial function is directing—making the decisions that guide the organization's human resources. The discussion is divided into two chapters. Chapter 15 shows how situational factors such as the leader, the organization's structure, and the organization's climate affect member performance, as do such individual factors as traits and aptitudes. Chapter 16 continues the discussion of directing by exploring motivational factors.

Chapter 17 covers controlling, the fifth function about which managers make decisions. The chapter explains what control means and describes different types of controls.

After completing Part Four, the student should understand clearly how managers make decisions within the five functional areas that comprise the manager's job.

11

planning

The emphasis of this book so far has been on managerial decision making as a general process. However, managers also need to understand and appreciate the specific *focus* of decisions. Managerial effectiveness rests not only on decision-making skill but also on an awareness of the context within which decisions are made. This context, depicted in Figure 1-1 (the management model) on page 20, consists of the five managerial process functions: planning, organizing, staffing, directing, and controlling. The most basic of these functions is planning.

After describing what planning is, this chapter will give six reasons why managers do *not* plan. The planning process itself will then be presented in detail. The chapter concludes by discussing standing plans (policies, methods, and procedures)—what they are, where they come from, and how flexible and detailed they should be.

WHAT PLANNING IS

Every organization has goals. Planning decisions aim toward the implementation of those goals by specifying what the organization is going to do, how it is going to be done, and who is going to do it. Decision-making activity is undertaken because of the gap between reality and the organization's goals; planning represents the way in which the organization's management hopes to close the gap.

The organization's plans serve to direct the activities that all organization members must undertake and successfully perform in order to move the organization from where it is now to its goals. Planning choices are difficult because no one knows for sure what the future may bring.

Plans and Objectives

Because plans are oriented toward action, they tend to be confused with operational or measurable goals. Actually, plans are the *means* and goals are the *ends*. In the discussion of means–end chains (Chapter 2), we showed how subordinate goals are interrelated with overall organizational goals. For example, if the organization's goal is to increase sales by 10 percent per year, this top-level goal must be translated into lower-level goals or subgoals for the organization's operating divisions, departments, and individual members. The achievement of these subgoals by the organization's subunits represents the means by which the organization will achieve its overall goals.

Planning a Vacation.   Plans relate to goals in a similar way. If the Johnson family's goal is to have an interesting vacation, the means for reaching this goal is to plan ahead. The Johnsons might decide that a motor tour of the northern West Coast could help them achieve their goal. In turn, this tour might be broken down into more specific subgoals: visits to the Redwood Park, Crater Lake, the Olympic Peninsula, and the cities of Portland, Seattle, Vancouver, and Victoria. The Johnsons would then engage in the planning process to tie the different subgoals together—determining arrival and departure dates and times, routes, motels, restaurants, and so on. In this instance, the gap between the Johnson family's goal and their present reality consists of the difference between their desired vacation and their present location in time and space. Plans are their means for closing the gap.

WHY MANAGERS DO NOT PLAN

Planning represents the way in which decision makers attempt to build bridges into the future. Since all organizations want a smooth transition from present to future, the planning process is an important phase of managerial activity. Yet, for several reasons, planning is not often given the attention that it deserves.

Planning Requires Time

Many managers claim that they simply do not have time for planning. To-day's emergencies usually take priority over a planning process that might enable the manager to avoid similar emergencies in the future.

Crisis Preferred? Strangely enough, some managers prefer a crisis atmosphere. They pride themselves on working well under pressure, reacting capably to problems thrust unexpectedly upon them because they have failed to plan. Managers also realize that time and effort spent in planning are often unrecognized by the organizational reward system. In fact, managers who look good under fire often gain more recognition than managers who run a smooth, well-planned operation. A dramatic turnaround in an organizational trouble spot is more likely to be noticed than a smoothly running, ongoing operation.

The apparent need to handle today's activities and problems almost always pushes planning into the background. Most managers give today's fires priority over planning for tomorrow's fire prevention. However, one test of good managers is the ability to distinguish the important from the urgent, and it is very important that the manager manage the job through planning rather than having the job manage the manager by crisis.

Planning Requires Thought

Good planning requires not only time but thoughtful analysis as well. Most managers find it easier to *do* something than to *think* about the best way of doing it. They are usually action oriented. They want to dig in, to get on with it, to get the job done.

Doing Nothing?   Thought requires time, quiet, and the ability to shut out the immediate situation. Few managers are willing to sit back and think through the problem at hand in order to come up with the best plan. Even fewer managers have the courage to sit quietly in their offices, giving the outside world (and the boss) the appearance of doing nothing. Most managers get greater gratification out of solving an immediate problem or handling an

FIG 11-1 Not a manager.

immediate crisis, and then watching normalcy return in front of them. They do not get as much satisfaction out of sitting quietly, thinking through the operation's activities, and planning with such skill that emergencies seldom arise.

A glance at any issue of *TV Guide* will forcefully make this point. People prefer to focus their attention on *doers* rather than on thinkers. Managers know this. It was not a manager who sat as a model for Rodin's "The Thinker."

Planning Requires Paperwork

Managers perceive that planning will increase their paperwork. Most managers already feel overloaded with forms, letters, memos, and reports, paperwork that they think often hampers them as they use their finely honed managerial skills to cope with one crisis after another. One university uses a long form called a Planning Authorization Request, a request for authorization to begin planning. The form must pass through numerous strands of red tape and must gain approval at several administrative levels before planning can even *begin*. Rather than go through such a process, many managers simply avoid planning altogether.

Planning Requires Forecasts

Managers also tend to resist planning because they cannot see much use in trying to outguess the uncertain future. Planning always involves making some assumptions about the future state of the world. Since change and uncertainty are constant facts of organizational life, guesses about the future are probably going to be incorrect. So why make plans?

Many managers complain about the impossibility of forecasting the future and therefore dismiss the possibility of making sensible plans. Yet goals must be established, forecasts must be made, and plans must be conceived and implemented. Not to do so is to place the organization totally at the mercy of the future, rather than planning for future possibilities and probabilities. The future must be anticipated to as great an extent as possible, and the actions of the organization must be planned accordingly.

Planning Requires Commitment

Thorough planning requires commitment. Once a plan of action is determined, the possibility of making other choices is greatly reduced. In fact, one purpose of plans is to limit alternatives and prescribe action. Once the Johnsons committed themselves to a northern West Coast tour, they almost eliminated the possibility of side trips to Reno, the '49 Gold Rush country, or many other interesting places.

Flexibility? Obviously, all plans should be flexible enough to allow unforeseen opportunities and delays to be worked into the schedule. On the other hand, if the Johnsons do not feel strongly committed to their vacation plan, they will not meet the subgoals (seeing Redwood Park, Crater Lake, the Olympic Peninsula) that are designed to accomplish their overall goal. In short, the more flexibility you want—or the less you are committed to the specifics of your plan—the greater must be the slack time built into the plan, and so the less useful your plan becomes. Later in the chapter we shall talk more about planning flexibility.

Planning involves the structuring of activity over a future period of time. Once this structure is chosen, once the plan is adopted, the organization must communicate its expectations of future behavior to all people affected by the plan. A problem may arise at this point because many people have a great need for autonomy and freedom in both their personal and their working lives. They may not want to behave as the plan says they must behave. Their resentment may be reduced by having them participate in the planning process.

Cost–Benefit Relationship Unknown

The costs of planning are identifiable. The costs of *not* planning and the benefits of planning are both difficult to determine. Planning requires thought, paperwork, and forecasts. All these elements take time and cost money. The cost of planning is arrived at by adding up the hours expended by each planner and multiplying the hours times the wage rates.

Planning costs, then, are clear, precise, and known. The costs of *not* planning are unclear, difficult to blame on a lack of planning, and frequently unknown. What is the cost of an unexpected problem, a missed deadline, a forgotten part, or many similar "natural" problems of doing business that planning might prevent? What is the benefit of heading off these problems before they arise? The precision of the cost and imprecision of the benefit make it hard for many managers to see the real benefits of thorough planning.

Total Time Versus Planning Time. In addition, planning is similar to searching for alternatives in that it is difficult for managers to know when to stop, when they have planned sufficiently. Figure 11-2 pictures the planner's dilemma. The early units of planning time, from point x to point y, are well spent, because up to point y they reduce total time required to complete the project. From point y to point z, the manager is overplanning. In this part of the curve, the improvement in results does not justify planning time and costs. Beyond point z, the manager has spent so much time on planning that total time spent on the project is higher than if no planning at all had been done.

When managers cannot clearly measure the benefits of *not* having problems, and when they are never sure just when they have planned enough, the

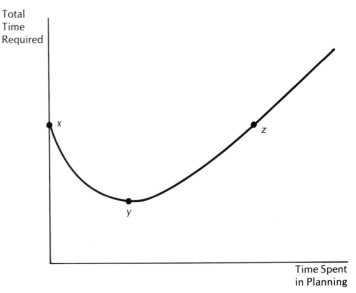

FIG 11-2   Total time versus planning time.

advantages of planning never seem to be worth the identifiable costs of planning thoroughly.

Up to this point, planning seems to have more drawbacks than advantages. Yet we all know intuitively that people and organizations cannot get to where they want to go without plans. Perhaps a description of the planning process will make the benefits of planning more clear.

THE PLANNING PROCESS

Planning has many advantages if it is well done. Sound plans enable a manager to delegate authority. Plans in the form of guidelines or rules enable the subordinate to work without the manager's direct personal supervision. Clear plans enable persons of limited experience to fulfill useful organizational functions. Plans improve the quality of decision making. They permit more effective supervision and control. Without plans, the manager becomes a free-lancer, an improviser.

Planning: An Overview

Planning is an important part of the management job. Whether you are planning for a large corporation, a nonprofit hospital, a Boy Scout troop, or your personal career, some fairly specific steps are involved. These steps are diagrammed in the flow chart appearing as Figure 11-3. At the upper right are the organization's goals. The rest of the planning process is designed to

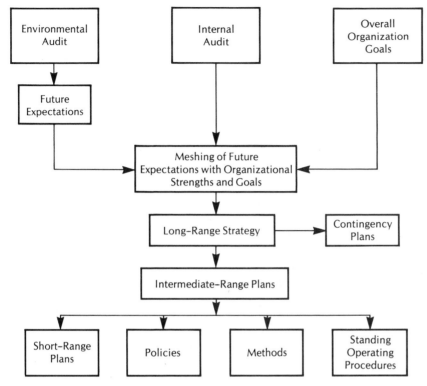

FIG 11-3 The planning process.

achieve them. The organization should be engaged in ongoing environmental and internal audits, keeping track of what is happening inside and outside of the organization. The future is forecast with respect to environmental influences. The large block at the center of the chart symbolizes the point at which future expectations, organizational strengths (identified during the internal audit), and organizational goals are considered together.

Out of that consideration arise the organization's long-range strategy, along with contingency plans, and its intermediate-range plans for achieving its goals. Intermediate-range plans are fulfilled by implementing short-range plans, policies, methods, and standing operating procedures.

Of course, Figure 11-3 is an oversimplification. For example, since some policies might arise directly out of organizational goals, a "policies" box could be attached to the "overall organizational goals" box. Methods and procedures often come about as a result of habitual practice or tradition, rather than being established as a specific means for implementing intermediate-range plans. However, the overview of the planning process is accurate in its general outlines and should be helpful. The different stages in the process will now be discussed in detail.

Internal Audit

An early step in the planning process is the internal audit of organizational resources. The organization must study itself thoroughly and objectively to identify its strengths and weaknesses. To plan realistically, the organization must capitalize on its strengths and overcome (or at least recognize) its weaknesses.

Personnel.   The planner must first focus on personnel. Many questions must be answered. What skills do the people have? What contributions to the organization are they making now? What inducements keep them working for us? What are their age distribution, talents, potential, and interests? Briefly, what are they good at doing, and what are they not so good at doing?

Other Resources.   Physical and financial resources should also be examined. What are the advantages and disadvantages of the organization's physical location, its design, and its equipment? Does the organization have the capital resources that would permit something other than continuing on its present course? If not, can it get those resources? What are the organization's arrangements, reputation, commitments, and contracts with its suppliers, customers, distributors, employees, and with the community? Are these relationships assets or liabilities?

These kinds of questions allow a management planning team to make a realistic and intense internal audit that will form the basis for future planning. Such an audit can help the organization to find the right fit between itself and the future. A realistic appraisal of advantages and disadvantages will enable the organization to exploit its strengths. A person weak in mathematics but strong in athletics should probably enter a physical education degree program rather than an accounting degree program. Similarly, an organization that has operated ocean liners successfully for many years should probably not begin making chemicals and consumer products.

Environmental Audit

Another ongoing process that takes place along with the internal audit is the environmental or external audit. Chapter 10 offered the image of the organization as a balloon, floating within the space of its social system and surrounded by different forces—social change, population and demographic trends, foreign factors, market developments, governmental influence, and others. The task here is to assess what is presently going on within the organization's environment and to forecast what influences and trends will be important in the future. Table 11-1 outlines the kinds of factors that will be examined by means of the environmental audit.

TABLE 11-1 From Environmental Audit to Long-Range Strategy

Key Factors	Present Trends	Forecasts of Future Direction	Relationship (Opportunity or Threat) to Organizational Goals and Strengths	Long-Range Strategy
Competition	Growth or decline of competitors	More	Production methods	
	Complementary goods	or		
	Substitutes		Marketing	Marketing
	Price–quality	less?	channels	strategies
	Foreign			
Customers	Demographic changes		Employee relations	
	Age, marital			
	status, number of	Up	Customer	Financial
	children		wants	strategies
	Income levels			
	Life style		Product	
	Expenditure patterns	or	position	
Technology	Research and		Social	
	development	down?	responsibility	
	expenditures			Organizational
	New products		Financial	design
	New processes		structure	strategies
Government	Employee-related		Job	International
	legislation		design	strategies
	Market-related			
	legislation			
	Regulatory decisions			
	International trade			
	position			
	Monetary policy			

Competition. The organization must assess its competitive market position. Are competitors growing or declining? What developments are occurring with respect to complementary goods? That is, if the organization makes bread, what is going on within the butter business? If the organization makes tires, what is happening in the auto industry? What substitutes for the organization's goods or services seem significant? A copper company will want to assess trends in the aluminum industry to the extent that aluminum products are used as substitites for copper products. What are the price and quality trends within competing organizations? Such competitive factors must be assessed, and their future trends must be forecasted.

Customers. Table 11-1 indicates some characteristics of customers that must be assessed as part of the environmental audit. Organizations must acquire and interpret demographic and social facts about their customers or clients.

For example, grocery stores have known that more and more women are joining the work force, but they have not recognized the trend's importance until fairly recently. Working wives are less able or willing to cook, so more meals are eaten away from home. Therefore, grocery stores have lost an increasingly larger share of the food dollar, and the fast-food chains have benefited dramatically.

Other demographic and social trends are important aspects of the environmental audit for many organizations. For example, the number of single heads-of-household is increasing because of rising divorce rates. The average population age is shifting upward as the postwar baby boom ages, the average life span lengthens, and reproduction rates decline. Many businesses and industries must assess these and other subtle but predictable changes in the nature and character of customers.

Technology.   Technological changes are also somewhat foreseeable, at least in the short run. For example, the development of semiconductors (tiny discs that make possible pocket calculators and digital watches) has meant important changes for many industries. Some giants in the calculator field disappeared almost overnight as large desk calculators achieved instant obsolescence. Anyone with responsibility for planning must try to foresee the potential applications of technological developments.

Government.   National and international political and legal developments may have an impact on the organization. However, the numerous rules and regulations that may affect the conduct of organizational affairs are seldom unpredictable. For example, in the United States, the very structure of our national government makes the sudden appearance of legislation or new policy unlikely. The energy policies that emerged in 1979 were formed over a five-year period. The oil embargo of the early 1970s was a politically motivated decision that might well have been foreseen (and in fact was foreseen by numerous oil companies, who did not tell what they knew).

Forecasting Premises

Once the environment has been assessed, the organization can construct some planning premises or assumptions, labeled "future expectations" in Figure 11-3. These assumptions should spell out how the findings of the present environmental audit may change over the future. If a grocery chain concludes that more and more people are going to be eating out—because working wives and single heads-of-household do not have time to cook meals—then the chain may consider adding a restaurant, delicatessen, or fast-food window to keep pace with the changed nature of its market. On the other hand, the grocery chain may conclude that the trend is going to reverse itself. Increasing restaurant prices, in combination with a rise in personal income insufficient to match the inflation rate, may force more people to cook at home.

Matching Present and Future

At this point in the organization's planning process, three questions have been answered: What is going to happen in the future? What are we good at? What are we trying to accomplish? The answers to these questions must be blended with skill and objectivity.

One hard part of this planning step may be abandoning certain organizational strengths of the past in light of future expectations. Dropping people, ideas, and products that have been successful in the past, but that cannot succeed in the future, is difficult. Yet an automobile company had better not count on large future sales of gas guzzlers just because the company happens to be good at making huge cars.

Table 11-1 shows that, at this planning stage, the key factors in the organization's success (column 1) whose present trends and future directions have been assessed (columns 2 and 3) must now be related to the organization's goals and strengths (column 4). Out of this process arises the organization's long-range strategy (column 5).

Long-Range Planning

Long-range strategy is designed to reach organizational goals by matching future expectations with present capabilities. This long-range strategy becomes the organization's working model. It allows the managerial group to make decisions that will keep the organization pointed toward definite goals over an uncertain future. Long-range strategy is the tool used to evaluate various alternative policy decisions. The key question applied to each alternative is: How will this course of action help meet what the future may bring?

Contingency Plans.   Contingency plans are various options within the organization's overall long-range strategy. The organization has made certain assumptions about the future, but future uncertainty does not go away merely because assumptions are made about what might happen. Consequently, contingency plans are necessary to enable a rapid and effective organizational response to a variety of foreseeable outcomes.

The Defense Department provides a model that all organizational planners might examine. The Department allocates considerable time and personnel to war games in which various enemy action strategies are forecast and appropriate responses are developed. These responses are designed to maximize defense and minimize surprise. Civilian organizations can use this same process to maximize management's ability to cope with likely and unlikely future events.

Finding the Niche.   Potential niches or gaps in the organization's markets should also be included in the organization's master strategy. What special roles may the organization play? What special products and services will fill the market's future needs? What future market trends will create niches that this organization, by virtue of its unique organizational talents, can fill successfully? Without a consideration of special niches that may need filling, the organization's master strategy might turn out to be little more than a projection of present trends into the future.

The pursuit of a particular potential niche may involve a total reconsideration of organizational goals. Such a step would be drastic, and yet the opportunity presented by some foreseen, unsatisfied demand for a product or service may be so compelling that reconsideration is justified.

In our discussion of the organization's internal audit, we said that an organization that has operated ocean liners successfully for many years should probably not go into chemicals and consumer products. Yet that is exactly what the W. R. Grace Company did. The company looked at its corporate strengths and objectives, forecast its future environment, and chose to get out of the ocean liner business on which it was founded. Today the company is primarily a chemicals and consumer products business without an ocean liner to its name. W. R. Grace found such a promising market niche that it completely reallocated its assets from one industry into two others.

Planning for Competition.   If the organization does well, it will inevitably attract competition, no matter whether the organization is a business, a hospital, or a club. Even government monopolies draw competition. For many years, the privately owned United Parcel Service has been beating the U.S. mail's parcel post service at its own game. The revenues generated by the United States Collectors Series stamp program encouraged Monaco and several Central American republics to begin similar extensive and profitable operations. In the same imitative way, hospitals compete with each other for low-risk, short-term surgical patients who attract outstanding doctors and high revenues. At the same time, they try to minimize their efforts in obstetrics and emergency room activities because these hospital services lose money.

The point is simply to realize that today's success will surely bring tomorrow's competition. Therefore, the strategic planning process must not only develop today's strengths and successes but also must look for tomorrow's possibilities.

Once the organization has developed its master strategy by appropriately meshing the environmental audit results with organizational assets, goals, potential niches, and contingency plans, managers are ready to construct intermediate and short-run plans, consisting of policies, methods, and procedures.

Although the foregoing discussion of the planning process has been in terms of overall organizational planning, smaller units (or even individuals) can adapt the process to their own needs.

STANDING PLANS

Need and Origin

Why Organizations Need Plans. *Standing plans* consist of the organization's *policies, methods,* and *procedures.* Standing plans are necessary for any organization. They are designed to deal with problems that occur over and over again. Standing plans avoid the need to go through the problem-solving process every time a problem appears. These plans are also needed for another reason. Since by definition an organization consists of more than one member, the people making up the organization must have some standing plans that define how they are to work together and what they can expect from each other. Without standing plans that ensure reasonable cooperative consistency of behavior, no member will know what to expect from other members.

Where Plans Come From.   Figure 11-3 implies that the meshing of future expectations with organizational strengths and goals leads to long-range strategy and intermediate-range plans. Arising out of intermediate-range plans are the organization's standing plans. In real life, the planning process is not always as structured and orderly as the flow chart suggests. For example, many organizational policies may have evolved from earlier decisions that proved to be successful, rather than resulting from the formal planning process.

Every organization develops its customary, traditional ways of doing things. At some point, certain customs and traditions become so clearly defined and widely used that they become part of the organization's standing plans. On the one hand, such plans may be quite satisfactory because they have evolved from the practicalities of daily organizational activity. On the other hand, just because a plan has become well-established over time does not mean that it is the best plan to use. Frank Gilbreth examined the bricklayer's craft and came up with a better method. Frederick Taylor studied Schmidt's performance and devised a better way to load pig iron. Organizations should not assume that standing plans should stand for all time. Planners should be sure that the traditional, customary ways are in fact the best ways.

Policies

An organizational policy is a statement of organizational intent. It is designed as a guide to handling a recurring organizational problem or as a means of avoiding potential problems. "No ticket, no wash," "Satisfaction guaranteed or your money back," "No checks cashed," "No one under 18 admitted," and "Closed Sundays" are all organizational policy statements for dealing with customers. They answer such recurring questions as, Can I give this customer her laundry if she does not have her laundry ticket? Shall I give this dissatisfied customer a refund? He has an honest face; should I cash his check? Should I let that young child come in to watch this X-rated movie? Should I go open the store tomorrow? Organizations may also have many internal policies, such as "We promote from within."

Policies may be broad or narrow, specific or general. The nature of an organization's policies will depend on the kinds of problems that the organization customarily faces. Since they are a guide as to how employees should *think* about problems, managers should be sure that the policies they establish give employees the kind and amount of guidance they need.

Since policies are guides to thinking, they usually allow organization members to exercise some discretion. Standing plans that allow for no flexibility of application are *rules*, not policies.

Methods

The difference between a policy and a standard method is not clear-cut. Both guide employees in the solving of recurring problems. Policies tend to tell employees *what* to do (or not to do); standard methods give more specific instruction in *how* to carry out an activity.

The best known use of standard methods is the automobile assembly line. The parts on which the employee works are standardized, as are the employee's tools. It follows that the method of using the tools to assemble the parts should be standardized for greater overall efficiency.

If an organization is going to standardize a method, it of course wants the chosen method to be the best one possible. Industrial engineers may have to spend many hours in determining the best way to carry out one organizational operation, and the organization may have hundreds of operations. Therefore, determining the "one best way" to perform every function may be too costly.

However, once standard methods have been worked out, they can be useful to managers trying to plan the work flow. Standard methods often take a standard length of time to perform and are accompanied by a standard cost. Therefore, the manager can plan how long a job is going to take and how much it will cost.

Procedures

The main difference between a standard method and a standing operating procedure (SOP) is that a procedure usually involves *several people* carrying out a *sequence of activities*. Each organizational member gives specialized attention to one function that needs to be done. In addition, these functions must be coordinated to accomplish the organization's day-to-day activities. Procedures tie all the organization's working parts together. Most organizations have dozens or hundreds of standing operating procedures. If they did not, they would have to determine new routines and standards every time a problem recurred. Standing operating procedures make it unnecessary to reinvent the wheel continually. Here is an example of a standing operating procedure.

WELDING PERMIT PROCEDURE

In light of the serious fire hazards involved in welding and cutting with acetylene gas torch or electric arc equipment, a Welding Permit Procedure has been established. No work of this nature—by the Maintenance Department or by outside contractors—may be done without this permit. The *only* exception is in the maintenance shop where adequate welding space and protection have been provided.

No compressed gas cylinders are to be left either on transport carts or on the floor unless they are securely supported by chains to prevent them from falling.

Specific Instructions

1. The Fire Chief is responsible for administering this procedure.
2. Permits are to be issued by Watchmen, who must keep a log of all permits issued. Permits are good for *one day only.*
3. Permits may be obtained by Maintenance Foremen or Project Engineers (or Tower Foremen when the Maintenance Foremen are not available). The permit must be signed by the person obtaining it after indicating by check mark that all precautions listed on the back of the card have been taken.
4. Permits must also be signed by the Department Head, Operating Supervisor, or Foreman of the department where work is to be carried out, indicating that the person in charge is aware of such work going on.
5. A helper *must* be present to act as a fire watch while the work is being carried out.
6. When work covered by the permit is complete for that day, the permit must again be signed by the person obtaining the permit, signifying that the work area was inspected for fire hazards.
7. The permit must then be returned to the Watchman for recording completion of the work in the log.
8. The Watchmen will inspect all areas where welding equipment has been used, on all plant tours on the second and third shifts. A record of inspections must be kept in the log.
9. Should a permit not be returned at the end of the day, the Watchman will try to locate it at the earliest opportunity.

Procedures are essential to the smooth-running organization. Yet they can overwhelm employees and customers if they become too elaborate, as anyone knows who has tried to cut through governmental red tape. The skillful manager will establish only those procedures that facilitate achievement of organizational objectives and will get rid of the rest.

The Flexibility and Detail of Plans

Flexibility.   How flexible should standing plans be? The main reason for standing plans is so people can depend on each other, can predict each other's behavior. If a plan is too flexible, it does not provide enough guidance.

Unfortunately, the best answer to the question of how flexible plans should be is, "It depends on the situation." Take standard selling methods as an example. Telephone solicitors often read exactly the same sales pitch to everyone who picks up the phone, because managers in the business of telephone sales have found that, if solicitors will only stick with the pitch, a certain percentage of persons called will place orders, year in and year out. Door-to-door sales personnel may have five or six different sales pitches, the one used being determined by the age, sex, or other characteristics of the person opening the door.

In some kinds of selling, the approach is much more flexible. The standing plan might simply be that the salesperson must cover the five standard selling steps in some fashion.

Guides or Rules?   Managers must know how flexible they intend their plans to be and must communicate the degree of flexibility to subordinates. In particular, they must let subordinates know whether the plans are designed to serve as *rules* or as *guides*. If possible, plans should be expressed as guides. People and circumstances change over time. A rule that seemed sensible in the past may be silly today. Personnel who implement a plan are often in a better position than the planner to determine how the plan should be applied.

Sometimes rules are preferable to guides. If personnel lack the judgment necessary to use flexible guidelines, strict rules may be needed. Or if the plan is a procedure involving the interaction of several people, rules may be necessary so that the steps in the procedure can be coordinated.

Detail.   How detailed should plans be? Employees like to use their jobs as a means of self-expression, as a way of growing. If plans are so detailed that growth and self-expression are stifled, then employees will be dissatisfied. Yet plans lacking in sufficient detail may not supply the guidance that employees need in order to work confidently. The manager's dilemma is how to make plans detailed enough, but not too detailed.

All the manager can do is take into account the nature of the work and the nature of the workers. If consistency or close coordination is required—as in accounting for financial transactions, establishing wage scales, or in executing a triple reverse off a Statue of Liberty formation with a flea flicker

---

RULES FOR EMPLOYEES

Carson, Pirie, Scott Co., Chicago 18--

1. Store must be open from 6 A.M. to 9 P.M.
2. Store must be swept, counters and base shelves dusted. Lamps must be trimmed, filled, and chimneys cleaned. A pail of water and also a bucket of coal must be brought in before breakfast.
3. Store must not be open on the Sabbath Day unless necessary and then only for a few minutes.
4. The employee who is in the habit of smoking Spanish cigars, being shaved at the barber shop, or going to dances and other places of amusement will surely give his employer reason to be suspicious of his honesty and integrity.
5. Each employee must pay not less than $5 per year to the church and must attend Sunday School regularly.
6. Men employees are given one evening a week for courting and two if they go to prayer meeting.
7. After 14 hours of work in the store, the leisure time of employees should be spent mostly in reading.

SIGNED: THE MANAGEMENT

---

option—then a detailed plan is essential. If the people implementing the plan lack ability, motivation, maturity, or experience, again a detailed plan may be called for.

SUMMARY

This chapter first explained what planning is and showed the relationship between organizational goals and plans. Six reasons why managers avoid planning were then presented: planning requires time, thought, paperwork, commitment, and forecasts, and the cost–benefit relationship of planning is difficult to determine.

The steps of the planning process were then put forth. The external and internal organizational audits should be ongoing processes. Future projections based on these audits are analyzed in light of the organization's long-range goals. Out of this process arise long-range plans, contingency plans, intermediate-range plans, and the organization's various standing plans: policies, methods, and standing operating procedures.

The chapter concluded with a discussion of how detailed and flexible plans should be.

DISCUSSION QUESTIONS

1. What is planning? Why are plans important?
2. How does planning tie into the management model of Chapter 1 and into the decision-making approach used in this book?
3. Why don't managers plan?
4. How can the relationship between the cost of planning and the cost of not planning be expressed?
5. What is the importance of the internal and external audits to successful planning?
6. Distinguish between policies, methods, and procedures.
7. What is the importance of a potential niche to a firm's strategy?
8. How flexible should plans be? How detailed should they be?
9. How can plans help an organization to match the present with the future?
10. Since no one ever knows for sure what the future will bring, why plan at all?

AT&T

In 1968, the Federal Communications Commission handed down a landmark decision against the American Telephone and Telegraph Corporation. From that time on, competition would be permitted between companies wanting to supply telephone instruments and other communications terminals. After 1968, consumers could decide whether to use AT&T phones or to acquire phones from other sources.

After the commission's ruling, AT&T president John deButts considered the situation. The organization must obviously develop new strategies. What courses of action were open to him? Where should he begin?

LEVIN GAS STATIONS

Harry Levin started in 1960 with a single gas station. By virtue of hard work, he continued to expand until by 1972 he controlled a regional chain consisting of 22 gas stations.

Harry kept up with the petroleum news. He was well aware that the Arab oil-producing states were not satisfied with the prices they were getting for their crude oil. Harry had also obtained data on crude oil reserves and had compared that information with data on the rapidly expanding demand for gasoline and other petroleum products. With demand increasing and supply apparently about to decrease, Harry saw trouble ahead later on in 1972 and thereafter.

He wondered what his next step as owner of Levin Gas Stations should be.

12

organizing: differentiation

The previous chapter explained the importance of organizational planning and showed how managers plan. They assess the organization, its environment, and its goals, and then put together the firm's master strategy. The organization's structure is the subject of this chapter and the next. That structure must fit the organization's strategy. *Organizing* is the study of how to establish and maintain the structure that will help achieve organizational goals, given the master strategy that managers have devised.

Our discussion of organizing is divided into two chapters. This chapter discusses *differentiation*—how the organization differentiates or divides up its work. The next chapter discusses *integration*—how the organization coordinates the units into which it is divided.

This chapter will first discuss why people organize, offering a street-corner gang as an example of a basic organization. The steps in organizing a profit-making concern are then illustrated in the founding and development of a hypothetical wine company. This example introduces the concepts of organizational levels and departmentalization.

Major sections of the chapter then cover three further methods of differentiation: specialization of labor, decentralization–delegation, and the line–staff distinction.

WHY PEOPLE ORGANIZE

People organize at every level of human activity. People in an organization have these characteristics:

1. A common, conscious purpose.
2. A willingness to accept authority relationships.
3. A willingness to interact in order to achieve the common purpose.
4. An ability to communiate.

These characteristics are shared by people in all organizations, ranging from such simple ones as the street-corner gang or the community bowling league to the complex bureaucratic structures found in the American Telephone and Telegraph Company and the United States government.

Street-Corner Gangs

In their role behavior and authority relationships, those informal social groupings known as street-corner gangs seem remarkably similar to any large business organization. Although no gang member draws up an organization chart on the sidewalk, each member knows his functions and his level within the authority hierarchy.

Figure 12-1 shows the members in the Norton gang, their relative positions, and the lines of influence running from member to member. Here is

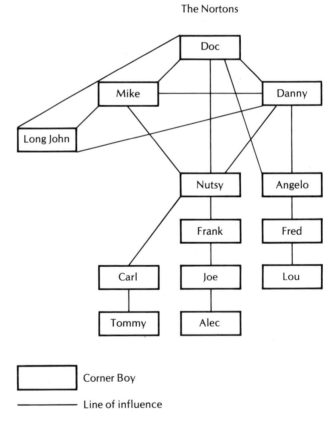

FIG 12-1 The Norton street corner gang. (*Source:* William Foote Whyte, *Street Corner Society,* 2nd ed. Chicago: University of Chicago Press, 1955, p. 13. Used by permission.)

William Foote Whyte's account of the gang's relationships. In age, the gang ranged from 21 to 28.

> The men became accustomed to acting together. They were also tied to one another by mutual obligations. In their experiences together there were innumerable occasions when one man would feel called upon to help another, and the man who was aided would want to return the favor. Strong group loyalties were supported by these reciprocal activities.
>
> There were distinctions in rank among the Nortons. Doc, Danny, and Mike held the top positions. They were older than any others except Nutsy. They possessed a greater capacity for social movement. While the followers were restricted to the narrow sphere of one corner, Doc, Danny, and Mike had friends in many other groups and were well known and respected throughout a large part of Cornerville. It was one of their functions to accompany the follower when he had to move outside of his customary social sphere and needed such support. The leadership three were also respected for their intelligence and powers of self-expression. Doc in particular was noted for his skill in argument. On the infrequent occasions when he did become involved, he was usually able to outmaneuver his opponent without humiliating him. I never saw the leadership three exert their authority through physical force, but their past fighting reputations tended to support their positions.
>
> Doc was the leader of the gang. The Nortons had been Doc's gang when they had been boys, and, although the membership had changed, they were still thought to be Doc's gang. The crap game and its social obligations prevented Danny and Mike from spending as much time with the Nortons as did Doc. They were not so intimate with the followers, and they expected him to lead.
>
> Long John was in an anomalous position. Though he was five years younger than Doc, his friendship with the three top men gave him a superior standing. . . . Nevertheless, he had little authority over the followers. At this time he was accustomed to gamble away his week's earnings in the crap game, and this was thrown up against him.
>
> There is an important social distinction between those who hold crap games and those who play in them. The game-holders enjoy something of the standing of businessmen; the "shooters" are thought to be suckers. The Nortons as a group considered themselves above the crap-shooters' level, and at this time Long John was trying unsuccessfully to break away from the game.[1]

As the chapter proceeds, we shall see that large corporations and street-corner gangs are designed according to similar principles.

THE TIPPLE WINE COMPANY

Three Necessary Functions

Here is a fictitious example to show how organizational design typically develops. Assume that George Tipple has inherited some land filled with grape vines. He decides to begin making wine for profit. Here are the tasks that any organization offering products for sale must accomplish:

---

[1]William Foote Whyte, *Street Corner Society*, 2nd ed. (Chicago: University of Chicago Press, 1955), pp. 12–13.

1. *Production.* The product must be produced.
2. *Distribution.* The product must be distributed to customers.
3. *Finance.* The funds needed to produce and distribute the product must be secured.

In George Tipple's case, funds must be secured to produce and distribute Tipple Wine. Since George Tipple is the owner–manager–employee of the business, he fulfills all tasks by himself. He uses his savings to produce wine, and he sells it from his roadside stand. The road alongside which George Tipple has his stand is I-90, a major route between Syracuse and Buffalo. Customers are numerous, and business is good.

Basic Organization Chart.   At this point, George Tipple is a one-man organization. He performs and coordinates all functions. His organization chart appears in Figure 12-2. An organization chart pictures the organization's parts and shows how they are related to each other. Since George Tipple is performing and coordinating all functions himself, he probably sees no need for distributing this chart to the organizational membership.

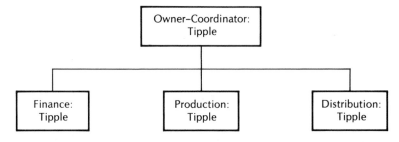

FIG 12-2   Organization chart for a single proprietorship: the Tipple Wine Company.

The early American industrial pioneers organized their enterprises in this same way. In his silver shop, Paul Revere had to organize his time to produce and sell silver goods, and to finance the ongoing operation.

Growth Strategy

George Tipple decides that he wants his business to grow. Several strategies are available. He can buy more land and develop more efficient means of production and distribution. That strategy would permit growth without additional employees. Or he can add more personnel to increase employee hours available for production and to benefit from specialization in his work force. He decides to do both. He buys more land and hires an employee: James David.

Up to now, Tipple's only managerial problem has been management-of-things. Although hiring James David does not increase organizational complexity dramatically, it does introduce a management-of-people problem for the first time. Tipple must define David's organizational role and must teach David the responsibilities and tasks associated with the role. Tipple's business has now become a formal organization. Two people are united in a mutual effort to reach a goal.

New Organization Chart.   Tipple maintains control over the finance function. He decides to keep handling wine production, and he assigns wine distribution to James David. The new organization chart in Figure 12-3 looks just like the first chart, except that David's name appears in the "distribution" box.

At this point, assigning functions (and their accompanying tasks) to *people* becomes useful. Most organization charts are made up of rectangles that show who is assigned to which function. However, organizing and organization charts are designed primarily to reflect which *tasks* must be accomplished (rather than which people are assigned to accomplishing them) if the organization is to achieve its goals. The assignment of people to the tasks is a staffing function, to be covered in Chapter 14. Placing people's names on an organization chart is usually a convenience to show areas of responsibility.

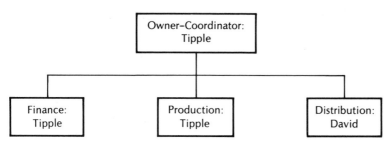

FIG 12-3   Organization chart for a two-person firm.

Differentiating and Integrating.   Organization charts and the organizing task itself involve two specific activities:

1. *Differentiating.* Dividing up the tasks that the organization must accomplish if it is to succeed.
2. *Integrating.* Coordinating the tasks for a united effort.

In simple organizations like Tipple Wine, the owner–manager does all the integrating. In large organizations, differentiating and integrating may each require an elaborate, detailed managerial system and communication mechanism. The larger the organization, the more important the integrating function becomes. After a certain point, George Tipple will no longer be able to coordinate single-handedly the many complex activities required for reaching the organization's goals.

Corporation Organization Chart.   Assume that George Tipple and James David have worked hard and successfully. After several years, the need for additional capital has caused George Tipple to *incorporate* the company. The corporation organization chart appears in Figure 12-4. In the interests of simplification, this chart omits some vital functions, such as quality control, auditing, computer operations, and maintenance, to name a few.

DIFFERENTIATION AND THE CHART

Organization Levels

The Tipple Wine Company, Inc., chart has numerous different *levels* into which organizational tasks are differentiated. These levels will now be discussed in turn.

Stockholders.   Under the corporate form of organization, the stockholders own the company. George Tipple has been sensible enough to retain 51 percent of the company's common stock, so he has majority control over the firm's policies and direction. Tipple probably needs 51 percent in order to control the company. In some cases, such as the Ford Motor Company, corporate control can be maintained with much less than 51 percent of the stock. As little as 5 percent will often establish control, because the remaining 95 percent is spread out among so many stockholders.

Board of Directors.   The board of directors is elected by the stockholders to represent their interests in guiding and criticizing the firm's management. The board is responsible for establishing the company's master strategy, as described in the preceding chapter. Then the board keeps watch to be sure that the company's management and employees implement board policy properly. Former owner–entrepreneur (and now chief stockholder) Tipple can easily justify appointing himself as company president and board chairman, because he has the most to gain and the most to lose.

President.   The president is the organization's principal operating officer. The president is responsible for executing board policy and for coordinating and allocating organization resources so as to achieve organizational goals. The president cannot pass the buck to anyone else; it stops at the president's desk.

Managerial Levels.   Below the president, the Tipple managerial levels range from the vice-presidents on down to the foremen. Tipple Wine Co. has three vice-presidents. The vice-president for distribution is responsible for five distribution areas, each with its own manager. Within each region (although the chart is extended downward only for the Eastern Region), the sales function is

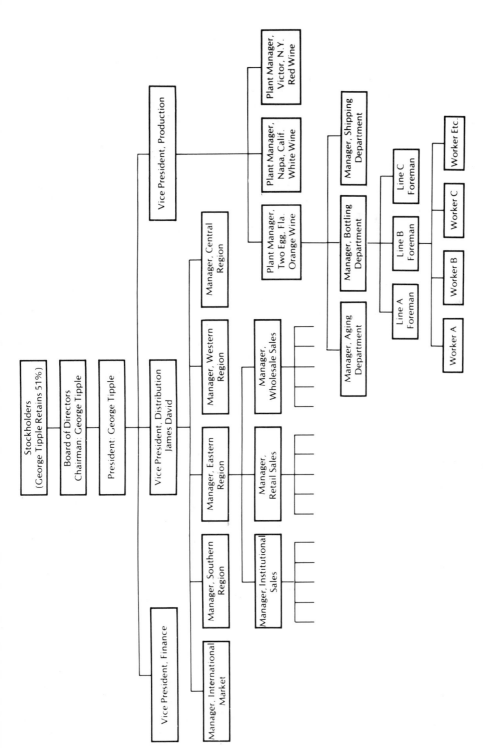

FIG 12-4 Tipple Wine Company, Inc., organization chart.

divided up into institutional sales, retail sales, and wholesale sales—each with a manager. Each manager is responsible for a group of salespeople. Three plant managers report to the vice-president for production. Each plant manager supervises one plant's aging, bottling, and shipping departments. The foremen and workers in the bottling department are included on the chart, and the foremen and workers in the aging and shipping departments are not.

Tipple's department foremen represent the lowest level of management, or what is commonly called *first-line management*. This group of managers is in direct contact with the people who actually produce the organization's product or deliver its services. Blue-collar units usually use the term "foreman," and white-collar units usually use the term "supervisor" for this managerial group. Whether the term used is nursing floor supervisor, production line foreman, or child care service supervisor, the job is managerial in that it represents the first point of formal organizational coordination and supervision for a group of employees.

Task Importance.   One function of organizational levels is to reflect the hierarchy of managerial authority. Each organization member reports to one person at the next higher level of authority. Another function of organizational levels is to show the relative importance of each task or function in light of the organization's goals. For example, a ball-bearing manufacturer and a hospital might both operate a food service, but the food service function would be more important, and consequently higher, on the hospital's organization chart than on the ball-bearing manufacturer's organization chart.

The level of a function on the organization chart reflects management's opinion of its importance. Top management maintains immediate and direct control over those functions that contribute directly to achieving organizational goals. Less vital functions are placed farther down the chart.

Personnel departments are currently higher on organizational charts than they have ever been before. Their new position reflects the increasing importance of personnel activities in complying with new laws and regulations. Top managers feel the need for immediate and close contact with the personnel department in order not to break the law.

Span of Control

The organization chart reflects vertical authority relationships. It also illustrates a related concept: span of authority or span of control. This term refers to the number of subordinates directly controlled or supervised by one manager. In the Tipple Wine chart, the span of control ranges from three to five.

Greater Span, Fewer Levels.   Organizational levels and span of control are directly related. The wider the span of control is, the fewer the organizational levels will be—with a fixed number of employees. If span of control is re-duced, each manager has fewer subordinates. If span of control is increased, the number of managers and the number of levels on the chart will both be reduced. Organizations with many levels and relatively few employees re-porting to one manager are called *tall* organizations, because their charts look tall. Organizations with relatively few levels and many employees reporting to one manager are called *flat* organizations.

The more levels within the organization, the greater the communication, coordination, and integration problems. The fewer levels, the more people each manager must supervise. The organization must keep both the number of levels and the various spans of control as small as practical, which is difficult because reducing one increases the other.

Span of control is an integrating concept rather than a differentiating concept, so it will be discussed at greater length in the next chapter.

Departmentalization

In the Tipple Wine chart, the next level below the presidential level represents the three functions essential to success in the wine business. The *functional* approach is one way of departmentalizing or dividing up the organization's tasks. Other common ways of departmentalizing an organization are used in lower levels of the Tipple Wine Company. Three plant managers, represent-ing three different product types, report to the vice-president for production. This form of departmentalization is *product based*. Five regional sales managers report to the vice-president for distribution. This form of departmentalization is *geographical*. Another common form of departmentalization is seen in the positions reporting to the Eastern Region sales manager. These positions are departmentalized by *type of customer*. Each sales group is responsible for sell-ing to a specific part of the entire wine market.

Other ways of departmentalizing are by *numbers* (4th squad, 7th-grade teachers, 9th battalion), by *time* (first shift, second shift), and by *process* (dril-ling division, planning office, polishing department).

Dividing up the Tasks. Departmentalization is a logical, easily understood strategy for differentiating the organization's tasks and grouping related tasks together. It enables several departments to be controlled at the next higher level by a person whose interests and competence are related to the de-partmental functions. James David, for example, the Tipple Wine Co. vice-president for distribution, understands and has sympathy for sales problems in the five markets served by Tipple. The vice-president for production would not have such understanding and sympathy. Indeed, some classic organiza-tional conflicts have come about because marketing, production, and financial departments have failed to understand and appreciate each other's point of view.

Further Differentiation

Information Channels.   The Tipple organization chart shows how knowledge is differentiated into specialized information channels. No single organization member needs all organizational information. The organization's structure allows information to flow in a systematic way to where it is needed. For example, information related to marketing would routinely flow through the boxes on the chart attached to the distribution function. All personnel needing, using, and affected by this information would have regular routine access to it.

Differentiating the flow of organizational information also lets people outside the information channels know where to look for it. In smaller organizations, if people outside the marketing function want marketing information, they merely inquire of the person likely to have the information. If the organization has outgrown informal information relationships, the differentiation and dissemination of knowledge through channels reflected in the organization chart can make acquiring information relatively simple. For example, a research and development employee in Tipple's Two Egg plant can quickly get marketing information from the home office by checking the organization chart and routing an inquiry to the proper office.

Promotion Requirements.   The organization chart enables all employees to know what the requirements for promotion are. The chart shows hierarchical relationships and reflects logical job knowledge specialization. Subordinates can look upward at the requirements of the manager's job to see what job knowledge, skills, training, degree, or other credentials they will need in order to be eligible for promotion. The person wishing to move up the organization ladder can effectively allocate time and effort to acquiring the qualifications demonstrated by persons at higher levels on the chart.

SPECIALIZATION OF LABOR

Although it is usually discussed from the standpoint of the worker, specialization of labor is an important differentiating concept at all organizational levels.

Advantages of Specialization

Simplification.   Specialization of labor means that each job should be made as simple and straightforward as possible. This idea has a long history, and Chapter 1 described two instances: the Arsenal of Venice and Adam Smith's pin-making example. Some scholars believe that the efficiencies arising out of this concept are primarily responsible for the vast rise in the standard of living experienced by industrialized countries in the first half of the twentieth century. When specialization of labor was applied to agriculture in the 1940s to 1960s, further increases in the standard of living occurred.

Here are seven specific advantages that arise from specializing and simplifying the work.

1. *Time required to learn the task is reduced.* The more specialized a job is, the simpler it generally becomes, and consequently the faster it can be learned. Many workers could never learn how to build an engine or a transmission, much less an entire car. Almost any worker can rapidly learn a highly specialized task such as tightening a nut on the fourth bolt of each automobile coming down the assembly line. Not much time will be required to learn the three steps in the operation: locating the bolt, locating the nut, and turning the wrench.

2. *Waste created by learning the task is reduced.* The easier the job is to learn, the fewer mistakes will be made, and consequently the fewer production defects will occur. This principle applies not only to the quantity of defects but also to their cost. If Bob Workman is trying to learn how to build a car engine, he will destroy many intricate, costly engines while he learns (*if* he learns). If he is trying to learn the simpler operation of drive shaft construction, his learning will produce fewer, less costly defects.

3. *Skill is gained by repeating a task.* In general, the more times we do something, the better we become at it. This gain in skill can be represented by a *learning curve.* Psychologists developed these curves to show the relationship between number of attempts and level of skill achieved. A typical learning curve appears in Figure 12-5. The fact that employees repeating a task get

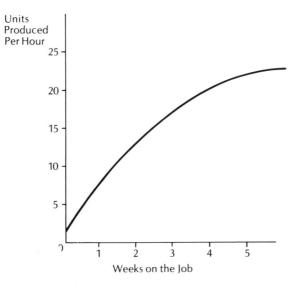

FIG 12-5 A typical learning curve.

better at it is not surprising. What is significant is that improvement in performance often follows such a regular pattern that it can be predicted. These predictions are very helpful in pricing and production planning because they can be used to estimate how long a new project will take and how much it will cost.

During the aerospace boom of the 1960s, companies bidding on large government contracts used learning curves to decide how much to bid. Any company wanting to build a bomber or missile would have to start at the least productive point on the curve. Yet a bid based on the cost of producing the first unit would be unrealistic and noncompetitive, because production costs would eventually drop as workers learned their tasks. Therefore, standard learning curves were used to calculate what the time and costs of the work force would be as they learned by producing 100 planes, 1000 missiles, or whatever.

Similar curves can be used to describe the learning of the shade tree mechanic who rebuilds a carburetor more than once, the do-it-yourselfer who builds several room additions, and so on. Skill gained in repeating a task is one of the greatest and most obvious benefits derived from specialization of labor.

4. *Time lost in changing from one task to another is reduced.* No matter how simple a task is, it requires some concentration and a certain mind set. Whenever workers move from one task to another, they must shift their mental gears. Even if the tasks are similar, the mind requires adjustment time. As an example, consider a student taking notes on one professor's lecture and then moving along to take notes on another professor's lecture. The tasks are similar, but the mind adjusted to the style, gestures, tone, humor, volume, and subject matter of the first lecturer must readjust for the second lecturer. Time is lost whenever anyone assigned two tasks must drop one set of procedures and skills and then adopt another set.

5. *Time lost in changing tools is reduced.* The more specialized the task, the less likely the need to change tools.

6. *The likelihood of specialized tools and methods being developed is increased.* The more specialized the task, the easier it is to focus on it and to think about just what is being done. True, many people doing highly specialized jobs (such as assembly-line work) learn their jobs well enough to do them while daydreaming. However, many workers do think about their jobs, especially about how to make them easier.

Workers like to "tinker" with their jobs, to outdo the "experts" who designed them. Workers often consider the perfectly engineered job with its ideal tools as a challenge to their ingenuity. They make modifications or invent their own do-hickies, gadgets, or gizmos that speed up the operation and increase efficiency far beyond the engineered standard. Most of these unauthorized, effective tools and tricks are securely hidden when the plant efficiency expert walks by. Nevertheless, if they really are an improvement, they eventually find their way into common, widespread use. These innovations are a direct outgrowth of greater intimacy with the job, natural human curiosity, and the thinking time available when doing a highly specialized, routine task.

7. *Individual skills are used more efficiently.* When work is highly specialized, the employer need hire only the amount of skill or ability that each job requires. This idea is attributed to scientific management pioneer Charles Babbage, who said about 150 years ago,

> The master manufacturer, by dividing the work to be executed into different processes, each requiring different degrees of skill or force, can purchase exactly that precise quantity of both which is necessary for each process; whereas if the whole work were executed by one workman, that person must possess sufficient skill to perform the most difficult and sufficient strength to execute the most laborious of the operations.[2]

As an example of this advantage, consider the *word processing center* concept in the modern office. Under the older, more customary practice, five managers would have five secretaries, each one performing all secretarial functions. A word processing center is essentially a centralized secretarial operation. The five personal secretaries would be arranged in a *pool,* and each would specialize in a particular function. One would answer the phone, one would type, one would transcribe, one would take dictation, and one would file. Each secretary would become more skilled at one function but, more importantly, the cost of the overall secretarial operation would decrease because the costs of hiring would vary from secretarial function to function. A personal secretary must meet certain minimal typing, dictating, and filing qualifications. The cost of the most expensive necessary skill will determine the secretary's hourly wage for each hour on the job, whether or not the expensive skill is being used.

For example, if a certain full-time secretarial job requires one hour a day of exceptionally fast, accurate typing, and an exceptional typist gets $7.50 per hour, the secretary filling the position is going to be paid $7.50 per hour for answering the phone and for filing, as well as for typing.

In a word processing center, the exact needed amount of each skill can be purchased, so the cost of overall secretarial support can be reduced. However, in practice, this idea is one that is good for subordinates but not for bosses. *They* must obviously have personal secretaries. The personal secretary is a status symbol that most managers will not willingly give up. Therefore, attempts to set up word processing centers are usually pushed down the organization and wind up at the lowest level of management.

The foregoing seven advantages of specialization have been overwhelmingly important in increasing the productivity of organizations, industries, and societies. From automobile assembly-line workers to heart specialists,

[2]Charles Babbage, *On the Economy of Machinery and Manufactures* (London: Charles Knight, 1832), p. 176.

from Midas Muffler to Burger King, the advantages of specialization to society seem clear.

Disadvantages of Specialization

Worker Dissatisfaction.   On the other hand, specialization has a cost in human terms: the dissatisfaction created by the routine, repetitive, highly specialized job. Here is Donald F. Roy's description of what he experienced as he used a punching or "clicking" machine to punch shapes out of plastic.

It was evident to me, before my first work day drew to a weary close, that my clicking career was going to be a grim process of fighting the clock, the particular timepiece in this situation being an old-fashioned alarm clock which ticked away on a shelf near George's machine. I had struggled through many dreary rounds with the minutes and hours during the various phases of my industrial experience, but never had I been confronted with such a dismal combination of working conditions as the extra-long workday, the infinitesimal cerebral excitation, and the extreme limitation of physical movement. The contrast with a recent stint in the California oil fields was striking. This was no eight-hour day of racing hither and yon over desert and foothills with a rollicking crew of "roustabouts" on a variety of repair missions at oil wells, pipe lines, and storage tanks. Here there were no afternoon dallyings to search the sands for horned toads, tarantulas, and rattlesnakes, or to climb old wooden derricks for raven's nests, with an eye out, of course, for the tell-tale streak of dust in the distance which gave ample warning of the approach of the boss. This was standing all day in one spot beside three old codgers in a dangy room looking out through barred windows at the bare walls of a brick warehouse, leg movements largely restricted to the shifting of body weight from one foot to the other, hand and arm movements confined, for the most part, to a simple repetitive sequence of place the die, _____ punch the clicker, _____ place the die, _____ punch the clicker, and intellectual activity reduced to computing the hours to quitting time. It is true that from time to time a fresh stack of sheets would have to be substituted for the clicked-out old one; but the stack would have been prepared by someone else, and the exchange would be only a minute or two in the making. Now and then a box of finished work would have to be moved back out of the way, and an empty box brought up; but the moving back and the bringing up involved only a step or two. And there was the half hour for lunch, and occasional trips to the lavatory or the drinking fountain to break up the day into digestible parts. But after each momentary respite, hammer and die were moving again: click, _____ move die, _____ click, _____ move die.

Before the end of the first day, Monotony was joined by his twin brother, Fatigue. I got tired. My legs ached, and my feet hurt. Early in the afternoon I discovered a tall stool and moved it up to my machine to "take the load off my feet." But the superintendent dropped in to see how I was "doing" and promptly informed me that "we don't sit down on this job." My reverie toyed with the idea of quitting the job and looking for other work.

The next day was the same: the monotony of the work, the tired legs and sore feet and thoughts of quitting.[3]

[3]Donald F. Roy, " 'Banana Time': Job Satisfaction and Informal Interaction," in William B. Wolf (ed.), *Management: Readings Toward a General Theory* (Belmont, Calif.: Wadsworth Publishing Company, Inc., 1964), p. 128.

Overcoming Worker Dissatisfaction. Three basic strategies and miscellaneous other plans have been used to reduce the negative aspects of job specialization:

1. *Job enlargement.* "Unspecialize" by adding more tasks to the worker's job (for example, instead of having one person put on the wheel and another tighten the bolts, have one worker do both).
2. *Job rotation.* Switch people from one specialized job to another, allowing them to learn and use different skills rather than concentrating on only one (for example, a utility infielder).
3. *Job enrichment.* Develop employee ego involvement in the work, so the employee can take pride in the product of personal skills, rather than turning out an anonymous, mass-produced item (for example, look at the bottom of a grocery bag and you may see the name of the worker who produced it).

Other Methods. More and more firms are adopting new work schedules such as the 4-day work week. About 1,200,000 workers (2 percent of the nation's work force) now work only 4 days a week, and the number seems certain to increase. Although the automobile and steel unions are trying to achieve a 4-day, 32-hour week for their members, most firms using the 4-day week require that each work day be 10 hours long, with half an hour for lunch. Firms using the system say that it reduces absenteeism, boosts productivity, and improves employee morale.

Another widely used method is *flextime.* Under this approach, all employees work during a core of hours in the middle of the business day. But employees may adjust their start and stop times to suit their individual preferences. Some employees might work from 6 until 2, while others might work from 9 until 5.

Now that fringe benefits are worth several thousand dollars a year to each employee, how these benefits are packaged has become a matter of increasing employee interest. A final inducement being offered by more and more organizations is the cafeteria approach to fringe benefits. The organization presents employees with a list of benefits, each with a money value attached. The employee's job level, seniority, or the union contract determines the total dollar value of the benefits package that the employee can put together. The employee then selects the most attractive combination of benefits. Management hopes that this combination will make specialization's disadvantages more tolerable.

Job Enrichment. Of these techniques, management scholars most frequently advocate job enrichment. Job enlargement and job rotation can be carried only so far before they eliminate the economic benefits of specialized labor. In addition, merely adding more tasks or rotating jobs inevitably leads to as much monotony and boredom as was present in the original job design.

Furthermore, employees accustomed to daydreaming on the job may resent having to *think* as they do more tasks or change routines. They may also view job enlargement as a "speed-up" attempt to get more work out of each worker.

The efforts to increase ego involvement through job enrichment strategies have had mixed results. Predictably, some workers want more involvement on the job, and some do not. So even when employees are not suspicious of management's motives, reactions to job enrichment programs vary. However, from the human relations point of view, any management effort to decrease monotony and job boredom is probably worthwhile.

An Example: Volvo.   A classic illustration of job involvement has been occurring in Sweden at the Volvo plant in Kalmar. The traditional assembly line was broken down into work centers, with employee teams deciding about production rates, individual tasks, team membership, break times, and so on. From both the morale and economic standpoints, results have been mixed but have tended to be positive.

The human-related costs associated with highly specialized jobs are high absenteeism and turnover, more supervision needed, product defects, equipment damage, and some vandalism. The benefits of higher morale, generally felt to result from a decrease in job monotony, are the inverse of these costs, although these benefits are obviously harder to measure than the costs. The difficult task for managers is to use job enrichment to achieve both employee job satisfaction and economic validity. Satisfied workers do no good if the organization is failing. Conversely, in the present social setting, firms that fail in their responsibilities to workers cannot expect economic success.

Specialization and the Service Industries.   During the first half of this century, specialization of labor led to astounding productivity gains. These advances have leveled off over the past 20 years or so. One reason is said to be that applying specialization principles to a product-oriented economy is much easier than applying them to our present-day service-oriented economy.

Most service industry jobs, like food stamp disbursement, beauty parlor permanents, and plumbing, defy specialization. "Service" implies individual attention to customers, and rising labor costs will make individual attention more expensive. Our social values demand that food stamp personnel give individualized interviews and reviews. Hairdressers would lose business if they set up assembly lines. And the only way to make plumbers more efficient is to take plumbing problems to them.

The service sector of our economy is not very adaptable to the efficiencies arising from specialization of labor. As the service sector continues to grow, its inability to gain greater productive efficiency from service employees will become an even more significant concern.

The Usefulness of Specialization.   Apparently, specialization can be both useful and not useful. Clearly, the *market* will determine whether the organization should specialize or not. If you want to specialize in servicing Rolls Royce wheel bearings, you must be prepared to spend a lot of time (traveling to Rolls Royces) or a lot of money (advertising to convince Rolls Royce owners to travel to you).

Both alternatives are ludicrous. Rolls Royce owners are not going to drive all over the country to consult dozens of specialists. Nor can specialist mechanics afford to remain on call, waiting to display their specialized repair skills on Rolls Royces only. While waiting for a Rolls Royce wheel bearing job, they must repair Chevrolet disc brakes and change the oil in Fords. In short, specialization in service organizations can only be carried so far. No manicurist specializes in right thumbs.

Manufacturers handle the varying demand for their products by building up an inventory. Farmers store grain in silos. Most services cannot be stored. It is impossible to store a haircut, a gasoline tank fill-up, a shoeshine, an empty motel room, a kilowatt, or an extra airplane seat. Therefore, the people and organizations providing these services must maintain expensive and often unused capacity. That capacity takes the form of either extra capital equipment (such as spare electrical generating capacity, unused buses, and empty hospital beds) or additional personnel costs (such as cross training people in a variety of tasks and skills, using people's talents inefficiently, or underutilizing people). Ineffectively matching the demand for a service with its supply has a human cost. In addition, the cost of maintaining unused capacity must be passed along to those who do use the service.

DECENTRALIZATION AND DELEGATION

A second major differentiating concept is decentralization and delegation. Delegation is usually thought of as a one-to-one relationship. Manager A delegates some authority to managers B, C, and D. Practiced as an organizational philosophy, this orientation toward delegation is called *decentralization*. The idea of decentralization is to push decision-making power *down* through the organization. Especially in large organizations, decentralization provides a practical means for coordinating the organization's activities.

The Specialization of Authority

Consider a purchasing officer responsible for buying equipment and supplies. The purchasing officer becomes overwhelmed with purchase decisions and so delegates authority for making purchases in amounts of less than $100 to a subordinate. The senior manager has given up some authority to a subordinate in order to have time for more important matters.

New managers soon find that a relatively small part of the total managerial job requires most of the manager's time. The wise manager delegates the routine, uneventful portion of the job in order to focus on the more troublesome part. The problem, of course, is determining which activities should be delegated and which should not or, more generally, how much decision-making power should be decentralized.

Delegation and Human Relations

Another aspect of the decentralization issue is the positive impact on the organization's resources that comes from increasing the involvement of lower-level personnel in decision making. According to the human relations school, participation improves organizational health.

Chris Argyris makes the case for decentralization as opposed to a centralized hierarchy. He finds hierarchy incongruent with the needs of a mature personality. In a hierarchy, members are "*dependent* upon, *passive* toward, and *subordinate* to the leader. As a result, the individuals have *little control* over their working environment . . . and exemplify dimensions of immaturity, not adulthood."[4]

Delegation and Information. Another argument for decentralization is the quantities of information handled in the modern organization. The amount of information available to modern executives is so great and diverse that they cannot possibly cope with it all and at the same time oversee the operation and coordinate the activities of organizational members. Decentralization helps to combat the problems arising out of information overload.

Decentralization at General Motors

Peter Drucker has studied decentralization at General Motors by interviewing GM executives. He reports that in their opinion, decentralization has these advantages:

1. The speed with which a decision can be made, the lack of any confusion as to who makes it, and the knowledge of the policies on which the decision is based by everybody concerned.
2. The absence of any conflict between the interests of the divisions and those of General Motors.

[4]Chris Argyris, *Personality and Organizations* (New York: Harper & Row, Inc., 1958), pp. 50–51.

3. The sense of fairness in dealing among executives, the certainty that a good job will be appreciated, the confidence and feeling of security that comes when personality issues, intrigues, and factionalism are kept under control.

4. The democracy of management and its informality. Nobody throws his weight around, yet there is never any doubt where the real authority lies. Everybody is free to criticize, to talk, and to suggest; yet once the decision is taken, nobody tries to sabotage it.

5. The absence of a gap in the executive group between the "privileged few" and the "great many." The president does not arrogate to himself any right he does not accord to his associates.

6. There is a very large management group. Thus there is always a supply of good and experienced leaders, able to take top responsibility.

7. Decentralization means that weak divisions and weak managers cannot ride for any length of time on the coattails of successful divisions, or trade on their own past reputation.

8. Decentralization means the absence of "edict management" in which nobody quite knows why he does what he is ordered to do. Its place is taken by discussion and by policies which are public and which are arrived at as a result of the experiences of all the people concerned.[5]

Decentralization at General Electric

Another classic illustration, General Electric, shows additional advantages of decentralization as developed on a return-on-investment (ROI) basis. The GE approach allows decentralized decision making without losing top management coordination.

Until the late 1940s, General Electric was highly centralized. The company was organized into *functional* departments such as manufacturing, sales, and engineering. As a result, the engineering department might design a dishwasher without the advice of the marketing department. The manufacturing division might produce too many or too few dishwashers because information from the sales division was lacking. As a result, new president Ralph Cordiner reorganized GE in the early 1950s into 100 *product* departments. Each product manager was responsible for a given product's design, manufacture, and sale. Here is what Cordiner had to say about the new arrangement:

> Today, General Electric's products are engineered, manufactured, and marketed by nearly a hundred decentralized Operating Departments, each of them bearing full operating responsibility and authority for the Company's success and profitability in a particular product or service field. The special skills and knowledge required for each operating business are thus brought to bear by a local business managerial team which can concentrate on the opportunities of a specific product or marketing area. Through these integrated managerial teams, each with a specific profit-and-loss responsibility for the operation of a defined

[5]Peter Drucker, *The Concept of the Corporation* (New York: New American Library, 1964), p. 51.

business, we achieve the flexibility, drive and "human touch" that comes from direct participation in the daily problems of a business.

To demonstrate that the responsibility, authority and accountability of these Operating Departments is real, not window dressing, consider their pricing authority. The price of a product can be raised or lowered by the managers of the Department producing it, with only voluntary responsibility on their part to give sensible consideration to the impact of such price changes on other Company products.

As further evidence of the freedom provided by decentralization to the Operating Departments, consider the fact that the operating budget of the General Electric Company is not a document prepared by the Executive Offices in New York. It is an addition of the budgets prepared by the Operating Department General Managers, with the concurrence of the Division General Managers and Group Executives. These budgets include planned sales volume, product development plans, expenditures for plant and equipment, market targets, turnover of investment, net earnings, projected organization structure and other related items.[6]

Decentralization is not the automatic answer to a company's problems. Later events showed that GE had gone from the extreme of too much centralization to too much decentralization. If decentralization is too complete, the company's right hand does not know what the left hand is doing. As an example, in the late 1950s, the Convair Division of General Dynamics Corporation surprised both the stockholders and top management by reporting a loss of over $400,000,000. General Dynamics almost went bankrupt.

Centralization Versus Decentralization

The manager's problem, then, is how to find the best balance between centralization and decentralization. Figure 12-6 shows the centralization–decentralization continuum. The figure reflects the fact that most decisions can either be made at the top or delegated downward. Since top managers are ultimately responsible for coordinating the organization's progress, they must retain the right to make certain decisions and to review others. On the other hand, the figure shows that totally centralized decision making is impossible. Unless an "organization" is a one-person operation, it is literally impossible for one individual to make all the decisions.

Although no certain formula exists for finding the perfect balance of centralization and decentralization, here are some guidelines that have proved useful.

Information.   First, who has the information necessary for making the decision? Decision making should not be pushed down the organization to the point where necessary decision-making information is not customarily available.

[6]Ralph J. Cordiner, *The New Frontiers for Professional Managers* (New York: McGraw-Hill Book Co., 1956), pp. 58–60.

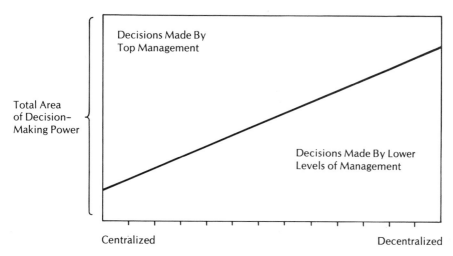

Total Area
of Decision–
Making Power

Decisions Made By
Top Management

Decisions Made By Lower
Levels of Management

Centralized   Decentralized

FIG 12-6 The centralization-decentralization continuum. Reprinted by permission of the *Harvard Business Review.* Adapted from Exhibit 1 of "How to Choose a Leadership Pattern" by Robert Tannenbaum and Warren H. Schmidt (May–June 1973). Copyright © 1973 by the President and Fellows of Harvard College; all rights reserved.

Ability.   Second, who has the ability—the training and experience—to make the decision? Key-punch operators who know nothing about either electronics or cost–benefit analysis should not be asked to decide which key-punch equipment to buy. Decisions should not be delegated to people without the expertise to make them. On the other hand, for the general operating manager *not* to decentralize the key-punch equipment decision to the engineering department would be just as foolhardy, because that department does have the required expertise.

Timeliness.   How fast must decisions be made? Some situations, especially in the retail sector of business, require rapid responses to changes in market conditions or social trends. Decentralization lends itself to quick decision making.

Here is an example of how a decentralized operation can get the jump on a highly centralized competitor. Company X was market testing a new soap in a small southern town. The company put the soap in grocery stores and interviewed people who either bought it or chose another brand. A company Y sales representative noticed the product and the interviews, reported the situation to the boss, and was told to observe soap sales and customer reactions. By being observant, the company Y representative learned as much about customer preferences as company X did. And customers did like company X's soap.

Company Y was highly decentralized. The soap product manager used the market test information and quickly introduced a soap just like company X's soap. That soap captured a large part of the national market while highly centralized company X's lower-level managers were still analyzing and consolidating data, before forwarding it up the chain of command to the policy makers at the senior-management level.

In the grocery business, the increased use of computerized inventory control tends to concentrate management attention on high-turnover items. Consequently, the stocking patterns of all grocery stores in a chain come to resemble each other over time, creating a market gap that can be exploited by shrewd independent operators aware of local conditions. A grocery chain closed one of its stores in a large city because of low volume and profits. The new independent owner recognized that the elderly customers living in the neighborhood simply wanted to buy smaller portions than the average buyer that the grocery chain had in mind. The independent grocer took local conditions into account, stocked items in smaller portions, and began to make money.

Degree of Coordination.   How much coordination is required? Activities that require coordination of many elements do not lend themselves to decentralization. For example, an automobile assembly line cannot delegate to each worker the decision about what time to come to work. The more interdependent the organization's tasks are, the more centralization is required. If tasks are independent and autonomous, decentralization may be appropriate.

Significance of Decision.   How significant is the decision to the organization? Critically important decisions should not be delegated. The nation's president would not let a junior-level State Department employee conduct official negotiations with a belligerent nation. On the other hand, not every decision is a life-or-death issue. Managers must learn to distinguish between levels of decision significance.

Time Available.   How much decision-making time is available to the manager? Some managers let subordinates make some decisions simply because the managers do not have time to make all decisions personally. These managers often find themselves second-guessing their subordinates, reviewing their decisions, and then taking piles of work home because they have not had time to do their own jobs.

In a misguided attempt to be helpful, many managers keep looking over the shoulders of subordinates, rather than coordinating the group's efforts, disseminating information, and offering training. Such managers usually feel overworked and underappreciated.

Actually, as we shall see in a moment, piling work on managers is one way to force them to delegate. The less time a manager has available, the more delegation must necessarily occur.

Effect on Morale.   What effect will decentralization have on morale and on-the-job initiative? People like to participate in making decisions that affect their jobs. Decentralization of decision making often improves morale and initiative.

The owner of a large New York City apartment complex noted poor morale and high turnover among his janitors. He had tried to make the janitorial job as simple and structured as possible. He made the decisions about products and processes and then laid them out in a basic janitorial manual. However, the janitors did not do a very good job, and tenants often complained.

One day, by chance, the owner asked the men to try out a new wax product and report back to him on their findings. To the owner's surprise, they tested the wax enthusiastically and thoroughly. He then turned the entire supply budget over to the janitors, which led to substantial and sustained improvements in morale and initiative.

Although decentralization and employee participation do not automatically improve morale, considerable research evidence suggests a connection between high decentralization and high morale.

How to Decentralize

Once top management has decided to decentralize, they need to encourage lower-level managers to cooperate in the decentralization program. Since many managers like to keep decision-making power once they get it, top management must use techniques ranging from gentle persuasion to high pressure.

Decentralization Techniques.   One way to encourage decentralization is to run a training program. Show managers how to decentralize and convince them of decentralization's benefits in terms of time saving, increased morale, and so on.

Along with the training program, top managers must serve as models for their subordinates. If top managers delegate responsibility, they begin a chain reaction. Managers at the next-lower level find that they simply do not have time to do their previously defined jobs plus their new responsibilities. They must delegate responsibility to their subordinates in order to perform their new roles effectively.

Another device is to increase managerial span of control, holding each manager responsible for the performance of more subordinates. When managers find that they do not have enough time to second-guess the larger number of subordinates, they will conclude that they must (1) inform subordinates of their job goals and responsibilities, (2) train and treat them well, and (3) give them enough decision-making freedom to get the job done.

Another technique is to inform all managers that they can obtain promotion only if subordinates are trained to replace them.

Achieving Balance.   Centralization and decentralization both have their advantages and disadvantages. The organizational task is to decentralize enough, but not too much. Organizational efforts at every level must be coordinated. Most coordinators are middle-level and lower-level managers, who cannot coordinate efficiently unless delegated sufficient authority. On the other hand, decentralization has its dangers and costs. If all managers have the authority to establish their own policies, then policies will not be uniform. Given too much authority, some managers tend to build small empires. Too much decentralization eventually leads to loss of organizational control.

Astute top managers decentralize decisions of many kinds but retain control by making and enforcing decisions about such matters as financing, budgeting, overall organizational goals, compensation plans, basic personnel policies, and capital expenditures.

LINE AND STAFF

As organizations grow beyond the point where a few people can do all things, they must differentiate their tasks and people into specialized parts. So far, this chapter has covered four means of differentiation: by organizational level, by department, by job specialty, and by decentralization and delegation. Another classical strategy for dividing up the organization's work is the differentiation between line and staff. *Line* positions are concerned with the organization's main operations. They are those positions in the organizational hierarchy that contribute directly to achieving the organization's primary goals. *Staff* positions are those that offer *advice* and *service* to the line. These general distinctions seem clear enough. However, the distinctions become blurred when we examine specific situations.

Look back at the Tipple Wine chart in Figure 12-4. Many management writers would maintain that the chart includes line relationships only. The chart represents those functions necessary for wine production, distribution, and financing. Some writers would consider financing as a staff function, since it is not directly involved in making and selling wine.

Staff functions are of two sorts. First, persons fulfilling high-level line functions may have personal staffs to assist them. For example, the president might have a staff of three, headed by an executive assistant to the president. In the street-corner gang described earlier, Danny was on Doc's personal staff. His job was to help expand Doc's time available for supervision by doing much of Doc's "leg work."

Another type of staff function is the specialized staff department that serves the entire organization. Tipple Wine might set up departments of personnel, research and development, training, and accounting to help any line department or position in need of advice or service.

Army Staff Principles and Procedures

The line–staff distinction can perhaps be seen most clearly in the military. A staff of officers is specifically assigned to assist every commander. The com-

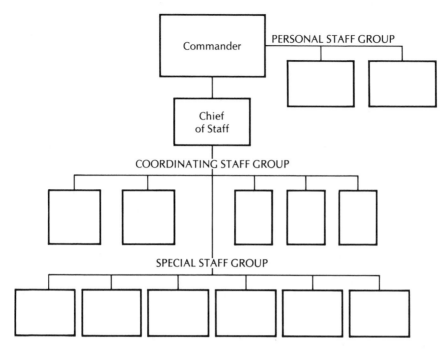

FIG 12-7 Military commander's staff structure.

mander commands the staff, but it is directly supervised by a chief of staff or executive officer.

Staff Functions. The staff has five functions: providing information, making estimates, making recommendations, preparing plans and orders, and supervising the execution of plans and orders. All staff actions are designed to help the command carry out its mission and to help the commander fulfill his responsibilities.

Staff Structure. The staff may include three different groups: coordinating, special, and personal. Each *coordinating* staff officer is concerned with one of these five fields: personnel, intelligence, operations, logistics, and civil–military operations. *Special* staff officers deal with technical and administrative matters. *Personal* staff officers assist the commander in personal matters and report directly to him, rather than to the chief of staff. Figure 12-7 shows a typical military staff structure. All of the 14 officers in the organization chart have one primary function: to help the commander to do a better job as commander. George Tipple, president of the Tipple Wine Company, might have a similarly organized staff of 14 people to help him to do a better job as company president.
The successful experience of the military with staff structures has led many other organizations to apply staff principles to their own situations.

267

Functional Authority

Staff members are sometimes delegated *functional authority* over their specific areas of expertise. The line manager gives up some control over an area and assigns it to another person or department. For example, the executive vice-president might give a staff purchasing expert control over the purchasing department. The purchasing expert will then be held accountable for the purchasing department's performance. The executive vice-president retains ultimate responsibility for task performance in that department but may lack expertise, ability, time, or interest to supervise purchasing directly.

Three types of functional authority may be assigned: advisory, concurrent, and full.

Advisory. A staff member with advisory authority supplies advice to any line department requiring it. For example, the public relations department might have a speech writing staff to give members of other departments advice on public appearances.

Concurrent. Concurrent authority means that the line manager and a staff member of another department must both approve certain line activities. For example, an equal opportunity compliance officer in the legal department may have to countersign all hiring decisions. The staff with concurrent authority does not control the line. It serves as a check on the line officer's actions to be sure that the staff's expertise has played a part in the decision.

Full Functional Authority. Staff members with full functional authority can make decisions in their areas of expertise, rather than merely offering recommendations. For example, Tipple Wine Company's market research department is a staff department, because it has nothing directly to do with producing, distributing, or financing wine. That department may have formal authority to carry out, interpret, and publish any market research project it deems useful. The Tipple safety officer has full authority to shut down production whenever unsafe conditions exist. In a specific area of expertise, the staff member with full functional authority can make all the decisions.

Line–Staff Problems

Textbooks can provide clear-cut illustrations of how line personnel and staff personnel should be used. In practice, this differentiation of tasks can create problems. Line workers are often hostile to staff workers, feeling that they are interfering meddlers. Staff workers often have less job satisfaction because they feel out of the organization's mainstream and less important. By definition, they depend on somebody else's acceptance of them and their work.

Assistant-to.   Managers want to increase their capacity for directing and controlling tasks and people. Therefore, many managers have created a staff position called an "assistant-to" themselves, as in "assistant to the executive vice-president." The assistant-to provides a second set of eyes, ears, and legs, serving as helper and "go-for." The assistant-to has no formal organizational power, is not expected to make decisions, and is not supposed to affect the behavior of anybody but the boss. The assistant-to-'s main function is to observe, collect, and disseminate information to and from the boss. The manager's capacity to process information is expanded by having an effective assistant-to.

The assistant-to staff function seems harmless enough, but in reality most organization members see the assistant-to as the "spy" or "enforcer" of the boss. In fact, many assistants do acquire much more authority than their formal job descriptions suggest that they should have. As an information sender–receiver, the assistant-to observes and interacts with many organization members. The manager's power frequently becomes associated with the subordinate assistant. As was shown in an earlier chapter, authority is attributed by the receiver of a communication to the sender. An order is not an order until it is obeyed. If the organization's members attribute authority to the assistant-to, that person begins to assume authority and make decisions. Rather than merely supplying the information that will help the boss to make better decisions, assistants begin to make decisions themselves. If a boss becomes aware of the situation and says nothing, then decision making has been informally delegated.

Recognizing that the assistant-to role can get out of hand, many organizations have tried to eliminate it. One way is to limit each manager's tasks so that areas of responsibility and accountability can be specifically designated and recognized throughout the organization, rather than being informally exercised by an assistant-to. Another way is to create a new, lower level of management for the assistants-to, with areas of specific responsibility and accountability that are recognized throughout the organization.

Nixon's Assistants-to.   To cope with the enormity of the job, President Nixon created two assistant-to positions and gave them to John Ehrlichman and Robert Haldeman. These men acquired tremendous authority from their ready access to the president and their power to filter information. If it was true that the Nixon administration was "out of touch with reality" and that persons needing access to the president could not gain it, the powerful assistants-to may have been one reason.

A related example is provided by the reclusive Howard Hughes. He so isolated himself and gave so much power to assistants that rumors of his death persisted long before he actually died.

Production-Oriented Firms.   Line–staff conflict is more pronounced in stable, traditional, production-oriented industries. In these industries, especially those with a tradition of formal line–staff distinctions like the steel and automobile industries, line–staff conflict is more likely than in the newer service-oriented industries.

Tipple Wine Company is production-oriented. Within that company, tasks can be easily classified into line operations (those responsible for achieving the organization's goal: producing wine for profit) and staff activities. Production workers are line personnel, and cafeteria workers, housekeepers, and maintenance personnel are staff workers.

Service-Oriented Firms.   A Holiday Inn (a service organization) would have far greater difficulty in separating line from staff. The Holiday Inn "product" is a contented customer, and virtually all the organization's activities contribute directly to customer contentment.

Blurred Distinctions.   The Holiday Inn situation illustrates the fact that the historical conflict between line and staff will become less and less important in the future. Organizations must recognize the interdepartmental, interrelated nature of the activities necessary for achieving organizational goals. Obviously, no job exists in the organizational structure unless it contributes something toward achieving the organization's ends. As dynamic, social, system-wide relationships are increasingly recognized, the line–staff distinction must become increasingly blurred.

SUMMARY

This chapter covered the organizing principle of *differentiation*. Two differentiation principles were illustrated in the progress of the Tipple Wine Company: organizational levels and departmentalization. The chapter then presented the advantages and disadvantages of another differentiation principle: specialization of labor.

Delegation and decentralization represent a specialization of authority. Delegation was seen to have beneficial effects on organizational human relations and information flow. The chapter described decentralization at General Motors and General Electric, and then discussed how to achieve a proper balance between centralization and decentralization.

The chapter's last major section explained the line–staff distinction.

The next chapter will show how organizations integrate the different units into which tasks have been differentiated.

DISCUSSION QUESTIONS

1. Why are the methods discussed in this chapter called "differentiating" methods?
2. Why do people organize anyway?

3. Why does an organization need to consider both differentiating and integrating strategies?
4. What does it mean to departmentalize?
5. When does decentralization work best? Why?
6. What is specialization of labor? What are its advantages?
7. What disadvantages are associated with specialization of labor? How might they be overcome?
8. Do you think the assistant-to role is a good idea?
9. How do you tell the difference between line and staff in the Ajax Ball Bearing Company? In the Holiday Inn?
10. What is functional authority? How does it help to solve the line–staff problem?

FIDELITY INSURORS

Fidelity Insurors is one of the largest insurance companies in the world. Sybil Rose, underwriting manager of the southern regional office, has a problem. The executives and the sales force want the applications for new insurance to be processed by the underwriting department much more quickly. Rose finally concludes that the typing section is a bottleneck in the process.

The section has 11 typists. Most of them are recent high school graduates with no prior work experience and only minimal typing skills. The company starts them at a level 1 salary of $120 a week. One senior typist receives a level 2 salary of $145 a week.

The section has an average daily backlog of about 600 cases, and most cases sit in the area for from 3 to 8 days before being typed. An experienced typist can handle 70 or 80 cases a day, but because of the inexperienced staff, output in the typing section averages 50 cases a day. The typists work mandatory overtime 2 nights a week and every other Saturday.

Not only is inadequate output a problem. Quality is also below Sybil Rose's standards. Many cases must be retyped, and much correspondence goes out untidy or even unintelligible.

The typists know that their performance is not good, and their morale is very low. Their supervisor argues that the root of the problem is inexperience and says that everything will improve "in time."

Sybil Rose has tried various solutions designed to increase the volume handled, without success:

1. Overtime has not improved matters. In fact, Rose realizes that mandatory overtime has decreased morale and increased turnover.
2. Temporary help from other departments has not helped. Temporary people are not sufficiently familiar with forms, procedures, and terminology.

Rose recently interviewed a group of typists and gathered these comments:

1. We are ranked at level 1, the lowest in the company. Since we have a marketable skill, we feel that we should make more than unskilled employees (mail openers and messengers) make. Yet they are also at level 1.
2. Although we type the work of the underwriters, we are physically and psychologically isolated from them. Our only contact with them is negative—when they point out our errors. They do not know us individually and have no sympathy with our problems.
3. We do not get enough instruction and training. We have no idea how our work relates to the work of other sections. We are part of the underwriting division, but we do not even know what "underwriting" is.
4. Our work is monotonous. Most of what we do is to fill in blanks and type names and addresses on preprinted forms.
5. We have little opportunity for advancement. All we can hope for is advancement to level 2.
6. We are constantly pressured and criticized. We are told that because of the high work volume, nobody has time to train us. Because we do not have enough training, we make errors and are criticized. We are always rushed, so we make more errors. If we slow down to improve quality, the work piles up and we are criticized for that.

Sybil Rose considered what she might do to straighten out the situation in the typing section.

THE HAPPY FEET SHOE COMPANY

The Happy Feet Shoe Company is a large producer of such shoe accessories as shoe polish, boot cream, suede spray, and shoe dye. The largest of the company's ten plants is located in Brunswick, Georgia. That plant employs 2500 people. The company's headquarters is in Charleston, South Carolina.

The Brunswick plant has grown steadily. This growth has brought problems. It seems that every time the formal organization structure is defined and charted, new changes occur that necessitate a reexamination of the relationship between the plant manager and the department heads reporting directly to him.

When the Brunswick plant opened in 1965, the plant manager had one assistant (who acted primarily as a staff person) and 12 department heads. Figure 12-8 depicts this situation.

In 1975 staff activities were added, and the number of departments was increased to 16. The assistant plant manager gradually became an operating person, to whom six department heads reported directly. The others continued reporting to the plant manager. Figure 12-9 depicts these new relationships.

The company's continued growth put increasing pressure on the plant manager, since his office was a channel through which flowed a growing number of communications from Charleston to the different departments. The 1975 additions of staff helped to relieve some pressure, but the plant manager still had to be kept informed about home office–plant dealings. As a result of the position's pressures and responsibilities, the plant has had eight managers in the past ten years. Although

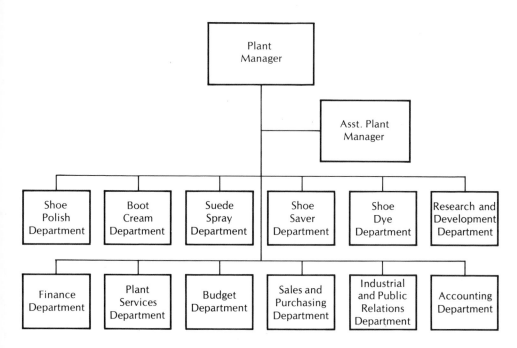

FIG 12-8 Happy Feet organization chart: 1965.

the Brunswick plant remains very profitable, the high turnover of plant managers has undoubtedly had a negative effect on profitability and management morale.

Fred Johnson took over as plant manager 3 months ago. He consolidated accounting and finance under one supervisor and combined industrial relations with plant services. These changes helped a little, but they did not decrease the number of decisions that Johnson must make.

Johnson struggled to deal with ever-increasing communications. His problems seemed to be compounding. To a lesser extent, the department heads have recently begun feeling the same pressures, so several have quit. Now not only is Johnson faced with a pyramid of decisions and projects that need coordinating; he also has some inexperienced subordinates. Johnson cannot seem to keep in touch with what is going on.

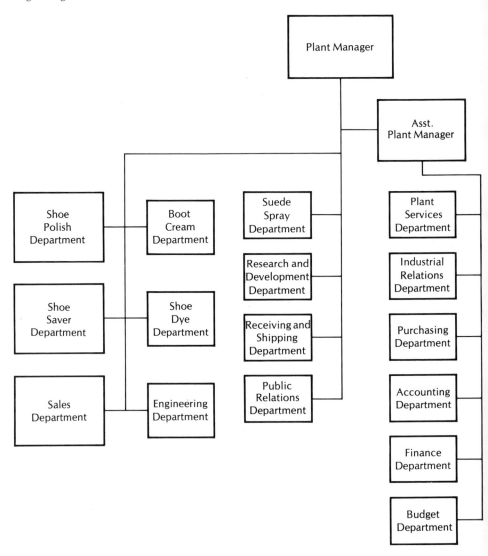

FIG 12-9   Happy Feet organization chart: 1975.

13

===

organizing: integration

The previous chapter presented several strategies for dividing the organization's work into pieces. This chapter describes procedures for integrating the work—bringing the pieces back together again. Five approaches will be covered: coordination by hierarchy, coordination by committees, span of control, project management, and linking-pin coordination. These five approaches are not mutually exclusive. An organization may use one, several, or all five of them. Then the contingency approach to organizational design will be presented. Finally, the chapter describes the organizational pattern known as bureaucracy.

COORDINATION BY HIERARCHY

Small organizations depend almost entirely on the force of personality to keep members heading toward the organization's goals. In a production organization of fewer than 50 people or so, using relatively simple technology at a single location, one person can keep track of all the people and their tasks. As the organization grows, or the production process becomes more complex, or the industrial rate of change increases, the need to keep the organization's components unified and coordinated becomes critical—and more difficult. The previous chapter's Tipple Wine Company, responding to the dynamics of growth and change, specialized the firm's efforts to obtain maximum efficiency. However, the other side of the coin is to coordinate those specialized activities so they all keep heading toward the organizational goal.

Coordination by hierarchy is the first obvious solution to this problem. The classical school of administrative theory maintained that organizational efforts could best be coordinated by means of a rigidly enforced chain of command. The owner–entrepreneur at the top of the hierarchy hired people, told them what to do and how to do it, and disciplined those who did not comply.

The Supervisor of Supervisors

As an organization grows so large that the owner–entrepreneur cannot directly supervise those doing actual production work, the owner–entrepreneur hires supervisors and becomes a supervisor of supervisors. The owner–entrepreneur retains the formal authority and power but delegates direct supervision to others. These people become responsible for observing and directing the work of production employees, perhaps making minor personnel decisions like assigning break times. If an unplanned event occurs in the workplace, the supervisor evaluates it and either makes a decision or passes the matter upward to the owner–entrepreneur.

In other words, the owners or managers give up some power to subordinates by defining for them the limits of their authority and responsibility, training them to be supervisors, and holding them accountable for performance. The boss can choose to delegate much discretionary power to subordinates or very little power.

Delegation: A Grim Necessity?

In classical management theory, delegation was a grim necessity rather than a desirable end in itself. The owner wanting to maintain tight control should give up as little decision-making power as possible. After all, the competitive market place was lying in wait to punish the owner for bad decisions and to reward the owner for good ones. The owner puts up the money and takes the risks, so the owner should run the show, according to this theory. Delegation is undesirable because it places decision-making power with people whose capital is not on the line and whose information is not as complete as the owner's.

As family-run organizations expanded, this argument lost considerable clout. No one person could single-handedly manage a large firm, making all the decisions and effecting all the coordination. Managers of growth organizations came to see that, far from being a grim necessity, delegation was a natural outgrowth of organizational dynamics. Risky as it was to the classicist, delegation became more prevalent as organizations grew. Managers found that without delegation, they got so bogged down in detail that they could not function.

COORDINATION BY COMMITTEES

Committees are sometimes accused of causing more problems than they solve. Nevertheless, they are used in most organizations as a means for coordinating and integrating the group's activities. An early advocate of coordination by committee was Alfred P. Sloan. While reviewing his career at General Motors, he had this to say about committees:

I feel that a proper balance can and must necessarily be established in the course of time between the activities of any particular operation and that of all our operations together and as I see the picture at the moment no better way or even as good a way has yet been advanced as to ask those members of each organization who have the same functional relationship to get together and decide for themselves what should be done where coordination is necessary, giving such a group the power to deal with the problem where it is felt that the power can be constructively applied. I believe that such a plan properly developed gives the necessary balance between each operation and the corporation itself and will result in all the advantages of coordinated action where such action is of benefit in a broader way without in any sense limiting the initiative or independence of action of any component part of the group.

Assuming that this is correct in principle, I might set forth specifically what the functions in the case of the General Technical Committee would be, although this discussion would, I think, apply equally well to other committees dealing with all functions common to all manufacturing enterprises.

1. The committee would deal in problems which would be of interest to all divisions and would in dealing with such matters largely formulate the general engineering policies of the corporation.

2. The committee would assume the functions of the already constituted patent committee which would be discontinued and in assuming these functions would have the authority to deal with patent matters, already vested in the patent committee.

3. The committee would not, as to principle, deal with the specific problems of any individual operation. Each function of that operation would be under the absolute control of the general manager of that division.[1]

Committees can be temporary (*ad hoc* or *special*) or permanent (*standing*), large or small, policy making or investigative, elective or appointive. They are used throughout religious, educational, and social service organizations, as well as in business and industrial firms.

Consider their typical uses in a corporation. The stockholders elect a committee to represent them, called the board of directors. The board may be further divided into an executive committee, a compensation and benefits committee, a finance committee, and so on. The board appoints a president, who is advised by a variety of committees: a management committee, a policy committee, a grievance committee, and numerous other standing committees, special committees, and task forces. Below the presidential level, committees of many sorts engage in a wide variety of coordination activities.

Advantages of Committees

Communication Benefits.   Committees are used for many good reasons. Their major advantage is their communication benefits. Many meetings are held primarily to communicate and discuss information. Although a memorandum might transmit the information as well, the committee meeting gives

[1]Alfred P. Sloan, Jr., *My Years with General Motors* (Garden City, N.Y.: Doubleday & Company, Inc., 1972), pp. 121–122.

everyone concerned with the project or problem a chance to explore, inquire, elaborate, and clarify the information.

More Knowledge Available.   Committees are often used for defining problems, listing alternative solutions, and specifying the advantages and disadvantages of alternatives. This use of committees reflects the old idea that two heads are better than one. The group brings to the problem more experience, ideas, facts, expertise, and training than any one member can offer. If a problem is at all complex, a committee's vastly greater information, experience, and judgment may be required for its solution. Surprisingly enough, if committee members are properly selected, they may identify and resolve problems faster than one person can.

Fair Representation.   A third reason for using committees is to be sure that all persons interested in an issue or a decision are fairly represented. For example, if a proposed policy is going to affect seven departments, a policy review committee including members from those departments will ensure that all affected points of view are considered.

Coordination.   Committees can often supply the coordination required for planning and carrying out programs. The complexity of modern organizations is a real problem to managers responsible for integrating activities and plans. A committee may help the manager to coordinate numerous plans, specialists, expenditures, and activities.

Participation.   Committees encourage people affected by decisions to participate in making them. We have already described participation's many benefits. People participating on a committee are involved in the final outcome and feel committed to the chosen course of action.

Disadvantages of Committees

Committees are not without their disadvantages. However, if the committee chairperson and members are familiar with the techniques of small group discussion, these disadvantages can often be overcome. Committees are said to have five major disadvantages: (1) high cost, (2) mediocre decisions, (3) unresolved conflict, (4) lack of follow-up, and (5) lack of accountability.

Cost.   The most frequently cited disadvantage of committees is their high cost in time and money. Bringing the committee's members together is expensive. The cost of a one-hour meeting is not merely the total salaries of the members for one hour but also includes the cost of their *not* doing other things with that hour.

In addition, committees are formed and meetings are called to handle topics that require a sharing of different viewpoints. Much time will be required to hear all these viewpoints. Discussing an issue in an open forum takes longer than for each person to read a concise, well-constructed position paper. Furthermore, variations in comprehension ability, background, preparation, and communication skills make it unlikely that committee meetings will ever be as *efficient* a communication device as the written word.

Cost is important when forming the committee and assigning tasks to members. Keeping costs down, by selecting the right members and assigning appropriate tasks, is usually the committee chairperson's responsibility.

Mediocre Decisions. A second major criticism of committees is that, rather than finding the best decision, they tend to compromise—to reach a decision that is no one's best choice but that everyone can live with. Since committees are typically designed to represent various interests, concerns, and personal values, coming to a decision that every member favors equally is difficult. The difficulty is compounded if the problem is vague or poorly defined in the first place or if hard data are not available, making it necessary to rely on value judgments.

The classic disagreement between the sales manager and the finance manager illustrates this problem. If credit is extended to more customers, the sales manager is happy because sales will rise, and the finance manager is unhappy because the firm's financial stability may be endangered. If credit is restricted, the sales manager is unhappy and the finance manager is pleased. Now picture a committee discussing this problem. Both managers sit on the committee. The group may decide on a compromise that does not best serve organizational goals. Even worse, the committee may decide in favor of the manager who is the louder, talks more smoothly, or has more political clout.

Group decision making may be better than the decision making of the average group member. It may not be better than the decision making of the group's best decision maker. In fact, if the group's decision-making performance is superior, that performance may result from the efforts and influence of one superior decision maker.

Poor Conflict Resolution. Sometimes, a committee cannot resolve an issue. Hung juries are not uncommon, because people will draw different conclusions from the same set of facts and opinions. Conflict on a committee is natural and desirable. The chairperson must see to it that the horsetrading characteristic of committee deliberation leads to sound, effective consensus—rather than to a bad compromise or to interminable bickering.

Lack of Follow-up. Follow-up and control procedures are usually accomplished not by the committee but by individual managers at the point of implementation. Of course, a decision-making group can keep watch over decision implementation, and perhaps it should. Still, the direct responsibility to ensure an outcome that will meet the original objective lies with the individual manager, who may or may not follow up effectively.

Lack of Accountability. The final major disadvantage of committees is that they can divide up the responsibility for a decision. All too often, managers pass the buck on politically sensitive issues to a committee. The problem with this practice is not so much that the committee may make a bad decision but that, if the decision *is* a bad one, no one person can be held accountable for it.

We spoke earlier about the *risky shift*—the tendency for groups to make riskier decisions than individuals make. A risky decision is more likely if no individual is held accountable for results. Therefore, many organizations allow committees to obtain information, share opinions, and discuss options—but not to make decisions.

Advantages Versus Disadvantages. If committees have these major disadvantages, why are they used? The answer is that they have proved their worth in terms of making information available, allowing full consideration of alternatives, and giving organization members an opportunity to participate. By being involved in issues that directly concern them and their jobs, participants in committee discussions gain real satisfaction. Most organizations believe that these and other advantages outweigh the committee's disadvantages.

Structuring the Committee

Here are some suggestions for structuring the committee, to gain that form's advantages and avoid its disadvantages.

Clear Task Definition. A committee's first rule is to *know its task*. If the committee's charge is to generate alternatives, the committee should not try to redefine the problem or evaluate alternatives, and a good chairperson will insist that the committee sticks to its assignment.

Selecting Members. The successful committee is made up of the right number and type of members. The committee's *size* will influence its effectiveness. Each additional member contributes some information and insight, but each additional member means one more idle person while another person speaks. If every affected group is represented, the committee may be too large. Yet not representing all affected groups may leave the committee's decision open to criticism.

The most common guidelines for committee size are (1) how many people can reasonably interact, (2) which groups must be represented, and (3) who has important expertise to offer the group. Estimates of appropriate committee size made by small group researchers often range from 5 to 15, with groups near 5 tending to be more effective than groups near 15.

The matter of "representation" is often stressed too much. If the members of a small committee are objective and well prepared, they will arrive at a better decision than would a large committee consisting of persons determined to represent their special interests.

Importance of the Chairperson.   The most important determinant of a committee's effectiveness is its chairperson. The chair must know and clearly express the committee's goal, scope, and authority. The chair must ensure that committee disagreement is constructive, not destructive.

In hopes of encouraging everyone to talk, the chairperson may be tempted to let the discussion wander. Part of the chairperson's art lies in knowing when this wandering aloud stops being productive and starts wasting time. Most committee members do not like to waste time or have their time wasted. The more productive they are, the more they resent wasting time. Since productive people are important to a productive group, the chairperson must maintain the enthusiasm of the group's productive members by running the committee efficiently.

Discussion leaders must have many skills. They must remember what has already been said in order to provide helpful summaries and reviews. They must pay attention to what is being said at the moment. They must be aware of nonverbal communication signals by persons other than the present speaker. They must perceive where the committee is going and keep an eye on the clock. They must keep the gates of communication open, give everyone an equal chance to participate, and maintain impartiality by accepting rather than judging the opinions expressed. Persons are usually appointed committee chairpersons because they have higher rank or status than other committee members do. Therefore, to gain the advantages that can come out of open discussion, they must do everything possible to see that their higher status does not inhibit the free flow of ideas.

Some committee leaders seem to feel that their main task is to set the meeting time and place. Actually, the leadership position is crucial to group success. Enormous skill and effort are required to ensure that each committee member's time and energy are used productively.

SPAN OF CONTROL

The third way of integrating the organization's tasks, energies, and efforts is through span of control, a term referring to the number of people supervised by one manager. However, the issue of concern is not the absolute number of persons reflected on the organization chart as reporting to a manager, but the number that a manager can supervise *effectively*. Span of control can be determined merely by counting people. *Effective* span of control is a more complex issue.

Early Approaches

The Classical School.   The classical school of organizational theory had the most direct approach for deciding how wide a span of people should be controlled by one manager. Existing successful organizations were examined, the numbers of subordinates supervised by managers were counted, and the results were taken to be ideal spans of control. One prominent writer stated that the ideal span of control at higher organizational levels was four and the range at lower levels was eight to twelve. This drive to find a specific number tied in well with the "principles" approach to management. Derive and apply the right principles and numbers, and everything will fall into place.

The difficulty with this approach is that successful organizations vary greatly in their spans of control. Although the mean number at higher levels might be four, spans of control in successful organizations might range from two to twenty.

The Graicunas Formula.   In 1933, V. A. Graicunas showed mathematically how adding subordinates to a manager's span of control quickly complicates the manager's ability to maintain control. Consider a manager with two subordinates. According to Graicunas, that manager is involved in six supervisory relationships. First and obviously, the manager supervises subordinate A and also supervises subordinate B. The manager may also supervise AB as a pair and may supervise the relationship between A and B as well. Here are the relationships. The manager may:

Supervise A
Supervise B
Supervise B with A in attendance
Supervise A with B in attendance
Supervise B when B consults with A
Supervise A when A consults with B

Although one may argue that some of these relationships are more similar than different, Graicunas maintained that each relationship has different psychological shadings.

Graicunas developed a formula to show how number of subordinates and number of relationships match up. The results of the formula appear in Table 13-1.

Of course, as Graicunas acknowledged, the formula and table do not take the *quality* of subordinates into account. Managers with four independent, intelligent subordinates formally reporting to them (44 relationships) may not spend as much time in supervision as managers with three barely competent subordinates (18 relationships), each performing a function vital to organizational success.

TABLE 13-1   Results of Graicunas Formula

Number of Manager's Subordinates	Number of Relationships Manager Must Supervise
1	1
2	6
3	18
4	44
5	100
6	222
7	490
8	1,080
9	2,376
10	5,210
11	11,374
12	24,708
18	2,359,602

The Graicunas results and the classical attempts to find an ideal number are interesting but not very instructive. The variation in organizational circumstances makes it unrealistic to expect that the effective span of control will be the same for a surgery team, a telephone switchboard group, a prison farm, and U.S. Steel's long-range planning committee. What might be more helpful is an identification of the variables upon which an ideal span depends.

The Contingency Approach

Frustration at finding a single best span of control has resulted in the contingency approach to the problem. The contingency approach states that the right answer to any organizational design problem depends on the important factors bearing on *that specific problem,* not on some general theory or principle. What are the important factors upon which appropriate span of control depends? Six factors are of obvious importance, with a mixture of other factors having some importance.

Subordinates.   The most important factor governing effective span of control is the ability and characteristics of subordinates. If subordinates are trained, competent, and job involved, a manager can effectively supervise more of them than if subordinates are untrained, incompetent, and uninterested. Consider the job of managing highly trained, dedicated research scientists. Their manager might casually oversee their activities, but the main managerial task is not to supervise the scientists; it is to connect them with the organizational resources they need to do their jobs. Rather than "manage," the group's manager should coordinate and facilitiate, seeking organizational solutions to the group's problems. If the group's work is largely self-paced

283

and independent, the manager may supervise several dozen subordinates effectively and comfortably.

On the other hand, consider a manager responsible for teaching entry-level employees a new and complex task. The employees have little knowledge and limited ability, so the manager must spend much instruction and coordination time with them. To do the job properly, the manager must have a small span of control.

Managerial Ability.   The manager's ability is a second important determinant of the optimum supervisory span. If managers have inadequate leadership skills and job knowledge, faulty understanding of organizational resource location and availability, or an inability to communicate with superiors and subordinates, they will have difficulty in managing themselves, much less anyone else. A good personnel department will probably keep most such unqualified people out of managerial positions.

Different from lack of managerial ability is a managerial style that disapproves of authority delegation. Managers who train their subordinates and then let them exercise their skills can manage many subordinates. Managers who insist on keeping the authority, looking over each subordinate's shoulder, and checking all the work before it goes out only have time to supervise a few subordinates effectively.

Job Complexity.   Another important factor in determining the optimum span of control is the complexity of the jobs being supervised. Supervising a professional football team is more difficult than supervising switchboard operators or ditch diggers. From the standpoint of task complexity, the potential for coordination problems is much greater with the football team than with the operators or diggers. When more things can go wrong, the manager is less able to coordinate a large number of people. More will be said later in the chapter concerning technological complexity and the contingency approach.

Rate of Change.   The greater the rate of change in a job, the narrower must be the management span for the supervisor of that job. This statement is true because a rapid rate of change increases the demands on the supervisor as teacher.

The manager is always doing some teaching in the ongoing process of developing subordinates. The manager of a group experiencing rapid job change must spend much time keeping up with change and teaching subordinates new tasks. These activities chop away at the time available for overseeing and coordinating, thereby reducing the manager's effective span of control. Because of relatively constant technology, a salt mine supervisor can supervise more workers than a manager in a semiconductor manufacturing plant can.

Interdependence of Units.   Supervisors coordinating the activities of their units with the activities of other units cannot effectively control many subordinates. The interdependence of an assembly-line unit is determined by the sequence of the work. Therefore, the supervisor of any given unit on the line can support, coordinate, and direct that unit's activities almost exclusively. That situation makes supervising a fairly large number of workers possible.

In contrast, consider training director Shirley Jones, trying to secure the support of several departments for a training program she wants to offer next month. Jones must spend time away from her own department. Her absence reduces her time available for supervising her own people and, therefore, her effective span of control.

Measurable Results.   Another important influence on span of control— perhaps more because it reflects the nature of the task rather than being a unique factor in itself—is the degree to which job results can be measured. If the output of subordinates can be measured precisely, the supervisor will have less need to observe *how* subordinates reach their goals.

If you tell your sales force that they must sell 30 elephants by the end of the month, you probably turn them loose to sell the elephants in any way they can. You then spend your time in familiarizing new sales people with the product, reviewing corporate goals, methods, and policies with the present sales force, and counting order tickets at the end of the month. If the tickets total 30, you need not change your style. On the other hand, to supervise a group of reference librarians, a head reference librarian would have to watch them locate materials, listen to them advise library patrons, and so on. In other words, the supervision focus would be on observing the *process* rather than the *output*, because the reference librarian's output is so intangible.

The effect on span of control is obvious. The less measurable the results, the narrower must be the span of control.

Other Factors.   Top management must also consider various other factors when determining the optimum span of control. First, geographical distance separating subordinates will influence the number of subordinates that a manager can direct effectively. Activities that are spread out are harder to coordinate than activities that are bunched together.

The repetitiveness of the decisions that subordinates make also affects span of control. If the same decisions must be made repeatedly, the manager can structure programs, policies, and standing operating procedures for subordinates to use in solving recurring problems. If problems are more varied, subordinates will have to refer more decisions upward to the manager.

Finally, the similarity of tasks performed by different subordinates affects span of control. If each subordinate is doing a different task, the manager's coordination problems may be great and span of control must therefore be narrow.

TABLE 13-2 Lockheed Study: Factors Influencing Span of Control, Level of Difficulty, and Factor Weight

Factor Influencing Span of Control	Level of Difficulty Plus Factor Weight				
Similarity of functions	Identical 1	Almost alike 2	Similar 3	Different 4	Totally different 5
Geographical nearness	All together 1	All in one building 2	Separate buildings, one plant location 3	Separate locations, one geographical area 4	Different geographical areas 5
Complexity of functions	Simple and repetitive 2	Routine 4	Slightly complex 6	Complex 8	Very complex 10
Direction and control	Minimum supervision and training 3	Limited supervision 6	Moderate periodic supervision 9	Frequent continuing supervision 12	Constant close supervision 15
Coordination	Minimum relation with others 2	Some relation with others 4	Moderate relationships, easily controlled 6	Considerable close relationships 8	Extensive relationships 10
Planning	Minimum scope and complexity 2	Limited scope and complexity 4	Moderate scope and complexity 6	Much scope and complexity 8	Very large scope and complexity 10

Under the contingency approach, the manager would examine those factors having a bearing on appropriate span of control and would decide that a certain span was appropriate in this particular situation. More will be said about contingency theory near the end of this chapter.

The Lockheed Study

The optimum span of control depends on several variables. How do these variables influence the span—from industry to industry, organization to organization, and department to department? During the middle 1960s, Lockheed Missiles and Space Company attempted to answer some of these questions.

Lockheed identified six important influences on span of control: similarity of functions, geographical nearness, complexity of functions, direction and control (how much supervision and training do subordinates need?), coordination, and planning. The company then divided each influence up into five levels of difficulty and assigned weights to each level of difficulty to reflect the relative importance of each influence. Table 13-2 summarizes these preparations. After each position was analyzed in terms of the table, the results were corrected to take into account how much assistance each manager had.

Comparison with Standard.   Results were then compared with a standard. This standard, developed by observing the spans of control in well-managed units, appears in Table 13-3. A manager supervising subordinates whose characteristics are, let us say, those described in column 2 of Table 13-2 would receive a span factor weighting of 22 (arrived at by adding up the weights in that column). According to Table 13-3, that manager should be able to supervise from 8 to 11 people effectively.

As a result of this study, Lockheed increased its average span of control and eliminated one level of management.

TABLE 13-3   Lockheed Study: Factor Weighting Totals and Suggested Span of Control

Total of Factor Weightings	Suggested Span of Control
40–42	4–5
37–39	4–6
34–36	4–7
31–33	5–8
28–30	6–9
25–27	7–10
22–24	8–11

MATRIX AND PROJECT MANAGEMENT

The classical school of organization provided many useful structural devices to handle the surge in size of the average business organization near the turn of the century. The human relations school added advice for dealing with the more recent surge in human expectations. Nevertheless, classical or conventional schemes for integrating human and material resources are inadequate at times. Managers need supplemental strategies to deal with multinational, multiproduct, multiform organizations in the present dynamic environment.

Two such strategies are *project–matrix management* and *linking-pin theory*. Project–matrix management helps organizations to cope with rapidly changing product or technological situations. Linking-pin theory is designed to avoid communication breakdowns. Both strategies are meant to enhance the organization's integration efforts.

Matrix Management

Matrix management and project management are so similar that the terms are often used interchangeably. Matrix organization forms are used for temporary organizational projects requiring the short-term services of specialists who, for the duration of the projects, report to more than one boss. For example, an engineer might be working on three different projects under three different project directors, as well as reporting to the head of the engineering department. This situation violates the unity-of-command principle and is upsetting to classical theorists who cannot imagine keeping four bosses happy.

Matrix management gets its name because the chart for that organization form looks like a grid or matrix. Figure 13-1 shows a typical arrangement. The design, electrical, chemical and civil engineers working on projects A, B, and C all report to their respective project directors, as well as to their chief engineers.

Matrix management can work only if the authority and responsibility of all managers are clearly defined. Consider ABC Company project X. Project manager Brown, chief design engineer Jones, and design engineer Smith must work together and must agree on their authority relationships. Manager Brown has authority for the overall design and execution of the project. If the project is being undertaken for a customer, manager Brown deals with the customer. Manager Brown also handles the project budget (using it to "buy" people from the departments) and works with chief Jones to coordinate engineer Smith's time on the project and on other work. If manager Brown and chief Jones disagree about when and how much engineer Smith should work on project X, the chief engineer settles the matter.

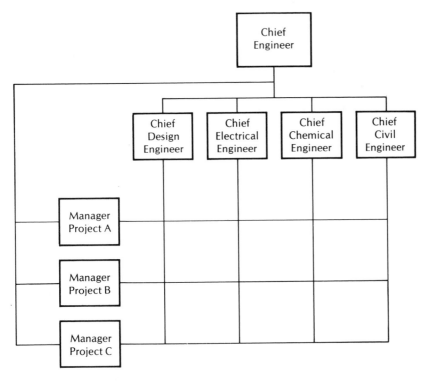

FIG 13-1 Typical matrix organization.

Project Management

Matrix organizations are temporary structures, usually built to solve specific problems. Project management is used when the organization needs a longer-run structuring of people. A project team is formed by borrowing employees from their regular work units and assigning them temporarily to the project manager's authority. The project manager must use these employees to complete the project on schedule and within cost and performance standards.

Jetcraft Company

As is true of many modern management concepts, project management was a logical solution to a problem faced by aerospace organizations. To illustrate, consider an imaginary manufacturer of long-range passenger jet planes: Jetcraft Company. Jetcraft's present structure, straightforward and functional, is shown in Figure 13-2.

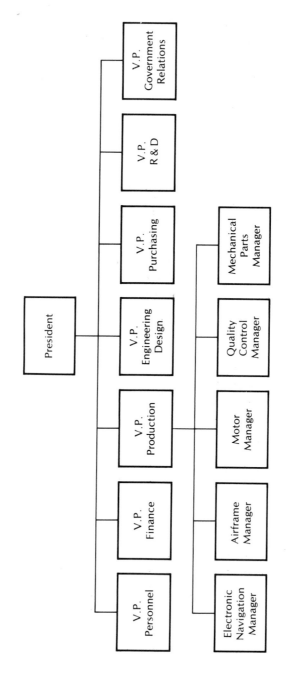

FIG 13-2 Jetcraft Company organization chart.

Creating a Temporary Organization.   Companies producing salt and snuff do not have to deal with obsolescence. In the aerospace industry, rapidly advancing technology inevitably forces almost every product into obsolescence. Jetcraft's management realizes that the firm's continued existence depends on its ability to keep securing contracts for new products to replace expiring contracts for obsolete products. To get a contract, Jetcraft must submit the low bid.

Let us suppose that Florida Airways wants a new and different passenger plane. Rather than form a new division to produce an aircraft that may not yet be more than a drawing on a piece of paper, and for which a competitor may win the bid anyway, Jetcraft creates a temporary organization. People are borrowed from the company's functional areas long enough to prepare a bid.

The Project Manager.   The project manager asks for the necessary people: (1) a personnel specialist, to estimate whether the current work force has the necessary skills, what it would cost to train new people, and so forth; (2) a research and development specialist, to estimate the time, money, and people required to develop the project; (3) an engineer, to match equipment with expected needs and to estimate the costs of R&D designs; (4) a finance specialist, to determine the project's expected costs and benefits; and so on. In short, the project manager assembles a miniature organization—perhaps even a duplicate in structure of Jetcraft itself.

Submitting the Bid.   The specialists put their talents together, and a bid is determined and submitted. The project organization disbands, and people go back to their regular jobs. If Jetcraft does not win the bid, the company has made a large investment of money for nothing. However, human costs and disruption to the organization have been minimal. No large division is standing by, waiting to spring into action if the bid is successful, or waiting to be laid off if the bid is unsuccessful. Project management is the only way for Jetcraft to get involved in large-scale bidding without relying entirely on outside expertise or temporary employees.

If Jetcraft wins the bid, the organization will follow through on the project in whatever way seems best. For a very large project, Jetcraft might set up a separate, nearly self-contained division to handle it. If the project is small, another project team might be assembled. Project size, then, largely determines how the group working on the project should be structured.

Guidelines for Using the Project Form

The project form of organization can generally be used for a one-time undertaking that is (1) definable, in terms of a specific goal, (2) unique, or unfamiliar to the parent organization, (3) large or complex, and (4) quite important. If the undertaking does not have these characteristics, the organization's regular structure should be able to take care of it.

Table 13-4 compares the functional and project viewpoints. Examining a proposed undertaking in light of these viewpoints should help to determine whether it is adaptable to the project management form.

TABLE 13-4 A Comparison of the Project and Functional Viewpoints

Organizational Characteristic	Project Viewpoint	Functional Viewpoint
Life–staff organization	Line functions become support positions. A web, rather than a chain, of authority–responsibility relationships exists.	Line functions are directly responsible for accomplishing objectives. The line commands, the staff advises and supports.
Scalar principle	Some vertical authority relationships, but emphasis is on a horizontal and diagonal work flow.	Chain of authority runs through organization from superior to subordinate. All important business is conducted up and down the chain.
Superior–subordinate relationship	Superior–subordinate relationship not so important. Relationships are peer to peer, associate to associate, manager to technical expert.	Superior–subordinate relationship is most important. All important business is conducted through the superior–subordinate pyramid.
Organizational objectives	Multilateral objectives. Project is joint venture of many relatively independent groups.	Unilateral objectives. Parent unit defines objectives, uses subunits to achieve them.
Unity of direction	Project manager manages across functional and organizational lines to accomplish interorganizational objectives.	General manager manages "downward," heads up a group of activities that are part of the organization's plan.
Equality of responsibility and authority	Project manager's responsibility may exceed authority. Functional manager, not project manager, may have authority over pay, promotion, etc., of project members.	Attempt is made to equalize functional manager's responsibility and authority.
Time duration	Limited.	Unlimited.

(*Source:* Adapted from David I. Cleland, "Understanding Project Authority," *Business Horizons,* Spring 1967, p. 66.) Copyright 1967, by the Foundation for the School of Business at Indiana University. Reprinted by permission.

Advantages and Disadvantages. Project organizations have their advantages and disadvantages. The following advantages were claimed for project management in one survey:

1. Improved customer relations.
2. Lower program costs.
3. Increased control over the undertaking.
4. Better coordination of company units working on the undertaking.

5. Higher morale (because job goals and task responsibilities are well-defined for project employees).
6. Faster development of managers.

Reported disadvantages included the following:

1. Poorer coordination within the project unit itself.
2. Ineffective use of personnel assigned to several projects.
3. Employees working for more than one manager affected by managerial inconsistency in applying company policies
4. More difficult to manage, because unity-of-command principle is violated.[2]

Diversity of Command. The last disadvantage listed is said to be the biggest problem in using project and matrix management structures. Many managers have difficulty in understanding and accepting partial loss of control and direction over an employee who has been assigned to a project. This difficulty is especially acute if employees work on projects while sitting in their normal places. Functional managers face their own time pressures and deadlines. They must be trained to grit their teeth and accept the fact that they are not entitled to assign more than a prescribed part of each subordinate's duties.

If the boss cannot accept the situation, the project employee is caught in the middle. The boss makes pay, promotion, and other supervisory decisions, and yet the employee is also responsible to the project manager. Top management must ensure that functional managers understand and accept the dual authority structure.

The project manager must often be a diplomat, skilled in smoothing out the difficulties that temporary assignments and relationships can create. Project managers are frequently on an organizational level equal—or even subordinate—to the level of functional managers from whom they must borrow personnel. Yet they must ask for and get people, get the job done, and be sure that project members are not harassed or overworked.

LINKING-PIN COORDINATION

Rensis Likert developed the linking-pin concept to solve the coordination problems of large-scale, highly specialized, departmentalized organizations. The concept arises out of his System 4 management strategy.

The Four Systems

Briefly, System 1 is exploitative-authoritative, System 2 is benevolent-authoritative, System 3 is consultative (manager consults with employees but keeps authoritarian structure of Systems 1 and 2), and System 4 is participa-

[2]C. J. Middleton, "How to Set Up a Project Organization," *Harvard Business Review*, 45 (March–April 1967), p. 74.

tive. Under System 4, self-motivation is stressed, employees achieve their own goals by helping the organization to achieve its goals, communication goes up, down, and sideways, employees at *all* levels participate in decision making, and managers have full confidence in their subordinates.

System 4 Coordination

Under System 4, many employees will be members of more than one work group and will therefore have more than one manager. Consider Mary Ladd, a member of the marketing department who is also a member of the work group that designs cereal boxes. Ladd therefore can serve as a linking-pin to coordinate the activities of the two groups. If marketing considers taking an action that Ladd believes might be harmful to cereal box design, she must report her opinions to both managers.

System 4 assumes that organizational units use group decision making. The two groups to which Mary Ladd belongs will try to come to a decision that is best for the organization, rather than a decision that benefits one group more than another. Members of the two groups understand Ladd's position because many of them may serve as linking-pins between two or more groups. Just as work group members serve as pins to link horizontal groups together, so do work group managers serve as links in coordinating the organization's activities vertically.

Conditions for Success

System 4 and its linking-pins can work only if two conditions are met:

1. The organization must understand and accept that, along with the organization's functional structure, a new structure—different, overlapping across functions, and just as important as the functional structure—is also being used.
2. Within this second structure, group decision making—rather than person-to-person, superior-to-subordinate command giving—is to be used.

THE CONTINGENCY APPROACH

In this and the previous chapter, the strategies of organizational structure have been placed in two classes: (1) those that help the organization differentiate its tasks into more highly specialized parts, and (2) those that help to integrate the organization's efforts back together again. For review, here are the strategies.

Differentiation Strategies

    Specialization by organizational level
    Specialization of tasks by department
    Specialization of labor
    Specialization by decentralization and delegation
    Specialization by line or staff function

Integration Strategies

    Coordination by hierarchy
    Coordination by committees
    Coordination by span of control
    Coordination by matrix and project management
    Coordination by linking-pin

We have seen repeatedly that no one strategy is always the best. Which strategy or combination of strategies should an organization use?

Contingency Theory

Systems theorists have shown persuasively that every organization is a social system whose parts are interrelated and interdependent. The environment within which the organization operates can affect the organization's performance. A change in any part of the organization can affect the organization as a whole.

Consider the human nose: wide, narrow, short, long, Roman, pug, and so on. If something so basic as a nose varies so widely in response to the environment, it is understandable that organizations—presumably created in a much more haphazard way than noses—would show great variations from one situation, environment, or marketplace to the next.

Contingency theory recognizes that organizations are systems of interrelated parts. Since no two organizations (and no two situations within which an organization may find itself) are ever the same, the appropriate strategy can be determined only by looking at the unique situation in which the unique organization finds itself at the unique moment.

The Factors Involved. Unlike the factors determining nasal shape and structure, the factors determining organizational shape and structure are just beginning to be defined. For many differentiation and integration strategies, no theory or research exists. In such important areas as specialization of labor, the line–staff distinction, and departmentalization, little help exists for the manager seeking to trade off the benefits of these differentiation strategies with the losses in coordination that accompany the benefits. Contingency theory says that the organization's optimum design depends on various factors within and outside the organization. Unfortunately, these factors have yet to be specified and measured precisely.

Technological Factors

One group that has received attention is technological factors. The hope is that by investigating and classifying organizations in terms of their technology, some characteristics of successful and unsuccessful organizations may emerge. Three important efforts in this direction are those of James Thompson, Joan Woodward, and the team of Tom Burns and G. M. Stalker.[3]

James Thompson's Work.   Thompson classifies organizational technology into three types.

1. *Long-linked technology.* Each production unit gets its work from the previous unit, makes its contribution, and then passes the work along to the next unit. Typical would be the automobile assembly line. At its most technologically complete and successful, the production line would be totally automated.
2. *Mediating technology.* This type of technology acts as an intermediary between people outside the organization. A bank takes one customer's deposit and loans it to another customer. A bond dealer buys bonds from one client and sells them to another client. Telephone companies and the postal service also perform mediating functions.
3. *Intensive technology.* When technology is intensive, many technological devices and skills are brought to bear on a problem. Hospitals, research laboratories, and the space program use intensive technology.

According to Thompson, an organization's goals, methods, structure, social system, and management approach will be affected by the type of technology used in the organization. For example, the organization of a research laboratory and of a rock-breaking chain gang will differ greatly.

Joan Woodward's Work.   Throughout the 1950s, Joan Woodward studied the relationship between structure and technology in 100 British industrial firms. She found technology of three types: unit or small-batch production (such as

---

[3]James D. Thompson, *Organizations in Action* (New York: McGraw-Hill Book Company, 1967), pp. 15–18; Joan Woodward, *Industrial Organization: Theory and Practice* (New York: Oxford University Press, 1965); Tom Burns and G. M. Stalker, *The Management of Innovation*, 2nd. ed. (London: Tavistock Publications, 1966).

tailor-made clothes), mass production (such as assembly lines), and continuous process production (such as oil refineries). Unit production is technologically simplest, and continuous process production is most complex.

Woodward concluded that technology and organizational structure are directly related. She found that organizations with more complex technology have more management levels, more administrative and clerical personnel, more coordination by committee, and a larger span of control for the chief executive (unit production, 4; mass production, 7; process production, 10).

Burns and Stalker's Work.   Burns and Stalker examined about 20 firms that were moving from production with stable technology into a field with rapidly changing technology: electronics. They hypothesized that changed technological requirements would demand changes in organizational structure.

Before they went into electronics, the sample firms had traditional organizational structures with well-defined tasks, roles, responsibility, and authority. The chain of command was strong and direct. Upward communication consisted of information filtering to the top, and downward communication consisted of orders, instructions, and commands.

These firms had to change their style when they entered the electronics field, where change is rapid, problems are frequent and critical, and conditions are generally unstable. The newcomer organizations had to achieve greater structural flexibility. Communication and control had to move horizontally as well as vertically. People with technical expertise gained power, and managers with high places on the organizational chart but without technological know-how lost power. The highly structured hierarchy that worked when technology was stable and routine no longer worked when technology was dynamic.

BUREAUCRACY

"There's a new parlor game called Bureaucracy. The first person who moves loses."

To conclude this chapter on the integration of organizational roles, we now consider integration within those enormous public and private organizations called bureaucracies. A bureaucracy is a large and complex organization consisting of many skills used to carry out policies and decisions made by others. Bureaucrats are the more or less permanent subordinates who carry out the policies of impermanent superiors.

Bureaucracy has a long history. Any organizational endeavor needs rational, predictable behavior from its members. Since the earliest organized endeavors were the administrative and military branches of governments, the study and practice of bureaucracy as a means of rational administration arose in those areas.

Weber's Bureaucracy

German economist Max Weber saw the following as characteristics of large-scale twentieth-century bureaucracies:

1. *Hierarchy.* Personnel and bureaus are organized on a hierarchical basis.
2. *Rational job structure.* Jobs are structured and labor is divided on rational principles. Each position has sufficient authority to achieve its purposes.
3. *Written formalization.* The rules, decisions, and actions of the bureaucracy are formalized in writing.
4. *Owners and managers separated.* Owners hire managers to run the organization. In a public bureaucracy, the people elect representatives to make decisions (called laws). These representatives hire managers to run the government.
5. *Competence.* Organizational managers and workers are selected on the basis of their competence, rather than family, wealth, or some other characteristic.

As private organizations have grown, government has increased in size to keep pace. In 1900, only 4 percent of the entire U.S. labor force was employed by governmental units (including the military). By 1940 that percentage had doubled to 8 percent, and by 1965 it had doubled again to 16 percent.

Reasons for Bureaucratic Growth.   Several reasons exist for the possible continuation of bureaucratic growth. One reason is that the complexity of society often results in conflicts that can best be solved through governmental action or arbitration. Government impartially balances competing interests for the common good. Another reason is that societies are becoming larger and more wealthy. They want the mass-produced items that only large (and therefore bureaucratic) manufacturing organizations can supply. Third, technological advances have done away with many nonbureaucratic jobs, so the bureaucrats who remain hold an ever larger proportion of available jobs.

Reasons for Bureaucratic Shrinkage.   Yet evidence exists that the tendency toward bureaucratization as a means of integrating organizational tasks may be diminishing. First, rapid change seems to be a fact of life for contemporary organizations. But the strength of bureaucracies is their ability to handle routine, repeatable, unchanging matters. Second, although bureaucracies are designed to cope with organizational size, they may have limits as to the size they can handle. Our largest corporations continue to expand, particularly into international markets. Can bureaucracy work effectively in such gigantic, geographically dispersed organizations?

A third reason for the possible slowdown in bureaucratic growth is the increase in service occupations. We now employ more people in service occupations than in production occupations. In such service fields as education, health, and financial services, workers must achieve highly specialized competence. Service occupations tend to deal with nonstandardized products that do not lend themselves to routinization and bureaucratization. Whether bureaucracies can handle these trends toward service and specialization is open to question.

Finally, employees continually demand more opportunities for personal growth and self-actualization. Yet, by their very nature, bureaucracies demand conformity. Whether or not bureaucracies are equipped to resolve this conflict remains to be seen.

SUMMARY

This chapter has covered six integration strategies. Under *coordination by hierarchy*, the manager is viewed as a supervisor of supervisors, and delegation is often considered to be a grim necessity.

A second integration strategy is *coordination by committees*. Committees have five major advantages: communication benefits, increased knowledge available for decision making, fair representation of all parties, improved coordination, and heightened morale through participation. They also have their disadvantages: high cost in money and time, a tendency to make mediocre decisions through compromise, their inability to resolve conflict, and their lack of follow-up and accountability. However, a committee can avoid these potential disadvantages through clear task definition, properly selected members, and an effective chairperson.

A third integrating concern is *span of control*. The classical approach (find the ideal span by observing successful companies) and the formulaic contribution of Graicunas to the problem were described. Then the contingency approach to management span was outlined, with six factors shown to be important when determining span of control:

1. What are the abilities and characteristics of subordinates?
2. What are the abilities and characteristics of the manager?
3. How technologically complex are the jobs being supervised?
4. What is the rate of change for the jobs being supervised?
5. How interdependent are the jobs or units being supervised?
6. How measurable are performance results for each job?

Geographic spread, repetitiveness of subordinate decisions, and similarity of tasks performed by subordinates also affect optimal span of control. The Lockheed study showed how one company tried to combine six influences on span of control into a set of "standard" spans.

The *matrix* and *project management* methods are similar in that organizational authority relationships run horizontally and vertically, instead of just vertically. The Jetcraft Company illustrated how a project team assembles and prepares a major bid.

The important advantage of Rensis Likert's *linking-pin* coordination approach is the communication between work groups that it encourges. Any employee serving as a member of more than one work group helps to link group functions together.

The chapter then described the *contingency approach* to organizational design. This approach suggests that, rather than entering an organizational situation with a preconceived set of principles, the manager must objectively consider all factors influencing the organization at the moment, and then make the integrating choice that seems best. Much research needs to be done on factors that influence organizational structure. The chapter described efforts to tie the type and complexity of an organization's technology to its structure.

The final major section of the chapter discussed the bureaucratic form of organization.

For a given organization, the "one best structure" may exist. That structure may not be best for any other organization. All the manager can do is be aware of numerous differentiating and integrating strategies, then choose the combination that seems most likely to help the organization and its people to achieve their goals.

DISCUSSION QUESTIONS

1. What is coordination by hierarchy? How does it help to integrate the organization?
2. What are the advantages and disadvantages of committees?
3. How would you structure a committee to avoid the disadvantages?
4. What is the span of control problem? How can it be solved?
5. What is the contingency approach to span of control?
6. What are the uses and advantages of project management?
7. What is the linking-pin concept? How does it help to integrate the organization's members?
8. What is the effect of technological factors on organizational structure?

9. Why has bureaucracy come to be a bad word?

10. Differentiation and integration seem to be opposites in some ways. Why are both important?

THE INDUSTRIAL DIVISION

Until recently, the Industrial Division of Hamilton Ross & Co.: Architects-Engineers-Planners, Inc., consisted of two engineering departments: the mechanical department and the electrical department. Morale and enthusiasm among the engineers and draftsmen were good, and product quality was high. The division's organization chart looked like Figure 13-3.

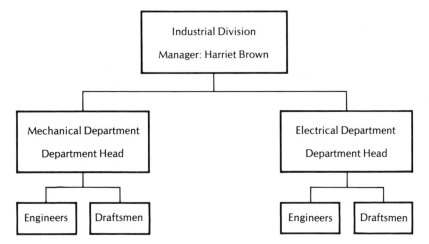

FIG 13-3 The Industrial Division: organization chart before reorganization.

Division manager Harriet Brown decided that the firm could achieve even better results by doing a little reorganizing. She thought that greater efficiency would be achieved by establishing drafting as a separate department. She explained the reorganization to the division staff and set up a time schedule for making the changes. After reorganization, the chart looked like Figure 13-4.

Under the new arrangement, the two engineering departments continued to operate more or less as they had before—preparing detailed technical specifications and rough construction drawings. Formerly, draftsmen within each department did the finished drawings. Under the new organization, the engineers submitted rough sketches to the head of the drafting department, who assigned them to specific draftsmen.

The written specifications and the final drawings of course had to match up. Before the reorganization, the heads of the mechanical and electrical departments were responsible for coordinating the writing and the drawing. But after the reor-

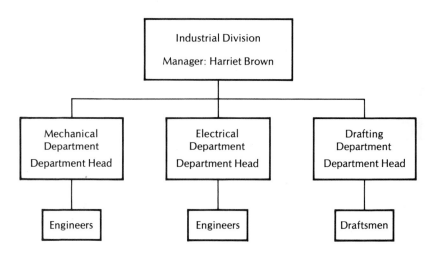

FIG 13-4 The Industrial Division: organization chart after reorganization.

ganization, division manager Brown noticed that the drawings were of lower quality than before and that discrepancies were beginning to appear between the specifications and the drawings. Brown wondered whether she should go back to the old form of organization or whether the new form could be made to work.

THE ELECTRIC AUTHORITY

The Electric Authority is departmentalized by function. Close coordination among the functional units is essential to good customer service, but coordination is not always easy because the functional units are spread all over the county.

Before the simplest job can be completed, it must pass through four geographically separated departments. First, the engineering department designs the job. Then the construction department does the actual work. Third, the customer service department verifies the customer's records. Finally, the meter department installs the meter.

Many times the authority must handle rush jobs. Under the functional departmentalization, four managers must be convinced that the job needs to be done in a hurry. More than once, a job has been rushed through engineering, only to sit for two weeks on a desk in construction. Customers must often call several phone numbers in order to find out how far along their jobs are.

Recently, the number of complaints has become so large that the local newspaper has begun writing editorials about the Authority's inefficiency. The Electric Authority board of directors now sees that action is essential.

14

staffing

Now we have covered two of the manager's major functions: planning and organizing. A third major decision focus is staffing.

Staffing decisions are of two kinds: (1) finding new organizational members, and (2) maintaining the existing membership. These efforts, usually coordinated by the organization's personnel department, include the following activities:

1. Personnel needs assessment.
2. Recruitment and selection.
3. Training and development.
4. Evaluation and compensation.
5. Other services (such as employee benefits, unions, and safety and health).

These five categories are the focus of this chapter.

PERSONNEL NEEDS ASSESSMENT

The key to any organization's continuing success is an accurate assessment of its present and future personnel needs. The organization must predict its needs in sufficient detail and with adequate lead time to recruit and train the required personnel.

Macro and Micro Needs

To oversimplify, macro means large and micro (as in microscope) means small. The organization's personnel needs must be assessed at both levels.

Macro Level.   The macro-level needs assessment refers to the future requirements across the entire organization. For example, if the firm anticipates great growth within a certain product category, it would have to assess present personnel and the local labor force to predict whether the needed skills and people will be available. Some organizations simply assume that the future work force will match organizational growth requirements. Sometimes organizations get away with this assumption and do indeed find the required personnel. However, the assumption often leads to lost growth opportunities and profits foregone, as the firm cannot locate people when and where they are needed.

For these reasons, the macro forecast is important. It ensures that the people required by future growth and organizational strategy will be available.

The Micro Level.   The micro forecast is a far more specific, short-term assessment of personnel needs. At the micro level, the organization is trying to match specific people with specific jobs. First, the organization must determine each job's requirements. Then it must train existing personnel to do their jobs more effectively; replace present job holders upon their promotion, retirement, or resignation; and fill new jobs that growth or new organizational directions have created.

Resistance to Micro Forecasts.   Getting managers to make macro forecasts is easier than getting them to make micro forecasts. Nobody minds speculating about future personnel requirements. But many managers are reluctant to make micro forecasts, especially within organizations whose people are concerned about job security.

Such concern will distort the needs assessment for existing personnel and for new hires. As Maslow's "needs hierarchy" suggests, people concerned with security tend to focus on preserving and securing their present situations. Insecure employees want to make themselves indispensable. Therefore, they try to ensure that the manager's needs assessment overstates each job's skill and training requirements. In such a situation, the manager should try to overcome the insecurity of existing personnel by creating a climate of mutual trust.

Needs Assessment Checklists.   A number of checklists are available for managers wanting to assess personnel needs at the micro level. These checklists enable managers to determine what personality characteristics, physical capabilities, training, and experience each job requires. The manager can then compare the job requirements with the characteristics of potential job holders.

These checklists force managers to evaluate the skills and talents actually necessary for job performance. Without such an assessment, it is too easy to believe that the only person capable of doing your job or a job that you supervise is Superman or Wonder Woman. When a job vacancy occurs, the personnel department may be asked to hire Superman or Wonder Woman at the minimum wage. Dissatisfaction and conflict between the operating department and the personnel department will result.

Table 14-1 shows a typical checklist that can be used to evaluate present and future personnel requirements. The list forces the requesting manager to consider the precise skill and experience that job candidates really need. Column 1 indicates the factors to be assessed. The manager puts points in column 2 to indicate the relative importance of each factor. For example, if the manager wants to hire a clerk–typist, "job-related knowledge" might get 80 points, with the other 20 points scattered throughout the column. The manager indicates in the last column how the factor will be measured. For example, in evaluating clerk–typist candidates, the manager might use the Minnesota Clerical Test and the SRA Typing Skills Test to assess job-related knowledge, might ignore decision-making talent as relatively unimportant, and might use the resume and an interview to evaluate self-reliance, social sensitivity, and emotional stability.

TABLE 14-1   Needs Assessment Checklist

Factor Required	Degree of Factor Required*	Measurement Technique†
1. Job-related knowledge		
2. Decision-making talent		
a. Analytical skill		
b. Conceptual skill		
c. Creativity		
d. Intuitive judgment		
e. Judgmental courage		
f. Open-mindedness		
3. Self-reliance		
4. Social sensitivity		
5. Emotional stability		

*Allocate 100 points throughout second column to show relative importance of each factor for job being assessed.

†Insert suitable measurement technique in third column.

Updating Job Descriptions.   If used throughout the organization, such checklists provide another benefit. They force managers to update and clarify existing job descriptions. These descriptions are a useful way of dividing up the organization's tasks and then defining areas of responsibility. However, organizations often let them become outdated or write them so vaguely that they fail to fill this important job delineation function. The continuing process of assessing personnel needs requires that job descriptions be clear, up to date, and verified.

Auditing of Task Requirements.   Job descriptions and personnel needs assessments provide a way for replacing departing employees and can serve as guidelines for redesigning existing jobs, as the organization adapts to its ever-changing environment. The organization must avoid two extremes. At one extreme is the manager whose job is so eroded by changes in organizational strategy and structure that little actual job content remains. At the other extreme, similar strategic and structural changes may have increased a job's scope and content so much that the manager becomes overburdened. Both situations are demoralizing. An ongoing needs assessment program will avoid this double demoralization by providing for automatic auditing of each job's requirements.

RECRUITMENT AND SELECTION

Every organization has a manager or department (usually the personnel department) responsible for recruitment. When that department recruits to fill a new job or a vacancy in an old job, the specific requirements of the job (derived through the micro needs assessment) become even more important, because they provide the standard used for screening applicants.

Inside Applicants

Applicants may come either from inside the organization or outside. Most managers believe that selection from within is best, because of its positive effect on morale. Many companies try to hire from the outside only for positions at the lowest entry level, filling all other jobs from within the organizational family. Robert Townsend, author of *Up the Organization* and successful president of Avis, suggests promotion from within:

> Most managers complain about the lack of able people and go outside to fill key positions. Nonsense. Nobody inside an organization ever looked ready to move into a bigger job.
> I use the rule of 50 percent. Try to find somebody inside the company with a record of success (in any area) and with an appetite for the job. If he looks like 50 percent of what you need, give him the job. In six months he'll have grown the other 50 percent and everybody will be satisfied.
> How to do it wrong: go outside and get some expensive guy who looks like 110 percent of what you want and a year later, after having raised salaries all around him, you'll still be teaching him the business. The people around him will be frustrated and ineffective.[1]

Companies who promote from inside must enable their employees to upgrade their skills in preparation for promotion opportunities. They must

---

[1]Robert Townsend, *Up the Organization* (New York: Alfred A. Knopf, 1970), p. 155.

also create detailed data banks on the talents, training, and skills of their employees. Such data banks may come in for increased legal scrutiny because of their potential for invasion of privacy. Nevertheless, if a large organization is to keep track of employees eligible for promotion, some data must be kept.

To complement such a data file, the organization needs a widespread and effective communication network to be sure that qualified candidates know about job openings. Many organizations use a special bulletin board, newsletter, color-coded memorandum, or other recognizable, accessible device for keeping potential job applicants informed.

Outside Applicants

When going outside to secure job applicants, the organization has several choices open to it, ranging from very informal to highly structured.

Ask.   The most informal method is to ask present employees if they know of anyone who might be qualified for a job. Employees will presumably recommend people more or less like themselves, people who would fit in with the present work force. Although equal opportunity legislation discourages this technique, it is still used—more often by small, privately held organizations than by larger, highly visible, or highly regulated ones.

Advertise.   A second technique for recruiting outside the organization is public advertising. Most often used is the newspaper. At one time or another, most people have looked in the classified section for job opportunities. Specialized professional publications reach such audiences as engineers, college professors, and city managers. At a broader level are advertisements in publications like the *Wall Street Journal.*

Even when the correct medium is chosen, advertising a job opening requires a careful description of the job's requirements. Figure 14-1 presents three good examples. The organizations placing the ads know what type of person they are looking for. The second listing demands qualifications that are unusually specific. Not many potential marketing managers will apply, once they read that "missile marketing experience is required."

These advertisements have a twofold purpose: to screen out unlikely candidates and to attract likely candidates. If the ad carefully specifies the job's responsibilities and the training and experience requirements, readers can evaluate themselves and self-screen. If an ad is too general, the organization will be overwhelmed with applicants to screen and interview.

Although detailed job specifications may cause the best candidate or two not to apply, because they modestly think that they cannot qualify, the costs of evaluating applicants are so high that the organization is justified in taking that risk.

ENGINEERING MANAGER

Excellent position available with a non-defense Fortune-100 computer manufacturer in San Diego, Calif., for an experienced Engineering Manager to direct an organization comprised of 50 engineers engaged in circuit design, product packaging and design automation. Must be technically abreast of the state-of-the-art in MOS, MSI, LSI and digital circuitry. This position requires demonstrated success as a manager, and a BSEE or MSEE degree.

Excellent starting salary, environment and benefits.

Send resume and salary history in complete confidence to: Box 211-0.

An equal opportunity employer

MARKETING MANAGER

A small, dynamic aerospace firm has a challenging position open for an aggressive individual to promote its products and services to potential customers in NASA, DOD and at military installations.

Missile marketing experience is required including ability to make market analysis, new business identification, bookings, forecasts, sales strategy plans, and extensive customer contact. Must be free to travel. College degree required with post graduate courses in Business or Aerospace Management desired. Applicants must be familiar with DOD and NASA organizations.

Particular attention will be given to otherwise qualified applicants with recent experience in Strategic Offensive and Defensive Missile Systems Development at the senior management level. Please submit resume and salary history to Box 242-0.

An equal opportunity employer

FIG 14-1   Advertisements for available positions.

Vice-President
Marketing
Electronics

This is an exceptional opportunity to direct the marketing and sales functions for a rapidly expanding division of a major electronics company. It will interest a successful marketing executive with solid experience in the sale of electronic products, systems and services to the financial community.

The individual best qualified to direct these activities should be thoroughly familiar with the electronic data processing field and ideally has a background in marketing to the leading brokerage firms. A good grasp of facts and figures and the capability of establishing marketing strategy and new product requirements are important qualifications.

Compensation will prove attractive to an executive whose current earnings are in the $35,000 area, and the company offers outstanding benefit programs. Your reply will be treated in strict confidence and should include experience, education and personal data, as well as present compensation and home telephone number.

Box 199 L.

FIG 14-1 (continued).

Selection, Testing, and Placement

A Subjective Process. Placement specialists have the difficult task of matching the right position and the right person. At the level of manual dexterity or manipulative skill, some available tests can logically and legally be used to screen job applicants. However, useful tests do not yet exist for confidently placing people in upper-level administrative jobs or in sophisticated specialist jobs. Tests can determine whether an applicant can type 75 words per minute or manipulate 14 gear assemblies per hour. These standardized, valid tests are properly used in the selection and placement process. In contrast, the tests and measurements experts do not yet have valid, reliable devices for predicting whether an applicant will be a good accountant, an effective supervisor, a competent sales manager, or a sound financial analyst. Consequently, above a fairly low organizational level, the selection and placement process tends to be very subjective.

Legal Restrictions.   Loosely defined jobs with subjective selection criteria are more open to legal challenge by persons not selected. For many years, managers got away with using intuition, judgment, or experience-based selection procedures to place people in ill-defined jobs. Several important laws and subsequent judicial rulings have sought to prevent the arbitrary use of non-job-related selection criteria. Some job appointments used to be based on such non-job-related factors as "Would he fit in?" or "Do I like her?" Employers no longer have the luxury of hiring in this casual way.

Antidiscrimination Legislation.   Subjective selection criteria can lead to discrimination in hiring, promotion, and compensation. Consequently, they have been challenged over the past 20 years, as the civil rights movement has made everyone aware of the subtle but effective means that have been used to exclude certain minorities from managerial and other high-level jobs. The Civil Rights Act of 1964 prohibits discrimination in personnel decisions on the basis of race, sex, religion, or national origin. To demonstrate that their hiring, promotion, and compensation practices are not discriminatory, organizations have had to replace subjective criteria with objective ones.

Test Validation.   As a follow-up to Title VII of the Civil Rights Act of 1964, the Equal Employment Opportunity Commission in 1970 issued its "Guidelines on Employment Selection Procedures." After 1964 many firms substituted "tests" for their previously subjective selection criteria. The EEOC determined that many of these tests had discriminatory effects and that the tests were being used as the basis for employment decisions without sufficient evidence of a connection between test performance and job performance. The new selection guidelines demanded that test performance and job performance must be highly correlated. Since such a close relationship is very difficult to show, these guidelines present an important challenge to personnel departments.

The guidelines insist that employers must take affirmative action to be sure that applicants and employees are treated without regard to race, color, religion, sex, or national origin. Furthermore, employers must take positive action in giving employment and training to the minorities protected by Title VII of the Civil Rights Act of 1964.

Interview Questions Not to Ask.   To avoid charges of discrimination, here are some questions and requests that should not be used by selection interviewers or on application forms:

1. Where were you born? Where was your spouse born?
2. Please send us a copy of your birth certificate.
3. What is your religious preference?
4. Please give us your pastor's name.

5. Are you a native-born citizen or are you naturalized?
6. Please enclose a recent photograph with your application.
7. Have you served in the armed forces of any country but the United States?
8. Are you willing to work on Yom Kippur?

The Assessment Center

The selection problems created by the federal guidelines have generated much interest in finding valid selection and placement measures. One approach to solving these problems is the assessment center. More and more organizations are using assessment centers (1) to evaluate the promotion potential of present employees, (2) to identify the training needs of employees, (3) to simulate job-related situations so that immediate constructive feedback can be provided, and (4) to select potential successful job applicants by using work-related criteria that have been shown to be related to future job success.

The In-Basket Test. At the assessment center, potential employees are given an interview, standardized tests, and an in-basket test. The in-basket contains a cross section of problems in memorandum form, just as they would appear in the manager's in-basket. Managerial prospects tell how they would deal with the problems, and their responses are evaluated by a team of trained assessors.

The in-basket and other assessment center exercises provide a reasonable facsimile of the actual job. Long-term validation data are not available because the assessment center technique is so new. However, the technique shows considerable potential for separating those who will do a particular job well from those who will not.

Personal Data

To aid in selection, personal data may be used as a predictor of future career success. Short women do not perform as well in professional basketball as tall men do. Someone who prefers to be alone will probably not do well at selling insurance.

Numerous studies have been conducted on the relationship between personal qualities and managerial effectiveness. These studies show that from 30 to 50 percent of managerial effectiveness is related to personal qualities that can be identified before hiring. Such qualities as intelligence, verbal skills, being well organized, working hard, and being active, confident, and dominant can be identified in advance and are good predictors of managerial success.

Biographical information can also be used to suggest managerial promise. A healthy applicant with high grades and leadership experience in extracurricular activities is a better managerial prospect than a sick applicant with low grades and no extracurricular activities at all.

The biographical–personal approach is not precise and needs to be refined. Eventually, placement specialists may be able to combine personal traits and qualities into legitimate selection devices for particular managerial jobs in much the same way that similar devices are presently used to place skilled production workers.

TRAINING AND DEVELOPMENT

The Importance of Training and Development

Once applicants are attracted to the organization and induced to join, they must be shown what they are supposed to do to help the organization reach its goals. While training new employees, the organization should also be developing present employees. These development needs are ever-present because the organization keeps confronting change and the employees keep needing job satisfaction and personal growth. True, the products, competition, processes, and technology of some organizations change little from year to year. Also true, some employees have no interest in any deeper association with the job than to put in their 40 hours. Yet most organizations face an ever-changing environment, and most employees seek more from their jobs than pay checks.

Reactions to Computerization. Organizations must continuously translate environmental changes into training for their personnel, so that people can go from obsolete jobs to new ones. The enormous changes brought about by computerization provide contrasting illustrations of how companies cope with change. Some companies saw the changes that computerization would bring, so they projected which jobs would become available and which jobs would become obsolete. After identifying the job types, they approached people in jobs that were sure to be phased out and offered them the opportunity to retrain.

The benefits of this strategy are obvious. The employees were familiar with the organization, fit in well, and were demonstrably loyal. All that needed to be done was to retrain, say, bookkeepers to be key punchers or programmers. In some cases, the retraining meant promotion and an upgrading of skills, with associated morale benefits. This type of program sent a clear and important message to employees: we are concerned about you, we value you, we want to keep you, and we will retrain you.

Other companies—lacking foresight or compassion—lost employee good will and loyalty by firing the obsolete work force and bringing in a new group of outsiders. Companies in the latter group may or may not have saved on their direct costs, but their indirect costs, resulting from lowered morale as loyal employees were laid off or shunted aside, were enormous. In this single stroke of technologically induced change, organizations had a chance to establish or reaffirm a solid bond with their employees—or quickly destroy a bond that may have taken years to develop.

Training and Development Techniques

Training and development programs are designed to increase the employee's knowledge, show the employee how to solve problems, or teach the employee how to interact more effectively with other employees. The techniques used to train and develop employees fall into three categories: information presentation, supervised instruction, and simulation.

Information Presentation. Information presentation techniques range from first-day orientation films and lectures to lengthy formal training programs run by the training department or by outside specialists. These techniques are the most efficient, most cost-effective training method. A lecture or a film can be presented to many people at once. Under this method, the organization has only limited opportunity to get feedback about whether the material is being learned. Therefore, the mere presentation of information may not work if the information is complex or the learners are not motivated. A modification of the lecture or film is self-paced learning or programmed instruction in which employees can keep checking themselves to be sure they have learned the skill or concept.

Other training methods that may involve some information presentation are conferences, T-groups, closed-circuit television, correspondence courses, and reading assignments.

Supervised Instruction. The second major training method is supervised instruction, often called on-the-job training (OJT). Ideally, all managers train and develop their employees by providing continual feedback on job performance. When the manager is not around, the employee learns by doing, through trial and error.

With OJT, the responsibility for training is placed squarely on the employee's manager. Since managers vary in their ability to train, and employees vary in their ability to learn, the effects of training will vary from situation to situation.

The costs of OJT, or the lack of it, are sometimes easy to measure. For an assembly-line job, the cost of ineffective instruction can be measured in terms of scrapped product, ruined assemblies, machine down time, and so on. At managerial levels, potential costs become far greater—and less quantifiable.

Poor training or no training (sink or swim) may be reflected in terms of long-time employees quitting, decisions that backfire, legal problems, and other types of costly errors.

The Bright Young MBA.   Here is a real-life example of what can happen when new managers are left to their own devices. The XYZ Company hired a bright, young masters in business administration graduate, fresh out of college, and made him a branch manager. At his first meeting with branch personnel, he complained about everyone's poor performance, stated his high expectations regarding future performance, and gave the "get tough" speech he had always dreamed of making. Within a week the division manager had received five letters of resignation and four transfer requests—quite a showing for a ten-person office. The division manager's response to this problem, generated by unsupervised on-the-job "training," was a telegram: "Get everyone back within 24 hours or you are fired."

Unfortunately, whenever on-the-job training is replaced by formal training programs, they are usually implemented at lower skill levels. At those levels, training gains are clearly measurable and training expenses are easily justifiable. At supervisory and managerial levels, the costs of poor or good training are less measurable, but far more meaningful.

Simulation.   Simulation or "pretending" has been used to teach many skills: driving a car, flying a plane, learning effective interpersonal behavior, making high-level decisions in a corporate management game, and so on. Modern technology has made simulation methods relatively inexpensive, and sophisticated design has made simulation extremely realistic.

Many variations exist. Hundreds of business games are available, some teaching facts and others teaching skills. The in-basket technique described earlier, the cases at the ends of this book's chapters, and any role play exercise are all simulations. The point of these exercises is to give managerial trainees practice in making decisions, but without letting poor decisions hurt the organization.

EVALUATION AND COMPENSATION

The next major group of staffing decisions is those regarding evaluation and compensation. Although these are two separate topics, they are almost always linked in practice. Evaluation presumably enables organizations to identify employees who are capable, loyal, motivated, doing a good job, and eligible for future promotion. Such employees should receive additional compensation as a reward for their performance. From the employee's point of view, evaluation provides feedback on performance, an indication of how the employee has performed relative to other employees, and information about areas that need strengthening.

In practice, evaluation and compensation are not as closely related as they might be. Organizations often need to increase employee compensation to keep valued employees or to stay even with inflation. So they may first decide on the compensation increase and then come up with the evaluation that justifies it. Such an "evaluation" program does not serve the purposes for which it was originally designed.

Evaluation: Performance Appraisal

Improving Performance Appraisals.   Most managers use the trait approach to performance appraisal. The typical evaluation instrument might ask managers to use a rating scale for evaluating subordinates on ten or twelve traits, such as attendance, work quality and quantity, leadership potential, appearance, attitude, and so on. An example appears in Figure 14-2.

Most managers find drawing the distinctions required by a rating scale extremely difficult. Should Betty Smith get a six or seven on "attitude"? Since Smith's salary and promotion potential are often directly related to the appraisal, a difference of a point or two here and there can be very meaningful.

The typical annual appraisal therefore becomes an all-or-nothing, make-or-break proposition. Consequently, both appraisers and subordinates approach the review period with uncertainty and fear. In this atmosphere, the appraisal process consumes more time and emotional energy than it should.

Increased Frequency of Appraisal.   Many appraisal problems stem from the manager's anxiety over completing a single, annual performance review. This anxiety can often be lessened by *increasing* the frequency of appraisals from once a year to, say, six times a year.

When managers realize that each appraisal on the bimonthly schedule represents only a small portion of the total yearly score, they will not spend so much time in soul-searching. Instead of agonizing over whether Smith and Jones should get a six or a seven on attitude, their managers call it as they see it for the shorter time period and quickly move on to the next trait. If Smith's attitude for the two-month period is "unsatisfactory," she finds out soon enough to avoid ruining her year's appraisal average.

Avoiding Performance Appraisal Errors.   More frequent performance appraisals can help managers avoid several typical performance appraisal errors. For example, more frequent appraisals can reduce the *halo effect*. This error reflects a managerial judgment about one part of the job (either negative or positive) that affects the manager's judgment about other parts of the job. For example, Betty Smith's attitude may be so poor that the manager fails to recognize her extraordinary output. Managers can be unduly influenced by personal appearance or a positive attitude while making a one-shot appraisal. Five or six appraisals a year will enable the appraiser to recognize how trivial certain traits are in the perspective of total, observable job accomplishments.

LAST NAME	FIRST	M.I.	Social Security No.	TYPE OF RATING	
				PROBATIONARY	
				ANNUAL	
JOB TITLE		ANNIVERSARY DATE	MOS.IN POS.	SPECIAL	

COLLEGE OR DIVISION	DEPARTMENT	SECTION

INSTRUCTIONS: Please complete this form by circling one of the numbers in the block for each rating factor that best describes the person being rated. The definitions in each block are to be used as _guides_ only to help you determine your rating. Please refer to Section 7.3 of the Personnel Procedures Manual for detailed information.

RATING VALUES	UNSATISFACTORY	CONDITIONAL	SATISFACTORY	ABOVE SATISFACTORY	OUTSTANDING
(1) Personal Appearance	0 Dress and/or personal grooming frequently below standards for job.	1 2 Dress and/or personal grooming at times below standards for job.	3 4 5 Dress and personal grooming equals expectations for job.	6 7 Dress and personal grooming consistently exceeds expectations for job.	8 Dress and personal grooming above expectations for job. Cannot be improved.
(2) Attendance	0 Frequently late and/or often absent. Completion of work assignments is drastically affected.	1 2 Frequently late and/or absent. Completion of work assignments affected.	3 4 5 Usually present at prescribed times. Absences and infrequent tardiness within prescribed standards.	6 7 Seldom is absent or late.	8 Extremely good attendance record.
(3) Attitude	0 Goes about work halfheartedly. Outlook detracts from organization.	1 2 Frequently appears indifferent. Outlook detracts from organization at times.	3 4 5 Shows normal interest in all that is ordinarily expected.	6 7 Shows more than normal interest in work. Promotes organization to coworkers and public.	8 Extremely interested in work and often makes very good suggestions. Exceptional in promoting organization to coworkers and public.
(4) Supervision Required	0 Needs constant supervision. Fails to follow instructions.	1 2 Must be prodded at times. Fails to follow instructions at times.	3 4 5 Follows instructions. Needs periodic checking only.	6 7 Needs very little attention. Accepts advice and suggestions.	8 Works independently and exercises discretion expected only of top workers.
(5) Knowledge of Job Duties	0 Has not gained adequate comprehension of job duties.	1 2 Insufficient grasp of some phases of job duties.	3 4 5 Adequate knowledge. Knows job duties well for time in job.	6 7 Thorough knowledge of all phases of job. Exceeds expectations for time in job.	8 Has remarkable mastery of all phases of job for time in job.
(6) Quality of Work	0 Completed assignments frequently unacceptable due to lack of neatness, accuracy, and/or compliance with instructions.	1 2 Occasionally assignments fall below standards, neatness and/or compliance with instructions.	3 4 5 Completed assignments fall within expectations for job.	6 7 Completed assignments are consistently above job expectations.	8 Completed assignments far exceed job expectations consistently.
(7) Quantity of work	0 Cannot or does not meet minimum acceptable requirements.	1 2 Works slowly or in short spurts. Produces only enough to get by.	3 4 5 Output equals job expectations in consideration of time in job.	6 7 Does more than share. Works rapidly and consistently.	8 Recognized as top worker. Consistently top performer.

FIG 14-2 Midwest University performance appraisal form.

Another common appraisal error is the *recency effect*. Many employees are convinced that managers evaluate them on the "what have you done for me lately" principle. If the manger appraises more frequently, the consistent performer will not be overshadowed by someone making a dazzling year-end stretch run.

Another error is *central tendency:* the appraiser's tendency to bunch all appraisals toward the center of the scale. Managers are sometimes reluctant to "punish" or "reward" subordinates unduly, so they do not use the full range of performance scores. More appraisals during the year would increase the likelihood of open, honest assessments.

Improved Appraisal Effectiveness.   If appraisals are frequent, managers can train subordinates by providing feedback shortly after a problem has developed. The boss often surprises employees by pointing out, at annual appraisal time, something that the employees have been doing wrong all year long—and could have corrected months before.

Evaluation: Management by Objectives

Another systematic approach to employee evaluation and development is management by objectives.

MBO Philosophy.   Management by objectives is based on Douglas McGregor's Theory Y philosophy. The Theory Y manager assumes that people like to work, derive real satisfaction from their work, and want to do a good job. A Theory X manager cannot use MBO effectively. Managers who feel comfortable with Theory Y assumptions may find MBO to be a simple, effective tool that aids them in doing what they have already been doing: motivating, evaluating, and communicating with employees.

MBO Process.   Peter Drucker explains MBO in terms of the "manager's letter." In the letter, subordinate Helen Coleman would specify:

1. What she believes the long-range objectives of her boss are.
2. What she believes her own job objectives are.
3. What performance criteria she believes her boss applies to her.
4. What subobjectives she must accomplish in order to achieve her job objectives.
5. What organizational resources and requirements either help or hinder her in accomplishing her sub-objectives and objectives.
6. What specific activities she will attempt in order to reach the sub-objectives, which will lead to achievement of her overall job objectives.[2]

[2]Peter Drucker, *The Practice of Management* (New York: Harper & Row, Inc., 1954), pp. 129–130.

Once Coleman writes the letter, she and her boss discuss it and correct it. After Coleman and her boss agree on the letter's accuracy and completeness, it becomes a performance "contract" for a set time period. At the end of this period, Coleman and her manager review her performance to see whether she has met the performance standards agreed to in the contract.

This review serves as Coleman's evaluation by her manager. The evaluation allows Coleman to find out her areas of strength and weakness. In a relatively objective way, the pair can determine how well Coleman has fulfilled the "contract."

Making MBO Work.   There are problems with MBO. First, it creates a lot of paperwork because specific objectives must be written down. Second, not all managers can verbalize their expectations, nor can all employees verbalize their objectives. Both skills take practice. Third, the manager may not know enough about the jobs of subordinates to help them set realistic objectives.

These problems must be overcome if MBO is to be used fairly as a performance evaluation tool. If managers and employees can learn to write down realistic objectives, the evaluation process goes much more smoothly because managers and employees have a standard—agreed to in advance by both of them—for appraising job performance.

Evaluation: Job Behavior Scales

A final evaluation method is the behavior scale. Employees and managers get together to define and describe effective and ineffective behaviors for each job. These behaviors are then placed on an evaluation form.

This method can be useful, but defining behavior and achieving mutual employer–employee agreement about effective and ineffective ways to behave take time. If an organization consists of few job groupings, each containing many employees (like nurses, department store salespeople, or insurance claim clerks), then the form may be worth generating. If the organization has many job groupings with few people in each job, generating the form will probably not be worthwhile.

Compensation

The ideal compensation plan would directly reflect the organization's judgments of employee effort and performance. However, other influences bear on what compensation each employee receives.

Influences on Compensation Levels.   Compensation levels are based on two influences: (1) the going market rate for a particular skill, and (2) the differential inside an organization between people having that skill. Both influences cause problems and complaints.

Different skills command different compensation levels. That is why a personnel department member who did a great job last year may be bitterly disappointed to find that the mediocre, uncaring computer programmer down the hall got a much larger raise.

The demand for engineers during the 1960s made for a classic compensation problem. Their salaries rose at incredible rates. Two results were (1) that other employees became demoralized as they saw even mediocre engineers receiving large raises, and (2) that the engineers expected their good fortune to be permanent. As the space program was cut back during the 1970s, demand leveled out and the engineers unhappily saw the big raises stop. Nonengineers were still unhappy because the salary differentials of the 1960s remained.

Whole books and entire courses exist on how to structure the organization's compensation plan. As a guiding principle, any good compensation plan will embody some behavior modification elements. The plan will reward desirable employee behaviors and will not reward undesirable employee behaviors.

Table 14-2 indicates the behavior modification implications of 14 incentive or compensation methods. Column 1 briefly describes the compensation methods. Column 2 indicates how long a time the employee must wait between the behavior and the compensation for it. Column 3 tells how predictable the compensation method is as a reinforcer. Column 4 specifies whether the compensation method appeals to an economic need, a behavioral need, or a combination of the two.

OTHER PROGRAMS

Important staffing decisions must be made in three additional areas: employee benefits, union matters, and safety and health.

Employee Benefits

Employee benefits are sometimes referred to as *fringe benefits*. From the employer's point of view, that term understates their importance because these benefits can be very costly. In fact, across many organizations and industries, these benefits average between 30 and 35 percent of wage payments.

Benefit Types. Employee benefits are of five types:

1. Retirement and insurance benefits required by law (workmen's compensation and Social Security).

TABLE 14-2 Common Compensation Methods Classified by Time Interval Between Behavior and Reinforcement, Predictability of Reinforcement, and Need Appeal of Reinforcement

Compensation Method	Time Interval Between Behavior and Reinforcement	Predictability of Reinforcement	Primary Need Appeal of Reinforcement
1. Daywork: employee is paid a daily wage.	Relatively short	Predictable	Primarily economic
2. Piecework: employee is paid a fixed rate for each unit of work performed.	Relatively short	Predictable	Primarily economic
3. Taylor piecework: above average output results in much better pay than average or below average output.	Relatively short	Predictable	Primarily economic
4. Halsey plan: a time-saved plan; actual hours worked are subtracted from standard time. Value of hours saved is split between employee and company.	Relatively short	Predictable	Primarily economic
5. Bedaux plan: based on time saved; employee splits bonus for time saved with indirect help.	Intermediate	Predictable	Part economic, part behavioral
6. Scanlon plan: bonus paid to group members on the basis of cost savings as some proportion of production value.	Intermediate	Predictable	Part economic, part behavioral
7. Yearly merit increases: above standard performance results in a yearly wage or salary increase.	Relatively long	Predictable	Part economic, part behavioral

8. Performance targets: target output is set; employees are rewarded for meeting or exceeding target goals.	Relatively long	Somewhat predictable	Part economic, part behavioral
9. Education plans: provide payment for education; improve promotional opportunities.	Relatively long	Predictable	Primarily behavioral
10. Competition: individual or team rivalry is encouraged; best performance is rewarded.	Long or short	Predictable	Primarily behavioral
11. Organizational recognition: outstanding performance is rewarded with non-monetary awards.	Relatively long	Largely predictable	Primarily behavioral
12. Supervisory recognition: outstanding performers are praised by their supervisors.	Relatively short	Unpredictable	Primarily behavioral
13. Promotion: good workers are promoted over poorer workers; new positions may or may not pay more.	Relatively long	Largely predictable	Part behavioral, part economic
14. Stock purchase: employees become "owners" and are motivated to improve production.	Relatively long	Predictable	Part behavioral, part economic

Source: Robert C. Ford and Ronald Couture, "A Contingency Approach to Incentive Program Design," *Compensation Review*, 10 (Second Quarter 1978), p. 40. Used by permission.

2. Retirement and insurance benefits not required by law (life insurance, health and accident insurance, pension plans).
3. Additional compensation (bonuses, profit sharing, stock options).
4. Compensation without work (vacations, holidays, sick pay).
5. Miscellaneous benefits (discounts on purchases, subsidized college courses, free tickets, company gymnasiums and cafeterias, flexible working hours).

Although organizations have willingly granted some of these benefits to employees, union pressure resulted in many of them. Organizations began offering benefits to employees so that they would not join unions, unionized organizations were forced to offer benefits, and employees came out ahead either way. Some organizations now allow employees to make up their own benefit packages (within set limits), taking the benefits they need or want because of age, life style, or family situations.

Unions

Because subordinates have only a limited opportunity to bargain individually with their managers, many employees have often joined together to bargain collectively. Managerial decision making in most organizations—public and private—is affected by either the *fact* or the *possibility* of unionization.

When an organization's employees form a union, the employees and the union negotiate together to arrive at a collective bargaining agreement. This agreement describes the conditions of employment for union members, specifies a procedure for resolving grievances, and places members under certain protections and obligations.

Unions are an extremely important influence on manager–subordinate relationships. They affect employee power, security, performance, motivation, wages, hours, and working conditions.

Safety and Health

Society expects that modern employers will provide safe, healthy working conditions. For many years, various state laws and regulations were designed to protect employees. As an attempt to increase protection, Congress enacted the Occupational Safety and Health Act (OSHA, usually pronounced *o-shuh*) in 1970. The act affects any business engaged in interstate commerce.

The Department of Labor and the Department of Health, Education, and Welfare administer OSHA. The research that forms the basis for safety and health criteria is performed by HEW. As these standards are established, HEW publishes them in the *Federal Register*.

The Department of Labor actually sets and enforces industrial safety and health standards. The department inspects employment locations and, if violations are discovered, imposes penalties and issues citations.

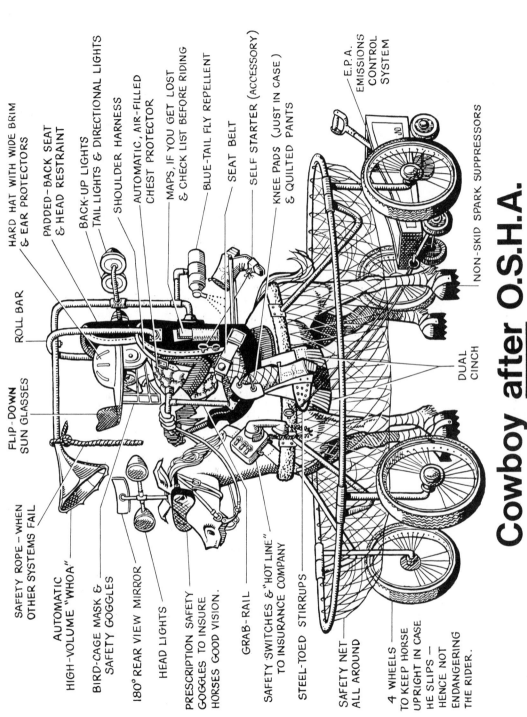

SAFETY ROPE – WHEN
OTHER SYSTEMS FAIL

AUTOMATIC
HIGH-VOLUME "WHOA"

BIRD-CAGE MASK &
SAFETY GOGGLES

180° REAR VIEW MIRROR

HEAD LIGHTS

PRESCRIPTION SAFETY
GOGGLES TO INSURE
HORSES GOOD VISION.

GRAB-RAIL

SAFETY SWITCHES & "HOT LINE"
TO INSURANCE COMPANY

STEEL-TOED STIRRUPS

SAFETY NET
ALL AROUND

4 WHEELS
TO KEEP HORSE
UPRIGHT IN CASE
HE SLIPS –
HENCE NOT
ENDANGERING
THE RIDER.

HARD HAT WITH WIDE BRIM
& EAR PROTECTORS

PADDED–BACK SEAT
& HEAD RESTRAINT

BACK-UP LIGHTS
TAIL LIGHTS & DIRECTIONAL LIGHTS

SHOULDER HARNESS

AUTOMATIC, AIR-FILLED
CHEST PROTECTOR

MAPS, IF YOU GET LOST
& CHECK LIST BEFORE RIDING

BLUE-TAIL FLY REPELLENT

SEAT BELT

SELF STARTER (ACCESSORY)

KNEE PADS (JUST IN CASE)
& QUILTED PANTS

E.P.A.
EMISSIONS
CONTROL
SYSTEM

ROLL BAR

FLIP-DOWN
SUN GLASSES

DUAL
CINCH

NON-SKID SPARK SUPPRESSORS

Cowboy after O.S.H.A.

FIG 14-3 (Copyright by J. N. Devin. Used by permission.)

SUMMARY

This chapter on staffing has included five major sections. The first section emphasized how important an ongoing assessment of personnel needs is to the organization at both the macro and micro levels.

Once the organization is aware of its personnel needs, applicants must be recruited from inside or outside the organization. Selecting people for jobs above the entry level was seen to be a subjective process, made more difficult in recent years by antidiscrimination legislation and requirements that personnel tests be validated. Because of these difficulties, more and more organizations are turning their selection and testing over to a specialized service: the assessment center.

Once employees are selected, they must be trained and developed. The chapter described three techniques: presenting information, supervised instruction (and on-the-job training), and simulation.

The next major section dealt with employee evaluation and compensation. Two evaluation programs were discussed in detail: performance appraisal and management by objectives. Although many organizations appraise the performance of employees annually, more frequent appraisals were shown to have several benefits. A third evaluation method, the job behavior scale, was mentioned briefly.

The chapter concluded by discussing three other staffing concerns: employee benefits, unions, and safety and health.

This chapter may seem to have covered a wide variety of subjects. However, they are all related to these three staffing principles: get the best people, help them to do their best in the job, and keep them satisfied while they are doing their best work.

DISCUSSION QUESTIONS

1. In a personnel needs assessment, what is the difference between the micro and macro levels?
2. What sources are available to the manager seeking new employees?
3. How should a manager assess the requirements of an individual employee position in order to tell the personnel department what kind of person to look for?
4. What are the legal constraints on using tests for selection?
5. What good is an assessment center?
6. What methods can be used to train and develop employees?
7. What are the common problems in performance appraisal?
8. What is management by objectives? How is it set up?

9. What should the relationship between evaluation and compensation be?
10. How can behavior modification principles be used in compensation programs?

Evon Street, president of the First National Bank, is not happy with the bank's performance appraisal system. The system makes use of the trait approach. Traits seen as desirable by the bank are listed, and managers evaluate their subordinates on how well they match these traits.

As Street views the system, it has four major flaws:

1. Most managers give favorable marks on *all* traits to people they think should be promoted. That practice makes identifying personnel weaknesses difficult, and in several instances people have been promoted without having their weaknesses corrected. They have then made serious errors that have caused great problems for the bank.

2. Many employees feel that the trait appraisals are unfair in what they measure and how they are administered. For example, young male employees think that their evaluations are lowered because they dress differently, talk differently, and wear longer hair than the managers evaluating them do.

3. Top management has difficulty in interpreting evaluation results because some managers evaluate everyone quite positively and other managers, maintaining that they have "high standards," evaluate everyone rather unfavorably.

4. The First National Bank has grown rapidly over the past few years. The bank now has 130 branches throughout the state. Branch managers complain that their district managers do not understand local conditions well enough to evaluate the branch managers fairly.

Evon Street has taken the problem to the executive group and has asked them for recommendations as to how, or if, the performance appraisal system should be changed.

During her first year as personnel manager of Great States Insurance Company, Olive Evans became increasingly aware of a possible morale problem within the company's clerical workers. Employee absenteeism and tardiness were rising. Coffee breaks were being extended beyond the allowed 15 minutes. According to the grapevine, employees were not happy with working conditions or with the work load.

Although Evans was aware that turnover had been rising, she was surprised that it had exceeded 50 percent at the clerical level over the past year. She reviewed the past year's resignations. They accounted for 95 percent of the turnover. The other 5 percent were workers who had been terminated as unsatisfactory.

The company employed 70 men and 140 women. The women were employed primarily at the clerical level. Approximately 25 percent of the resignations were for reasons in two categories: "husband being transferred to another city" and "wife leaving to devote more time to home and family." Evans viewed these resignations as beyond company control and ignored them. The remaining resignations occurred for four reasons, in the following frequency of occurrence: (1) left to get salary increase, (2) left to get greater opportunity for advancement, (3) left to get different type of work, (4) personal reasons.

Evans reviewed the criteria for hiring, from desirable to undesirable in the company's view: under 21; single or newly married without children; husband in armed forces or for other reasons temporarily in the area; divorced with children; early twenties to early thirties; family fully established; husband permanently employed in the area; children fully grown. The hiring policy was obviously designed to appeal to people who seriously needed an income but who did not need a high income.

How should Evans change the Great States hiring policies?

directing: situational and individual factors

A fourth managerial function is directing. The manager must make the decisions that direct the organization's human resources. Since no manager can achieve effective results through other people without this skill, directing is one of the most widely sought abilities in management today.

Much organizational direction is really self-direction. If employee goals and organizational goals are compatible, and if these goals are specific and measurable so that employees know whether they are reaching them or not, employees can largely direct themselves. That assumption is based on the Theory Y philosophy of Douglas McGregor: people want to do a good job and *will* do a good job if they know and agree to what is expected of them.

Many managers simply cannot accept this assumption about their employees (although they probably accept it about themselves). Nevertheless, although many exceptions exist, most people want to work effectively and productively, and the organization is responsible for helping them to do so. The organization fulfills this responsibility by ensuring that the right person is in the right place at the right time, heading toward the right goals, and provided with the right rewards.

Figure 15-1 shows the three forces that jointly and interactively determine effective employee performance. The present chapter discusses two of them: situational factors and individual factors. The next chapter discusses the third element in the performance triangle: motivational factors.

SITUATIONAL FACTORS

The factors making up the work situation are obviously important. They can structure the employee's behavior, and they can largely determine whether the employee is happy and effective within the situation. Some situational factors are objective; they can be observed and measured by anyone. Other situational factors are subjective. These factors, both tangible and intangible, are perceived differently by different employees.

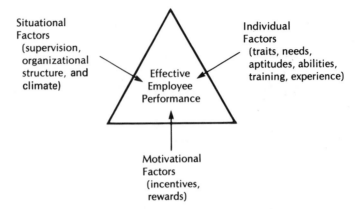

Situational
Factors
(supervision,
organizational
structure, and
climate)

Effective
Employee
Performance

Individual
Factors
(traits, needs,
aptitudes, abilities,
training, experience)

Motivational
Factors
(incentives,
rewards)

FIG 15-1 The performance triangle.

This section will discuss three major situational forces:

1. The leader
2. The organization's structure
3. The organizational climate

Leadership and structure will be dealt with separately, although they both contribute to the organizational climate as the worker perceives it.

The Leader

The Importance of Leadership.   The most important situational factor from the employee's point of view is the leader. That person structures the work environment; determines the appropriateness, fairness, and adequacy of organizational rewards; and provides the main linkage between individual members and the rest of the organization. The formal or designated leader explains their jobs to subordinates, shows how those jobs contribute to organizational goals, and makes clear how subordinates are supposed to act. The leader is the person who can do most to ensure a proper balance between organizational inducements and member contributions.

Organizations have always known that leadership positions are important. However, only recently have they begun to consider seriously what a drastic change in roles occurs when a former supervisee becomes a supervisor. Leader and follower behaviors are different. Making the position of new leaders even more difficult is the fact that they must now play two roles; they must lead their subordinates, and they must follow their own leaders.

The Study of Leadership.   Leadership has been studied in several ways. The sequence of study has paralleled the way in which the study of management and organizational theory has progressed. First came the "one best way" approach: What traits do the best leaders possess? Next came the human relations approach: How does the effective leader behave in relation to subordinates? Finally came a systems or contingency approach: What are the factors in the entire manager–subordinate environment that make for effective and ineffective leaders? These three approaches will now be described.

Trait Theory.   What is a leader? What does a leader do? A logical starting point for answering such questions is to find some leaders and study them to identify those physical characteristics, personality traits, or other factors that make for effective leadership. The early study of leadership paralleled the early work in scientific management. From roughly 1930 to 1950, researchers believed that one best way to lead must exist, so one universal set of leader characteristics must contribute to that best way to lead.

The longer this course of reseach was followed, the more contradictory the results became. One researcher would find that successful leaders were enthusiastic, friendly, affectionate, decisive, and sensitive. Another researcher would find that successful leaders had a sense of purpose and direction, physical and nervous energy, technical skill, intelligence and faith. A third would conclude that the successful leader must be moral, wise, determined, good looking, courageous, talkative, and tall. The list of important leadership traits grew longer and more useless for differentiating potentially good leaders from anyone else.

Even though the trait approach has been largely discredited, many people cling to a stereotype of the "managerial personality," perhaps derived from television and popular fiction. The stereotype does not hold up in real life. Peter Drucker cites the three greatest executives he ever met: Alfred Sloan and Nicholas Dreysenstadt of General Motors and General George C. Marshall. Their personal characteristics were as different as could be. Sloan was cool and reserved, Dreysenstadt was warm and bubbly, and Marshall was shy but charming.

Figure 15-2 shows one researcher's conclusions about which traits are important for managerial success. The positions of the traits suggest that one trait (supervisory ability) is essential, five are very important, three are of minor importance, and three or four are of little or no importance.

The trait approach failed for two reasons. First, traits are difficult to define and quantify in any useful way. Second, the leader's traits are only a part of the whole leadership environment. The leader possessing those traits necessary for success in one environment may fail miserably in another. Third, the trait approach ignores the specific task at hand. The person with more job knowledge or job skills is more likely to emerge as a leader, regardless of "traits." The basketball team captain will be a good player, not a poor one.

Even so, research suggests that most leaders in most situations must have four traits if they are going to succeed.

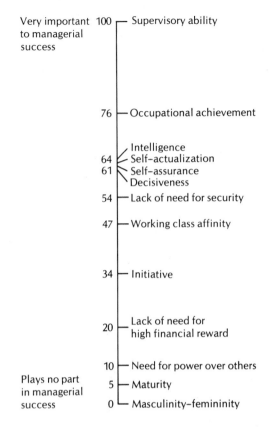

FIG 15-2 The relative importance of thirteen traits to managerial success. (*Source:* Edwin Ghiselli, *Explorations in Managerial Talent.* Pacific Palisades, Calif.: Goodyear Publishing Company, 1971, p. 165. Used by permission.)

One trait is *intelligence*. Leaders are usually more intelligent than their followers.

Another trait is *drive*. Leaders want to keep moving, to keep accomplishing.

A third trait is *emotional stability*. Leaders are not easily frustrated, and they have learned to roll with the punches.

A fourth trait is *human relations skills and attitudes*. Leaders know that their leadership success depends on how well they can achieve the cooperation of other people.

Most leaders have these traits, but many people who are *not* leaders also have them. So the usefulness of this trait list is limited.

The Behavior of Leaders.   The trait approach failed as a predictor of leadership success and as a guide to identifying those characteristics that, if developed, would result in effective leaders. Therefore, the emphasis of research into leadership shifted over to the behavioral orientation emerging from the post-World War II human relations movement. Researchers changed over from the study of leadership *traits* to leadership *behaviors*.

The Ohio State Studies. The most famous of these studies were carried out at Ohio State University during the 1950s. Researchers ignored personal or physical characteristics and sought to isolate and define the *behaviors* of successful leaders.

These studies resulted in a two-factor leadership theory. The two factors were called *consideration* and *initiating structure*.

Consideration includes behavior indicating trust, respect, warmth, and desire for rapport. The considerate leader is concerned about group member needs, establishes two-way communications, and encourages participation in decision making. The considerate leader is supportive, friendly, and approachable.

The leader also *initiates structure* by organizing and defining group activities, assigning job roles, establishing goals, scheduling the work, evaluating work quality and quantity, and generally attempting to satisfy organizational requirements.

These two dimensions of leadership are independent. A person may score high on both, low on both, or high on one and low on the other. In other terms, these two dimensions might be called *concern for people* and *concern for product*.

The University of Michigan Studies. Another set of studies, conducted during the 1950s at the University of Michigan, complemented the Ohio State findings. The Michigan researchers identified two distinct leadership styles, *employee-centered* and *job-centered*, that parallel the two Ohio State leadership dimensions, consideration and initiation of structure.

The job-centered manager emphasizes production, close supervision, specified procedures, and clear-cut rewards and punishments. The job-centered manager may be aware of human relations concerns but views them as a luxury and not a necessity. The job-centered orientation was a natural continuation of the historical industrial focus on production results. Followers were expected to obey the leader's orders without hesitation, question, or thought.

The employee-centered manager focuses on the work group and work environment. The employee-centered manager expects that production will be satisfactory if workers are content and the atmosphere is supportive. This orientation was a reaction against the earlier emphasis on production at all costs. Social philosophy was changing. Employees had feelings and rights. The emergence of the human relations philosophy was a logical product of its time. The surprising results of the Hawthorne experiments, confirmed in later studies, convinced managers in the 1950s that the best leader behaved so as to facilitate (rather than force) group formation, development, and performance.

The Michigan researchers studied 500 clerical employees over one year. Half of them worked for employee-centered managers, and half worked for job-centered managers. The researchers used such effectiveness criteria as productivity, job satisfaction, turnover, and absenteeism.

Productivity increased under *both* types of managers: 20 percent under employee-centered managers and 25 percent under job-centered managers. However, the nonproductivity criteria—job satisfaction, turnover, and absenteeism—increased under job-centered managers and decreased under employee-centered managers. The researchers concluded that the employee-centered approach was more effective, overall, because the short-run higher productivity of job-centered units was more than offset by the long-run negative attitudes brought about by job-centered managers.

The Ohio State and Michigan studies imply that the manager should concentrate on the "people part" of the organization. The continuum in Figure 15-3 spans the different leadership behaviors available. According to the Michigan and Ohio State results, managers should move as far to the right side of the continuum as they comfortably can.

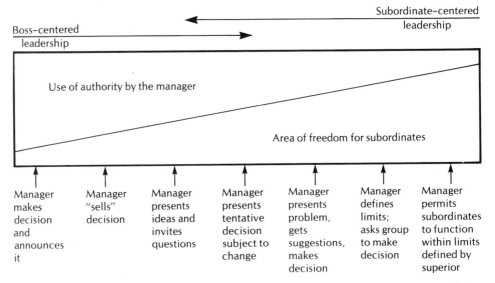

FIG 15-3 The continuum of leadership behavior. Reprinted by permission of the *Harvard Business Review.* Exhibit 1 of "How to Choose a Leadership Pattern" by Robert Tannenbaum and Warren H. Schmidt (May-June 1973). Copyright © 1973 by the President and Fellows of Harvard College; all rights reserved.

The point of the Ohio State and Michigan studies is that what the manager *does* is more important than what the manager *is*. Of course, traits and behavior cannot be totally separated. People with certain traits do tend to behave in certain ways.

Path–Goal Theory.   A leadership theory appearing in the early 1970s is path–goal theory. According to this theory, good leaders behave in these ways: (1) they make rewards available to subordinates, (2) they make sure that these rewards are tied to the accomplishment of specific goals, and (3) they continually clarify for employees what kind of behavior (or what path) will lead to accomplishing the specific goals and to receiving the rewards for goal accomplishment. According to the theory, the leader behaving in these ways will have motivated, satisfied employees who accept the manager's leadership.

Contingency Theory.   Most human relations writers send this message: participatory, employee-centered leadership is good and should be developed. Since the research on this point is ambiguous, the message is founded more on faith than on data.

The lack of empirical support for the human relations approach to leadership led to a new line of reasoning, ultimately called contingency theory. We have already discussed contingency theory as it relates to organizational structure. The contingency theorists concluded that universally accurate answers to the classical organizational questions did not exist. Instead, the "best" organizational approach varied from industry to industry, department to department, and person to person. Thinking of the organization as a system led to the conclusion that the answer to a particular question was contingent on the best fit or meshing of the forces and factors in a particular setting at a particular time.

This shift of emphasis carried over into leadership research. Investigators stopped studying what types of leadership behavior were *generally* appropriate and began relating leadership behavior to particular situations.

Fred Fiedler's Work.   The classic leadership studies in this area are those of Fred Fiedler. He tried to answer this question: What kind of situation requires what kind of leader? Fiedler discusses two leadership styles with which we are already familiar: job-centered and people-centered. Whether a given situation calls for a job-centered style or a people-centered style depends on three variables: the leader's position power, task structure, and leader–member personal relations.

Position power refers to the leader's degree of authority (by virtue of position) over the group. For example, an army captain has more position power than a bowling team captain. *Task structure* refers to the step-by-step definiteness of the task. A drill press operator has a structured task. A psychiatrist has an unstructured task. Leading is easier if worker tasks are structured. *Leader–member personal relations* refer to whether or not the group likes, trusts, and respects the leader.

Influential Variables.   Fiedler studied many groups and found out that the three variables rank as follows in terms of the influence that they give the leader over the group: (1) leader–member relations, (2) task structure, (3) position power.

Fiedler makes the following generalizations: (1) leader–member relations can be either good or poor, (2) tasks can be either structured or unstructured, (3) the leader's position power can be either strong or weak. Figure 15-4 shows the possible relationships among these generalizations. One obvious point is that the most influential leader has good group relations, a structured task, and strong position power. Not so obvious, but also proposed by Fiedler, is the idea that a leader with *weak* position power supervising a *structured* task has more influence than a leader with *strong* position power supervising an *unstructured* task. The degree of task structure, then, affects the leader's influence significantly.

Leader–member relations	Good				Poor			
Task structure	Structured		Unstructured		Structured		Unstructured	
Leader position power	Strong	Weak	Strong	Weak	Strong	Weak	Strong	Weak

FIG 15-4   Three variables affecting leadership effectiveness. (*Source:* Fred E. Fiedler, *A Theory of Leadership Effectiveness.* New York: McGraw-Hill Book Co., 1967, p. 34. Used by permission.)

Appropriate Leadership Style.   After studying 800 groups, Fiedler determined which situations called for job-centered leadership and which called for people-centered leadership. The results appear in Table 15-1. The eight possible "situations" (eight possible combinations of the three variables) are numbered in the first column. The manager takes a look at the group's leader–member relations, task structure, and the leader's position power, and

TABLE 15-1   Appropriate Leadership Styles in Different Situations

Situation	Leader–Member Relations	Task Structure	Position Power	Appropriate Style
1	Good	Structured	Strong	Job-oriented
2	Good	Structured	Weak	Job-oriented
3	Good	Unstructured	Strong	Job-oriented
4	Good	Unstructured	Weak	People-oriented
5	Moderately poor	Structured	Strong	People-oriented
6	Moderately poor	Structured	Weak	People-oriented
7	Moderately poor	Unstructured	Strong	People-oriented
8	Moderately poor	Unstructured	Weak	Job-oriented

Source: Fred E. Fiedler, *A Theory of Leadership Effectiveness* (New York: McGraw-Hill Book Co., 1967), p. 34. Used by permission.

then chooses the leadership style (or appoints a manager who has a leadership style) indicated in the last column as being appropriate to that combination. Surprisingly, the job-centered style is appropriate at the extremes. According to Fiedler, the leader with good leader–member relations, a structured task, and a strong power position *and* the leader with poor leader–member relations, an unstructured task, and a weak power position should *both* use the job-oriented style.

In Fiedler's view, leadership style depends largely on personality. To change one's style is to change one's personality—very difficult (possibly harmful) to attempt. Rather than change the leader to fit the job, Fiedler recommends changing the job to fit the leader or moving the leader to a more suitable job.

The Fiedler model describes only eight situations made up of three different variables. It offers only two leadership-style possibilities. Therefore, it is somewhat general and limited as to its real-life applications. Fiedler's contribution was to suggest that we cannot legitimately point to "good leaders" and "bad leaders." We must specify the leadership situation.

Environment and Structure

The second category of situational variables affecting employee performance is the physical environment of the workplace and the structure of the organization. The employee fits in a block somewhere on the organization chart, and certain aspects of the chart affect the blocks on it. Within the employee's block, the physical environment affects performance.

Physical Environment. Ever since the Hawthorne studies, researchers have been studying the influence of physical setting on job performance. For example, organizational psychologists determine part of the workplace mood by asking that the walls be painted in certain colors. Music may enhance worker satisfaction and performance. Room temperature, lighting level, work space size, cleaniness, and a drinking fountain may all affect the pleasantness of the job environment. Managers should do what they can to make the workplace physically conducive to top performance.

Organizational Structure. The influence of the organization's structural features on employee performance is still only partially understood. Table 15-2 summarizes some research findings on how structural factors are related to job satisfaction and performance.

As the table shows, research has confirmed some obvious probabilities. First, the employee's *level* in the structure makes a difference. People higher up in the organization are usually happier than people lower down. Supervisors get greater job satisfaction than workers do. In some firms, the higher

TABLE 15-2 Influence of Structural Factors on Job Satisfaction and Performance

Structural Factor	Satisfaction	Behavior and Performance
Organizational level	Higher satisfaction, better morale, at higher levels	Higher levels better informed, have more interpersonal relationships, make different types of decisions
Line and staff	Staff have less satisfaction than line	Staff are better informed, have higher turnover rate
Span of control	Inconclusive results; large span may have higher morale	No proven relationship between span and performance
Size of subunit	Smaller size produces higher satisfaction	Smaller size produces lower turnover, fewer absentees and accidents, and less labor strife.
Size of total organization	Ambiguous results; small companies, lower levels more satisfied; in large companies, higher levels more satisfied	Inconclusive results
Organization shape: tall or flat	In small organizations, flat structures produce greater job satisfaction; in large organizations, tall structures produce greater satisfaction	Large organizations tend to have greater productivity in tall structures
Degree of decentralization	Inconclusive results	Inconclusive results

Source: Adapted from Lyman W. Porter and Edward E. Lawler, III, "Properties of Organization Structure in Relation to Job Attitudes and Job Behavior," *Psychological Bulletin,* Vol. 64, No. 1 (1965), pp. 23–51.

(or lower) your position on the chart, the happier (or less happy) you are. However, in other organizations, the middle levels are less satisfied than organization members at upper and lower extremes.

Staff members are less satisfied than line members. Because they move about through different departments, staff members learn more about what is going on than line members do. Findings concerning how span of control affects performance and attitude are lacking. Workers in small work units are more satisfied and perform better than workers in larger units. However, the findings are not uniform on whether workers in larger organizations are more satisfied and perform better than workers in small organizations.

Organization shape (tall or flat) seems to affect both job satisfaction and performance. In small organizations, flat structures tend to produce more satisfied employees. In large organizations, tall structures seem to produce greater job satisfaction and productivity. No relationship can yet be shown between satisfaction or performance and the degree of organizational decentralization. Whether an organization is centralized or decentralized probably has an effect, but it is masked by the greater effect of other factors.

Inconclusive Data.   Much research is inconclusive. People and organizations vary so much that dependable generalizations are scarce. A work group of 10 may be too big for one worker and too small for another worker in the same group.

Furthermore, the objective data may not reflect the truth of the situation as it is experienced by the people in it. Supervisor Brown oversees her 15 subordinates so closely and constantly that they may wish for a wider span of control at Brown's supervisory level. Supervisor Green is never available for consultation and gives no direction. His five subordinates may think the span of control at his level is too loose.

As another example, an outsider judging the cleanliness of a particular steel mill would probably compare it either to other steel mills or to an "average" work environment. A given mill might be rated as "exceptionally clean" on a researcher's scale. However, an employee starting to work at the mill after having most recently worked at a milk processing plant or a hospital would consider the place absolutely filthy.

In short, some aspects of the job situation can be known, perhaps even measured, but they affect people differently. Therefore, most research findings in this area cannot help the decision maker very much.

Organizational Climate

Six Dimensions of Climate.   To overcome the foregoing problems with objective measures, some researchers tried to measure the subjective impact (on employees) of the objective factors. Investigations into "organizational climate" became an attempt to measure what the organization is really like as employees themselves see it.

"Climate" is a vague term. Every aspect of the work environment—including the two situational factors already mentioned, leadership and physical environment–structure—contributes to the climate. The term is helpful because it refers not to things as they really *are* but to the way things are *perceived* by the organization's members. Climate is really a kind of filter, through which the employee perceives the objective reality of the job situation.

One well-known definition of climate includes six separate dimensions:

1. Structure. The extent to which the employee feels bound by rules, regulations, and red tape.
2. Individual responsibility. The extent to which the employee feels independent and autonomous.

3. Rewards. The extent to which the employee feels that a good job is properly rewarded.

4. Challenge. The extent to which the employee views the job as a challenge.

5. Warmth and support. The extent to which the employee perceives good fellowship and friendliness.

6. Tolerance of conflict. The extent to which the employee feels that different opinions are tolerated.[1]

Problems in Assessing Climate.   The main difficulty in the study of climate is a lack of agreement on what climate is and a lack of sophisticated tools for measuring how the dimensions of climate (whatever the definition) actually influence employee performance. One person may find red tape, double-checking by supervisors, and punching a time clock necessary; another may find these elements of "climate" offensive. As so often happens, individual variations cause problems in interpreting research data.

The second problem is how to make the concept of climate useful to managers. Once the pluses and minuses in the job environment are identified, how can the employee's perceptions of climate be modified? Many employees hold to outdated and unjustified perceptions. Some older, more traditional organizations are still trying to dispel a climate of hostility and distrust that resulted from labor strife experienced decades ago.

The point is that, even if the dimensions of climate could be accurately identified, no one knows for sure what programs, procedures, or policies can change employee perceptions. However, as in many management situations, identifying the problem is at least a start. Managers can try different alternative strategies for modifying and correcting the unfavorable perceptions of employees.

INDIVIDUAL FACTORS

The second side of the performance triangle is individual factors. Because of variations in skill, aptitude, experience, training, physique, and intelligence, some people are obviously better at their jobs than other people are. A dwarf cannot be an effective center on a professional basketball team. An effective center cannot walk through a 5-foot pipeline to inspect it for leaks. Some students have an aptitude for quantitative concepts and choose college courses on quantitative subjects. Other students prefer qualitative ideas and enjoy discussing abstractions.

Characteristics of Success

Such differences are also found in job situations. Many assembly-line workers say they like what they are doing and are not bored. Some middle managers,

---

[1]George H. Litwin and Robert A. Stringer, Jr., *Motivation and Organizational Climate* (Boston: Harvard University Graduate School of Business Administration, 1968), pp. 67–68.

adequate at their mentally taxing jobs, drop out to become craftsmen because they find their true skills to be in the crafts.

The point of concern for decision makers, seeking to deal with all three sides of the performance triangle, is to place people in jobs for which their unique combinations of traits and attributes best suit them. Even if people are properly selected, the manager may not motivate them to perform their best. However, the organization should at least try to identify those individual traits associated with success, and then either select people with those traits or instill the traits within present personnel.

All too often, the Peter Principle seems accurate because an organization's leadership has not recognized that jobs at different *levels* require different skills. The skills required to be a salesperson and a sales manager, or a social worker and a social worker supervisor, are not the same. The different levels require different behaviors, training, interests, and concerns. People receiving promotions often need orientation programs to learn the new mental set and behaviors demanded at the next-higher level.

Managerial Success.   As the staffing chapter showed, individual factors and job requirements can be matched fairly well at lower job levels. Typing tests, manual dexterity tests, and measures of aptitude, intelligence, and creativity help the manager to place people in compatible jobs.

At the managerial level, such matching is more difficult. Managerial positions are more ambiguous, less easy to specify. Therefore, the individual factors related to managerial effectiveness have not yet been usefully defined.

The Exxon Studies

Some years ago, Exxon made a major attempt to match individual factors with managerial effectiveness. The company tried to answer two questions: (1) How should managerial effectiveness be measured? (2) How can potentially effective managers be identified early?

Measures of Managerial Effectiveness.   Exxon chose three measures of managerial effectiveness: (1) position level in the company, (2) salary history (to place a dollar value on each manager's "worth" to the company), and (3) an "effectiveness ranking" based on assessments by higher-level managers. These three criteria were combined into one "success index."

The 443 managers then took a battery of tests (verbal ability, personality, reasoning, etc.) and filled out biographical inventories (background, education, family, hobbies, finances, etc.). All this information was combined into a single score.

Results.   Overall, the best predictors of managerial effectiveness seemed to be the biographical surveys, a management judgment test, and intelligence. Exxon has not revealed the specifics, but the successful Exxon managers had a history of success in other areas. These managers did well in college, held leadership positions before arriving at Exxon, and viewed themselves as confident, assertive, and forceful people.

The Minnesota Study

Another study attempting to relate individual factors and managerial effectiveness was undertaken in the late 1950s at the University of Minnesota's Industrial Relations Center. Tests and a biographical survey were given to 452 managers. Just as in the Exxon studies, the managers were ranked for effectiveness by higher-level managers.

The Minnesota investigators studied 98 predictors of managerial success. Narrowing those to the 18 most statistically significant, they concluded that, compared to less successful managers, successful managers are more intelligent, dominant, and educated (as are their spouses). When younger, they were more active in hobbies and sports than less successful managers were.

The Chamber of Commerce Studies

In the Chamber of Commerce studies, 600 Chamber executives filled out an 11-page biographical questionnaire. The researchers wanted to find out whether any biographical data were correlated with executive success.

The study results showed that the successful Chamber of Commerce executive

1. Is from a middle class social background.
2. Had a happy early family life.
3. Is well educated.
4. Was involved in extracurricular activities.
5. Engaged in communications activities (debating, school paper, etc.).
6. Entered Chamber activities before age 35.

Individual Factors: A Summary

Successful executives have been shown to possess some characteristics in common: intelligence, a way with words, good managerial judgment, dominance, confidence, and skill at organizing. They are active, they work hard, and they are not afraid to take risks.

The backgrounds of these executives reflect a history of good health and energy, scholastic and extracurricular success and leadership, ambition, and active participation in community groups.

That people having such backgrounds should achieve managerial success is not surprising. They have a backlog of success and accomplishment. They enter the organization ready and able to be trained for further success.

Yet these studies are of limited help. They speak of "managerial effectiveness" as if all managerial jobs were quite similar. Obviously they are not. Furthermore, these studies stress what managers *are*, rather than what they *do*. Individual factors have a bearing on managerial performance, of course, but they are not nearly as important as *how the manager thinks about the job of running an organization or unit,* and *how the manager carries out that job.*

SUMMARY

This chapter has presented two sides of the performance triangle. The first side is made up of the three *situational* factors: (1) the leader, (2) the organization's environment and structure, and (3) the organization's climate. The manager who is directing the work of other people must always be conscious of situational factors and must adjust them so that they enhance employee performance.

The second side of the triangle is *individual* factors. Part of the directing function is to match aptitudes with jobs. The chapter presented the results of three major studies—Exxon, Minnesota, and Chamber of Commerce—to show what has (and has not) been done in the effort to find individual factors that are predictive of successful employee performance.

Motivation, the third side of the performance triangle, is the subject of the next chapter.

DISCUSSION QUESTIONS

1. What is directing? Why is it important to a decision maker?
2. What do you think is the most important influence on effective employee performance? Why do you think so?
3. Describe the different leadership theories. Which one do you favor, and why?
4. What is the significance of the Michigan and Ohio State leadership studies in our understanding of leadership?
5. What does Fiedler's leadership model show?
6. What is known about the relationship between organizational structure and employee performance and morale?
7. What is "organizational climate"? How would you measure it?
8. What individual factors are related to effective managerial performance?

9. What is the significance of the Exxon, Minnesota, and Chamber of Commerce studies of managerial effectiveness?

10. Relate the discussion of authority and power in Chapter 8 to the leadership discussion in this chapter.

FARNEY NATIONAL BANK

Sally Blade, supervisor in charge of inside tellers at Farney National Bank, has a problem with one of the tellers. All tellers are supposed to be at work by 8:30 A.M. They must have their windows ready for operation by 9:30 when the bank opens.

But Mary Lou Day is almost always late for work. She arrives any time between 8:40 and 9:15. Once she gets to work, she is excellent. She is easily the best teller in the bank and always gets her work done early, even after arriving late. She is qualified for a promotion except that she has not been in her present position long enough. She understands and accepts that situation.

Day's frequent tardiness is causing problems. Other tellers, without Day's willingness or ability, are using Day's lateness to justify their own. Sally Blade feels that she cannot crack down on the other tellers without cracking down on Day also.

Sally has had several talks with Mary Lou. She always promises to do better, but she never does. Sally has even suggested a different reporting and leaving time for Mary Lou, but Mary Lou does not like the idea of being treated differently. "After all," she says, "I always get my window open on time, and I always get my work done by quitting time, don't I?" Mary Lou has even suggested that she may quit if the bank cannot be "flexible enough to let one good employee be a few minutes late every so often, without bugging her about it."

DICKERSON REALTY

Dickerson Realty centers around Ms. Dickerson. She does the bookkeeping, controls the advertising, takes her turn at floor duty, and makes all the decisions about the firm's operations. She often works 15 hours a day, 7 days a week. She lives alone and usually takes paperwork home with her.

Some of the associate realtors at Dickerson Realty think the firm is in a real slump. Ever since last summer when Ms. Dickerson went out of town for a month, things seem to have changed.

The early summer is often the most active period of the real estate year. Many associates felt that while Ms. Dickerson was away not much could be accomplished. Even though she directed the office by long distance phone every day, many questions went unanswered and many decisions were not made. No sales meetings were held during her absence.

When Ms. Dickerson returned, she found that many associates were inactive. Some were much more involved in personal projects than they were in real estate. Listings were still coming in, but their level was far below last year's.

Ms. Dickerson seems to have too much to do. The associates often ask for her help in the field, but she gets "tied up at the office" and frequently shows up 1 or 2 hours late. Many associates feel that they have lost potential sales because of poor coordination at the office. Listings have been turned in promptly but not "worked" properly. Days often pass before Ms. Dickerson makes a file, then types, copies, and distributes the listing to other associates, and advertises the listing in the paper.

As a result, the sales force is very discouraged. Ms. Dickerson is discouraged, too. For the past 2 years, gross sales of Dickerson Realty averaged $1,500,000 a month. For the past several months, despite Ms. Dickerson's working harder than ever before, sales have averaged around $200,000 per month.

16

directing: motivational factors

But how do you motivate anybody these days? How do you get commitment? You know, they are growing up with a lot of their physical needs satisfied. They have good housing, they take a pretty good income for granted. And industry is going to need them. It's going to need them in management roles; it's going to need them in a lot of other places where somebody has to make decisions and take the initiative. And I don't think that industry with its "bottom line" incentives is going to attract these people.

They are going to say: "Goddamn, we already *have* enough money. What the hell do we need more for?" Look at the hippies. A lot of them are college students doing jobs as leather craftsmen and things like that, where they have control over their work, rather than doing some stupid little thing where they can see neither beginning nor end.

I don't think that overtime, all kinds of increased wages are really going to be an incentive. Even in labor unions. Wages don't mean all that much. I don't think they mean that much at all. I think it's more of a need to feel that they are having an influence on the system. I sense a whole different kind of motivation coming. We will, somehow, have to create opportunities for these people. But have we ever thought about how?[1]

The fourth of the five managerial functions is directing employees. As a device for explaining the manager's directing function, the last chapter described two sides of the employee performance triangle: situational factors and individual factors. The decision maker as director must also be concerned with the third side: motivational factors. Whether a person performs well or poorly in a given situation usually depends on motivation.

Motivation is a complex topic. The word has various meanings, depending on the context of discussion. It may be used in reference to the *direction* of someone's behavior. If several alternatives are available, motivation determines the one chosen. The term may be used to describe the *strength* of the initial response, once a response is chosen. Motivation is sometimes used to describe the *persistence* of behavior. Whatever causes the person to continue the chosen response is a quality called motivation. Managers also use the term

---

[1]Peter Cohen, *The Gospel According to the Harvard Business School* (Garden City, N.Y.: Doubleday & Co., 1973), pp. 225–226.

in several other senses. When they refer to the motivation level (or its lack) in their employees, they may be talking about apparent energy, effort expended, a spouse and family, ambition, and so on.

Most basically, a *motive* is a reason for doing something. *Motivation* is the act of supplying a motive. Some motives (called *extrinsic* motives) are supplied for us. For example, if you do your job so that you can get approved or paid by someone else, you are driven by extrinsic motivation. Other motives (called *intrinsic* motives) are derived from inner sources. If you do your job well because you find the job rewarding in itself, you are driven by intrinsic motivation. Some fortunate people have jobs that are *both* extrinsically and intrinsically rewarding. The jobs of some unfortunate people are neither extrinsically nor intrinsically rewarding.

After discussing a psychological concept called the law of effect, this chapter covers three groups of motivation theories: reward theories (Maslow, Herzberg, and behavior modification), the process approaches (equity theory, task motivation theory, and expectancy theory), and finally the Porter–Lawler model. This model offers assistance in understanding motivation, and it also joins and unifies the three sides of the performance triangle.

THE LAW OF EFFECT

Rewarding Situations

The simplest theory of motivation is based on the psychological law of effect: people tend to repeat rewarding situations, and they tend not to repeat unrewarding situations. This idea means that people build a wide range of responses into their behavior patterns over time. In a trial-and-error fashion, people decide what they like and what they do not like. Also, they constantly look for opportunities to behave in ways that provide them with rewards.

As time passes, certain behaviors become almost like a "knee-jerk" reaction because they are almost always elicited in certain situations. For example, sitting in church elicits quiet, somber behavior. Similarly, certain rewards will usually elicit certain behaviors, as parents who offer their children candy or an allowance know.

Job Behavior Reflects Life Experiences

These learned reactions are important when motivating people in organizations for two reasons. First, people bring to the organization certain ways of behaving that their life experiences have taught them are rewarding. The manager must take these ways of behaving into account when offering rewards or inducements. Consider an employee who has learned from life experiences that rewards come from hard work, commitment to the organization, loyalty, and other behaviors that any organization would find desirable. The experienced manager will not motivate that employee by supervising work closely but by setting goals, giving clear instructions, then turning the employee loose to accomplish the goals.

Other employees come to the same organization with different life experiences. If the resulting behaviors are not those that the organization wants to reward, the manager must teach the employee which behaviors the organization values by rewarding them.

Organizational Socialization. Each new employee's work group also shares in this socialization process. That group helps the employee to learn which behaviors are rewarded and which are not. But the major responsibility for adjusting the employee and the organization to each other falls to the organization's representative: the supervisor. The new employee experiments with a variety of behaviors, trying to find those that lead to rewards. The supervisor helps the employee in the search. Because people have different behavior backgrounds and experiences, managers must skillfully adapt the motivation to the person. Some employees need little supervision, and others need careful observation and control—in colloquial terms, different strokes for different folks.

Desirable Rewards

Different People, Different Rewards. Learned behaviors are important to the motivator–manager for a second reason. Different people are satisfied or reinforced by different rewards. Therefore, the manager must learn which rewards will motivate each employee to expend more and better effort.

Money. Some people are highly driven by a need or want for money, so they seek rewards measurable solely in financial terms. Often more money in exchange for better performance reflects the most popular understanding of motivation. Bonus, commission, and incentive plans appeal to money-motivated employees. They like to get a money payoff for their efforts.

Achievement. Other people get their most meaningful rewards from achievement. They like to accept challenges and try to meet them. For these people, the money incentive almost becomes unimportant—except perhaps as a measure of achievement.

Other Rewards. Some people find rewards in dominating and manipulating people, affiliating with people, achieving personal security, taking severe risks, and so on. They look for organizations that enable them to achieve these rewards. This whole process was described earlier in terms of inducements and contributions. People make intensely personal decisions about what things are important to them, they find situations that hold promise of offering these inducements or rewards, and then they decide how much of an effort or contribution they are willing to make to get these inducements or rewards.

Three Motivation Theories

How do people (and their managers) decide what is rewarding? How do people (and their managers) structure their behavior in order to achieve rewards? The rest of this chapter will describe three motivation theories designed to answer these questions. The first theory ignores motivation as a process and deals with the rewards themselves. The second theory ignores rewards as such and focuses on the motivation process: how people select the behaviors that they hope will lead to rewards. The third theory is exemplified by a path–goal model that ties together the situational, individual, and motivational factors affecting group member performance.

REWARD THEORIES

Early Research

The idea underlying reward-oriented motivation theories is that people are driven—for reasons that do not matter—to seek rewards. These theories try to identify (1) rewards that everybody would like to achieve, or (2) rewards that various people seek at various times.

For example, some early human relations research concluded that one reward sought by most workers is job autonomy. The more job autonomy provided by the organization, the more likely that employees would be motivated.

The Averaging Problem.   This type of research kept getting bogged down in *averages*. Some people are indeed happier and more productive if given more job autonomy. However, other people are happier but *less* productive, and still others are less happy *and* less productive. On average, people may be happier and more productive, but many exceptions may exist.

If you stick one hand in the oven and the other hand in the refrigerator, you should be comfortable—on average. In the same way, if you make some employees happy by pursuing one general motivational strategy, you may be making other employees unhappy. Because of the averaging problem, many early research studies on motivational strategy, job autonomy, job enrichment, participatory decision making, and so on, were inconclusive.

Maslow and Herzberg

Maslow. The lack of research support and the commonsense observation of individual differences on the job led to strategies based on rewards that might motivate people, depending on their past successes and failures. In Chapter 8 we discussed one such set of strategies: Abraham Maslow's hierarchy of needs (physiological, safety, social, self-esteem, and self-actualization). A given need in the hierarchy is motivating or nonmotivating depending on whether or not the needs below it have been satisfied. Maslow's reward categories are fairly general so that they can be applied across a broad range of employees. Yet they are more detailed than a single-answer motivational strategy, and so they allow the manager to pick the appropriate general appeal for each employee.

Herzberg. Frederick Herzberg's two-factor theory of motivation states that elements in the work situation are of two kinds: *motivation* factors (sometimes called *satisfiers*) and *hygiene* factors (sometimes called *dissatisfiers* or *maintenance* factors). Examples of both elements appear in the right side of Table 16-1. The motivation factors can lead to job satisfaction, but the absence of

TABLE 16-1   A Comparison of Maslow's Need Priority Model with Herzberg's Motivation–Hygiene Model

Maslow	Herzberg	
Self-realization	Work itself Achievement Possible growth Responsibility	Motivation Factors
Esteem and status	Advancement Recognition Status	

Belonging and social activity	Interpersonal relations
	  Superiors
	  Peers
	  Subordinates
	Supervisor—technical
	  relations	

Safety and security	Company policy and administration Job security Working conditions	Hygiene Factors
Physiological	Salary Personal life	

Source: Keith Davis, *Human Behavior at Work* (New York: McGraw-Hill Book Co., 1972), p. 59. Used by permission.

motivators will not lead to job dissatisfaction. The hygiene factors can prevent job dissatisfaction, but they cannot lead to job satisfaction. In other words, job satisfaction and job dissatisfaction are not at opposite ends of a continuum. The opposite of satisfaction is "no satisfaction" and the opposite of dissatisfaction is "no dissatisfaction."

Motivators (such as achievement, recognition, and advancement) are associated with job *content*. They are important because they can lead to job satisfaction, which motivates employees to perform well. Hygiene factors (such as company policy, working conditions, and salary) are associated with job *context* or environment. They are important because they can keep the employee from being dissatisfied. In the presence of dissatisfaction, employee motivation will be negative. If dissatisfaction and satisfaction are both absent, motivation will be zero. The most revolutionary implication of the two-factor theory is that improving the hygiene of the situation (by raising salaries, for example) will not improve performance. All it does is prevent dissatisfaction and poor performance. If employee satisfaction, motivation, and performance are all to be positive, the motivators must be present.

Herzberg's two-factor theory is widely known but not universally accepted. Other studies have suggested that such hygiene factors as salary and job security *can* motivate employees.

Although we do not know just how and to what extent Herzberg's motivation and hygiene factors actually influence individual behavior, his theory provides an even more detailed method than Maslow's for managers to use in fine tuning motivational strategies to suit individual employees. By providing a range of rewards that managers can offer to employees, Herzberg has extended Maslow's needs hierarchy to work motivation.

Table 16-1 places the Maslow and Herzberg models alongside each other. Herzberg's motivation factors overlap two Maslow categories, and Herzberg's hygiene factors overlap three Maslow categories.

Cafeteria Approach.   In the extreme, an organization may use a cafeteria of rewards to motivate employees. The organization may make available a variety of financial and nonfinancial rewards. Supervisors then become responsible for putting together the optimum tray full of rewards that will motivate each employee to expend the best effort.

Behavior Modification

As a reward-oriented motivation approach, Skinnerian behavior modification is an extreme. All approaches discussed so far have some theory or premise concerning *why* a certain reward has a motivating effect. For example, Maslow would maintain that food is a reward because it satisfies a primary drive: hunger. The behavior modification researchers ignore the *why* and concentrate on the *what*. Ignore motives, drives, needs and psychological processes. Simply find out what the employee values, and then provide it as a reward for good work.

Nature of Reward.   Any behavior modification program must consider four factors. First, the reinforcement or incentive offered to the employee *must truly be a reward to that person*. Laboratory scientists do not use birdseed to reinforce mice nor cheese to reinforce pigeons. Similarly, the manager may waste money by giving a pay raise to an employee who really wants recognition and praise instead.

Time Interval.   The length of time between the desired behavior and the reward will affect how quickly behavior is modified. During the training phase, that length of time should be as short as possible. That way, the employee has no doubt about which behavior leads to a payoff.

A new jobholder may have difficulty in responding immediately in the desired manner. In such situations, the manager may gradually shape the employee's behavior by rewarding behaviors that resemble those being sought. To illustrate, the supervisor may praise a machine operator for keeping the defect rate below 25 percent in the first week of the job. As time goes on, the supervisor reduces the defect rate that is praised—to 20 percent, 15 percent, and so on. The machinist gradually learns how to produce parts with few defects.

Once a behavior is learned, the organization can increase the length of time between the behavior and the reward. However, the length of time must not be so long that the employee loses track of which behaviors are being rewarded. The regularity of paydays is somewhat inconsistent with behavior modification, because the length of time between achievement and reward may be too short or too long. Having all employees paid on the same payroll dates may be convenient for data processing and for the personnel records department. However, regular intervals do not help the trainer to teach the new employee what the relationship is between a certain behavior and its reward. In a similar sense, employee-of-the-year awards and yearly performance appraisals represent an inappropriate focus on calendar time rather than on the time between good performance and its reward.

Fixed or Variable Intervals.   A third important factor in modifying behavior is whether the interval between the desired behavior and its reward is fixed or variable. Psychologists have found that variable intervals between rewards are more motivating than fixed intervals. An employee who knows that rewards are presented only every other Friday may let up just after receiving a reward and may intensify effort just before reward time. This psychological finding may explain "payday blues" or the hard work of average employees just before the annual performance appraisal.

Variable reward intervals work on the slot machine principle. Players know that the next tug on the handle may bring a payoff. Because they do not know which tug will pay, they are motivated to keep tugging. Although this principle is well known in Las Vegas, it seldom finds expression in motivational strategies. Typical recognition programs, awards for excellence, and paydays usually occur at well-planned, well-known, fixed intervals.

Extinction.   All learned behavior can be unlearned or extinguished. Extinction occurs when a given behavior is not rewarded. Learned behavior is extinguished slowly when the intervals between rewards vary. If workers do not know exactly when a reward will occur, they tolerate a longer time between rewards. Extinction occurs quickly if the biweekly payday passes without paychecks being issued.

THE PROCESS APPROACHES

The second major category of motivation theories is the process approaches. These approaches seek to explain the motivation process: why people behave as they do in general or specific situations. From among a wide range of such theories, the following section discusses three: equity theory, task motivation theory, and expectancy theory.

Equity Theory

Equity theory is based on the logical notion that people want the relationship between performance and reward to be fair or equitable. If a person's inner standard says that the relationship is equitable, the person will continue to behave in the same way. If the person feels inequity, the person is motivated to behave differently.

Getting What You Deserve.   Consider yourself. You have a certain set of beliefs about yourself, your capabilities, your worth, and so on. Whenever you expend effort, you want some kind of reward, either tangible (money, a medal, a trophy, a high test score) or intangible (satisfaction, pride, a feeling of accomplishment, a warm glow). If your rewards continue to match your expectations about what you deserve, you will probably be satisfied and will keep performing at about the same level. However, if you feel your reward is too large or too small, you will have a feeling of inequity and will change your behavior so as to reestablish an equitable relationship.

The Comparison Person.   People have inner standards of equity. They also compare their own performance–reward ratios with the performance–reward ratios of other people. Workers compare themselves to each other on the basis of inputs (talent, education, effort, experience, skill) and outcomes (pay, bonuses, promotions, praise, working conditions).

Equity theory includes the idea of a *comparison person*. Workers look around in the job setting and find roughly equivalent workers. As jobs are performed and rewards are made available, workers compare what they are getting with what their comparison persons are getting. If a worker and a comparison person are getting the same reward, the worker has a feeling of equity.

The comparison person probably works in the same location, but not necessarily. The comparison person might be a friend working for a different organization or even an idealized standard that serves as a personal yardstick with which the worker compares job opportunities, challenges, benefits, and salaries.

Reactions to Inequity.   Workers can react to inequity in various ways. If Jane Worker has low input–high outcome and her comparison person has high input–high outcome, she may "change her mind" about her input, deciding that she really is offering as much input as her comparison person. Or she may quit or request a transfer, change her inputs or outcomes, try to change her comparison person's inputs or outcomes, switch to another comparison person, or simply accept the inequity. A worker who has high input–high outcome versus a comparison person's high input–low outcome may prefer to accept the inequity rather than ask for the pay cut that would establish an equitable high–low versus high–low relationship.

Here are some research findings with regard to how workers react to inequity:

1. Piece workers perceiving themselves to be overpaid produce *less* work, of *higher* quality, than do piece workers perceiving themselves to be fairly paid.
2. Workers perceiving themselves to be underpaid do not work as hard as workers perceiving themselves to be fairly paid.
3. Workers perceiving themselves to be overpaid work harder than workers perceiving themselves to be fairly paid.
4. The greater the inequity, the greater will be the worker's motivation to reduce it.
5. People resist changing their perceived input–output ratios if the change would negatively affect their self-esteem.
6. People resist changing their comparison persons, once selected.

Importance of Equity Theory.   Equity theory is one explanation of why people behave as they do. If we do not get what our self-determined input–outcome ratios indicate that we should be getting, we will make a behavior change to balance the ratio, whether we are factory workers, charity volunteers, or school students. We may leave the situation, form a labor union, ask for a raise, slow down our work pace, or pick it up, but our behavior and job performance will reflect our desire for equity.

Managers naturally want a higher level of inputs. Therefore, they must first understand their workers well enough to know what the workers will consider to be a high reward level. Then they must try to supply those desired rewards for each worker individually, while at the same time carefully watching the inputs and outcomes of all workers to minimize actual or perceived inequities.

Equity theory is a variation of a theme that has recurred throughout this book: inducements–contributions. Inducements correspond to the outcomes of equity theory, and contributions correspond to the inputs. Equity theory adds the idea that organizational members want to keep inducements and contributions in balance.

Task Motivation Theory

The Task as Motivator.   Task motivation theory is another way of explaining how past experience or future expectations motivate us to behave in different ways. This approach centers on the motivational effects of the task itself.

The jogging craze illustrates how the task itself influences behavior. A person may want to achieve a goal—physical fitness, weight control, or whatever. The task selected to accomplish this goal is jogging. Some joggers hate jogging, but they keep at it in order to achieve their goal. Other joggers become so wrapped up in the activity that they continue jogging long after they have achieved their original goal—perhaps long after they have forgotten what the original goal was. For such joggers, the task itself has become motivational.

Continual Adjustment.   The influence of the task itself on a person's motivation level keeps changing. The person continually adjusts the levels of aspiration and acceptable performance to reflect satisfaction or dissatisfaction with the task. A jogger may modify the task by trying to run faster or by running longer distances. A production worker, salesperson, or student may continually revise performance goals, depending on the rewards derived from earlier performance levels.

To sum up, the task becomes motivating in itself as it provides an opportunity to satisfy personal objectives that may be unknown or unrecognized at the beginning of the task effort. You take a job because it pays well and seems appropriate for your skills. Then you find that performing the task appeals to you or satisfies needs beyond those you felt it would satisfy. Therefore, you exert additional effort. The task itself has become a motivational force.

The Nature of the Task.   Several characteristics of tasks seem related to their motivational effects, among them being the kind and level of skill required.

For example, if the worker perceives that a high level of skill is required, then completing the task successfully will be more rewarding than if a low level of skill seems adequate. Generally speaking, the more difficult the task, the higher will be the performance level, *if* the task performer views the challenge as possible and accepts it—to run so many miles, produce so many units, or make a certain examination grade.

Clarifying the Task.   Managers can influence the goal levels that people set for themselves. One way they do so is by making each worker's task clear, letting workers know just what they are supposed to do. The manager and the worker can discuss the task, problems that may come up, and strategies for solving them. Then the worker has a much better idea of how and where to expend effort. People in sales have a saying, "Don't work hard; work *smart.*" If two workers expend the same amount of effort, the one who works smart will have a better chance of meeting goals than the one who works hard. By clarifying the task, managers can be sure that their workers are working smart.

  In addition to influencing the goal levels that people set for themselves, managers can also offer support and can provide feedback on how well these goals are being met. Therefore, managers have considerable influence on how goals are set, how workers react to these goals, and whether the goals are met.

Expectancy Theory

The Expectancy Formula.   Expectancy theory holds great potential for explaining the motivation process. Here is the expectancy formula: a person's motivation to perform in a specific situation is a function of

$$(\text{incentives} \times \text{expectations} \times \text{motives}) - \text{fear of failing}$$

Incentives are rewards for performing tasks successfully. As an earlier section of this chapter showed, these rewards or incentives are of many kinds. Every item in Table 16-1 can act as an incentive. *Expectations* are of two kinds: (1) What are the chances that I am able to expend enough effort to accomplish the task? (2) If I accomplish it, what are the chances that the reward will actually be given to me? The *motive* is the strength of the person's need to succeed or achieve. If the reward itself (or simply the opportunity to achieve *a* reward) appeals to the person's underlying motive structure, the motivation to perform will be great. However, motivation will be reduced by the person's *fear of failing* to perform the task.

  The relationship between incentive, expectancy, and motive is usually described as multiplicative (incentive × expectancy × motive). Therefore, any time one factor is zero, the entire motivation equation goes to zero.

Elephants in Seattle.   As an example of how expectancy theory works, consider Mary Wilson, an elephant salesperson in Seattle. The sales manager sets her January quota at ten elephants and tells her that, if she exceeds her quota, she will get an expense-paid, month-long (for February) vacation to Puerto Rico. The company has provided its part of the expectancy formula: the incentive. Mary Wilson must estimate whether she can indeed expect to sell more than ten elephants during January, given her sales skill, what she knows of the Seattle elephant market, and so on. She must also decide whether she can expect the company to award the bonus if she exceeds her quota. Her prior experience with her sales manager and the company's credibility and financial status will influence that decision.

The third element in the situation is Mary Wilson's motive—her desire to succeed or achieve. Her job experiences with this organization and this sales manager will affect that desire. If in the past this sales manager has structured appropriate rewards, established and maintained credibility with Mary Wilson, offered training in the skills necessary to achieve job goals, and provided appropriate feedback on Wilson's prior expenditures of effort, then the job environment will add to Wilson's desire to achieve. If Wilson evaluates any of the three factors as zero, or if her fear of failing equals or exceeds her motivation to succeed, she will extend little or no effort. For example, if she hates Puerto Rico, the incentive may be zero. Similarly, if no salesperson has ever sold more than three elephants in any month, she may feel that extra effort would be wasted because achieving the goal is probably impossible.

Importance of Expectancy Theory.   Expectancy theory can be very useful to practicing managers because they can affect the influences on worker motivational level. They can find out which rewards induce their subordinates to contribute their best efforts. They can create an atmosphere of trust, confidence, and believability. And they can ensure that each employee's goals are congruent with that employee's abilities, training, and past experience.

Expectancy theory does not all by itself explain effective employee performance. However, it does offer insight into how effort levels are determined. A more elaborate model will now be described to explain in greater detail how effective job performance comes about.

THE PORTER–LAWLER MODEL

Goal Fulfillment

Figure 16-1 presents a model of employee behavior designed by Lyman Porter and Edward Lawler. The model is based on a simple concept: people choose paths or courses of action that they believe will lead to the fulfilling of their

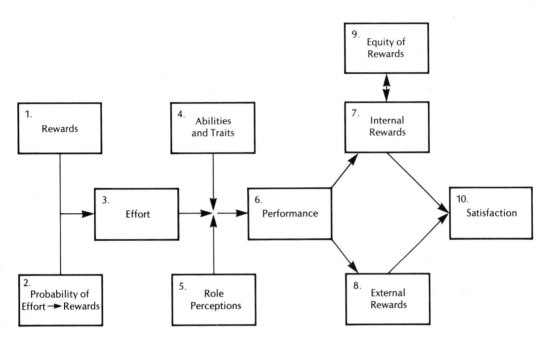

FIG 16-1 The Porter-Lawler model of managerial behavior. (*Source:* Lyman W. Porter and Edward E. Lawler, III, *Managerial Attitudes and Performance.* Homewood, Ill.: Richard D. Irwin, Inc., 1968, p. 17.) © 1968 by Richard D. Irwin, Inc.

goals. The model should help managers to discover how employees define their goals and how they decide what behavior will help them achieve those goals.

Is Reward Worth the Effort?

Block 1 in the figure is *rewards*. Based on their past experiences, people decide what rewards have value for them. The effort they expend on a given task (block 3) is determined by the value they place on the reward for the task (block 1) and the probability that their effort will actually result in the reward (block 2).

Traits and Role Perceptions

However, sheer effort is not enough. Role perceptions (block 4) and individual abilities–traits (block 5) also affect how successful the effort will be. Some people expend great effort to reach goals, but they simply do not have the inborn or learned ability to succeed. Similarly, if people misunderstand their organizational roles, their efforts may be wasted. Effort expended illegally, inappropriately, or contrary to company policy may be effort wasted. Effort, ability, and accuracy of role perception all result in a certain performance level. This level will then lead into a self-appraisal of how satisfying it has been to perform at that level.

External and Internal Rewards

The model divides rewards into internal (block 7) and external (block 8) rewards. Internal rewards are made up of feelings derived from doing a good or bad job and includes Herzberg's motivational variables (achievement, recognition, etc.) as listed in Table 16-1. External rewards include Herzberg's hygiene factors, such as pay, working conditions, interpersonal relations, and so forth. The person compares the sought rewards (block 1) with the achieved rewards (blocks 7 and 8) and also assesses whether these two reward types are equitable (block 9) in light of the effort expended (block 3).

Satisfaction?   At this point, people who have received rewards for expending effort decide whether they are satisfied with what they have done (block 10). This final, personal judgment serves as feedback that will guide behavior in future situations. It makes adjustments in several of the blocks possible. If the effort and reward have resulted in satisfaction, the person may make no changes. If the person expends the effort, achieves the reward, and is dissatisfied, the experience will lead to different behavior in the future.

Importance of the Porter–Lawler Model

This model explains how our efforts and goals are subject to continuous, dynamic interpretation and analysis. It also offers considerable insight into how people choose their levels of effort. For example, a manager may notice that a quality-control checker is making little effort to look for deviations from expected quality levels. If the checker receives no reward for finding errors, the model explains the checker's behavior.

The Porter–Lawler model ties together the three sides of the performance triangle: *situational* factors (blocks 1, 5, 7, 8), *individual* factors (block 4), and *motivational* factors (the model taken as a whole). It also shows the relationship between several ideas explained in the last two chapters: path–goal theory (the model can be viewed in path–goal terms), contingency theory (the model is a contingency approach), the influence of organizational structure on job satisfaction and performance (related to block 5: role perception), the law of effect (the process described in the model will be repeated or changed in future situations, because of the law of effect), the various reward theories (blocks 1, 7, 8), equity theory (block 9), task motivation theory (which would enter into this sequence of blocks: 1, 2, 3, 6, 7, 10), and expectancy theory (block 2).

SUMMARY

This chapter first explained the law of effect: if behavior is rewarded, it is repeated. The rest of the chapter discussed three motivation theories: reward theories, the process approaches, and the Porter–Lawler model.

Early research into reward theories was hampered by the "averaging" problem. Later reward theories described were those of Maslow, Herzberg, and Skinner (behavior modification). Attempts to modify behavior are affected by the nature of the reward and the time interval between rewards.

A second category of motivation theories is those that emphasize not the reward but the entire motivation process. Three examples were described. *Equity theory* assumes that people want to get what they deserve and to deserve what they get. A comparison person is often used to determine whether the relationship between inputs and outcomes is equitable. *Task motivation theory* shows that the task itself can be motivational. *Expectancy theory* includes the ideas of reward and desire to achieve, but maintains that motivation to perform hinges on the person's expectation of whether expended effort will actually lead to the desired reward.

The chapter concluded by presenting the Porter–Lawler model. That model does much to integrate numerous theories and concepts presented in the past two chapters.

The Ford Motor Company employs 200 robots in such jobs as stamping, spray painting, and die casting. General Motors employs about 150 robots in similar jobs, as well as in body welding. Since the robots never miss a weld, cars that they work on are less likely to develop rattles. Unless managers are supervising the work of robots, they must consider and understand the subject of motivation.

A final note: just as an undermotivated worker may not try hard enough, so may a worker try too hard. A very high state of motivation may produce excitement that can actually reduce efficiency. So the manager has yet another problem: how to motivate organizational members enough, but not too much.

DISCUSSION QUESTIONS

1. What is the difference between extrinsic and intrinsic sources of motivation?
2. What is the law of effect? How can the manager use it when performing the directing function?
3. How does the problem of averaging influence the manager's selection of one best motivational strategy?
4. What are the characteristics, strengths, and weaknesses of Herzberg's theory of motivation?

5. How can behavior modification be used to direct employees in the work setting?

6. Of the process approaches—equity theory, task motivation theory, and expectancy theory—which seems best? Why?

7. How is the equity of a situation determined?

8. How does the Porter–Lawler model tie in with the performance triangle discussed in the previous chapter?

9. The last point made in the chapter is that an overmotivated person's performance may be adversely affected. Can you offer some examples of that point?

10. Why does a manager making decisions care about motivating employees? After all, if they did not want to work, they would not have taken their jobs in the first place, would they?

NORTHERN TELEPHONE COMPANY

Wilbur Beck is manager of Northern Telephone's Traffic Order Production group. Reporting to Beck are four supervisors, each responsible for a district. Assigned to each district are a work group leader and a traffic engineer.

Northern Telephone uses the PERT technique to meet the need for future telephones. The process includes estimating future requirements, and then engineering, ordering, and installing all equipment. To meet this demand, the Traffic Order Production function is included in the PERT chart's *critical path*. Therefore, all work must be done on time.

Beck has decentralized and delegated as much as he can. Within each district, the work group leader is responsible for ensuring that all schedules are met.

Nelson Baldwin, supervisor of District I, has been on vacation for 2 weeks. A few days ago, traffic engineer Frank Diasi came into Beck's office, stated that seven District I engineering projects were critically overdue, and said that he could not possibly catch up without help. When Beck asked why the district was behind, Diasi said bluntly that work group leader Jim Clark devoted his time to "busy work" and did not do his job properly. Diasi said Clark had not performed satisfactorily at any time since his assignment to the district 4 months earlier.

Upon checking discreetly, Beck found that Diasi was apparently telling the truth. Everyone agreed that Clark was technically capable and personally likable, but for some reason he was not performing the duties required of his position. One employee commented that Clark did not seem to value his position very highly. Beck arranged to bail out District I by borrowing help from other districts, but something obviously had to be done about Clark.

When district supervisor Baldwin returned from vacation, Beck questioned him. Baldwin said he had only recently become aware that Clark was performing poorly. He admitted that he had not kept close track of individual performance within his district because the group as a whole had been performing fairly well. He asked Beck for help in determining what to do about Clark. They reviewed Clark's background together.

Clark is 54 years old. He was transferred to Northern Telephone from Southern Telephone 5 years ago. When he arrived, he and top management both anticipated that he would soon become a group manager in a position similar to Beck's. However, although he appears to be quite good technically, he simply has not lived up to expectations. For the past couple of years, he has obviously resented taking orders from younger managers. A year ago, when Clark was in another district, Beck decided that he was adequate in his present job but was not then promotable. Clark became quite angry when he heard Beck's appraisal. Since that time, his attitude has been barely acceptable.

NO MERIT INCREASES

Patricia Bley, a supervisor in the Department of Health, received the following memorandum from the department director on July 15, 19×6:

> In the 19×6 General Appropriations Act, the legislature stated specifically that "No appropriations in this act shall be utilized to grant merit salary increases for state employees." Therefore, no merit salary increases may be granted in the department during the fiscal year 19×6–19×7.
>
> Employees must continue to receive appropriate and timely performance evaluations in accordance with personnel rules and regulations. It is important to emphasize that the main purpose of such evaluations is to inform employees of their strengths and weaknesses, to recognize potential for promotion, and to inform employees of training needed and improvement expected.
>
> Employees under your jurisdiction should be made to understand that this austere financial action by the 19×6 Legislature has been made necessary because of the slump in the economy and its concomitant reduction of state revenue. The merit salary ban is an attempt to maintain services at the present level of salary funding, rather than reduce services and abolish positions.
>
> Please use whatever means you deem appropriate to advise employees under your jurisdiction of this ban on merit salary increases. Thank you.

Patricia Bley thought that salaries in her unit were already rather low. How was she to keep her people motivated to perform well in light of this unfortunate development?

controlling

Controlling is the fifth and last function about which managers make decisions. Control means *measurement* and *regulation*. It can be implicit or explicit, measured precisely or casually, useful or a nuisance, worth the cost or worthless. The organization's controlling systems directly affect how (or whether) the organization reaches its goals. The nature of controls is affected directly by the managerial philosophies of the persons designing them.

This chapter first contrasts control in mechanistic systems, social systems, and formal organizational systems. To make the idea of control more concrete, budgets and two types of production control models are described. After explaining Peter Drucker's seven requirements for controls, the chapter presents the PPBS control method briefly and the PERT/CPM method in some detail. The chapter discusses control measurement problems and offers some ways to solve them, and then concludes by exploring the human relations aspect of control.

THE RANGE OF CONTROLS

Controls are measurement devices. Ideally, they yield the information necessary for regulation. Control has two aspects: (1) performance is measured against a standard, and (2) performance is corrected in light of that measurement.

A wide range of techniques is available to bring about control of the organization's activities. The management task is to find the mixture that will give the control desired. Many control devices can be measured in monetary terms, such as budgets, return on investment, standard cost, and so on. Therefore, many people associate control with these tools and think that control is purely a function of the "controller's" office. Actually, control is much broader. It can range from the tight control of the mechanistic, straightforward, completely objective, closed-loop cybernetic system to the loose control of the unmeasurable, wide-open social system.

Mechanistic Systems

The simplest and classic illustration of mechanistic feedback control appears in Figure 17-1: the thermostat. It constantly compares actual temperature and desired temperature and, once set, controls the mechanism that maintains the desired temperature. When the air waves cool to a preset level, a metal spring in the thermostat contracts, contact between the two electrical circuits is made, and the furnace turns on. When the air waves warm, the spring expands the metal away from the circuit, contact is lost, and the furnace shuts off. The on–off cycle continues indefinitely.

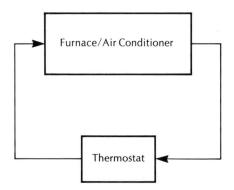

FIG 17-1　The thermostat: a simple mechanical control system.

In this simple system, measurement is precise, feedback to the temperature adjustment mechanism is prompt and undistorted, human error is absent, and the system is self-sustaining. True, forces external to the system cause temperature changes, and the system requires fuel oil and electricity external to itself. Nevertheless, temperature regulation by a thermostat is about as close to a completely closed control system as can be found.

Social Systems

Wide-open social systems are at the other end of the spectrum. They change constantly, measurement is vague, feedback within the system is open to many different interpretations, and regulation is subject to human error. Consider any social group, from a small club to a large nation. The group does have some control over its members, but the nature, use, and appropriateness of control can be interpreted in many different ways.

Formal Organizational Systems

A Mid-Range.　In between these two end points is the formal organizational system. As shown in Table 17-1, this system represents the middle range between the rigidly defined, measured, mechanical system and the shapeless,

TABLE 17-1 Three Points on the Continuum of Organizational Regulatory System Types

	Mechanistic System: Highly Bureaucratic, Highly Structured	Formal Organizational System: Some Structure	Informal Social System: Some Structure
Goals	Explicit	Some explicit, some implicit	Implicit
Measurements	Precise	Some precise, some vague	Vague
Feedback	Consistent	Some consistent, some erratic	Erratic, unreliable
Connecting mechanisms	Programmed responses based on automatic decisions Servomechanical	Decisions based on individual commitment to organizational goal Organizational power	Ostracism, praise, informal pressure, ethical judgment, accepted authority
Examples	Thermostat Computer program Automated equipment	Budget Management by objectives PERT/CPM Law	Norms of behavior Role sets Social responsibility

informally defined social system. The formal organization has many semi-mechanistic controls, such as budgeting devices, quality defect rates, turnover measures, return on investment, earnings per share, and so on. But humans interpret these controls to decide what is good and what is not so good. The controls used in organizational systems are a mixture of the mechanistic and the informal. They measure deviations, and then humans interpret the measurements and take corrective action.

Controls and Goals.   An organization's control systems will generally reflect the degree to which the organization's goals can be specified and measured with certainty. Of course, the degree of precision depends on many factors, among them the rate of change in the organization's environment, technology, market, and personnel. If these factors change rapidly, managers cannot set up rigid controls. They must rely on informal controls and on individual self-control. If change is slow, managers can use more mechanistic control systems.

BUDGETING

Within large formal organizations, the most widely used control device is the budget. The budget comes into being as a part of the organization's planning process. Each budget forecasts what the organization expects to happen within each budgeted area over a specific time period. Once the organization's financial plans are expressed in the form of budgets, they serve as control devices and as performance standards. Actual performance is periodically measured against the expectations reflected in the budgets, to let managers know how the organization is doing.

Revenue and Expense Budgets

The most common budget forms are the revenue (or sales) and expense budgets. The sales budget is an estimate of what the organization's sales will be over the budget period. All other financial budgets are based on the sales forecast embodied in that budget. The expense budget includes estimates of how much generating those sales will cost. Estimated costs for labor, materials, rent, and so on are included in the budget. Then unit managers try to keep expenses within the budgeted limits. Considered together, the revenue and expense budgets make up the organization's *operating budget*.

Cash Budget

The cash budget (derived from the revenue and expense budgets) is simply an estimate of how much cash the organization is going to need to meet its expenses over the coming budget period and where that cash is coming from. The organization must have enough cash on hand to meet expenses, but excessive cash on hand means that investment opportunities are being wasted.

Capital Expenditure Budget

Many organizations have long-term requirements to acquire, repair, or replace plant, machinery, equipment, and other physical assets. These long-term needs are expressed in the capital expenditure budget. As is true of the cash budget, the organization must use good judgment when setting up the capital expenditure budget. The organization does not want to tie up too much money in capital expenditures, because the payoff from such expenditures may be many years away. On the other hand, the organization must make capital expenditures sufficient to prepare for the future.

Balance Sheet Budget

Once the other budgets have been determined, the organization can prepare a balance sheet budget. Such a budget includes estimates of what the organization's assets, liabilities, and net worth will be at the end of the budget period—if the estimates in the other budgets turn out to be correct.

The budgeting process is an opportunity to involve all managers in planning and control. Budgets constructed with the help of all managers are likely to be realistic financial plans. Also, managers are more likely to adhere to budgets that they help to prepare.

PRODUCTION CONTROL MODELS

Two more examples of controls are the following production control models: quality control and work standards.

Quality Control

Any organization producing goods or providing services needs to establish quality standards. Organizational output is compared against the standard and is then classified as acceptable or unacceptable. Quality-control models fall into two general categories: acceptance sampling and statistical process control.

Acceptance Sampling.   Under acceptance sampling, the organization establishes a standard of what is an "acceptable" output of its production process. Samples of output are taken and compared against the standard. If more than a certain percentage are "unacceptable," the entire batch from which the samples were taken is rejected.

For example, bombs might be tested by exploding a random sample from a production lot. If more than a certain percentage are duds or misfires, the entire lot would be rejected.

Statistical Process Control.   Acceptance sampling is an after-the-fact procedure. Once the item is produced, it is judged to be either acceptable or unacceptable. In contrast, statistical process control provides a continuous monitoring of production. Managers can use process charts to detect variations in production output, and then determine whether variations are caused by workers, machines, materials, or a combination of these factors.

For example, a scale might be built into an assembly line that packs coffee into cans. Whenever a 1-pound can of coffee crosses the scale, the weight is automatically indicated on a graph. If a temporary malfunction causes the equipment to put too much or too little coffee in a can, it is automatically removed from the line.

The manager can watch the graph to see whether it is forming a trend line. Machines wear out or go out of adjustment. The graph reflects gradual deterioration of equipment and gives management an automatic warning signal that the time for repair is coming.

As is true of other automatic problem identifiers, quality-control techniques force managers to compare performance against a standard. When a deviation from the standard reflects a problem, then problem-solving activity can begin.

Work Standards

Work standards are another way of comparing what *does* happen with what *should* happen. For example, consider a production process that requires a worker to run a punch press. Management would like to know what a reasonable output for the punch-press operator is. One way to find out would be to measure the operator's average daily production for a period of time. Then whenever George P. Press exceeds his average, he is "overproducing," and when he falls below his average, he is "underproducing."

Is the standard "good" or "bad" in any absolute sense? Management may never know for sure. However, the average gives a rough indication of how effective George P. Press is over any given period, compared to his past performance. If the company employs several punch-press operators, the daily average of the group might be used as a standard to identify problem operators or problem days for good operators.

Managers can use a more sophisticated procedure to set standards for tasks like punch-press operation. Time-and-motion experts can analyze each job and determine the "normal" time, effort, and skill required to do it. Of course, "normal" is an extremely subjective word. Nevertheless, managers can use the established norm as a rough standard against which to measure performance. A substantial deviation from this standard signals a problem. The manager can then check on whether the problem lies in the machine, in personnel ability or effort, or in the standards themselves.

DRUCKER'S REQUIREMENTS FOR CONTROLS

Peter Drucker emphasizes that measurable results are history; they happened in the past.[1] Furthermore, measurable results usually occur within the organization, rather than outside it. Yet outside events, even though they may not be measurable, may affect organizational success importantly. For these reasons, organizations should keep themselves aware of results in both categories: measurable–internal and nonmeasurable–external. Drucker adds that organizations must resist the temptation to emphasize certain areas simply because they are measurable. Whether an occurrence is measurable or not may have little relationship to its importance.

Drucker offers seven requirements for controls.

[1]The following section is indebted to Peter Drucker, *Management: Tasks, Responsibilities, Practices* (New York: Harper & Row, Inc., 1974), pp. 498–505.

Economical

Controls must be economical, not just in the money sense but also in the sense of economical in number. Doubling the number of controls does not necessarily result in twice as much control. In fact, because of resulting confusion, excessive controls may cut control in half. The number of controls must be kept as small as possible.

Meaningful

Controls must be meaningful. They must measure performance in important areas. To establish meaningful controls, the organization's management must have a firm and clear understanding of what the organization's goals are. To be meaningful, controls should concentrate on measuring performance in those areas critical to the successful achievement of organizational goals.

If an activity is useful but not essential to goal achievement, it should be measured only occasionally. A standard for the activity should be set, and performance should be measured against the standard from time to time.

Appropriate

Controls must be appropriate. They must reflect fairly the events they are designed to measure. Drucker makes some generalizations about businesses.

1. Ninety percent of a firm's business is usually represented by 2 to 5 percent of its different products.
2. Ninety percent of the *number* of orders received by a firm typically makes up only about 4 to 5 percent of total volume.
3. Most research and development findings come from a relatively small percentage of the research and development people.
4. Twenty percent of a firm's distributors usually move more than 80 percent of the output.

Control measurements should fairly reflect these facts of business life. For example, in case 3 above, a report may indicate a 5 percent turnover rate in the research and development department. The 5 percent rate may sound acceptable, but the figure is not sufficiently self-explanatory. If 10 percent of the staff are doing the good work, and half of them leave to take jobs with the competition, the company is in trouble—even with a "low" 5 percent turnover rate.

Consider case 4. What if the firm has only five distributors and the largest decides not to carry the firm's products any more? The firm loses "only" 20 percent of its distributors, but loses 80 percent of its total distribution.

Sales are often reported in gross figures. Yet a firm with $200,000,000 in gross sales may be making or losing money.

An appropriate control mechanism will highlight the information that the manager needs to know.

Congruent

Controls must be congruent with the events they are measuring. By congruent, Drucker means as concrete and accurate as the events permit, but not deceptively concrete. For a firm to say "we have 26 percent of the market" is probably an example of "false concreteness." A less definite but more accurate statement would be, "We are not the biggest element in the market, but we are not the smallest either." Teachers may carry final grades out to two or three decimal points, forgetting that purely subjective judgments led them to assign points to the different assignments.

Persons designing and interpreting controls should be clear about which events can and should be expressed precisely ("The company earned $3.40 per share last year"), and which cannot and should not ("Morale seems a little better around here"). Of course, even so specific and universally used a number as earnings per share can be arrived at in many ways, because many accounting principles are in general use. Therefore, the manager needs to know as much as possible about the control process that results in an apparently precise measurement, in order to judge how meaningful that measurement is.

Timely

Controls must be timely. This principle does not necessarily mean that sheer speed and frequency of measurement are always desirable. Although the statement may not be very useful, the truth is that measurements must be made often enough, but not too often.

Consider a programmed learning machine that reports on performance to the learner every 3 years. Or a control mechanism that reports research progress to the research and development manager every 5 seconds. Both "controls" are absurd. Performance on a programmed learning machine should be measured almost instantly. The student needs to know whether a chosen response is correct or incorrect. In contrast, research results are usually a long time in coming. Two or three years of no apparent progress may be followed one morning by the big breakthrough that the work of two or three years has made possible. So monitoring research every 5 seconds makes no sense. The timeliness of controls depends on the nature of the activity being monitored.

Simple

Controls must be simple. Many elaborate control manuals sit unused on the shelf. If people are issued complicated control instructions, they either ignore them or get more involved with the procedures themselves than with the performance that the controls are supposed to measure.

The control should always be the servant and not the master. If controls are more confusing than helpful, they should be simplified or abandoned.

Operational

Controls must be operational. The end result of any control is action, although the action may be to continue on the present course. No results should be reported simply because they are "interesting."

Since controls should be oriented toward action, their measurement results should reach the person who can take action that is needed. Workers, supervisors, and managers therefore need to see the results of different control measures.

The operational significance of control is not that it is a means of dominating or restricting, but that it is a guide to rational and productive action. According to Drucker, the best controls lead to self-control.

The following sections describe two fairly detailed control procedures: PPBS and PERT/CPM.

PLANNING–PROGRAMMING–BUDGETING SYSTEMS

During the early 1960s, the Rand Corporation developed for the Department of Defense a control philosophy called planning–programming–budgeting systems. The philosophy was designed to encourage the different armed services to do more planning and to think in terms of programs before submitting budget requests.

Prior to this time, the services decided what they needed, asked Congress, and received appropriations. The specific requests often had little to do with important military programs. As the services began to place more emphasis on missions, programs, and projects, they realized that their budgeting systems needed to be changed.

PPBS required the services to think through their programs from idea to execution, with cost estimates for every stage along the way. A concept would be originated, then designed, produced, delivered, and used. The ordinary budgeting system stresses *inputs* (like materials, equipment, and personnel); PPBS stresses *outputs*. Furthermore, unlike the usual budget, PPBS typically spans a planning period of several years. It ties the budget to the organization's long-term goals, not to an annual time cycle.

PPBS was so successful in the armed services that in 1965 President Lyndon Johnson directed all branches of the federal government to use the method. Since that time, it has been adopted by organizations of many kinds.

PERT AND CPM

Development of PERT and CPM

PERT stands for Program Evaluation Review Technique. CPM stands for Critical Path Method. In the late 1950s the U.S. Navy first used PERT to accomplish the Polaris missile project. PERT has been credited with enabling the Navy to finish the project 2 years early.

At about the same time, the Du Pont Corporation and Remington Rand (later Sperry Rand) were developing CPM. They wanted a method for reducing the time required to build and maintain plants. CPM is credited with reducing maintenance time at Du Pont plants by one-third. As PERT and CPM have developed, their differences have disappeared and they are now essentially the same technique. PERT/CPM has been adopted by many business and governmental organizations, and many government contractors are required to use it.

Circles and Arrows

Figure 17-2 presents a simple PERT/CPM diagram made up of circles and arrows. The circles represent completed *events* (called *nodes*) and the arrows drawn to the circles represent *activities* that must be performed to yield completed events. For example, "finishing English 101" would be a circle. All the activities that must be accomplished to get through the course—reading the book, taking exams, writing a term paper, giving an oral report—would be arrows connected to the circle.

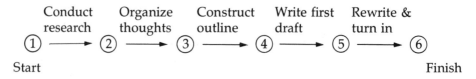

FIG 17-2   Simple PERT diagram: writing a term paper.

The completion of each activity may also be viewed as an event. For example, "writing the term paper" is one *activity* that will lead to finishing the course. But "completing the term paper" is an *event* on the way toward completing the course, and that event may be preceded by several related activities and events. The activities and events in Figure 17-2 include conducting research, organizing thoughts, constructing the outline, writing the rough draft, rewriting the paper, and turning it in. If the student can estimate the time required for each activity, the entire term paper process can be laid out and scheduled.

Steps in Building a PERT/CPM Network

Here are the four steps in building a PERT/CPM network.

Step 1: Activity–Event Analysis.   In step 1, the manager must define all events that must occur and all activities leading up to those events. As every amateur at home repairs knows, much project time is spent in rush trips back to the store to pick up items that should have been purchased on the first trip. Activity analysis forces the project manager to plan out all of a project's aspects before beginning.

Step 2: Activity–Event Sequencing.   Once the manager has defined the activities and events that must at some time occur, they are placed in proper sequence. Some activities must precede or follow other activities, and some activities can be done at the same time. The purpose of this step is to place the activities and events in order. However, this ordering process may reveal other necessary activities and events not perceived during step 1. Therefore, the sequencing of activities also helps to modify or confirm the planning process of the first step.

Step 3: Activity Time Estimates.   The manager must estimate how long performing each activity will take. Once these estimates are made, the manager can add them up and find out how long it will take to move through the entire activity–event network. Since steps 2 and 3 do not depend on each other, they can be done in reverse order.

Some managers use a simple formula for making time estimates. They first make three preliminary estimates: most optimistic time, most pessimistic time (the Murphy's law estimate), and most likely time. The most likely time is multiplied by 4, then added to the optimistic and pessimistic time, and the sum is divided by 6. The result is the expected time. Here is the formula:

$$\text{Expected time} = \frac{\text{optimistic time} + 4 \times \text{most likely time} + \text{pessimistic time}}{6}$$

Although the individual estimates may not be exactly correct, errors average out over the entire network.

The manager determines the expected time for the project by summing the expected times for the activities that fall on the *longest* path through the entire network. Since each activity on that path must be completed, the project cannot be completed more quickly than the sum of those expected times. That longest path is called the *critical path* because, if any event on it is delayed, the entire project will be delayed.

The critical path is the manager's greatest source of potential trouble. The manager may want to reallocate resources to activities along that path, to be sure they are done on time.

Once the total time is determined, the manager calculates the latest time at which each event can occur without delaying total project completion time. For events along the critical path, their expected and latest times are all the same. For events along other paths, expected time may occur before latest time, leaving slack time. Figure 17-3 shows how a network with several paths might look.

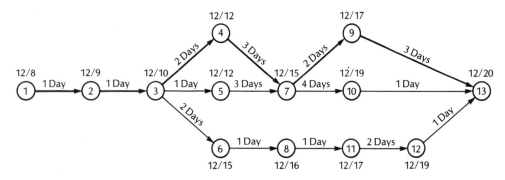

FIG 17-3   Typical PERT/CPM network: events, activities, time estimates, latest times, and critical path (darkest line).

Figure 17-4 shows an actual PERT/CPM chart used to build a service station.

Building a Barbecue

Activity Analysis and Time Estimates.   Here is an illustration of how Sam and Eileen Johnson might use a PERT/CPM network to build a backyard barbecue. First they determine all the activities that must be accomplished. Then they sequence the activities and make time estimates. Table 17-2 shows the results of these three steps.

Building the Network.   Now the Johnsons are ready to construct the PERT/CPM network. It will show the entire series of relationships, the estimated

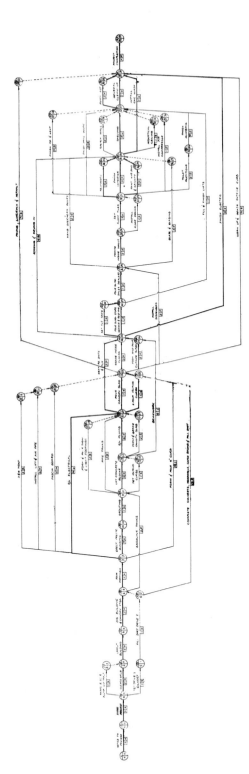

FIG 17-4 PERT/CPM chart for building a service station.

TABLE 17-2   Activity Analysis with Time Estimates for Building Barbecue

Activities in Sequence	Optimistic Time (days)	Most Likely Time (days)	Pessimistic Time (days)	Expected Time (days)
Draw design	0.5	1	1.5	1
Order and receive materials	1	3.5	15	5
Dig foundation	0.25	0.75	1.75	0.75
Build forms for concrete	0.5	0.625	3	1
Pour and set concrete	2	2.5	6	3
Lay brick	1	1.5	2	1.5
Set grate	0.25	0.5	0.75	0.5

completion time, the critical path, and a day-by-day plan for accomplishing the required activities. The network appears in Figure 17-5.

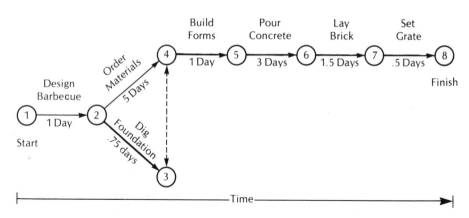

FIG 17-5   PERT/CPM network for building a barbecue.

PERT/CPM Benefits

The true usefulness of PERT/CPM is most fully found not in backyard activities but in very large projects. This powerful planning and controlling device forces project members to foresee problems before starting the project. Once the network is laid out, the controlling aspect of PERT/CPM becomes apparent. Project managers and workers can always compare where they are with where they should be. Problems are automatically signaled by deviations from the time estimates on the chart.

PERT/CPM requires thorough, rigorous planning. That planning pays off by providing continuous control for the project manager. PERT/CPM can be used to plan almost any project that consumes time. It can help managers know whether a project is going to be finished on schedule, can point up potential bottlenecks, and can enable managers to allocate people and materials where they are most needed. For example, consider this section of a network:

Event 7 is a potential trouble spot for two reasons: (1) four activities have to be completed successfully before event 7 occurs, and (2) event 7 must occur before four other activities can begin. the experienced manager's instinct may sense the potential problem. The PERT/CPM network highlights it for all to see.

PERT/CPM has become widely available in easy-to-use software packages requiring minimal computer time. However, for many projects, PERT/CPM can be done with paper and pencil.

PERT/CPM Limitations

PERT/CPM does have some limitations. First, it works best on one-time, large-scale projects. Second, the network may be costly to build. However, this cost may be deceptive. We have already mentioned that the costs of planning are easier to determine than the costs of *not* planning. The manager can readily add up the materials and hours required to build the network and then calculate the exact costs. The costs of delays, missed deadlines, and other expenses of not planning are less easily given a dollar value. Therefore, the initial cost of a PERT/CPM process may appear unjustified to the manager who is unwilling or unable to measure the costs of delays in project implementation. More often than not, the benefits of the advance planning required by PERT/CPM justify the costs.

MEASUREMENT PROBLEMS OF CONTROL

Some managers tend to view the responsibilities of their offices or positions as a personal test of their abilities and knowledge. The usual organizational reward systems reinforce this view. Therefore, the natural tendency of managers is to seek more control—preferably mechanistic, impersonal, and objective control—over the people and activities for which they are accountable.

Overstressing the Measurable

Since managers like precise controls and measurements, they tend to focus on those activities that can be measured and to deemphasize those activities that are less easily measured. They evaluate the measurable organizational resources used by themselves and by their subordinates, sometimes ignoring the less quantifiable aspects. If the nonmeasurable part contributes importantly to the achievement of organizational objectives and/or if the measurable part does not contribute importantly, then achievement of organizational goals is made less likely when managers stress the measurable.

Measuring Teacher Effectiveness. An example of this problem occurs in the field of higher education. The goal of education is usually said to be something like "helping people gain knowledge." This goal is nonoperational; no one knows just what it means or how to measure its achievement. Therefore, organizational control systems designed to ensure that schools produce educated people take on varied, usually irrelevant forms.

Universities want "effective" teachers. Since no one knows how to measure the qualities, traits, attributes, or behaviors of an effective teacher, universities sometimes shift teacher evaluation emphasis to something less relevant but more measurable: scholarly publications. Indeed, some institutions tie organizational rewards directly to the numbers of such publications.

That scholarly publications have some relationship to effective teaching and to the attainment of knowledge by students is debatable. That such activity—because it is measurable—should become the sole criterion when the time comes for tenure and promotion decisions is absurd. Students know only too well that, in some cases, scholarly publications lead to less effective teaching, as faculty members must prepare the articles on which their professional advancement depends rather than prepare for class.

Measuring Human Resources and Social Impact. Many business and nonprofit organizations tend to evaluate people based on those things that can be counted rather than on total job performance. Some profit-making organizations have tried to address this problem in two ways: (1) by quantifying the manager's ability to manage human resources as well as physical resources, and (2) by measuring the social impact of managerial actions.

The first technique seeks to quantify the very real expenses created by poor management of human resources. The second technique seeks to quantify the organization's costs and benefits from society's point of view. Both measures are attempts to establish explicit managerial control over vague, ill-defined, and frequently ignored areas that should be of concern to managers. The expectation is that if a reasonable system of numerical measurement can be devised, managers will devote more attention to the control of these important areas.

Human Resources Accounting

Overstressing Short-Run Performance.   Here are some questions that may be asked of any organization:

1. What is the productive capacity of organizational members? What are their skills, intelligence, and aptitudes?
2. How motivated are the organization's members?
3. How good are the organization's leaders?
4. How effective is the organization's communications?
5. How great is the spirit of teamwork and cooperation?

The answers to these questions are important to organizational success, and yet the answers cannot be reflected on the organization's balance sheet along with its other assets and liabilities because the answers depend on the organization's human resources, not its financial or material resources.

Rensis Likert proposed human resources accounting to measure each manager's ability in handling "people resources" as well as material resources. Here is a problem that sometimes develops in organizations. Managers receive quick promotion by taking over a department or division and, through highly autocratic, fear-oriented management, obtaining outstanding performance. By threatening and coercing their subordinates, such managers can frequently display very good short-run results. These results may lead to rapid promotions, so the managers go on to other departments, use the same methods, and obtain the same results.

Meanwhile, behind the star performer, several organizational units are a shambles because the people who have been threatened, frightened, and coerced have developed low morale and anticompany feelings. Any manager unlucky enough to follow such a star is doomed to look bad when judged by the conventional organizational performance measures of turnover, productivity, and job satisfaction. The better employees are gone, and those remaining wish they were. The star shines, and the organization is a mess.

A common organizational training practice is to rotate managers in order to spot potential stars. Under such a system, a star can turn in a brilliant performance according to conventional profit-and-loss measures while destroying human assets.

Quantifying Human Resources.   Human resources accounting quantifies human assets and includes their increase or decrease in value on the balance sheet. If a manager makes good use of financial and material resources but damages human resources in the process, human resources accounting measures that poor use and treatment of people.

Under human resources accounting, the organization's members are viewed as an investment, as are the organization's relationships with its suppliers, distributors, and customers. Human resources accounting attempts to place a dollar value on these investments by answering such questions as: How much are our members worth to the organization? How much did it cost to recruit, hire, train, and develop them, and how much is it costing us to keep them? If Bill Adams quits, what will it cost to replace him? If we spend $50,000 to improve customer relations, what dollar return can we expect? How much is customer loyalty worth? How much is stockholder loyalty worth? Some of these questions are answered in the conventional balance sheet. For example, most balance sheets include an entry called "good will." Also, expenses of hiring and training employees are included as costs of doing business. Therefore, human resources accounting simply expands on accounting practices in which organizations already engage.

No principles of accounting for human resources are generally accepted yet, but efforts in that direction are underway. Some organizations have actually tried to include the value of their human assets in their balance sheets. For example, as early as 1968, the R. G. Barry Corporation included in its balance sheet such figures as: replacement value of 96 managers = $1,000,000; book value of 96 managers = $600,000; investment in average first-line supervisor = $3000; investment in average top management member = $30,000. The company stopped using this system in 1974, because it lacked the resources to continue developing it and because other problems were more pressing.

As an external reporting device, human resources accounting has some problems. Who "owns" human resources? How is the value of a human resource to be determined: by capitalization of salary, acquisition cost, start-up cost, replacement cost, or present value of expected future contributions? How can the value of physical, financial, and human resources be fairly added together? How is the organization going to explain its accounts to the Internal Revenue Service? Since these difficulties have yet to be overcome, external systems for reporting human resources are rare.

If internal human resources accounting does become widespread, it will have an impact on organizational decision making. As human resources are managed more effectively, human decisions will be made differently.

Organizations have always kept close track of their physical and financial resources. In the past decade, more and more organizations have tried to measure their external and internal human resources. The occupational categories growing the fastest are the managerial and technical groups. Since they require the greatest organizational investment in human resources, methods of accounting for these resources can be expected to become more widely used.

The Social Audit

A second tool designed to bring a previously unmeasurable area within a management control system is the social audit. The attempt here is to focus managerial attention on the organization's social obligations.

Organizations—businesses in particular—are increasingly accepting the idea that they have responsibilities to the social environment. Therefore, the need to measure the organization's attempts to meet these obligations has become great. The social audit is designed to define and measure the organization's social impact.

One type of social audit has four steps.

1. List all organizational activities that may have a social impact.
2. Place a dollar value on each activity's social costs and social benefits.
3. Subtract costs from benefits to arrive at net cost or benefit for each activity.
4. Sum all costs and benefits to arrive at the organization's net social impact.

Here are some examples of items that might appear in the audit.

1. The organization uses public services but pays taxes. If taxes exceed services used, a social credit results. If services exceed taxes, a social debt results.
2. If the organization pollutes the environment, a social debt results. If it uses antipollution devices, it is in effect supplying a service to the public. The organization calculates whether, on balance, it is harming the environment or helping it.
3. Organization members work 10 percent over regular working hours without compensation. That 10 percent is considered as a "contribution" to the organization's customers and to the general public.
4. Organization members publish articles and pamphlets that add to society's knowledge. For purposes of the social audit, the publications are valued at the rate paid to free-lance writers for similar publications.
5. The company gives money to the local United Fund effort and to the local college. The dollar amounts are taken as a social credit.

Some companies have even found it possible to combine their human assets, social contributions, and financial assets into one balance sheet and one income statement. The bottom line of the income statement becomes "total net social and financial income."

Difficulties. The social audit and human resources accounting face similar difficulties in placing a dollar value on humans and their activities. Costs and benefits of activities having a social impact are difficult to measure. Also, who should prepare the audit? Management? Independent outside auditors? The public relations department? A consumer group? The government? The result of these difficulties is that the social audit is recognized as a useful concept and is described in management textbooks but is not yet used by many organizations.

The social audit is a direct response to the increasing demand that organizations be socially responsible. Chapter 19 is devoted to this subject.

CONTROL AND HUMAN RELATIONS

From the organization's point of view, controls are seen as necessary and advantageous. From the member's point of view, they are often seen as a basis for distributing rewards and punishments.

Control and Evaluation

Control systems are a way of evaluating performance. Goals and standards are established, and then performance is measured and compared with goals and standards. The organization member whose performance does not measure up receives a negative evaluation.

Bad Times.   Workers sometimes perceive that employers stress controls more when times are bad than when times are good. If sales and profits drop, controls are sure to receive greater emphasis.

Evaluating the Evaluator.   The persons designing controls must of course be evaluated by their supervisors. Ironically, they and their supervisors may feel that they are doing their controlling job *right* only if they can point out ways in which other people are doing their jobs *wrong*. Only by pointing up errors, weaknesses, and faults do some control systems justify their existence.

Control and Competition.   Control systems often cause an organization's people to compete rather than cooperate. All supervisors want their reported results to compare favorably with established standards. Any supervisor who avoids mistakes and meets production standards is happy, regardless of how well other departments are doing. In other words, some control systems encourage a work-unit or departmental orientation, rather than an organizational orientation.

Avoiding Human Relations Problems

Participative Decision Making.   The best way to avoid the human relations problems sometimes associated with controls is to ask the person controlled to participate in setting up controls. As is true with all organizational decision making, people will more readily accept controls if they play a part in determining them.

Human Relations Training.   A second step toward better results is to offer human relations training to people in charge of controls. Help them to see the human relations implications of the controls they are establishing. Show them how to "sell" their systems and procedures. Make them aware that their main purpose is not to point up failure but to stimulate success.

SUMMARY

This chapter first explained that control means measurement and subsequent regulation in light of measurements taken. Controls within three systems were contrasted: mechanistic, social, and formal organizational systems. To illustrate the concept of control, budgets were explained and then two production control examples were given: quality control and work standards.

The chapter's second major section explained Peter Drucker's seven requirements for controls. They must be economical, meaningful, appropriate, congruent, timely, simple, and operational.

Two fairly elaborate control systems were then discussed: PPBS and PERT/CPM. PPBS encourages managers to think through programs from original idea to execution. By using PERT/CPM, the manager can keep track of the many activities that add up to success for a complex project. Building the PERT/CPM network involves four steps: activity–event analysis, activity–event sequencing, estimating time for each activity, and determining the critical path.

The chapter then covered some measurement problems faced by persons responsible for controls. A dangerous possibility is that managers may stress and measure certain activities simply because they are easily measured.

The final section of the chapter described attempts to measure organizational activities that are obviously important but are also very difficult to measure. Human resources accounting attempts to place a dollar value on the organization's human assets. The social audit attempts to place a plus or minus dollar value on the social impacts of organizational activities.

In Chapter 1, Figure 1-1, the management model, pictured the five managerial functions. The fifth function in the model (control) is right next to the first function (planning), to make clear that the results of controls, measurements, and evaluations must be used in the planning stage, as a new cycle of decision making begins.

DISCUSSION QUESTIONS

1. What is control? Why is control necessary in managing?
2. Do people like to have controls placed on them? If so, how many or to what extent?
3. What are the differences between controls used in mechanistic systems, formal social systems, and informal systems?
4. Contrast acceptance sampling and standard process control.
5. What requirements does Peter Drucker set for controls? Why are they important?
6. Describe the nature, uses, advantages, and disadvantages of a planning–programming–budgeting system.

7. What is PERT/CPM? For what situations is it best suited?
8. What are the steps in building a PERT/CPM chart?
9. What is the purpose of a human resources accounting system? Do you think such systems can work?
10. What is the purpose of a social audit? Should all organizations, both profit and nonprofit, be audited in this way?

COUNTY HEALTH SERVICES AGENCY

Ann Rhoads supervises 12 case workers in the County Health Services Agency. Rhoads and the case workers are responsible for determining who is eligible for state aid and how much aid the eligibles should receive. The case workers must understand and enforce many rules and regulations to satisfy the intent of the law.

Rhoads was recently assigned a new employee, Jack Buckelew. He is a recent graduate of the state university's social welfare program. Rhoads assigned Buckelew to spend one week with an experienced case worker, and then she put him on his own. Her parting words before he left her office were, "My door is always open. Ask for help if you run into any serious problems."

Buckelew took frequent advantage of the invitation and, during his first month on the job, constantly asked Rhoads to review his case work decisions. Rhoads is now growing tired of Buckelew's insecurity. He is intelligent, personable, and hard-working. He should be able to do a good job on his own.

Last week, another new employee entered the agency, so Rhoads was forced to spend less time with Buckelew. Consequently, he had to make more decisions by himself. Shortly after she cut down on her discussions with Buckelew, Rhoads started getting phone calls and visits from some of Buckelew's clients. They complained that Buckelew was not giving them all the financial aid that was due them, and they asked Rhoads to make adjustments. In reviewing Buckelew's decisions, Rhoads found only one small error, which she immediately corrected.

At the end of the week, Rhoads sat down to think about the Buckelew situation. In particular, she wondered whether she should have changed the client's allotment, even though it was originally in error. Perhaps she should have backed all of Buckelew's decisions to give him the confidence he badly needed. In general, she wondered how much time she should spend in reviewing case worker decisions and what her role should be during those reviews.

URBAN NORRISTOWN, INC.

Urban Norristown, Inc. (UNI) was chartered in 19×8 by the state of New Jersey as a nonprofit corporation for supplying housing to low-income families. Here is part of the corporation's organization structure:

President: Marjorie Loth
Vice-president, finance: Tom Spain

Apartment manager: Dick Mowbray

Community organizer: Nancy Pritchard

UNI sponsors 96 rent-supplement apartments. Dick Mowbray has complete responsibility for these apartments, except for the accounting function. The corporation is also responsible for selling 200 houses, built under the federal HUD program for low-income families. Housing sales are handled (except for accounting) by community organizer Nancy Pritchard.

Tom Spain keeps all the accounting records personally. He will allow no one to help him.

Early in 19×9, UNI president Marjorie Loth became aware of several problems almost simultaneously:

1. Accounting reports designed to be done monthly were being done several months late or not at all.
2. UNI had an extremely large inventory of unsold houses.
3. The contractor who had constructed the houses presented Loth with a bill for $60,000, money due on the unsold houses.
4. HUD inspectors brought the deteriorating appearance of the 96 apartments to Loth's attention.

Loth called Spain, Mowbray, and Pritchard together for a meeting. No one would accept any blame. They all blamed each other for UNI's problems.

Upon further investigation, Loth discovered additional problems:

1. Tom Spain has no idea how much money UNI owes or is owed.
2. All 96 apartments have never been occupied at once. Yet, Mowbray has a long waiting list of people wanting apartments.
3. Mowbray is not following the formal procedure for collecting rent on the apartments.
4. Nancy Pritchard is making no effort to sell the 36 unsold houses.

President Marjorie Loth concluded that she had a control problem. She set about correcting it.

Part Four: Comprehensive Cases

CHARLES AND BAKER, INC.

Charles and Baker, Inc., is a multistate architectural, engineering, and planning firm. The power generation group is primarily concerned with the engineering design and specifications for steam and combustion turbine power plants, electrical power transmission systems, and electrical substations. The electrical division of the Power Generation Group is responsible for the electrical aspects of these projects.

The focal point of the electrical division's activities is the division manager. This manager has many responsibilities and needs to possess many skills: supervision, client contact concerning project design, some negotiation with clients, a heavy public relations effort, and continually updated engineering knowledge.

The division has 35 employees in three states. Up until 19×9, the division ran smoothly and morale was good.

In 19×9 the division got a new manager, Horace Beckwith. He is a hearty, confident man. C. J. Spino, vice-president for power generation, announced Beckwith's appointment this way: "Mr. Beckwith has had extensive experience with Northern Electric and with Southern States Electric in the design, manufacture, and marketing of electrical equipment. He is going to use his utility and industry contacts to obtain clients that we badly need in the substation and transmission areas."

However, the division soon saw that Beckwith had no real understanding of what the division did. They rapidly lost all confidence in his technical capabilities.

In the next 8 months, Beckwith also showed that he had no competence in obtaining new business or in establishing a reputation that might lead to new business. The division concluded that vice-president C. J. Spino either did not notice Beckwith's incompetence or noted it but did nothing about it.

Beckwith's communications with the division are strictly of the "do this" variety, with no opportunity for an exchange of ideas. This deterioration in communications has resulted in poor presentations to potential clients. The engineers used to "prep" the former division manager for these presentations, but Beckwith does not want any advice.

As a result of these developments, the division's employees have stopped trying to anticipate the needs of the company or its clients. They simply wait for instructions. The work continues to be satisfactory; the professional pride of the engineers and technicians will not have it otherwise. However, the division has lost its aggressiveness and responsiveness to client needs. The division's employees hope that the situation will improve, but they do not really think that it will.

NATIONAL BUSINESS MACHINES

National Business Machines branch office number 120 is a marketing and service organization consisting of nearly 200 employees. The data-processing division is divided into four sections: two marketing units and two systems engineering units. This arrangement is depicted in the organization chart.

The two marketing units sell new hardware. Each marketing unit has ten salespersons. The two systems engineering (SE) units provide technical assistance to the marketing units. They help in selecting hardware, systems design, computer programming, operator training, installed systems review, computer application development, and many other functions associated with selling and installing computer systems. Each SE unit has ten systems engineers.

The SE units are independent of each other. One unit supports marketing unit A, and the other unit supports marketing unit B.

Systems engineering includes three types of skills and knowledge: those associated with small, medium, and large computer systems. Small systems are usually purchased by the brand-new data-processing user getting first exposure to the world of automation. Systems engineers in this area must of course be skilled systems

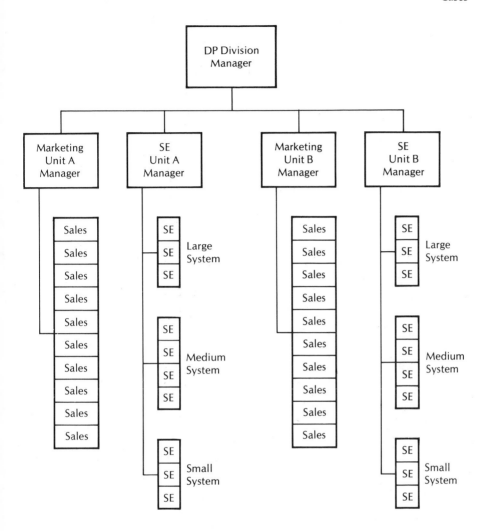

analysts and programmers, but they must also be educators and psychologists. New data-processing users know only as much about the machines as the marketing representatives have told them. They are often unsure about whether they can deal with the machines. The small-system SE's must expand their knowledge and help them build confidence.

The medium-system SE works with a larger, higher-priced machine that has probably been installed for a few years. Users have their own data-processing staffs. Instead of being concerned with programming and operator training, the medium-system SE spends time looking for more advanced applications, such as installing terminals in different user departments.

The large-system SE deals with sophisticated data-processing installations. Large-system users are data-processing professionals with high standards, internal education programs and staffs of 50 or more.

The small-system SE may be working on five or six accounts per day, while the large-system SE may spend a week at one location.

In NBM branch office number 120, both SE units have systems engineers of all three types. This organizational structure has several advantages, but it also causes several problems.

The first problem occurs because the three data-processing system types—small, medium, and large—represent three quite different technologies. The effective SE manager must be well-versed in the latest trends of three separate disciplines. Both SE managers do a good job, but communications problems sometimes arise because they do not have experience in working on data-processing systems of all three kinds.

For example, both current SE managers have backgrounds in medium and large systems. The common misconception is that they should thoroughly understand small computer installations because small systems must be easier to install than large systems. However, in addition to designing the system and writing the programs, the small-system SE performs tasks that the SE's working on medium and large systems never perform. The small-system SE has to explain why the new user must spell the customer's name in exactly the same way every time, or why the card punch operator cannot back-space and punch over an error in the card. Mistakes in these details can cause unbelievable delays in an installation and can be very difficult to locate.

Another problem is the division's sales quota. Since NBM makes more money when installing large machines, the manager naturally meets the quota faster by installing large machines. Of course, everyone realizes the advantages of selling small machines to many customers in the expectation that they will later graduate to medium and large machines. However, the short-run emphasis always seems to be on the large systems.

This situation causes a morale problem among the small-system SE's. They see the large-system people getting the bonuses and the recognition at branch office meetings. The small-system SE's also think that their compensation is not proportionate to the compensation of the large-system SE's. Actually, most large-system SE's have worked longer for NBM and have developed more skills, so their average compensation is justifiably higher. However, the small-system SE's tend to overlook this consideration.

Having two SE managers each control three SE classifications may be inherently inefficient. For example, imagine this situation. Manager A needs a small-system SE and does not have one available. Manager B has an available SE with the proper talents. Manager A asks to borrow the SE. If manager B allows the borrowing, the borrowed SE may be needed but unavailable the very next day. On the other hand, NBM is a service organization, so manager B probably allows manager A to borrow the SE.

Consider the borrowed SE. Once assigned to the project, the SE will probably have to stay with it until it is finished, even if an SE from unit A becomes available. Once the borrowed SE gets to know the people and situation at the new installation and begins to design systems and develop programs, manager B will be reluctant to make a change. So the borrowed SE will be working for a manager who does not appraise performance or make salary recommendations. The borrowed SE may work 60 to 80 hours a week on a crash project, and manager B may never hear about it.

CONSTRUCTION BATTALION UNIT 435

Construction Battalion Unit 435 is a small Navy organization engaged in general construction operations at naval stations in northern California. The unit's 45 enlisted men and one officer do all types of construction. They remodel old structures, and they build new structures, roads, and parking lots.

As the following chart shows, the organization of CBU 435 is relatively simple. Lieutenant Sykes, the officer in charge (OIC), relies heavily on the judgment and expertise of his subordinates. Job scheduling, personnel assignment, and job accomplishment are pretty much left up to the operations chief and the company commanders. Sykes has been successful in building and maintaining a spirit of cooperation—except in the mechanics shop.

Approximately 80 percent of the unit's capital assets are tied up in its automotive and heavy construction equipment. Five mechanics service this equipment, which ranges from pickup trucks to a 25-ton crane. Petty Officer Hall, the senior mechanic, supervises the shop. He reports directly to Chief Forrest, who, as Alpha Company commander, also supervises the equipment operators.

Construction Battalion Unit 435 Organization Chart

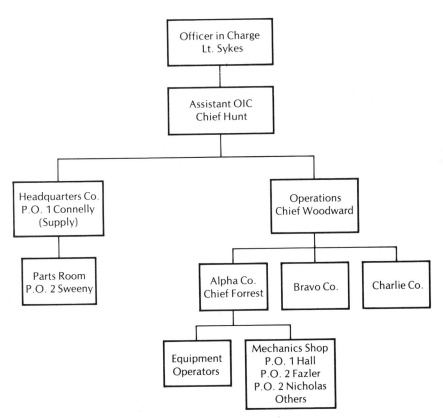

In the past few weeks, personnel in the mechanics shop have been restless and have displayed low morale. Several recent events have made Lt. Sykes realize that he must take action. Each incident seems to center on a single personality: Petty Officer Hall.

Sykes is not really surprised. Hall has been a first-class petty officer for 7 of his 14 years in the Navy. He has flunked five successive advancement examinations and was demoted one grade in Viet Nam for disobeying a direct order. Sykes has never seen Hall do a lot of supervising, much less get his hands dirty. Yet the unit's equipment is well-maintained, and Hall knows every detail about the mechanics shop.

Hall is overbearing and views leadership as a way of exercising power over unquestioning juniors. And his juniors produce, though not very enthusiastically.

Hall's naturally intimidating personality has generated several undesirable side effects beyond his own shop. First, Hall feels that, since he maintains the equipment, anyone wanting to operate it should come to him rather than to Chief Forrest. And many men, including some company commanders, do exactly that. Second, Hall argues incessantly (and often persuasively) with his seniors if they do not accept his suggestions and recommendations. Third, Hall is very active in the local petty officers club and has just been elected president. According to the assistant OIC, Chief Hunt, Hall has been using the unit's material and tools to fix up the clubhouse, but Chief Hunt cannot prove the charge.

Chief Hall has been involved in three recent personnel problems involving second-class petty officers Sweeny, Fazler, and Nicholas. Here is a description of these problems.

1. The spare-parts room is vital to the smooth operation of the mechanics shop. Petty Officer Second Class Sweeny administers this function. The spare parts room used to be a subsidiary area of the mechanics shop, and Sweeny used to report to Chief Hall. Inventory was being misplaced and incorrect parts were being ordered, so Lt. Sykes moved the parts room to the supply section of Headquarters Company, where matters have gone more smoothly. Chief Hall objected strongly to the move, saying that proper maintenance of the unit required the spare-parts room to be under his supervision.

Lately, Hall has been spending a lot of time in the spare-parts room, "because the supply section is not handling spare parts correctly and because I'm the only one who can keep the inventory straight." Sweeny has said privately that Hall is just trying to catch Sweeny in mistakes, so Hall can have him tossed out of the spare-parts room and put back in the mechanics shop as a mechanic under Hall. Sweeny is very discouraged at the prospect but feels powerless to stop Hall.

2. Petty Officer Second Class Fazler has been in the Navy for 8 years and has just been selected for petty officer first class. His supervisors very much want him to stay in the Navy. Friction between Fazler and Chief Hall has been apparent ever since Fazler began work in the mechanics shop, but Fazler has not complained and has done his job well.

His enlistment expires in 2 months, and he must reenlist in order to get his promotion and pay raise. When Chief Forrest asked him if he intended to do so, he said that Chief Hall had made life unbearable for him and that he had already accepted a civilian job.

3. Petty Officer Second Class Nicholas is not as good a mechanic as Fazler is,

but Lt. Sykes views him as quite competent. Nicholas has a compliant, unresponsive personality. He is nonaggressive, has no initiative, never questions an order, and never complains. Yet he does his job satisfactorily, or so Lt. Sykes thought.

Sykes was recently quite surprised to receive an evaluation in which Chief Hall gave Nicholas the lowest possible rating. Sykes called Hall in to ask for an explanation. Hall defended himself loudly and implied that Nicholas was hardly fit to wear the uniform.

Sykes then called Nicholas in. Nicholas said that he would not disagree with Hall's rating. He said Hall always chews him out no matter what he does and never offers any helpful advice or instruction. Furthermore, since no one in the unit seemed interested in his problems, he saw no reason to stay in the Navy and was getting out as soon as he could.

evolving topics in management

Part Five presents information about four special topics of concern to contemporary managers.

Chapter 18 discusses organizational development, the emerging field devoted to training and developing the organization's human resources.

Chapter 19 explores social responsibility. To what extent are the organization and the manager responsible to society? The chapter presents the cases for and against social responsibility. The issue is important because a sense of social responsibility will affect the decisions that the manager makes.

Chapter 20 presents information on international management. More and more organizations are becoming international in scope. International managers must remain aware of the cultural, economic, and legal constraints that international activity places upon them.

Chapter 21 takes a look at the future. The implications for future managers of eight changes already underway and expected to continue are discussed.

organizational development

As the people working in organizations and dealing with the organization from the outside have changed, the nature and design of organizations have also had to change. Society has new expectations about what the organization should do for its membership and for its community. These expectations have led to two new concerns for managers. One is organizational development (OD)—to address the expectation that organizations will adapt to changing human requirements. The other is social responsibility—to address emerging concerns about the organization's place in the entire social fabric. Social responsibility is the subject of the next chapter. This chapter explores the evolving topic of organizational development.

An *organization* is a group of people willing and able to work together to accomplish a common goal. *Development* is a process that seeks to promote growth or improvement. *Organizational development* then becomes the process of promoting the growth or improvement of organizations.

Although this definition is broad, at least it sets the stage for the kinds of activities, ranging from a 1-hour seminar to an intensive encounter-group experience, that are commonly considered as being part of organizational development. This chapter consists of major sections on OD's history, assumptions, methods, and problems.

The day has long passed when the organization could take its human assets for granted. OD reflects the new emphasis on the importance of these assets.

HISTORY

The history of organizational development is usually traced back to the work of psychologist Kurt Lewin (1890–1947), a pioneer in the practical application of theory. His "action research" sought to apply laboratory-based theories to ongoing enterprises. He influenced a number of behavioral scientists to undertake studies in organizations, where they could see the real-life effects of experimental changes.

Laboratory Training

Lewin's action-based research resulted in two related OD approaches that have essentially merged today. One approach is *laboratory training* or *T-group training,* a method of developing the organization by developing its individual members. T-group training borrows concepts from a wide variety of fields (among them group dynamics, learning theory, personality theory, clinical psychology, adult education, and personnel training) and applies them in the training laboratory setting. Participants are placed in small, unstructured training groups (T-groups), interact with other participants under the supervision of a trainer or facilitator, and then give and receive feedback on the experience. T-groups are far different from ordinary classes. Rather than having discussions or lectures, the groups engage in interaction exercises and other experiences.

Early T-group results were exciting. The National Training Laboratory was founded in Bethel, Maine, in 1947, and the T-group training method was on its way. Thousands of persons have attended NTL labs, fully one-third of our largest firms use T-group programs in some form, and many universities include T-group sessions in their academic programs.

Increased Sensitivity.   T-group training is sometimes called sensitivity training, because its basic idea is to develop an increased sensitivity to others and to the effect we have on others. The group is unstructured and ambiguous. Since most group members do not like lack of structure and ambiguity, they usually become anxious. The hope is that the ambiguous, anxiety-producing situation will lead to self-exploration and self-awareness. T-group members try to become more aware of the verbal and nonverbal messages they send, their behavior patterns, their defense mechanisms, and the way they come across to other participants. The members of a particular lab group may come from a wide variety of organizations. They join together in a laboratory experience, learn from it, and hopefully carry their learning back to the job. If training has been successful, people go home with greater awareness, sensitivity, better human relations, and better attitudes toward managing.

From Laboratory to Job.   From its beginnings in 1946, the T-group movement faced a major problem: how to transfer laboratory learning back to the job. People underwent impressive changes at Bethel and put their learning to work back home, only to find that their changed behavior confused their co-workers and upset the organization's dynamic social equilibrium. Their fellow organization members had not gone through the same experience, did not understand the manager's attempts to practice T-group learning, and did not trust the manager's new openness and empathy as being sincere. In subtle and unsubtle ways, co-workers sent their newly trained managers this message: "You may not have been so great before your T-group training, but at least we all knew where we stood. Now we don't know what's going on, and we don't believe the change in you is real." The managers often became frustrated and relapsed into the old behavior patterns with which everyone was familiar and comfortable.

Two Variations.   These difficulties with permanent learning transfer led to two new laboratory approaches. One approach was to bring the organization to the laboratory. That way, managers and co-workers would all understand what the T-group experience was all about. The other approach was to take the laboratory to the organization. Company trainers could be sure that co-workers throughout the organization understood and accepted the T-group learning.

Further Difficulties.   These approaches had some unfortunate aftereffects. T-groups encourage subordinates to be frank and open with managers about their shortcomings. Some managers displayed long memories about what subordinates revealed during the training sessions. Other managers, shocked to learn that their subordinates viewed them as less than ideal, lost their managerial effectiveness or quit altogether. Many organization members found it difficult to face each other on the job in daily working relationships after having shared their innermost feelings in profoundly emotional T-group sessions.

   A second major difficulty resulted from the mass-production, come-one-come-all approach. Since little screening was done, a few persons emotionally incapable of handling the T-group experience became seriously disturbed.

   The last, and probably most critical, difficulty was lack of top management participation. Their attitude seemed to be, "I don't need it, but my subordinates sure do." Few subordinates deviate significantly from the behavioral style of the boss. When the subordinate learns a new style in the T-group and the boss behaves in the same old way, the new style withers away from disuse. As is true of any major organizational change, laboratory training simply will not work unless top management is *actively* involved.

In-House Change Agents.   These disappointments led T-group enthusiasts to broaden the concern and coverage of T-group training. The initial focus had been individual change. The new realization was that the entire organizational system had to be developed. Changed behavior patterns could not be maintained unless the organizational culture was ready and receptive. Therefore, the organization had to be developed by changing the entire system's way of looking at things.

   One means for accomplishing these far-reaching objectives is to acquire a corps of in-house change agents or trainers. Rather than being content with short seminars or weekend laboratories, these specialists in organizational development constantly work from within the organization to encourage preferred management styles. They offer the continuous reinforcement that can make learning stick.

The Managerial Grid.   The early laboratory training was unstructured. Robert Blake and Jane Mouton added some structure by offering measurement-based feedback to trainees. They used their "managerial grid" to demonstrate pre-training managerial style in terms of the manager's orientation toward people and toward production. Then they used the grid to show managers how their learning would influence their managerial performance.

The grid appears in Figure 18-1. It has two dimensions: (1) the manag-

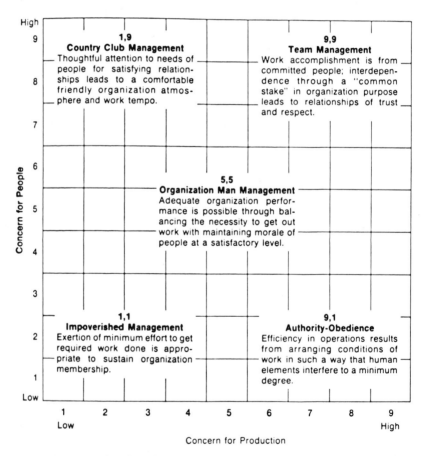

FIG 18-1   The Managerial Grid®. (*Source:* Robert R. Blake and Jane S. Mouton, *The New Managerial Grid.* Houston, Texas: Gulf Publishing Co., 1978, p. 11. Used by permission.)

er's concern for getting the work done, and (2) the manager's concern for the people who get the work done. Management styles are given numbers ranging from 1,1 to 9,9. The 1,1 manager is not much of a manager, having a low concern for both people and product. The 1,1 manager is just putting in time, going through the motions of managing. The 9,9 manager has a high concern for both people and product, and the 5,5 manager, with a moderate concern for each, does not want to appear too soft or too tough. The grid approach strongly favors the 9,9 managerial style.

The grid training program has six phases.

Phase 1. Learning the grid, so that managers can perceive their own managerial styles.

Phase 2. Developing the work team, defining the organizational climate, understanding how the organization's parts are related.

Phase 3. Training in intergroup relationships to achieve better problem-solving coordination between the organization's related parts.

Phase 4. Analyzing the organization, establishing a blueprint for attaining the organization's long-term goals, redefining relationships, learning new problem-solving skills.

Phase 5. Implementing the blueprint.

Phase 6. Reinforcement to stabilize new management patterns and to encourage continuing organizational self-examination and development.

The grid training program cannot be accomplished quickly. In fact, it may stretch out over 5 to 10 years.

Data-Based Action Research

The second important organizational development group, led by Rensis Likert and Chris Argyris, worked out of the University of Michigan's Institute for Social Research. This group was more directly influenced by Lewin's action research concept. Rather than using laboratory training, it conducted research from the very start within the organization itself.

These behavioral scientists conceived of organizational development as the organization-wide learning, acceptance, and practice of the human relations point of view. They believed that all personnel department staff had to teach the human relations philosophy and management style to managers at all levels.

The Institute for Social Research group wanted answers to three questions:

1. What are the general principles that underlie management activity?
2. Once discovered, how can these principles be put into practice?
3. Which principles and practices are appropriate in the organization under study?

Survey Feedback. To make training specifically appropriate for the organization being studied, the Institute used *survey feedback*. Under this method, surveys containing relevant questions about the organization are distributed to members, and responses are summarized for each work group, area of responsibility, department, and the organization itself. The summaries are then distributed to survey participants. With the help of outside consultants or in-house trainers, supervisors discuss survey results with their subordinates. All organization members commit themselves to resolving the issues raised, by using standard problem-solving techniques.

The Major Groups: A Comparison. Although laboratory training and data-based OD are different in approach, they have similar goals. Both want to help the organization move ahead from its present status to greater self-awareness and more effective use of human resources. Both recognize that the organization is a system in need of development, rather than a mere collection of individual elements. For the OD job to succeed, managers at all levels must understand human relations concepts and be committed to them.

Organizational Development Today

Problem Solving and Change. In its most fundamental sense, OD is the process of teaching problem identification and resolution skills to organization members. We have maintained that the manager's main job is to make and implement decisions. The most effective way to implement decisions is for the manager to use the philosophy and techniques of member participation in decision making. Thus OD becomes the process of teaching managers how to recognize problems and resolve them through the participation of those affected by the problems. Human, societal, technological, and other influences continually require that organizations change, and OD helps the manager to develop the ability to use human resources to plan and implement inevitable changes.

An organization involved in continuous change must have a mechanism for coping with it. Organizational development is the process of maintaining this continuous response. It is all the techniques used to teach managers how to implement change through their human resources. It is a long-range plan for integrating individual goals into the organization's goals.

Although OD has come to include a variety of purposes, methods, goals, programs, and activities designed to improve the organization, it has a few distinctive features.[1]

Behavioral Base.   Organizational development is based in the behavioral sciences. The OD consultants bring to the training a knowledge of psychology, sociology, education, management, and other behavioral disciplines.

Long-Range.   An OD program is not just a series of miscellaneous development exercises. It is a long-range, planned effort, based on an overall strategy.

Use of Consultants.   Consultants or change agents, either from within or outside the organization, run the program. The consultants and the trainees collaborate to build trainee skills.

Skill-Building Activities.   Activities are distinctive in that they help trainees to build skills in self-examination and in dealing with people.

ASSUMPTIONS

Effective Human Relations

Organizational development has risen rapidly as an important field for the modern decision maker. Arising from the behavioral school of management thought, OD's assumptions represent in their cumulative effect the assertion that the human relations approach to managing is the most effective.

Few empirical data exist to support this assertion. Nevertheless, management and workers are increasingly accepting this philosophy as the best way to administer human organizations.

Many OD assumptions come from Douglas McGregor's classical work on Theory Y management, and it is no accident that McGregor was an OD pioneer. The assumptions can be grouped under three broad categories: those about people, people in groups, and people in organizations.[2]

Assumptions About People

In its assumptions about people, OD endorses the following ideas.

[1]These features are taken from Wendell L. French, Cecil H. Bell, Jr., and Robert A. Zawacki (eds.), *Organization Development: Theory, Practice, and Research* (Dallas, Texas: Business Publications, Inc., 1978), p. 11.

[2]The following discussion is indebted to Wendell L. French and Cecil H. Bell, Jr., *Organizational Development* (Englewood Cliffs, N.J.: Prentice-Hall, Inc., 1973), Chapter 6.

Growth.   Most people seek personal growth and development in all aspects of their lives. They are most likely to fulfill themselves in an environment that supports and challenges them.

Involvement.   Most people want to be involved in their activities. They do not want simply to go through the motions. They want to identify with the products, services, or functions of organizations to which they belong. They are not satisfied just to meet externally established quotas or performance standards. They want the personal satisfaction that comes from meeting internally established standards of excellence.

Goals.   Most people prefer to be goal-directed. They set internal or external goals for themselves. They behave in ways that they think will lead them toward their goals.

Assumptions About People in Groups

Organizational development assumes the following ideas about people in groups.

Acceptance.   Most people need to feel accepted by at least one small group. This group is usually the family or the work group.

Work Group Influence.   Most people spend about half of their waking hours in a work group. Therefore, the work group's values and beliefs greatly influence each member's behavior, both on and off the job.

Commitment to Work Group.   Most people are more committed to solving work group problems than they are to solving organizational problems. They are more loyal to the work group than to the organization.

Leadership.   For a group to be effective, all members, not just the formal leader, must assist in leading and directing the group's efforts. Leadership in the effective group rotates from member to member, depending on the situation.

Assumptions About People in Organizations

Organizational development makes several assumptions about how people behave within the larger organizational setting.

Organizations as Systems.   Because the organization is a system, anything happening anywhere throughout the system is going to affect other parts of the system. For example, technological developments will affect the social and administrative subsystems. Relatively minor decisions made in the president's office may affect many work groups.

Feelings Matter.   Most organizations encourage their members to suppress, rather than express, their feelings and "stick to business." If, instead, organizations would encourage the expression of feelings, members would experience greater personal growth and job satisfaction, and organizational cooperation, morale, and communications would improve. Because most organizations sorely lack frank and honest expression, OD interventions often focus on this important problem.

The Value of the Individual

The cumulative impact of these assumptions is a belief in the value of the individual within the organizational environment. The OD people recognize that all organization members must satisfy their needs, or they and the organization will fail each other. If members are encouraged and equipped to reach individual and group goals, the organization will perform more effectively.

The organization's true goals are rarely printed in the annual report or contained in press releases. Instead, each organization's goals represent the complex meshing of many individual and interdependent group goals. Individuals give up control over their behavior and act collectively to accomplish more than any one person could.

Organizational Productivity

Organizational development helps managers to become aware of why people join organizations. They are then encouraged to seek new ways of incorporating individual goals into group goals. The quest for joint goal satisfaction should result in higher organizational productivity. If people feel that the organization actively helps them to reach their own goals, people will be happier and more involved, committed, and productive. If the organization becomes internalized within its members, they will produce as carefully and lovingly on its behalf as if they were producing for themselves. These are the goals of OD.

METHODS OF ORGANIZATIONAL DEVELOPMENT

The OD process is a simplified version of the problem-solving process. It consists of three stages: diagnosis, action, and process maintenance.

Diagnosis

Managers become aware about OD in various ways—through reading professional literature, attending a T-group session, talking with a personnel director, and so on. Once top management decides that organizational problems
may be reduced or solved through training, the outside OD consultant or
company staff begins to diagnose the organization's present situation. The
organizational climate is monitored continuously for a time. Information is
collected from morale and attitude surveys, absenteeism and turnover reports, interviews, and other sources. The information-collection system is
vital to OD success. It not only points up problem areas needing intervention,
but also provides continuous feedback concerning how successful the chosen
intervention strategy has been.

Action

The second OD step is action or intervention. Based on the information
gained through diagnosis, OD specialists devise appropriate training
strategies.

Change Agent.   The change effort is usually best spearheaded by someone
from outside the group that is trying to change. This person might be a
personnel department OD specialist or an outside professional. The change
agent must be able to perceive the underlying problems in the system, communicate these perceptions persuasively to the group, and facilitate the
group's learning of new behaviors that can resolve problems. Although some
problems may be caused by lack of funds or physical resources, OD change
agents ignore those matters and concentrate on behavioral training of members, groups, or the entire organization.

A professional change agent will insist on participation by each affected
unit's top manager. No program involving behavioral change can succeed
without top management's active support and participation.

The Depth of Intervention

Behavioral change of different kinds and degrees is probably desirable within
numerous areas of any organization. Change agents want to show results to
the organization. Yet few organizational systems can tolerate severe, abrupt
change. How much change should the change agent strive for? What depth of
intervention is best?

Resisting Change.   Individuals, groups, and organizations resist change for
many reasons. Any OD intervention strategy is going to change the system

somehow. Professional skill is required to introduce enough change to be recognized but not too much to be tolerated.

For example, consider this situation. A company's top management group wants an outside OD specialist to offer a human relations training program for supervisors. During the diagnostic step, the change agent recognizes that the organization's real problem is lack of human relations skills, not within the supervisor group but within the top management group itself. Human relations deficiencies among the supervisors are symptomatic of the real problem, and treating the symptom may not help much.

The trainer must decide whether the organization can handle the depth of intervention required to make a real difference. If it cannot, the change agent and the organization must be content with moderate intervention.

The Range of Strategies: The Organizational Development Cube

The OD cube is shown in Figure 18-2. The left edge of the cube lists the problems that may surface during the diagnostic stage. The upper left edge of the cube shows where intervention action can be focused.

The major OD strategies appear along the top edge of the cube. These strategies are:

1. *Training.* Training may range from T-groups or other experiential learning to standard lectures and readings.
2. *Process consultation.* Trainers watch the organization's day-to-day processes and then offer suggestions for improvement.
3. *Confrontation.* The trainer brings the parties to the problem together, offers data and interpretations, and then helps the group achieve a workable solution.
4. *Data feedback.* Information is collected, analyzed, and presented to units or persons having problems.
5. *Problem solving.* Some organizational problems require that the full problem-solving process be undertaken.
6. *Plan making.* Some problems are best solved by drawing up definite plans and setting goals.
7. *Establishing OD task force.* Different task forces can be assigned different problems.
8. *Technostructural activity.* Changing the organization's structure, work flow, or methods is sometimes best.

Somewhere within the large OD cube lie the small cube or cubes that best represent a given organization's problem–focus–intervention combination. Finding that small cube is the trainer's task. For example, the OD

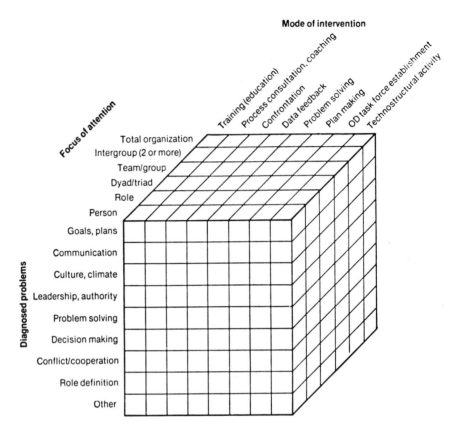

FIG 18-2 The organization development cube. (Reprinted from Richard Schmuck and Matthew Miles, *Organization Development in Schools.* San Diego, CA: University Associates, 1978. Used with permission.)

specialist may decide that the main problem in the Tipple Wine Company is vice-president for distribution James David's inability to make plans and establish goals. The trainer may prescribe some reading, attendance at a weekend seminar on goal setting, and follow-up sessions with the trainer. That combination of problems and solutions is represented by the small upper left front cube: goals, plans/person/training (education).

Process Maintenance

The last OD step is process maintenance, following up and sustaining the OD accomplishments. Once change occurs, it must be reinforced. Feedback loops must be established. The organization must be continually encouraged to analyze and reflect on its accomplishments.

Persons and groups going through laboratory training are usually excited at first about the possibilities of a new managerial style; then, like makers of New Year's resolutions, they tend to backslide. Many influences will encourage a return to the status quo before development. To combat these influences, the OD process must be encouraged, extended, reinforced, and maintained.

CRITICISMS OF ORGANIZATIONAL DEVELOPMENT

Organizational development has come in for criticism. Since OD exponents come from different backgrounds and orientations, controversy is perhaps to be expected. This last major section of the chapter will present some of the problems and criticisms that OD has experienced.

General Criticisms

Some say that organizational development is merely a 50-cent term for human relations training and that most OD interventions have no real hope of changing basic managerial attitudes, a necessity for true organizational growth. Others say that OD is merely an excuse for college professors and high-paid consultants to meddle in organizational affairs without having to take any responsibility for organizational changes and decisions that do not turn out right. These outsiders preach from an ideal world and fail to take the organization's structural, physical, and environmental constraints into account. Furthermore, they are usually behavioral scientists who overlook non-behavioral considerations.

Finally, some critics say that whether OD interventions actually increase productivity or improve organizational performance in any way has not been proved. No methods yet exist for estimating how much time must pass before an OD intervention has impact or for measuring the degree of impact.

Further Criticisms

In addition to these general criticisms, OD has received some more specific criticisms.

Development?   Some say that organizational development does not deserve to be called "development." The objectives of the approach are unclear, the processes are not well understood, many trainers are not qualified, and hardly any OD people really comprehend what is going on, especially within the unstructured, "anything goes" T-groups.

Psychological Damage.   Another criticism is that OD participants may be damaged psychologically. Not only is anxiety in OD sessions not avoided; to an extent it is sometimes sought. Participants may become highly anxious and very uncomfortable, especially in T-groups. The hope and expectation, of course, is that as the training draws to a close, group members will have gained deeper insight, will understand and come to terms with their anxiety, and will end up with an emotional (rather than intellectual) learning that makes any discomfort worthwhile. The successful OD "graduate" is said to be more sensitive, less dependent, a better listener, and a better communicator and group member in general.

Actually, few cases of severe psychological reaction to OD have been documented, and most of these cases had histories of psychological problems. Therefore, proper screening should minimize the possibility of psychological damage.

Some Questions for Managers.   In light of the foregoing criticisms and problems, managers considering OD for their organizations must ask themselves some serious questions.

1. If OD "works," can our organization handle the kinds of people coming out of the organizational development experience? Can the organization stand all that openness, frankness, independence, and sensitivity?
2. Can the organization's members tolerate the anxiety that OD sometimes produces?
3. Do managers have the *right* to ask or demand that the organization's members endure such anxiety and soul-searching?

Organizational development, and T-groups in particular, are powerful methods, not to be used lightly. But sometimes organizations and their members have big problems that require powerful methods for solution.

SUMMARY

This chapter first presented a brief history of organizational development. Two early approaches have essentially merged into what today we know as OD: laboratory training and data-based action research.

Organizational development makes several assumptions about people as individuals, people in groups, and people in organizations. The underlying assumption is that the human relations management style is the most effective.

The three steps in the OD process are diagnosis, intervention, and process maintenance. The consultant or change agent must gather data, diagnose organizational difficulties, decide how deep and intense the OD intervention can and should be, and choose from the range of available OD strategies: training, process consultation, confrontation, data feedback, problem solving, planning–goal setting, an OD task force, and structural or methodological change. Once change has been brought about, it must be reinforced and maintained.

The chapter concluded by examining some criticisms of OD.

DISCUSSION QUESTIONS

1. What does it mean to "develop" an organization?
2. What is the point of laboratory training? Does it seem to you that this method achieves its goal?
3. What are the limitations of laboratory training? What methods are available for overcoming them?
4. What is the purpose and usefulness of the managerial grid? What other factors, if any, would you add to the grid? Why?
5. What are the advantages and disadvantages of data-based action research, compared to laboratory training?
6. What assumptions does OD make about people, about people in groups, and about people in organizations? Do these assumptions seem valid?
7. What are the steps in the OD problem-solving process?
8. What are some criticisms of OD?
9. Can individual managers practice OD in their own departments? Explain.
10. How much organizational commitment does an organization have the right to generate within employees? Is there a point beyond which the organization should not seek to gain further employee identification with itself? Why or why not?

THE PUBLIC WELFARE AGENCY

Mack Morris is a manager at the Public Welfare Agency. Among other administrative duties, he hires and trains entry-level employees.

The typical Agency job applicant is fresh out of college, eager, idealistic, and confident of solving the world's problems. In return, the Agency offers minimal training, little chance for advancement, considerable job security, low pay, and a lot of paperwork to take home at night and on weekends.

For a couple of decades, job applicants have been plentiful. Over the past several months, the number of applications has dwindled.

Morris recently expressed his concern to Mary Ammerman, sitting at the next desk. "Where are we going to get fresh new employees? How can we keep the good people we have at the lower levels? I can't for the life of me see why so many stay with us. Of course, the best ones go somewhere else for more money and faster promotions. But I'm surprised that any of them at all stay. I wonder what they get out of it? And how can we help them to get more out of their jobs?"

Mary Ammerman said she didn't know. As a matter of fact, she thought to herself, she wasn't getting all that much out of her own job.

TILLEY MOVING COMPANY

When Sarah London came in as president of Tilley Moving Company, one of the first things she noted was the high turnover rate among employees. Once they were thoroughly trained, most clerks and other workers resigned to take jobs with competitors.

Before London came in, Al Tilley, Sr., had the final say-so on all matters. He did most hiring and firing, knew the old-timers by name and kept track of their families, dug into his own pocket to help employees in time of need, and had no personnel policies to speak of.

Employees got 2 weeks of vacation and a Christmas bonus and party. Sick leave was granted on a case-by-case basis. The company paid for most of each employee's medical insurance and provided a $2000 life insurance policy for each employee. Pay was at the industry's lowest levels.

Sarah London raised salaries up to the industry average, set definite policies on sick leave and other time off, opened a cafeteria for employees, and increased their medical and life insurance benefits. The employees were overjoyed. Turnover dropped sharply. The Tilley family, owners of the business, went along with the changes and were satisfied with the results.

The managers and supervisors were not happy at all. They had received very small adjustments in pay, and they resented the fact that salaries for their subordinates had been raised without consulting them. Soon, some managers and supervisors began to quit and take jobs with competitors.

social responsibility

In the past several decades, social responsibility has become an important concern for modern decision makers. Social responsibility is an important issue because it can affect how decision makers evaluate the alternatives available for solving problems. If an organization has a strong sense of social responsibility, its decision makers must not only try to make those decisions that will encourage profit, growth, and survival, but decisions that are socially responsible as well. This attitude may cause an organization to avoid actions that might be profitable but that might also harm society. Furthermore, the organization may make some socially beneficial decisions that result in no profit or even in a financial loss.

This chapter will first present some background on the social responsibility controversy. Then the cases for and against social responsibility will be made.

BACKGROUND

Meeting Society's Expectations

Social responsibility is a relatively recent concern. In 1953, Harold Bowen spoke of social responsibility as "the obligations of businessmen to pursue those policies, to make those decisions, and to follow those lines of action that are desirable in terms of the objectives and values of our society."[1] Over the past 25 years, the term has become widely used by managers and management scholars. Unfortunately, the term does not mean the same thing to everyone.

Social Responsibility and the Management Model. The manager's philosophical approach forms the base of the comprehensive management model presented

[1]Harold Bowen, *Social Responsibilities of the Businessman* (New York: Harper & Row, Inc., 1953), p. 6.

411

in Chapter 1. That approach greatly affects the manager's decisions within the five functional management areas. Some interpretation of what social responsibility means is a part of each manager's philosophical approach and thereby influences the manager's decisions.

The Cost of Social Responsibility.   Consider a manager who needs a new plant. The manager can of course simply build a totally functional, traditional plant. If at no extra cost a plant can be built that is functional *and* attractive, then the "socially responsible" decision to build an attractive plant is easy to make. But what if the attractive plant will cost twice as much as the functional plant? The manager must decide whether the organization can afford to be socially responsible.

Such dilemmas occur frequently. One manager may have to decide between keeping a plant in a high-unemployment area that really needs jobs, or building a new plant in an area with relatively full employment but slightly lower property taxes. Another manager may have to decide whether to spend funds on more efficient equipment, or on ramps that would permit hiring handicapped persons.

Yardsticks for Success.   The beauty of classical economics is that the yardstick of *profit* can be used to evaluate such managerial decisions. Under classical economics, society expects Harry of Harry's Pizza Parlor to sell a tasty pizza at a fair price. Every day the marketplace gives Harry a score on the on-going economic test. If Harry's pizza is not tasty or his price is not fair, he flunks the test. If he continues to flunk, he eventually goes bankrupt.

If Harry engages in activities unconnected with pizza making—such as supporting a Little League team, contributing to the United Fund, or planting beautiful and expensive trees around the parlor—he does so with full knowledge of the impact that these activities will have on the parlor's profitability.

Imagine that Max Prophet opens a competing pizzeria next door to Harry's. Max supports no team, makes no charitable contributions, and plants no trees. He merely makes a very tasty pizza and sells it at a lower price than Harry's. Now Harry must reduce or eliminate his socially responsible activities so that he can reduce his pizza price to meet Max's. Or he can sustain his socially responsible activities, lower his pizza price to meet Max's, and accept a lower return on his investment.

No Free Lunch.   The point is simply this: someone must pay for socially responsible activities. There is no free lunch. If an organization loans an executive to the United Fund for two weeks, someone must pay. The stockholders pay if the company absorbs the cost, the customers pay if the company passes the cost along to them in the form of higher prices, or society pays if it absorbs the cost by giving the organization a tax deduction.

Every year, major corporations such as General Motors, IBM, Prudential, General Electric, Ford, and AT&T distribute publications that reflect their social responsibility. These publications include a wide variety of activities, ranging from the development of a softball that bleeps so blind children can play the game, to pollution control, to charitable contributions, to a program for rehabilitating the inner city of Newark. How can we decide whether these activities really are socially responsible?

Society's Expectations.   Although many definitions of social responsibility exist, any valid definition should include the idea of *society's expectations*. Society has allowed the formation and development of economic and other institutions. We collectively define the rules of the game for these institutions, and we collectively agree on what constitutes good and poor performance.

Each institution performs a valuable social function. For example, society has given economic organizations such as businesses the task of allocating scarce economic resources efficiently. At an earlier point in history, society's expectations for business organizations did not go beyond efficient resource allocation. The rules reflected these expectations, and the classical evaluation criterion of *profits* reflected success or failure. Now, society's expectations of business organizations have changed, and modern businesses must think beyond the simple notion of profit maximization.

Defining social responsibility in terms of society's expectations is more vague than such definitions as "maximize profits without breaking laws." Yet the latter definition is not sufficiently broad in the current social context. As managers face their choices, they must try to use society's expectations as a criterion for determining whether a choice is socially responsible. However, society's more recent expectations are often non-operational, contradictory, or even impossible to meet. Even so, today's business organizations must try to meet them. They must consider the human, social, political, and environmental results of their economic choices. Businesses must be good citizens.

Profiting from Social Responsibility.   Some companies have achieved the best of both worlds by making a profit out of social responsibility. IBM has engaged in many activities that might seem detrimental to short-run profits. Yet, IBM earnings and stock prices have risen steadily for many years. Selling used computers cheaply to universities may not maximize this year's profits, but over the long run it yields a large group of people who are both familiar with IBM equipment and grateful to IBM for providing it. These same people may well be in the position someday to order computer equipment for their organizations.

The Beginnings of Social Responsibility

A Noncompetitive Market.   The initial interest in social responsibility came about during the early 1950s. At that time, academics and other observers became concerned that our economic system was no longer regulating private enterprise properly. The classical competitive market regulatory forces—perfect market information, free and easy entry into the market, and enough competing firms to keep any one firm from controlling the market—seemed unable to contend with such corporate giants as the Generals Electric, Motors, and Foods. By 1968, 100 corporations controlled half the assets of the nation's 1,500,000 corporations. We now have corporations whose gross annual income exceeds the gross national product of such nations as Denmark, Switzerland, Belgium, and Portugal. In the absence of a truly competitive market, perhaps moral persuasion in the form of social responsibility can bring about appropriate organizational behavior.

At about the same time that this hope was emerging, management theorists and writers were shifting emphasis from studying the individual firm or industry in isolation to studying the firm or industry as a member of a social system.

Trusting the Corporations.   These two movements held the joint hope that people in business would adopt the idea of social responsibility. And why not? Modern management theory maintains that individuals in corporations can be trusted to work appropriately and productively, once they understand the organization's goals. Since managers who make organizational decisions are also members of the larger social system, it follows that they can be trusted to perform their economic functions in a socially beneficial way, once they understand their social obligations. Economists of the postwar period were tackling the problem of enormous corporate size by advocating splitting up the large corporations or divesting them of some assets. Management writers were offering the concept of social responsibility as a reminder of the moral constraint that would keep large organizations from taking advantage of their size and power.

Giving Money to Princeton.   In 1951, a landmark decision permitted corporations to make gifts to educational institutions. Prior to that time, the courts had held that corporations are profit-making institutions whose profits, if distributed, should go only to stockholders. To test this position, several large corporations and foundations arranged that the A. P. Smith Manufacturing Company, a small New Jersey corporation, should give $1500 to Princeton University. The stockholders took the case to court.

In defending the gift, Judge J. C. Stein found that gifts to colleges and universities were of direct benefit to corporations and in fact promoted the welfare "of everyone anywhere in the land." Since 1951, corporate giving to educational institutions has been viewed as lawful and appropriate.

The Spotlight of the Evening News.   As the 1950s wore on, many organizations began to embrace the social responsibility concept for a variety of reasons, but primarily because organizational decision makers recognized that their every move might be reviewed by the public on the evening news. The massiveness of many corporations enables them to dominate market forces, rather than being regulated by them. Their very massiveness means that such organizations are highly visible and closely watched.

The Force of Society.   The doctrine of social responsibility made organizational managers aware of an obligation that did not always have the force of law and did not have the competitive market's power to punish. However, the call to ethical and principled decisions did have behind it no small strength—the full force of society. That force could be expressed through legislation (such as laws mandating better gas mileage for automobiles), through product boycotts (such as the classic grape boycott led by Cesar Chavez), or other means. If an organization did not behave in accordance with the social system's expectations, it might not merely lose its market share or face another piece of legislated control; it might lose its very right to exist.

The possibility of condemnation by society provides a striking constraint on decision makers to choose among various alternatives. Indeed, a profit-maximizing decision under competitive market conditions might be a catastrophic choice in light of social responsibility.

A Changed Level of Need.   The movement toward social responsibility can also be explained in terms of Abraham Maslow's hierarchy of needs. Businesses exist to make money. Employees receive part of that money and, with it, they try to meet their basic physical and security needs. In earlier times, society accepted the pollution resulting from manufacturing processes because cleaning up the air and water was too expensive; society could not afford both a clean environment and relatively full employment. Now, as a society, we have perhaps arrived at the point where our lower level needs are largely fulfilled. Now we can afford to allocate resources to cleaning up the air, making cars safe, and reducing the danger level of jobs. We have expectations of fulfilling our social needs and improving the quality of our social existence. These expectations are going to persist until the new needs are fulfilled, or until a severe economic downturn forces us to focus once again on the lower-level needs until the crisis passes.

Socially Responsible Activities

Practice Versus Importance.   The discussion of social responsibility has been general so far. What specific activities do firms and managers view as socially responsible? Table 19-1 lists 15 of them, ranked in order of how many firms in the sample actually *practice* them and in order of *how important* managers believe the activities to be.

TABLE 19-1 Socially Responsible Activities as Seen by Managers

Activity	Rank in Terms of Firms Practicing	Rank in Terms of Managers Considering Activity Among Top Three in Importance
Contributions to education	1	4
Minority hiring	2	1
Ecology	3	2
Minority training	4	3
Arts contributions	5	9
Hard-core hiring	6	12
Hard-core training	7	10
Urban renewal	8	6
Civil rights	9	7
Consumer complaints	10	5
Truth in advertising	11	11
Clear accounting statements	12	15
Fixing product defects	13	8
Guarantees and warranties	14	14
Consumer-oriented label changes	15	13

Source: Henry Eilbirt and I. Robert Parket, "The Current Status of Corporate Social Responsibility," *Business Horizons,* 16 (August 1973), p. 10. Copyright, 1973, by the Foundation for the School of Business at Indiana University. Reprinted by permission.

According to the table, the relationship between how important a manager thinks an activity is and whether the manager's firm actually engages in the activity is close but not identical. For example, contributions to education are the most common socially responsible practice, even though that activity is only fourth in importance. In contrast, dealing with consumer complaints is fifth in importance but only tenth in practice.

This listing indicates activities that are sometimes viewed as socially responsible. However, the question remains whether *not* engaging in these activities is socially *ir*responsible. An organization can have a negative impact on society if it fails to act when it perhaps should.

Social Irresponsibility.   Some corporate activities can clearly be viewed as socially irresponsible. In their book *In the Name of Profit,* Robert L. Heilbroner and others[2] give detailed evidence that some of America's largest corporations have engaged in such practices as knowingly selling defective aircraft

[2]Robert L. Heilbroner et al., *In the Name of Profit* (Garden City, N.Y.: Doubleday, 1972)

brakes to the Air Force, purposely cheapening the product in order to make it wear out sooner, refusing to repair dangerously faulty products, paying off local politicians in order to receive favorable zoning rulings, heavily advertising drugs with known serious side effects, manufacturing cruel antipersonnel weapons (phosphorus mines, pellet bombs, and fire bombs) in the name of patriotism, knowingly emitting dangerous pollutants into our atmosphere and streams, and selling products overseas that have been banned as dangerous in this country. In these instances, pressures to maximize profits took precedence over the vague, ill-defined concept of social responsibility.

SOCIAL RESPONSIBILITY: PRO AND CON

Perhaps it appears obvious that business organizations should be socially responsible. Yet, many people, ranging from a Nobel Prize-winning economist to practicing corporate managers, deny that business has social responsibility. The rest of this chapter will cover the arguments in favor of and against social responsibility.

Business Managers Should Assume Social Responsibility

Success of Business Managers.   A basic argument favoring the assumption of social responsibility by organizations is that the good organizational managers (especially business managers) have passed the market's tests. They have proved that they can get the job done effectively. Rather than continuing to turn social concerns over to ineffective governmental bureaucracies, perhaps we should let proven business managers handle them. The really *good* managers are in business. If society's problems can be better dealt with by good managers, logic suggests recruiting these managers from business.

Business Resources.   Companies like IBM, General Motors, and American Telephone & Telegraph have enormous resources. According to some observers, they make so much money from society that they should use their financial resources to deal with social concerns.

Business Accountability.   Organizations are people, too. Most business and nonprofit organizations have developed ongoing identities. Just as ordinary citizens are held accountable for behavior and activities that must meet certain standards, so should business managers be held accountable. Society permits organizations to exist as legal "persons." Therefore, organizations should behave at least as responsibly as individuals should.

Cleaning up the Mess.   Business managers have caused many social problems. Therefore, they are responsible for helping to clean up those problems.

Long-Run Advantage to Business.   Behaving in a socially responsible way is to the long-run advantage of business managers. Modern social institutions—business and nonbusiness—are highly interdependent. Businesses cannot afford to take a short-run perspective that would damage their long-run relationships with other institutions. An umbrella shop can perhaps get away with charging higher prices during one or two sudden showers. However, customers would recognize the shabby treatment and would react in one or more of several ways. They could refuse to shop at the store, tell their friends about their unfair treatment, picket the shop to discourage other customers, or even encourage the passage of laws controlling umbrella prices. The umbrella shop's short-run profit-maximizing view would probably not lead to its long-run survival. The same would hold true if Ford sells defective Pintos or if Firestone sells defective tires.

Long-run common sense means that the organization may have to pass up some short-run profits in order to maximize long-run profits.

Profitability of Social Responsibility.   Social responsibility may be good business. A computer company may loan an executive to teach computer applications at a struggling small college. This action may be either a clear and noble illustration of socially responsible behavior or a shrewd strategy calculated to maximize long-run profit. Loaning a teacher today may pay off in computer orders down the road when the students graduate and take jobs in which they can order computer equipment.

In a general way, almost anything that the organization does to benefit society may accrue to the organization's long-term benefit. "Society" consists of the organization's customers, employees, associates, neighbors, government, and so forth. Anything the organization can do to improve the prosperity of the larger community and to increase the good will that the community holds toward the organization may eventually work to the organization's economic benefit. This attitude is an ultimate expression of the "systems" philosophy.

The point is that many decisions may be simultaneously altruistic and economically sound. Making the socially responsible decision may ensure the organization's economic validity and continuation. Therefore, the strongest, least contradictory reason for making socially responsible decisions may be that such decisions will maximize long-run profits. In short, *enlightened self-interest* should lead businesses to help the community.

Conserving What We Have.   We all have too much to lose by allowing businesses to ignore their social responsibilities. In terms of culture and wealth creation, our accomplishments are considerable. We do not want business managers to jeopardize our accomplishments by selling dangerous products or polluting the environment.

Avoiding Government Control.   If business managers do not accept their social obligations voluntarily, some other group—probably the government—will make business managers accept them. A powerful incentive toward social responsibility is that government controls (expensive and restrictive for everyone) may be imposed on the firm or industry acting irresponsibly. Organizational leaders know that once control is lost—to the government or to anyone else—getting it back is nearly impossible. Acting in a socially irresponsible manner is one way to lose control.

Ideally, controls are designed and imposed by informed persons who have society's best interests at heart. Actually, they may be imposed either by sincere persons who do not really know much about how business works or by crusaders who do not really *like* business. In either event, business managers lose a flexibility that may be desirable or—to meet the competition—necessary.

Two Trends

Most of these several reasons in favor of social responsibility are derived from one of two trends: the *size* of modern organizations and the *interdependence* of modern social institutions.

Size.   One major attitude involves organizational size. Since many modern organizations have become so large, wealthy, and powerful, their managers should be willing or required to share their good fortune with the society that has made it possible. Therefore, if they wish to remain large, wealthy, and powerful, organizations should willingly provide good jobs, safe and reliable products, and a clean environment. They should also loan executives to schools, hire and train the hard-core unemployed, deposit money in minority banks, give employees released time to work on urban problems, help combat drug abuse and crime, raise the level of public taste, and so on.

Interdependence.   Modern social institutions are increasingly interdependent. Business, labor, and government activities affect everyone. Although we have so far spoken only of the effects that large organizations may have on society, effects in the opposite direction are also possible. That is, nonbusiness organizations have a social responsibility to act appropriately toward the business community as well.

Business Managers Should Not Assume Social Responsibility

The weight of opinion in favor of social responsibility seems overwhelmingly compelling. Many persons consider it self-evident that business managers should protect the consumer, control pollution, hire disadvantaged workers, lend executives to universities as teachers, help set up business systems in city governments, and so on.

Yet the case for social responsibility is not so clear-cut as it might seem. The following section presents several arguments against social responsibility on the part of business managers.

The Business of Business Is Business.   The most basic statement against the assumption of social responsibility by business managers has come from economist and Nobel Prize winner Milton Friedman. He says that the *only* social responsibility of business is "to use its resources and engage in activities designed to increase its profits so long as it stays within the rules of the game, which is to say, engages in open and free competition, without deception or fraud."[3] In brief, the social responsibility of all corporate officials is "to make as much money for their stockholders as possible."[4]

Businesses are economic institutions, designed to produce goods and offer services at a profit. Managers are employees, responsible not to the public interest but to stockholders. When business people drift away from their plain and simple responsibility to stockholders and begin to think in social and political terms about the "public interest," they are moving into inappropriate areas. Businesses exist to make money. Businesses fulfill their social role best by sticking to the mission for which they were formed.

Friedman seems to assume that "society," through its governmental regulations and laws, sets up and enforces the rules of the game independently of the businesses who play the game. In fact, business often affects the rules by exerting influence on legislators and on such regulatory bodies as the Federal Power Commission, Federal Communications Commission, Civil Aeronautics Board, Interstate Commerce Commission, and the Securities and Exchange Commission.

Need for Plurality.   We need multiple, competing social institutions. Our important social and economic achievements have come about because different institutions have competed for people's affections, wealth, time, and commitment. Social pluralism is desirable. Like its economic counterpart, market competition, pluralism encourages institutions to grow and change.

Persons who argue that business managers should have social responsibility are actually asking that business become a more dominant force in our social system. Do we really want to be dominated by business values? No society's values should be dominated by one institution. We need the pluralistic values that the government, colleges and universities, the military, organized religion, business, and all of our major institutions can offer us.

Business Lacks Social Competence.   Business managers are not competent to make decisions in nonbusiness areas. Top managers do not really have their

---

[3]Milton Friedman, *Capitalism and Freedom* (Chicago: University of Chicago Press, 1962), p. 133.

[4]*Ibid.*

hearts in activities that are not for profit. They cannot be properly committed to such activities, probably do not understand the problems, will not assign the best people to them, and will probably not offer these people the necessary support. Business involvement under those conditions will be more harmful than helpful.

If no other institutions existed for dealing with important nonbusiness concerns, then perhaps businesses might be justified in their nonbusiness activity. However, our society has many persons and groups qualified to work on social problems.

Business Lacks Social Authority.   This book has shown that some reasonable relationship must exist between the manager's authority and responsibility. The same holds true for business institutions. To state that business has a social responsibility is to imply that business has at least some social authority. By what authority does business become involved in social matters? If business feels that it does not and should not have authority in a field, it should keep out of that field.

However, if a given social problem is one which a business manager understands and can perhaps solve at a profit, the manager may appropriately take responsibility and assume authority. For example, many managers have hired and trained the hard-core unemployed—to the financial benefit of business and employee, and to society's benefit.

Negative Aggregate Effect.   Since research data are scarce, the effects of "socially responsible" activities by business firms are not easy to measure. However, some evidence suggests that activities having socially beneficial effects if engaged in by a few firms at certain times may have negative aggregate effects if engaged in by many firms at other times.

For example, Table 19-1 showed that managers view philanthropic activities like contributions to education and the arts as socially responsible. Since 1935, the Internal Revenue Code has permitted businesses to deduct up to 5 percent of their pretax income for certain charitable contributions. Corporations have averaged about 1 percent of their profits in contributions, instead of the 5 percent allowed by law.

Studies have shown that corporate philanthropic contributions correlate closely with indicators of business prosperity such as corporate profits, gross national product, unfilled new orders, and capital expenditures on new equipment. When business is good, "socially responsible" contributions increase. When business is bad, these contributions decrease.

An argument can be made that swings in the business cycle are aggravated by such timing of philanthropic activity. Businesses encourage upward swings by contributing most when the economy is already healthy. They encourage (or do nothing to diminish) downward swings by contributing least when the economy is in recession. When philanthropic contributions are probably most needed by educational and arts institutions, they are least available. Therefore, a general recommendation that corporations increase their charitable activity may be poor advice from the standpoint of aggregate economic health.

Competitive Disadvantage.   What if some firms act in a socially responsible way, but not all firms? Those firms acting responsibly then place themselves at a competitive disadvantage when compared to firms refusing to accept social responsibility. Socially responsible firm ABC may be contributing to charity, hiring untrained minority workers, giving employees released time to work on urban renewal projects, and buying much more antipollution equipment than required by law. Firm XYZ, totally without social conscience, may be using surplus funds to make capital improvements and to intensify research and development efforts. Firm XYZ is strengthening its competitive position with respect to firm ABC and may force ABC either to stop being so socially responsible or to go out of business.

Some of these arguments against the assumption of social responsibility by business managers are quite powerful. The closing section of this chapter will summarize the pros and cons of social responsibility and will draw some conclusions.

SUMMARY

After presenting some background on the social responsibility controversy, this chapter described the arguments for and against social responsibility on the part of business managers. Although the chapter concentrated on the extent to which business managers should become involved in socially responsible activities, the same problem exists for managers of many nonbusiness organizations like hospitals, universities, and churches.

These arguments were offered in favor of business being socially responsible.

1. The best managers are in business. Therefore, business managers are best equipped to solve social problems.
2. Business has the resources necessary to solve social problems.
3. A business has many characteristics of a person. Since persons must be socially accountable for their actions, so should businesses be.
4. Business should help solve the social problems it has helped to cause.
5. Social responsibility is to the long-run social advantage of business, as it interacts with other social institutions.
6. Social responsibility is to the long-run financial advantage of business. Enlightened self-interest demands that business managers should be socially responsible.
7. We all want to conserve our nation's culture and wealth. We should not

allow socially irresponsible businesses to jeopardize what we have achieved as a society.

8. Business managers must be socially responsible in order to avoid more government control.

The following arguments were offered against the social responsibility of business managers.

1. Social institutions can best serve society by specializing in the functions for which they are designed. Businesses are designed to serve an economic function, not a social function. The only social responsibility of business managers is to make as much money for stockholders as possible, within the rules established by society.

2. We all benefit from a diversity of institutions, each with its own activities, efforts, and values. Whenever one institution becomes dominant—whether it be the church, the military, or business—society suffers.

3. Business people lack the competence to move outside the business sphere and into the social sphere. Business methods work best when goals can be set, tasks can be identified, and criteria for successful performance can be established. Many social problems, being intangible, political, and emotional, do not lend themselves to this approach.

4. Business people lack the authority to move into the social sphere.

5. Some activities (such as philanthropy) that seem socially responsible when undertaken by a few firms may have a negative effect if undertaken by business firms in the aggregate.

6. The firm that ignores social responsibilities achieves a short-run competitive advantage over the socially responsible firm.

Even if sticking strictly to business were desirable, that course is not possible in our society. All our institutions are adversely affected by our social problems, and so all institutions must be prepared to take on some social responsibilities beyond the functions they are designed to serve. At best each institution can translate social problems into opportunities to fulfill institutional functions. For businesses, social problems can legitimately be tackled if they can be converted into profit-making opportunities.

Today's manager must be concerned about social responsibility. Arguments in favor of social responsibility have greatly influenced attitudes toward the role of business managers in our social system over the past two decades. Regardless of whether a manager agrees or disagrees that businesses must practice social responsibility, that issue has become a part of today's decision-making environment. As such, it must be considered when the manager chooses between alternative solutions to organizational problems.

DISCUSSION QUESTIONS

1. Give your own definition of social responsibility.
2. Do you agree with Judge Stein's decision to allow the A. P. Smith Manufacturing Company to give money to Princeton University? How would you persuade a group of A. P. Smith stockholders that company profits should be used in that way instead of as dividends?
3. Look at Table 19-1. Why do you suppose "contributions to education" is the most frequently practiced socially responsible activity?
4. Give a critique of this argument in favor of the business manager's assuming social responsibility: "America's corporations make so much money from society that they should use their financial resources to solve social problems."
5. How can a sense of social responsiblity help business organizations to avoid more governmental control?
6. Argue against Milton Friedman's position.
7. Do you believe that the socially responsible organization is at a competitive disadvantage when compared to the organization that refuses to accept social responsibility? Explain.
8. To what extent do you think business managers have helped to cause social problems?
9. Do you think business managers have helped to solve more social problems than they have helped to cause?
10. Give several examples of how a business might turn social problems into profit-making opportunities.

SUPER SALES CO.

When Gary Holmes joined the Super sales force, his manager John Rose said, "Gary, we deal with a fast, prosperous, young clientele. You're going to have to do a lot of entertaining. These people drink and they also enjoy smoking cigarettes filled with nondomestic tobacco, if you see what I mean. Is that kind of life going to be a problem for you?"

Holmes assured Rose that he had no strong feelings about drinking or smoking. "I can take it or leave it," he said.

After 6 months on the job, Holmes was an alcoholic and a drug addict. Following many months of rehabilitation, he was pronounced cured. He then brought suit against Super Sales Co., maintaining that his alcoholism and drug addiction were a result of the life he had to lead in order to keep his job with Super.

John Rose did not think that Super had any legal responsibility for Gary's problems. He expected the suit to be thrown out of court. But he wondered about the company's moral responsibility.

THE WILTON STEEL COMPANY

The Wilton Steel Company is a large, multi-division iron and steel manufacturer, incorporated in the early 1900s. As the demand for steel increased in the growing nation, Wilton continuously built new plants when and where they were needed. As the population moved westward, so did the company.

The technology of steel manufacture changed little over the years, so many of the plants resembled each other. The major difference was that the original eastern plants had a firmly entrenched union, a higher paid labor force, higher cost land and facilities, and less efficient equipment. Indeed, some of the older plants were not only fully depreciated (so they represented little tax advantage) but were also the physical structures most needing repairs.

One prime example was Wilton's Belden smelter, located on the banks of Lake Erie. The plant had brought in 600 employees when it was built in 1925, and Wilton had created the company town of Belden, Michigan. As time passed, the company turned the town over to individual ownership. The town's population is now about 25,000, most of whom directly or indirectly get their living from the smelter payroll.

In the late 1970s, the Environmental Protection Agency told the Wilton Steel Company that its Belden smelter was polluting the air and water. Wilton Steel either had to clean up the smelter quickly or close down. The demand for Wilton steel had leveled off because of a recession, and Wilton's price had not been competitive with the price of Japanese steel for some time. Therefore, Wilton had excess steel production capacity in the late 1970s. Wilton management estimated that the cost of cleaning up the old plant would be roughly equal to the cost of building a new plant (at which labor costs would probably be lower). However, Wilton management realized that if the plant closed down, the entire town of Belden, Michigan would close down too.

After hearing about the clean-up order, union officials offered to settle for an extremely reasonable union contract, just to help the company stay. Belden city officials offered to reduce Wilton's property taxes to the minimum. Yet, these measures were not nearly enough to offset the high cost of cleaning up the smelter.

What should Wilton Steel do now?

international management

As world trade approaches $1.2 trillion annually, decision making within international businesses and governmental agencies becomes increasingly important. Many principles of managing and decision making apply equally to both national and international organizations. However, the management of international enterprises—those operating in more than one country—involves two new dimensions: cultural differences and international economic and legal constraints. Therefore, the international manager may have to use different techniques for setting and achieving goals, depending on the organization's location.

This chapter will first comment generally on the international environment. Then, eight cultural factors that may affect decision making will be covered: language, religion, values and beliefs, customs, legal traditions, political traditions, status and social relationships, and material symbols. The chapter's last major section will discuss such economic and legal aspects of international management as personnel, tax, and trade regulations, international laws and agreements, and U.S. government aid to international business.

THE INTERNATIONAL ENVIRONMENT

The Multinational Manager

A major challenge for any manager is to help the organization and its members interact in order to reach their respective goals. This process is enormously complex for Americans to perform in American enterprises. Yet this complexity is small compared to the problems of overseas managers. They must consider the implications of their decisions within a foreign cultural context, and they must also be able to explain their decisions to the main office back home.

For example, consider a manager who makes a decision appropriate to the Marxist philosophy of the communist state in which the subsidiary organization operates. The manager must be able to justify the decision to the home office in America and perhaps also to the right-wing military government of another country in which the parent organization also operates. The situation is complicated enough if the foreign subsidiary is, let us say, simply a relatively independent, self-contained manufacturing operation. If the manufacturing output from country A must then go to countries B, C, and D in the manufacturing chain, the managerial complexities become even greater.

Multinational managers must be able to keep all the organizational units heading in the same direction. People with this unique ability cannot always be found in the host country, so the parent organization may have to transfer executives to the foreign subsidiary and hope they are sensitive and skillful enough to make the pieces come together.

Three factors seem to distinguish multinational business from single-nation business: international risk, multinational conflicts, and national variations.[1] Each factor presents multinational managers with special problems.

International Risk. International risk is of four kinds: financial, political, regulatory, and tax. Financial risk comes about because of the rates at which foreign currencies are exchanged for each other, the different effects of inflation on countries, interest rate fluctuations, and similar matters. Political changes can result in effects ranging from mild nuisance to direct take-over.

Regulatory and tax risks occur simply because regulation and taxation in foreign countries are usually different from those in the home country, and they sometimes change without warning.

Multinational Conflicts. When the owners, employees, customers, and suppliers of an organization may all be of different nationalities, conflicts can result. Some conflicts occur within the firm, as when host-country employees work for foreign owners and managers. Others occur because of differences between the multinational firms and the governments or officials of countries within which they operate.

National Variations. Some countries will allow private enterprises of only limited kinds. For example, most nations do not permit private ownership of utilities, transportation companies, or communications systems. Cultural variations, showing themselves as differences in language, religion, customs, and values, affect the ways in which multinational organizations can operate.

Specific examples of these three factors—international risk, multinational conflicts, and national variations—will be covered later in the chapter.

[1] These factors are taken from Stefan H. Robock, Kenneth Simmonds, and Jack Zwick, *International Business and Multinational Enterprises* (Homewood, Ill: Richard D. Irwin, Inc., 1977), pp. 9–12.

Universality of Decision Making

Although differences exist between nations, managing national organizations and managing international organizations are similar because the decision-making process is essentially the same wherever an organization is located. No matter whether an organization is in Tahiti, China, or the United States, it must still try to reach its goals by choosing the best alternatives from those available. The organization's goals may be expressed in terms of social welfare, economic repression, communal cooperation, or profit maximization. The nature of goal-seeking organizations requires management to pursue these goals by making the choices that use available resources most effectively. In other words, the decision-making process is universal to all cultures and important in all cultures. The five functions about which managers must make decisions—planning, organizing, staffing, directing, and controlling—are also universal to all organizations.

Judgmental Differences. Though the decision-making process does not change from culture to culture, the constraints placed on the manager's ability to choose freely among alternatives do change. Acceptable, ordinary business practices in one country may be illegal in another. For example, kick-backs and bribes are customary in some countries. Should American companies operating in those countries pay off? If they do, they may run the risk of moral condemnation or legal prosecution back home. If they do not, they are at a competitive disadvantage compared to companies that do pay off. Worse yet, the foreign country may accuse them of trying to impose American moral standards. Such dilemmas make managing multinational companies a difficult task.

Managerial Sensitivity to Differences

The decision-making environment, then, becomes the important consideration for international decision makers. Not only must they have those skills required of good managers in the American business environment. They must also be sensitive to the cultural and economic differences existing from nation to nation. The problem is essentially one of communication. The international manager must serve as a linking pin between the parent company, its foreign subsidiary, the home nation, and the host nation.

CULTURAL DIFFERENCES

Figure 20-1 reflects the complexity of the multinational manager's task. The parent organization and its multinational affiliates all have goals, cultural biases, personnel policies, and so forth. These goals, biases, and policies may

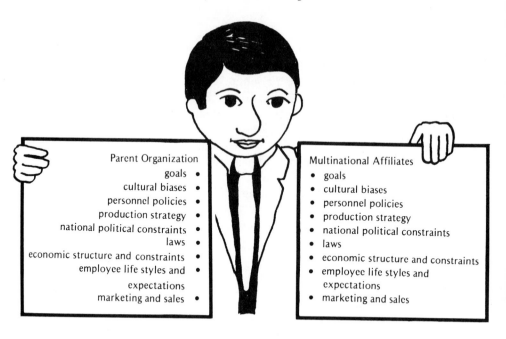

FIG 20-1 The linking-pin function of the international manager.

be different in the setting at home and the setting abroad because of cultural differences. A nation's culture is made up of its language, religion, values and beliefs, customs, legal traditions, political traditions, status and social relationships, and material symbols. This section will show how these cultural elements can affect the multinational manager's freedom to choose among alternatives.

Language

The overseas manager must be able to understand and use the host country's language. Organizations doing business overseas must either select local managers or train American managers in the host country's language. Manager–subordinate communications are as important overseas as they are at home. Just as American workers would be insulted if their manager could not speak English, so too are overseas workers insulted when an American manager not knowing their language is rotated in for a 1-year tour of duty. Nationalistic pride is as strong abroad as it is in the United States. Managers must know the host country's language so they can communicate with employees and also to show their respect for the host country.

Religion

The good decision maker must respect the host country's religion. The manager of an American firm who asks Christian employees to work on Christmas can expect labor–management difficulties. So too should the international manager be sensitive to the importance of the host country's religious holidays.

The manager must also be aware of other religious practices and beliefs. In some countries, people of different religions do not care to associate with each other. An unaware or unthinking manager who mixes such people will have problems. Depending on their religions, people may place high or low value on material possessions, may gain satisfaction in different ways, or may place different values on the worth of the individual. Again, the manager must understand these religious differences and be sensitive to their implications.

Values and Beliefs

The variations in cultural values and beliefs from nation to nation are really quite phenomenal. Many American companies have tried to do business in other countries without considering these variations, with negative results.

One company lost a business opportunity in South America because the company's salesperson wanted to stick strictly to business, rather than doing some of the socializing to which the South American national was accustomed. Another company shipped sewing machines to an emerging nation. The products rusted because the natives drank the lubricating oil as a fertility potion. To avoid such fiascos, the international manager must understand and respect the host country's values and beliefs.

Customs

From one culture to another, vast differences exist in accepted business clothing, the form of greeting, the patterns of interaction between business people, and generally in the way things get done. Although we in our society share a common language and a common cultural heritage, we still make many social blunders. An international manager is in danger of making many more blunders by being unaware of host country customs.

In our country, we may congratulate someone with a pat on the back and "You did a heck of a job." In a different culture, that behavior might represent a termination notice. Americans occasionally shake hands with the left hand, if the right hand is otherwise occupied. In some Arabic countries, that gesture is an extreme insult.

Sitting with the legs crossed is considered rude in Thailand. In some Moslem countries, it is against the law to put your arm around your spouse's shoulders in public. Managers in South America must expect to be embraced repeatedly. In most countries, business acquaintances are entertained in restaurants, not at home. In some countries the bargains are in the basement and the executive suite is on the top floor. In other countries the reverse is true. In Northern Europe, the custom is to arrive before the scheduled time of a business appointment. In Eastern countries, the appointment may often begin an hour or two after it is scheduled. And after showing up late, the Eastern manager may sign a contract just to be polite—with no intention of abiding by it. Since managers cannot and should not change these customs, they must adapt to them.

Legal Traditions

Legal traditions are based on cultural values, as each society codifies its strongly held customs into a formal body of law. International managers must know the host country's laws as they apply to the organization's efforts and must also understand the society's *attitude* toward the law.

Tax Laws. Consider the different attitudes toward tax laws. In countries like the United States, the government relies heavily on a high level of integrity as organizations report their earnings. In other countries, tax agencies know that most organizations keep one set of accounting records for themselves and another set to show the agencies. Organizations and taxation agencies in many countries consider the taxation and reporting system as a game. They try to outsmart each other in ways that U.S. organizations and the Internal Revenue Service would consider illegal or immoral. Managers of American subsidiaries in such countries are placed in the difficult position of making tax reporting decisions based on two different sets of standards. Which rules should they use?

Other Laws. From one society to another, great differences exist in the laws on industrial spying, restraint of trade, safety of drugs, working conditions, the rights of workers, the rights of privacy, truth in advertising, and so on. The international manager's continuing dilemma is how to follow the rules of both the host country and the parent country.

For example, a bribe may be very illegal at home but only slightly illegal (and very expected) abroad. Many foreign governments pay their civil servants poorly, because they know the workers will supplement their incomes with bribes that are viewed as fair payment for services rendered. Should the manager pay the bribe or not?

Political Traditions

Tradition and the Future.   Although many political traditions are reflected in a country's laws, they should also be discussed as a separate cultural factor. A manager planning for the future must consider a country's political traditions. The manager may choose one decision over another, depending on an assessment of the nation's political stability or instability. If a nation has a history of revolutionary governments that take over foreign companies, an American company would have to foresee a very high return on investment and a period of relative political calm before investing much capital in that nation.

The Government and the Governed.   The international manager must always remain aware of how the people in the host country react to their government. If they view the government negatively, they may not work effectively for an organization closely identified with that government. Some political traditions take a casual view of kidnapping executives, terrorist activities, or another country's intervention in the host country's affairs. American organizations must decide whether to risk operations in such uncertain political climates.

Ability of Political Leadership.   How able and willing is the host country's political leadership to work on social and economic problems? Some national leaders seem unconcerned about inflation. To gain votes, some leaders support all labor demands, regardless of their merits. Multinational managers must assess ongoing events in light of political traditions and their own projections about the future.

Status and Social Relationships

Status.   Status and social relationships are another important aspect of each nation's cultural heritage. People have expectations about how other people should behave toward them. People have ways of communicating their relative social positions to each other. These understandings about status affect business and organizational dealings.

In some countries, people simply will not deal with persons of lower status. For example, the president of a trade organization may refuse to do business with a subordinate manager of another organization. In some societies, people deal only with other people who have equal business status. In other societies, social status determines business status.

Social Relationships.   Social relationships can cause trouble for managers unaware of a nation's unique cultural environment. In some social systems, people ignore price and deal only with friends and acquaintances. They feel that friends will not cheat them and that, if a product or service proves unsatisfactory, a friend will make it right. An American chain store operation will not do well in such an environment, despite its lower prices and modern facilities.

Social Status and Managerial Decisions.   Status relationships and social interaction patterns have considerable impact on many managerial decisions. For example, in some parts of the world, managers may have to modify personnel practices in order to prevent employees of different castes from working together—or, worse yet, to keep a lower-caste employee from supervising an employee of higher caste. The current U.S. movement to promote female managers may create problems in the international divisions of multinational corporations. Females are often relegated to low status abroad, and a female executive would be unthinkable in some countries.

Material Symbols

The last culturally based variation to which the multinational manager must be sensitive is material symbols: those objects that represent in a physical way the society's beliefs, attitudes, and values.

Things Represent People.   A society's material culture includes those things, whether computers or totem poles, that the people feel represent themselves. Those objects make the people feel comfortable and secure, while other objects may make them feel uncomfortable and insecure.

Some primitive people cannot comprehend the notion of modern industrial equipment. An organization wanting to hire them in a factory must first change their orientation from the tribe to the factory, and then break down their fear of the factory machinery.

A tractor factory in a foreign country failed because the primitive farmers did not trust something that was not alive. They preferred their animal-powered farm implements.

Variations in Material Culture.   If you move from one part of our own country to another, you will see many differences in material culture. People in the new area will prefer different cars, houses, and clothing. These differences are large enough within our common culture. They are magnified many times when the manager moves out of our culture and into another one. Even so, the American manager in a foreign country must adjust. Developments in communications and the spread of international organizations are perhaps reducing the differences between cultures, but managers must not try to rush the process. When in Rome, not doing as the Romans do can be embarrassing and costly.

ECONOMIC AND LEGAL ASPECTS

In addition to the cultural aspects, the international manager must master the economic and legal aspects of doing business in more than one country. The manager of a firm in Springfield, Massachusetts, doing business solely in southern New England, does not have to be greatly concerned about exchange rates, tariffs, protectionism, the balance of payments, or International Monetary Fund decisions. Although some of these factors may affect the firm's success, they probably do not enter into the manager's decision making.

In contrast, the multinational firm and the managers of international subsidiaries must be concerned with a wide variety of economically based laws and political influences. Cultural differences usually impose *informal* constraints on decision making. Economically based laws and regulations are *formal* constraints on the manager's ability to choose freely among decision alternatives. The most important of these constraints are regulations affecting personnel, taxes, and trade.

Personnel Regulations

Many U.S. firms mistakenly assume that they can manage their people in foreign settings just as they do in the United States. From one country to another, great variations exist in the laws and rules governing union rights, worker rights, layoffs, conditions of employment, and so on. The decision maker must be sensitive to local conditions and must adjust organizational personnel policies to them.

"Yankee Imperialist."   Some organizations think that if a personnel practice works in the United States, it will work anywhere. That mistaken attitude can be especially costly in an unstable political setting, where any foreign firm provides a convenient scapegoat on which to blame difficulties. Many times the cry "Yankee imperialist" is heard just before the host country's government takes over the Yankee subsidiary.

Helping Others.   The universal philosophy of helping those who are helping you may provide some protection against takeovers. The corporate parent that invests time and effort to match its foreign organization with the local culture—in terms of operating practices, personnel training, and development—will probably do well.

Conflicts in Training Expectations.   Many foreign nations want training provided so that their local workers can match the performance (and compensation) of the imported American workers. Yet the American parent company may not have included training costs in its budget. Training costs could add greatly to the expense of doing business, especially in an underdeveloped nation with an unskilled population.

The parent company may see no need to train local workers, preferring to bring in its own people for jobs requiring skills. Indeed, the parent company may have gone abroad originally in order to find cheap, unskilled labor. So the company may be trying to keep its labor costs low by using low-skill, low-expectation, low-cost labor, while the host country exerts pressure on the company to upgrade the status, education, and wage level of local workers. The goals of the host country and the foreign parent obviously conflict.

Enlightened Personnel Development.   Whenever a host country is angry at a U.S. corporation for refusing to train and develop local workers, that corporation's investment in money and time is in danger. Therefore, the visiting company should not be so shortsighted as to deny training and development to local workers. In the United States, even the least enlightened managers do some personnel development, if for no other reason than to keep unions from taking over managerial prerogatives. The parent firms of multinational operations must also recognize that personnel development programs are good business.

Discriminatory Labor Laws.   Managers going abroad should know that many foreign countries have hiring laws that discriminate in favor of local residents. The law may be like Brazil's, which requires that two-thirds of any company's employees be locals and that they receive two-thirds of the company's payroll. Costa Rica and Mexico require that 90 percent of a company's employees be locals. Once hired, local employees in many foreign countries may not easily be dismissed. They keep their jobs unless they are proven thieves, saboteurs, or flagrant insubordinates.

These labor laws are understandable from the host country's point of view. Foreign nations prefer that their own people be hired and trained, so they pass laws designed to have that effect.

Tax and Trade Regulations

American companies in foreign lands often complain that they have to pay more than their fair share of taxes. To the extent that they do, they are at a competitive disadvantage compared to host country firms.

Numerous Taxes.   Organizations operating abroad can expect to pay at least as many different taxes as they pay at home. Among the customary taxes are property taxes, payroll taxes, income taxes, social security taxes, and sales and excise taxes.

Barriers to Trade.   Like tax laws, trade rules and regulations also vary from country to country and reflect each country's political and cultural traditions.

These rules and regulations often make more sense to the country imposing them than to the visiting firm facing them. The Florida citrus grower fails to sympathize with the Japanese government's regulations limiting the importation of foreign citrus fruit. Yet all the Japanese are doing is trying to protect the tangerine-like mikans produced by Japanese citrus farmers.

Similarly, Japanese television manufacturers may be angered by U.S. "antidumping" regulations. Before these regulations were passed, Japanese television manufacturers making more sets than they could sell at home and elsewhere would "dump" them in the United States at prices far below their cost of manufacture. To the Japanese, that was a sensible way of maintaining full employment and making full use of manufacturing capacity in Japanese television plants. United States television manufacturers were understandably unsympathetic to the Japanese problem.

Such trade and tariff barriers exist throughout the world, as nations channel their cultural traditions into formal regulations. These barriers are of three kinds: tariffs, quotas, and exchange controls.

Tariffs. A tariff is a government-imposed tax on goods leaving or—more often—entering a country. These taxes are of two kinds: protective tariffs and revenue tariffs.

A *protective* tariff is designed to keep goods out of a country. The idea is to set the tariff so high that foreign countries cannot afford to make the goods, ship them, and also pay the tariff. These tariffs are obviously designed to protect the home country's manufacturers and farmers from foreign competition. A *revenue* tariff is designed to produce as much income as possible. The tariff is set high enough to produce revenue but not so high as to discourage trade.

By using tariffs, a country can to an extent control the activities of visiting companies. For example, if Antipodes wants to encourage foreign manufacturers to make Antipodal television sets, the government will place a very high protective tariff on imported television sets and a very low tariff on television components. If the labor force and other factors are suitable, that tariff policy encourages foreign companies to come into Antipodes, build plants, import components, and manufacture television sets.

Quotas. A quota is a limit on how much of a given product can be imported. Quotas and protective tariffs have the same purpose: keeping goods out. If the country does not want any importation of a product, it can set the quota at zero.

Quotas can cause problems. For example, if a widget manufacturer persuades the government to impose a very low widget import quota, the manufacturer may be able to price widgets unreasonably high. If a company uses a low-quota item in its manufacturing process and the quota is used up, the company may have to stop producing or ask the government for special treatment.

Regardless of the problems, quotas are a fact of business life, and international managers must learn how to deal with them.

Exchange Controls.   *Exchange* is the process of shifting funds from country to country or from one currency into another. Exchange and capital controls limit the free shifting of funds. A company may have millions of rupees in a Calcutta bank and may need millions of pounds in a London bank, but may be unable to exchange the rupees into pounds if an English or Indian regulation forbids the exchange.

Trade Rules: A Summary.   Trade rules either stimulate or restrict imports or exports. The matrix in Table 20-1 illustrates some regulatory strategies that a host country can use in pursuit of its goals. As political pressures and realities change, so do the rules of trade. The manager stationed in the foreign subsidiary must keep the home office informed so that the parent company can adjust its long-range planning strategy in light of political and economic changes.

TABLE 20-1   Types of Trade Rules, Laws, and Regulations

	Stimulation Strategy	Restriction Strategy

Import	Open trade channels
	Government loans to importers
	Government transportation
	  subsidies
		High tariffs
		Quota restrictions
		Monetary exchange
		  controls

Export	Tax rebates for exporters Vacation ads and trade promotions Loans to foreigners to buy Price subsidies	Exit taxes Monetary policies

Balance of Payments.   An important economic concern for companies operating abroad is the balance of payments issue. Just as the Smiths may look down on the Joneses for living beyond their means, so do companies look down on other companies whose liabilities outweigh their assets. In a similar sense, countries evaluate each other's financial stability as reflected in each country's balance of payments position—the balance between the country's payments made for purchases and payments received for sales.

If a country keeps buying more goods and services in the international market than it sells, it will eventually run out of trading currency for conducting further international business. If a country owes more than it is owed, other countries will hesitate to do business for fear they will not be paid.

Although all nations can borrow some money, each nation—like each

Visa or Master Charge card holder—tends to have a limit beyond which it cannot buy goods without prompt payment. Managers of foreign subsidiaries can perform a valuable function by studying the country and its government, and then reporting developments to the home office that may affect the country's balance of payments position.

International Laws and Agreements

Each country passes laws, regulations, and rules with which the foreign subsidiary manager must be familiar. In addition, a large body of international laws and agreements affects trade between countries.

Treaties. A treaty is an agreement between two governments. Although most treaties are not designed specifically to deal with business matters, they may contain business agreements.

Countries often make individual agreements with each other about tariffs, quotas, and customs procedures. In addition, 99 nations participate in a large and complex international trade pact called the General Agreement on Tariffs and Trade (GATT). The first GATT was signed in 1955. The Tokyo Round of GATT trade talks, begun in 1973, set as a goal the establishment of more liberal, more definite international trade rules by the 1980s. Earlier agreements had reduced the number of tariffs significantly, but many non-tariff barriers (such as arbitrary technical standards for imports and government subsidy of exports) remained. The new GATT, signed in 1979, removed many nontariff trade barriers. At the same time, the United States signed separate agreements with 41 countries.

UN Agencies. Through its agencies, the United Nations influences international trade by encouraging its members to agree on issues and trade standards. Some of these agencies are the Food and Agriculture Organization, the Intergovernmental Maritime Consultative Organization, the International Civil Aviation Organization, the International Telecommunication Union, the Technical Assistance Board, the Universal Postal Union, and the World Meteorological Organization. For international business the most important agency is the United Nations Conference on Trade and Development (UNCTAD).

Fully developed nations are the dominant forces in GATT. They have pressed for free trade because it is generally to their advantage. The dominant forces in UNCTAD are the developing nations. They have felt that their emerging industries need protection, so they have not been as ready to liberalize trade as the GATT member nations have. As a result of UNCTAD's efforts, many developing countries pay reduced tariffs on goods imported from them by the more developed countries.

U.S. Government Aid

In a wide variety of ways, the people and government of the United States have supported the international activities of U.S. corporations. To some extent, this support reflects our desire to help other nations achieve a higher standard of living. We also want to demonstrate our belief in our own economic system by exporting it.

Memberships in International Organizations.   By virtue of its UN membership, the United States holds memberships in the International Bank for Reconstruction and Development (IBRD, often called the World Bank) and the International Monetary Fund (IMF). Since funds are contributed to the IBRD and IMF in proportion to member nation size, the United States is the largest supporter of these economic agencies.

The IBRD or World Bank has 75 member nations and primarily lends money to members (or to private firms in member nations if the government guarantees loan repayment). The World Bank loans hundreds of millions of dollars each year for such projects as electric power, flood control, and iron and steel production. If a government will not guarantee a loan to a private company, a World Bank subsidiary called the International Finance Corporation (IFC) may make the loan. IFC loans are much smaller than World Bank loans. These two agencies make loans very cautiously, so defaults are almost unknown.

The International Monetary Fund is designed to provide short-term funds that member nations might need to keep a reasonable balance of payments. If a country suddenly finds itself in balance-of-payments difficulties, it can draw on the IMF.

Other Financial Aid.   The U.S. government engages in several international programs that benefit American firms. For example, most American foreign aid is *tied* aid, meaning that the aid money sent to a foreign nation can be spent only in the United States. Our exporters receive obvious benefit from this policy.

The Export–Import Bank's function is to help American exporters by enabling foreign firms to make purchases in the United States. The Bank does so by extending credit and by guaranteeing transactions and loans.

The Agency for International Development (AID) also assists American exporters. In addition, AID encourages American firms to make foreign investments. AID will insure American investments abroad against such political and business risks as confiscation, war, and revolution.

SUMMARY

This chapter on international management first described the international environment in general. Although the decision-making process can be used in any nation, environmental differences from one nation to the next often restrict the alternatives available for solving problems.

A major section of the chapter described different aspects of culture to which managers must be sensitive. Eight aspects were presented and their importance for overseas managers discussed: language, religion, values and beliefs, customs, legal traditions, political traditions, status and social relationships, and material symbols. Although a manager's cultural sensitivity may not solve all the foreign subsidiary's problems, it is certainly a prerequisite for designing strategies appropriate to the social system in which the subsidiary operates.

The chapter's last major section described the economic and legal aspects of international management. The host country will often impose personnel and tax regulations that favor local people and businesses. Every international manager must be aware of such trade regulations as tariffs, quotas, and exchange controls that may affect a firm's activities.

The chapter concluded by covering international agreements and organizations such as the General Agreement on Tariffs and Trade, the UN agencies, the World Bank, the International Finance Corporation, and the International Monetary Fund. Also described were two U.S. agencies that assist American multinational firms: the Export–Import Bank and the Agency for International Development.

More and more companies are operating in countries other than their own. Until local people can be trained to take on managerial roles, the home office may have to "export" managers to foreign subsidiaries. If these managers are unskilled, insensitive, ugly Americans, they can quickly damage or destroy valuable international business relationships. If they are sensitive and skilled, they can serve as international linking pins.

DISCUSSION QUESTIONS

1. How do cultural differences affect the multinational manager's freedom to choose among alternatives?
2. The chapter says that the basic principles of decision making can be used anywhere in the world. Do you agree?
3. Discuss the international manager as a linking pin.
4. If you were an American manager in a foreign country where bribes are common, would you pay them? Why or why not?
5. The text has said that a female executive would be unthinkable in some countries. Would you appoint a woman to an important managerial position in such a country?
6. Training expectations of the visiting company and the host country often conflict. What can be done about that problem?
7. Distinguish between a protective tariff and a revenue tariff.

8. Why have tariffs at all?

9. Describe the different ways in which the U.S. government assists international business.

10. "When in Rome, do as the Romans do" is an old saying. To what extent is it good advice for the international manager?

GENERAL MOTORS AND THE COMMUNISTS

In a General Motors annual meeting notice, the company announced that a stockholder planned to introduce the following resolution:

"BE IT RESOLVED BY THE STOCKHOLDERS:

"1. to amend the articles of incorporation by adding, 'The corporation shall avoid business dealings with the Communist countries.'

"2. to recommend the following policy be implemented:

'Any and all direct business dealings and trade relations, and indirect business and trade relations thru intermediaries, between this corporation, its affiliates, or joint ventures (hereinafter referred to as "the corporation") and any of the Communist countries or combination thereof shall not be expanded, shall be decreased to the extent reasonably possible, and shall be terminated as soon as reasonably and legally possible.

'The board of directors shall prepare and deliver to the stockholders within six months of the adoption of this policy, and thereafter in each of this corporation's annual reports, a complete report describing the extent of the corporation's business dealings and trade relations with Communist countries and the actions taken to implement the reduction thereof, provided that no information be divulged that is proscribed by law.

'The term "Communist country" shall mean any of the following countries: Soviet Union, Lithuania, Latvia, Estonia, Poland, East Germany, Czechoslovakia, Hungary, Yugoslavia, Romania, Bulgaria, Albania, Cuba, Red China, North Korea, Mongolia, Macao, Tibet, Vietnam, Laos, and Cambodia.'

"3. to direct this corporation expeditiously to exercise its stockholder rights in the corporations in which it owns stock to cause the adoption of this same three-part proposal in such corporations."

The stockholder has submitted the following statement in support of such resolution:

"We stockholders have the responsibility to counter the unquestionably greatest threat to our cherished human rights: the Communist Bloc regimes. We should not even consider supplying advanced technology, strategic goods, valuable capital investment, or scarce natural resources to these Iron and Bamboo Curtain tyrannies.

"Dealings with them give moral support to imperialistic governments that have enslaved over one billion lives, slaughtered millions of innocent victims, and suppressed rights of religion, migration, life, liberty, and property. The Communists' political intrigues show they cannot be trusted.

"General Motors has paid too much attention to the criticisms of its commercial relations with South Africa. In comparison, the Communist Bloc presents vastly higher dangers to the world community and vastly lower standards of living for its subjects than does South Africa. GM should boycott the Communists first.

"We should instead direct our resources toward our own economy and our Free World allies.

"If you are considering voting against this proposal merely out of an abstract sense of political tolerance, consider further that you would be voting against the best long-run interests of yourself, your family, your corporation, and your free country.

"Your *yes* proxy is exceptionally important!"

How would you vote, and why?

SUDAMERICA COFFEE CO.

Here is part of a report from Sudamerica Coffee Co. manager B. J. Robertson to the home office.

Our labor problems are becoming more severe. Sudamerica has recently passed a law stating that 90 percent of any company's employees must be Sudamericans. The law also requires that at least 70 percent of the payroll must go to Sudamericans.

The new law is a real difficulty for us because our operation is so highly automated. The machinery does just about everything. Actually, we only need 30 people, and they have to be highly skilled. Yet the necessary skills are not available in Sudamerica, so we use skilled employees from back home. We have to hire 270 Sudamericans to fulfill the 90 percent requirement. And almost all of them do nothing but sit around, because there is really nothing for them to do.

We have tried training the brighter Sudamericans, but we have had no luck because they would rather be paid a low wage for doing nothing than to be paid a higher wage for doing something.

The new law has made things too tough for us. I think we should get out of Sudamerica.

management and the future

Predicting the future managerial environment is not easy. In the 1940s and 1950s, who would have predicted that space exploration technology would result in so many new products, industries, and career opportunities? Several decades ago, the nuclear submarine existed only in Jules Verne's novels. As recently as 20 years ago, the hand-held calculator, digital watch, and minicomputer were available only in science fiction.

Other present-day realities such as the militance of public employees in wage contract negotiations, the drop in the birth rate, the incredible number of working wives and mothers, the weakness of the American dollar, and persistent inflation would have been difficult if not impossible to predict with confidence.

Nevertheless, preparing tomorrow's managers today demands prediction, difficult as it is. Changing social and economic forces are already forming tomorrow's challenges and opportunities. How these forces will affect private and public organizations is conjecture, but the preparation for tomorrow must begin today. To get ready for the future, some estimates must be made.

Eight kinds of changes, already underway and expected to continue, provide the framework for this chapter:

1. Increased worker expectations of self-actualization.
2. The changed character of the work force.
3. Increased centralization and bureaucracy.
4. Greater public scrutiny of organizational morality.
5. Less governmental intrusion.
6. Greater recognition of international interdependence.
7. Restructured life styles.
8. Change in the rate of change.

These projected developments will be treated separately, although some of them are related to each other.

INCREASED WORKER EXPECTATIONS
OF SELF-ACTUALIZATION

The first future projection is based on current demands by workers for more enriching experiences in the work situation. Inflation has threatened the jobs of many workers, so this demand has quieted somewhat. If inflation is brought under control, workers will reassert their demand for self-actualization opportunities. For future managers, this demand will mean redesigning jobs to make them more challenging.

Self-Actualization and Bureaucracy

The prediction that workers will want more opportunity for self-actualization conflicts with another prediction to be explained shortly, that bureaucracy will increase. On the one hand, increased bureaucratic rigidity and greater capability of information-processing equipment will diminish initiative, freedom, and decision-making opportunities in lower organizational levels. On the other hand, individuals will demand greater autonomy, responsibility, and on-job satisfaction. Rather than remaining as small cogs in the machinery of mass production, workers may want a return to more craft-oriented jobs in which the product made or service rendered more directly represents their skills.

Middle managers will probably get caught in the squeeze between top management's drive for control (through massive MIS efforts and bureaucratic organizational designs) and worker demands for self-actualization. A possible outcome will be the evolution of craft-type jobs within a bureaucratic structure.

Hospitals.   To some extent, today's hospitals illustrate that outcome. Professional specialists, working in small teams, use their expertise to accomplish individual and organizational goals simultaneously within the hospital's bureaucratic and centrally directed structure. The professional and the hospital understand each other's goals, and the goals are compatible. Therefore, the hospital's managerial structure facilitates and supports individual nurses, doctors, and other professionals as they use their special skills to produce the hospital's product: healthy patients.

Volvo.   The Volvo plant in Kalmar, Sweden, represents an attempt to permit more independence within a bureaucratic structure. Volvo has tried to set up an arrangement to meet worker needs for social interaction, peer recognition, and, to a lesser extent, self-actualization. Volvo has broken up the depersonalized automobile assembly line into segments. Each segment is the responsibility of a small work group. Within these work groups, workers can use their creativity to get the job done, meet their social needs by interacting with other work group members, and achieve status or esteem because the group is small enough to know, appreciate, and informally reward everyone.

Management sets goals (average output required), defines the rules (rate of absenteeism permitted, and so on) and provides tools and equipment. The work group makes decisions about work pace, work hours, breaks, and allocating specific jobs to people. This arrangement allows workers to satisfy their own needs while they are helping the organization to meet its goals.

Worker Distrust. Some research indicates that the typical American worker might find such increased autonomy unnecessary or even unwelcome. Lack of confidence in management's integrity, industry instability, or the impermanence of specific jobs could easily lead workers to concentrate on making as much money as they can *today.* They may feel that they can satisfy their higher-level needs outside of the uncertain organizational setting.

This attitude could be particularly prevalent in organizations characterized by sudden changes, relocations, layoffs, job eliminations, and labor–management strife. The idea that workers have a right to know anything other than their job duties and the size of their pay checks is still revolutionary in many organizations. Not every employer recognizes the advantages of participatory management practices and the human relations philosophy. In such organizations, worker distrust of management is understandable. Trusting a manager or an organization enough to put one's ego into the job requires a new (and probably still uncommon) relationship between management and the worker.

Power Over the Job

In addition to greater job satisfaction, tomorrow's workers will expect more power over the job. If managers want workers to "identify" with the organization, they must be prepared to give up some traditional management rights and powers.

Managerial Prerogatives. Managerial prerogatives are generally believed to include the right to decide when, where and how the job is to be done, and by whom. If managers and workers are to participate jointly and meaningfully in organizational decision processes, some of these traditional prerogatives must be shared. The more participation management offers to encourage greater employee identification with organizational and job goals, the greater must be the sharing of traditional management prerogatives. Otherwise, workers will perceive an offer of "participation" as just another management trick to get more work done for less money.

Power and Human Relations. Many human relations programs have been sold to management as techniques, rather than as a philosophy for making employees co-partners in the attainment of organizational goals through the simultaneous attainment of individual goals. Many managers are skeptical that individual and organizational goals can be meshed. If skeptical managers are told to implement a human relations program, structured by the personnel department and complete with a ten-page manual, their enthusiasm and the payoff to the organization will both be questionable.

"Human relations" is a philosophical position. If managers already hold the position, some tools are available to help them put the belief into practice. Too often, the hope has been that the tools will *generate* the belief within skeptical managers. This confusion of philosophy with tools has probably hampered the long-range development of human relations practices and programs more than any other factor.

Many employees have been on the receiving end of human relations devices used by skeptical managers. They have learned to distrust management's intentions and sincerity with respect to these programs, so a cooperative climate is difficult to create. To encourage employee trust and acceptance, organizations must not only be convinced that the human relations philosphy is best, but they must then convince employees that the organization's managers *are* truly convinced, and not just playing games.

CHANGES IN THE WORK FORCE

The second fundamental influence on the way in which future managers are going to make decisions is the changing nature and composition of the work force itself. Not only are the aspirations and expectations of the workers changing, but their very nature as well.

More Female Workers

The most significant change is perhaps the increase in female workers, particularly female managers. Women have long been members of various organizational work forces and even the majority members of such traditionally female careers as elementary education and nursing. Now women can no longer legally, ethically, politically, or economically be excluded on the mere basis of sex from traditionally male dominated professions and career tracks. Nondiscrimination throughout the organizational hierarchy is essential. Organizations must adapt their informal social structures and formal organizational structures to match this new reality.

Demands for Equal Treatment.   Nearly two-thirds of women now work. However, the problem for organizations is not the *numbers* of women working but what *kinds* of work women want to do. In the past, women workers served as a shock absorber for the economic system. They entered the work force when jobs were plentiful, and they left when jobs got scarce. Consequently, the traditional male head-of-household enjoyed some job security, and the economy's labor supply could be matched to its labor needs. The women making up this flexible labor supply filled low-skill, entry-level positions for the most part. They played the role that other minorities have played (somewhat less willingly) in recent years.

During the 1960s, women began to demand equal pay and opportunity. Their demands were enforced by legislation. They began to do different kinds of work and to assume higher-level responsibilities. They refused to be shunted aside arbitrarily during economic downturns.

Other Demographic Trends

Accompanying the demand by women for equal treatment came three new important demographic trends:

1. The high divorce rate resulted in a large number of single heads-of-household.
2. The low birth rate of the Depression was followed by the high post-World War II birth rate, which was followed in turn by the decreasing birth rate in the 1950s. So the population of persons at certain ages has bulged greatly, while the population of persons at other ages has shrunk greatly.
3. Both males and females are obtaining more formal education in traditionally male careers and professions such as law, engineering, management, and so on.

Unmarried Workers.   The implications of these trends for society as a whole and for management in particular are enormous. First, the increase in full-time women employees requires a rethinking of the traditional and now outmoded differences between careers for men and women. As both sexes engage in the same careers, managers will have to handle problems ranging from redesigning the executive washroom to far more touchy and difficult issues. Can male–female teams be sent away to training schools far from their spouses and families? Can women make insurance collections or sell door-to-door in rough neighborhoods? What about normal job rotation policies? The single head-of-household is usually a divorced person with children. That group probably has family, financial, legal, and social constraints prohibiting free transfer by the organization.

Single males are also increasing in numbers and may create problems for organizations. A single male may have no ties and may be willing and able to move whenever the organization says the word without worrying about wife and family. On the other hand, the very rootlessness of the transient existence required in some jobs may bring about emotional difficulties for the single male. Single workers are going to provide increasing dilemmas for organizational decision makers seeking the best use of personnel resources.

The Population Bulge.   The second demographic reality—the population bulge caused by a high birth rate during the 1940s and 1950s—will continue to create significant problems for managers. The simple fact of fewer births during the Depression of the 1930s has already caused a shortage of top-level, seasoned managers in their forties. Organizations competing for the limited supply of experienced managers have bid up their salaries unrealistically. In contrast, the middle-management level suffers from a surplus of qualified managers born in the 1940s who are now in their thirties. Many capable people, now augmented by minority groups demanding correction of previous discrimination in promotion policies, are all competing vigorously for middle-level positions. In fact, some say that the explosive growth in middle management and professional jobs reflects not an organizational need for these jobs but a demand for them by increased numbers of qualified applicants.

For whatever reason, middle management positions have increased greatly in number. But the declining birth rate of the 1960s and 1970s means that fewer persons will be available to replace these middle managers when they retire early in the twenty-first century. Future decision makers will face difficulties and opportunities arising out of the population bulge.

Education.   The population as a whole is becoming more highly educated and feels entitled to advancement by virtue of acquired education. This third demographic trend will influence future decision makers importantly. During the 1950s and early 1960s, a bachelor's degree was desirable but not essential for the manager. A master's degree was respected, but the benefits of hiring a master's degree holder might not have been viewed as worth the pay premium demanded.

The new trend seems to be that a master's degree is required for more and more general management jobs, both private and public. The cynical observer may insist that requiring an MPA or MBA degree merely represents a personnel department tool to reduce the number of applicants and interviews. Yet, increasingly higher educational levels do seem required for managerial success in an increasingly sophisticated and technically complex world.

As employees become better educated, they expect more money and more fulfilling job content. College graduates now enter the work force with the same arrogance that their fathers felt after graduating from high school and that their forefathers felt when they learned to read. A college degree symbolizes accomplishment in meeting challenges. The graduate immediately feels ready for bigger and better things. No wonder the turnover rate within first jobs is so high. Like marriage, the first job often cannot match expectations. Frustration and dissatisfaction cause an organizational divorce rate that is at least as high as the marital divorce rate.

The challenge for future organizations is to find ways of matching employee expectations with organizational realities. Solid, realistic orientation programs can accomplish this matching in the short run, but redesigning jobs (in terms of job content, responsibilities, and reporting relationships) may be the only practical long-run solution. Decentralized, profit-center organizational forms, with their emphasis on lower-level decision-making responsibility, may represent a solution to the problem.

Nondiscriminatory Selection Practices

Another challenge created by the changed nature of the work force will be how to find legally defensible selection devices, so that promotion practices will be nondiscriminatory. More middle-level managers, knowing their legal rights, will be competing for the relatively small number of senior management jobs. They are going to put more and more heat on organizational promotion practices. Therefore, organizations are going to have to find more effective, more objective ways to evaluate managerial talent. Until now, assessing performance and defining the qualities needed in senior management jobs have been vague sciences, forcing most managers to rely on intuition and highly subjective appraisal practices. Consequently, the public and private organizations of the future must find more objective means for differentiating between good and poor middle-level managers and for specifying more precisely the criteria and characteristics required of top-level managers.

More Staff Professionals.   Based on demographic factors, one additional challenge to future managers will arise because staff professionals in organizations are becoming more numerous. This growth has been caused primarily by the increased complexity of the internal and external organizational environment. In the good old days, money could be borrowed at 3 percent; the government had only minimal interest in equal opportunity, pollution, and competitive practices; technology was simpler; and consumers were satisfied with a few brands of cars, cigarettes, and breakfast cereals. Under those conditions, running a business or a nonprofit organization was relatively straightforward.

Now even the small organization, the local hospital, and the city government need sophisticated professional employees to administer and interpret governmental restrictions, operate computerized information systems, and to purchase, install, maintain, and run complex modern equipment. These developments amplify the perennial problem of how to satisfy professional people and keep them on the payroll.

Retention and Recognition.   The problem sometimes takes the form of the question, "What can you do with good people but turn them into managers?" In the typical pyramidal organizational structure, the normal way to improve in salary and status is to move upward from one level to the next. This progression would entail promoting the best expert, specialist, or professional to the job of managing other experts, specialists, or professionals. But the best salesperson, social worker, computer specialist, or English professor may not make the best manager of other salespersons, social workers, computer specialists, or English professors. Outstanding professionals may be satisfied to remain outstanding professionals and may not even *want* to manage other professionals. How is the organization to retain and recognize such people?

The classical organizational pyramid is sorely taxed as it tries to handle this problem. Career, nonmanagement professionals feel that, as their performance improves and seniority increases, they are entitled to pay and status increases. What is the organization to do with these engineers, data processors, salespeople, accountants, and others? This problem will become intensified in the future.

INCREASING CENTRALIZATION AND BUREAUCRATIZATION

Incompatible Needs

The third change that decision makers must face is the continuing trend toward organizational centralization. This trend was made possible by large-scale computerized information systems and was made necessary as organizations grew through acquisition and merger and as governmental regulation of business and nonbusiness enterprises increased. When this need for organizational control over far-flung, complex activities is set next to the increasing need of organization members for autonomy and self-direction, a dilemma becomes apparent. Since these two needs are incompatible, either one need must give or a reasonable compromise must be found.

Profit Centers.   The most likely compromise is the profit center or return-on-investment center form of decentralized structure, as General Motors deemed appropriate years ago. This structure allows top management to establish profit center goals, objectively evaluate the accomplishment of profit center managers, and still maintain control over the allocation and use of overall organizational resources. The result is a decentralized group of minicompanies, each with a manager who makes decisions and is held accountable for performance. At the same time, top management retains centralized control and direction.

This structure may become very popular in the future as organizations try to avoid the me-too, organization-man, gray-flannel-suit environment that stifles creativity, impedes change, and reduces flexibility. These minicorporations will appeal to managers with the entrepreneurial spirit and human relations ability so necessary for top management success.

Organizations as Good Citizens

As organizations become increasingly large and bureaucratic, they will face greater challenges from society itself. Any large organization must *appear* to be a good citizen, whether it wants to or not. Since the large organization is so visible, its decisions must comply with society's expectations.

Technological Blandness.   While this requirement is in itself a special challenge to organizations, the problems created for them by the feeling that someone is constantly looking over their shoulders is more profound. That problem is the tendency toward cultural and technological *blandness.* When an organization's every action is subject to immediate public scrutiny, the organization may tend to make nothing but least-risk/least-return (or minimax) decisions. If many organizations fall into that pattern, our economic system will lose much dynamism and vibrance. The decision processes of economic organizations will resemble those of many noneconomic institutions; they will be slow, tedious, and conservative.

Although the economic structure will always permit the eventual rise of another Xerox, the nation's need for economic and market stability makes it unlikely that large organizations will provide the dramatic and dynamic upward thrusts that they once did. Instead, they will provide the on-going economic stability that will hopefully prevent prolonged and severe economic downswings. *New* small businesses will probably continue to provide technological daring and competitive opportunities for those possessing the entrepreneurial spirit.

A Two-Tier System

First Tier.   In effect, our economy may well evolve into a two-tier system, requiring two entirely different management personality types and organizational styles. In the first tier would be the governmental and business giants that will fulfill society's basic needs for products (cars, steel, soap), services (welfare, old age and retirement programs, insurance), and stabilization programs (unemployment insurance, Federal Reserve Board, Federal Deposit Insurance Corporation).

Second Tier.   In the other tier will be the economic and social change agents, the people and institutions with a drive toward uniqueness in a world of conformity. This group will develop the new products (like Xerox and Polaroid, which have now moved up to the first tier, and like Bucklin, an innovative car company that has moved down and out of the second tier and into bankruptcy), new services (like condominiums for people who do not want to mow lawns, car and van customizers, and public television), and new social accomplishments (like California's Proposition 13, ERA, and homes for battered wives). These enterprises fall beyond the interests of the first-tier, status quo organizations. They are risky and initially appeal to a small element in society for economic, political, or membership support. Many second-tier members will catch fire and move to the first tier, in a way that roughly parallels the transition from first-generation, entrepreneurial management to second-generation, professional management.

Avoiding Risk.   Large, first-tier organizations shy away from risky projects, sensitive social concerns, and controversial services. They are in the public eye, and they want to avoid governmental regulation or social censure. Enormous amounts of money are invested in large-scale, multi-industry firms. Therefore, these firms will avoid risky projects that could damage their reputations or product images. What large corporation would buy a highly profitable agricultural operation dependent upon migrant farm workers, knowing that the public outcry about deplorable working conditions could endanger profits throughout the rest of the corporation? Picketing or boycotting a small Florida orange grower is more difficult and ineffectual than getting television coverage of a protest march on the large corporation's New York headquarters. Once the orange grove operation is assimilated into the corporate family, the firm may have every intention of eventually improving the working and living conditions of the employees. But the initial entry cost in immediate bad publicity may be too great to risk.

In other words, the risk of public censure, government action, or some other adverse outcome may bring about the ultimate social irresponsibility: an unwillingness to do anything. The only migrant worker worse off than the present one is an unemployed migrant worker, and the increased bureaucratization within larger-scale organizations discourages involvement in such situations. It encourages a no-risk, don't-rock-the-boat, stick-with-the-status-quo philosophy. The declining rate of productivity in our economy and the incredible lack of technological advancement in the older, concentrated, large-scale bureaucracies are perhaps a result of this new public visibility.

GREATER PUBLIC SCRUTINY OF ORGANIZATIONAL MORALITY

Ethical Behavior Demanded

Related to the visibility derived from increased size and centralization is the increased public demand for ethical behavior. This demand began to intensify as business made disturbingly amoral responses to critics during the Viet Nam war era. Then the excesses of political intrigue culminating in the Watergate investigations further focused public attention on our codes of conduct and standards of behavior for all types of organizations.

The public now demands a high level of integrity in its institutions. It backs up these expectations with consumer rights laws, consumer advocate groups, and class action suits. The public demands a car that is safe from serious engineering error, a government that deals impartially with legal offenders, a business that delivers what its advertising promises, and medical personnel who pay for their mistakes.

An Educated Public

Consumers and employees are more highly educated than they used to be. Communications media have learned to uncover and report excesses, deceptions, and illegal behavior. Amorality and immorality are now more likely to be found out and to be very costly. In the past, corporations could justify most actions by saying "business is business." The electronic media and the post-Watergate backlash make that attitude impossible to hold. Managers in public and private institutions cannot afford to ignore the morality of their decisions, products, public statements, advertising, or even their personal behavior without risking adverse effects on themselves and their organizations.

Decisions have moral dimensions, and future managers at *all* levels must keep moral implications in mind. As many top managers have learned too late, even the first-line supervisor can get the organization into serious political and even legal trouble by ignoring the enterprise's moral and ethical dimensions.

DECREASED GOVERNMENTAL REGULATION

The past four decades have seen ever greater regulation by governmental agencies. Yet, even in this age of big government, big business, and big labor—all seeking more, not less, control over the other two—the future growth of government seems less certain today than it has in some time.

California's Proposition 13, restricting local government's power to tax property, has given all governments something to think about. The reaction by Californians may have had such a simple explanation as the economic crunch created for homeowners by the meteoric rise in property values. Yet the situation seems more complex than that.

The Burdens of Regulation

The expenses of being regulated have become extremely burdensome to many persons and groups, especially small businesses. The one-person or two-person shop cannot afford the technical expertise, pollution-control devices, modernized record-keeping equipment, or even the time to fill out all the reports and forms required by the government. Consequently, the choice becomes either sticking to the regulations (and forcing small businesses, farms, and nonprofit organizations to shut down) or revising governmental requirements. If the next few years do not see an outright decrease in governmental intervention, at least a leveling off can be forecast as organizations demand a relaxing of restrictions.

The Government as Referee

The future manager will look back on the decade beginning with the Great Society legislation of the 1960s as a period marked by unprecedented changes in social and economic expectations. Groups that had experienced discrimination sought immediate redress for injustice and instant change in patterns that had existed for centuries. Other groups discovered the perils of environmental pollution and also sought immediate removal of garbage piles that had been accumulating since the industrial revolution. One element of society sought firmer military–industrial linkages to solve the American dilemma of the 1960s: who and what to protect, how, and from whom. In addition, groups outside our country—third world countries, underdeveloped nations, our industrial trading partners, and the oil-producing nations—strained our economic system.

Historically, the government had been a referee in conflicts between different interest groups. During the 1960s and 1970s, government became an advocate of social change. Organizations had to change rapidly to keep pace with an activist government.

Reaction Against Regulation.   However, much of what was needed appears to have been accomplished, and a reaction may be setting in. People, groups, and organizations want government to leave them alone. Government has done its job. It has established the guidelines for redressing social injustice, written corrective regulations, and has refereed the resulting conflicts. The hope and expectation of the people now is that governmental interference will diminish while the new order is being emplaced.

Organizations seem to be saying to government, "Hands off, and we'll try to play fair." If decision makers of the future do not play fair, governmental intervention will again intensify.

GREATER RECOGNITION
OF INTERNATIONAL INTERDEPENDENCE

The 1970s taught us how interdependent the whole world is. The Arabs get angry at Israel, and the price of American gas jumps 20 cents per gallon. The Japanese economy slips, they ship their surplus production to us, and the dollar falls against the yen. Toyotas, Datsuns, and Hondas get more expensive. The Arabs do not want to take a devalued dollar, so the price of gas rises again. Meanwhile, Joe and Mary Smith, with their 10 shares of IBM and $10,000 per year in retirement income, watch in bewilderment as economic downswings diminish the value of one and inflation erodes the purchasing power of the other. The economy is becoming more international all the time.

Politics and Economics

Decisions by the United States have international repercussions, and overseas decisions have repercussions here. In the future, the political ties between countries will become even greater as the ties between economies become tighter. The instantaneous connection of foreign capitals, industries, and banking centers through computer links, communication satellites, and multinational corporate goals will make the world's economies even more interdependent.

Economic forces may eventually overcome the political differences of various nations, as they increasingly recognize and adjust to the international economic community. Present economic alliances among the Western European nations will become stronger, and the awareness of economic interdependence will diminish nationalistic stubbornness. Nations will find it ever more difficult to make war on nations that help them meet payrolls. Woodrow Wilson's dream of one world is still a long way from reality, but international economic interdependencies are taking all of us in that direction.

The manager of the future must be multilingual, perhaps multicultural. Today's manager may think it difficult to relocate from New York to California because of distances, cultural differences, and personal adjustment problems. Moving from Omaha to Belgrade, Paris, Oslo, or Sidney will be even more challenging for tomorrow's manager.

RESTRUCTURED LIFE STYLES

Working Spouses

Changing employee life styles have been an undercurrent theme of several future projections already discussed. These changing life styles also deserve separate and specific consideration because they are going to become a significant constraint on managerial action.

Most employees of the future will have working spouses. That fact will greatly reduce an employer's ability to move employees around the country in today's typical cycle of transfers for training purposes.

Organizational Loyalty?

Commitment to the Organization.   A second changing pattern is the building conflict between the degree of commitment and loyalty that employees are willing to offer and that the firm expects. Large firms encourage their people to associate and identify within the "corporate family," by establishing corporate gyms and social events, and by encouraging the periodic job transfers that make lasting community ties impossible. The trend is for companies to demand more time from their personnel, especially middle and top management. Companies ask people to pay their dues, to show their loyalty by sacrificing their time.

Commitment to Self.   On the other side are the emerging professionals committed to their professions, themselves, their families, and their private lives. The spirit of the 1960s lives on in this vast middle-management group. They want a full life beyond the organizational doorway and resent the increasing demands on their time.

Older, Depression-bred managers were willing to make great sacrifices out of gratitude to their employers. Younger managers have never felt the pain of total economic disintegration nor any deep sense of gratitude to the organization. Older and younger managers may both be willing to work hard for the good of the organization, but for different reasons. Their needs and expectations are not the same at all. They are not even thinking within the same frame of reference.

The upshot is that organizational and employee expectations of employee commitment may continue to diverge as younger employees try to satisfy their needs by engaging in a broad range of life experiences.

Self-Actualization.   New life styles emphasize that people have the right to self-actualization. This right is reflected in many ways, ranging from television commercials to minority group demands for equal treatment. Employees feel entitled to become the best that they can become, and organizations must do their best to help employees be their best. Younger employees are tending to be more egocentric and demanding of their rights and opportunities. This egocentrism may cause problems for managers trying to match organizational needs and goals with employee needs and goals.

Affluence

The Effects of Financial Security.   The general level of affluence will cause employees to look more critically at the compensation and benefit packages offered to them. In addition, working spouses and a tendency to save money have improved the financial status of employees. No longer is the threat of being fired always sufficient to make employees do things they really do not want to do.

The financial security that permits employees to risk being fired, coupled with higher employee expectations and higher ethical standards demanded by society, may usher in a new emphasis on moral decision making within organizations. In this atmosphere, the manager of the future will be coordinating, directing, and motivating new types of people. To succeed, the manager must learn even more about human behavior, interpersonal relationships, and satisfactions derived from the job itself.

The Organizational Pyramid

Not so far in the future will come problems created by the organizational pyramid itself. Pyramidal structure and span of control mean that only a few middle managers can become top managers. Those who do move up must be prepared to deal with the vast number of bright, hard-working, frustrated, discouraged people who do not. Counseling will become increasingly important as organizations try to help maintain the peak performance of employees experiencing middle-age menopause, the stresses of everyday organizational life, organizational stagnation, and strains caused by such social changes as dual career tracks for husband and wife. The high costs of replacing employees with mental disabilities are already being recognized. More and more organizations will realize that implementing successful counseling problems can avoid the expense of discharging or sidetracking problem employees.

Past Rootlessness

One interesting phenomenon that will cause future change is the rootlessness of the past. Over the last several decades, people have been physically and emotionally on the move. We have been a nomadic nation, moving into and out of countless transient suburban neighborhoods. Now people are searching for roots and emotional anchors. This quest can be seen in the researching of family trees, parts of the drug culture and the religious movement, and much of the national introspection reflected in the news media. The value structure emerging out of this wide-scale search for roots and for meaning is going to influence the degree to which employees are willing to commit themselves to organizations.

A Service-Oriented Economy

Finally, increased affluence and changing life styles will accelerate the economic system's tendency to become service oriented. As people gain affluence, they can afford to seek self-expression through individualized attention and specialized service. In many of these services, productivity cannot easily be increased. Face lifts and hair transplants, college degrees, car tune-ups, and haircuts cannot be mass produced. Future decision makers must cope with the increased demand for services that will arise out of increased affluence.

THE RATE OF CHANGE ITSELF

Slowing Down or Speeding Up?

Some say the rate of change is slowing down. This group points to such factors as the depletion of petroleum energy sources and raw material supplies and the need to stand pat for a while in order to clean up the messes that prior generations have left on this "spaceship Earth." Others say the rate of change is speeding up. Change has always occurred at an ever-increasing pace. Change feeds on itself, and each new development leads to several others.

Both positions are logical and have merit, and future managers must prepare for either outcome. Most likely are different rates of change for different parts of the social and economic system.

Technological and Social Change

Technology will continue its rapid rate of change, impelled by additional space exploration and an energy policy that may eventually achieve coherence. However, social change will probably slow down as the social system digests and reaffirms the dramatic changes occurring since the 1954 Brown versus School Board desegregation case. Political change will diminish as the nation continues to absorb the dramatic governmental growth of Lyndon Johnson's Great Society era. International change will be rapid as national economies build more ties and as national political systems recognize reality by cementing those ties politically.

Predicting is an amusing and harmless sport. If enough predictions are made, some will be correct. However, the point of our predictions, of this chapter, and indeed of this book is to prepare decision makers for tomorrow, so they can use the decision-making process to make the best choices among available alternatives.

DISCUSSION QUESTIONS

1. As a manager, how would you try to meet the increased expectations of self-actualization that future workers will have? Or don't you believe they will have such expectations?

2. As a manager of the future, which traditional management prerogatives would you be willing to share with workers wanting more "power over the job"? Which ones would you not be willing to share?

3. What will be the impact on organizations of more female organization members?

4. A bachelor's degree used to be the "union card" for entering a management training program. Now a master's degree is often required. Does that change make sense to you?

5. According to the chapter, the profit center form of decentralized structure will become more popular in the future than it is now. What disadvantages of that form do you see?

6. According to the chapter, our economic system will always permit the eventual rise of another Xerox. Will such a rise be harder or easier in the future?

7. Explain the arguments in favor of decreased governmental regulation in the future.

8. According to the chapter, most employees of the future will have working spouses. Attack or defend that statement.

9. If you moved successfully to the top of the organizational pyramid, how would you deal with the vast numbers of bright, hard-working, frustrated, discouraged people who did not?

10. Is the rate of change slowing down or speeding up?

information resource guide to management topics

Accountants Index	An index of English-language periodicals, books, pamphlets, and government documents in the fields of accounting, auditing, data processing, financial reporting and management, investments, and management and taxation. Entries are listed alphabetically by subject and author. Published by the American Institute of Certified Public Accountants.
American Statistical Index	(Washington, D.C.: Congressional Information Service.) A comprehensive two-part annual index to the statistical publications of the U.S. government. Part 1 includes an index of information, economic, and geographic categories. Part 2 provides abstracts, which are listed by executive departments and independent agencies.
Bibliography of Publications of University Bureaus of Business and Economic Research	(Boulder, Colo.: Business Research Division, University of Colorado.) Issued annually; $7.50. A bibliography of publications by bureaus of business and economic research and by members of the American Assembly of Collegiate Schools of Business that for various reasons do not appear in the traditional library indexes.
Bureau of the Census Catalog of Publications	(Washington, D.C.: U.S. Department of Commerce, Bureau of the Census.) Issued quarterly with monthly supplements and accumulated to an annual volume; $14.40 annually. An index of all available Census Bureau data, publications and unpublished materials. Its main divisions are Publications, Data Files, and Special Tabulations.
Business Periodicals Index	An index of English-language periodicals covering the fields of accounting, advertising and public relations, automation, banking, com-

munications, economics, finance and investments, insurance, labor, management, marketing, taxation, and specific businesses, industries, and trades. All entries are listed alphabetically by subject.

Business Statistics

Provides historical data in table format of economic analysis in such areas as domestic and
foreign trade, commodity prices, general business trends as well as figures on most major
industries, e.g., finance, transportation and
communication, petroleum, coal, textile products, chemical and allied products, etc. Prepared by the Federal Bureau of Economic
Analysis and published biannually.

Dissertation Abstracts International

A monthly compilation of abstracts of doctoral
dissertations submitted by over 310 institutions
in the United States and Canada. Separate indexes are provided for the areas of humanities
and social sciences and the sciences and engineering.

Dun and Bradstreet Directory

Provides information on businesses having a
net worth of more than $1,000,000, such as full
legal name, state of incorporation, headquarters address, telephone number, annual sales,
total employment, line of business, and names
of executives.

Encyclopedia of Business Information Sources, 2nd
edition

(Detroit: Gale Research Company, 1970.) Two
volumes. Edited by Paul Wasserman et al.;
$47.50. A listing of primary subjects of interest
to managerial personnel, with a record of bib-
liographies, directories, handbooks, organizations, periodicals, source books, and other
sources of information on each topic.

Encyclopedia of Management

Contains over 300 comprehensive and authoritative discussions ranging in length from concise half-page entries to discussions of 25 to
30 pages. All entries are fully cross-referenced
with additional sources of information on the
subject provided. Topics include such areas as
group dynamics, labor arbitration, linear programming, patents, and production, planning
and inventory management.

Encyclopedia of Professional Management

(New York: McGraw-Hill Book Co., 1978.)
Edited by Lester Robert Bittel. Purpose is to
provide managers in all kinds of organizations
with (1) clear explanations of fundamental concepts and widely practiced techniques and

(2) specific advice about how to apply them successfully. Scope covers three areas: (1) primary management functions, (2) major business activities, and (3) environmental resources and constraints. Over 250 comprehensive entries contain nearly 2300 specific definitions. Each major entry provides (1) the definition of the underlying principle or concept, (2) application opportunities, techniques, procedures, and examples, (3) an evaluation of the usefulness of the concept or technique, and (4) a list of other information sources.

F & S Index of Corporations and Industries

(Cleveland, Ohio: Predicasts, Inc.) An index that covers company, industry, and product information from more than 750 business-oriented newspapers, financial publications, special reports, and trade magazines. The *F & S Index of Corporations and Industries* provides information about the United States; the *F & S Index of International Industries, Countries, Companies,* covers information on the rest of the world. Information is arranged by SIC number, by company alphabetically, and by company according to SIC groups.

How to Use the Business Library with Sources of Business Information, 4th edition, by H. Webster Johnson

(Cincinnati, Ohio: South-Western Publishing Company, 1972.) $2.80. A guide for learning the use of a business library.

Journal of Economic Literature

(Nashville, Tenn.: American Economic Association.) Subscription joint with *American Economic Review.* Issued quarterly; $34.50 annually, single issues $5. An annotated listing of new books and current periodical articles in economics, finance, management and labor, and trade and industry.

Management Information Guides

(Detroit: Gale Research Company.) $14.50 per volume. A group of bibliographical references to information sources for various business subjects. Each volume includes books, dictionaries, encyclopedias, film strips, government and institutional reports, periodical articles, and recordings on the featured subject. Selected volumes include:

Accounting Information Sources, edited by Rosemary R. Demarest, 1970, 420 pp.

American Economic and Business History Information Sources, edited by Robert W. Lovet, 1971, 323 pp.

Commercial Law Information Sources, edited by Julius J. Marke and Edward J. Bander, 1970, 220 pp.

Communication in Organizations: An Annotated Bibliography and Sourcebook, edited by Robert M. Carter, 1972, 286 pp.

Computers and Data Processing Information Sources, edited by Chester Morrill, Jr., 1969, 275 pp.

Electronics Industries Information Sources, edited by Gretchen R. Randle, 1968, 227 pp.

Ethics in Business Conduct: Selected References from the Record—Problems, Attempted Solutions, Ethics in Business Education, edited by Portia Christian with Richard Hicks, 1970, 156 pp.

Food and Beverage Industries: A Bibliography and Guidebook, edited by Albert C. Vara, 1970, 215 pp.

Insurance Information Sources, edited by Roy Edwin Thomas, 1971, 332 pp.

Investment Information Sources: A Detailed Guide to Selected Sources, edited by James B. Woy, 1970, 231 pp.

National Security Affairs: A Guide to Information Sources, edited by Arthur D. Larson, 1973, 400 pp.

Occupational Safety and Health: A Guide to Information Sources, edited by Theodore P. Peck, 1974, 262 pp.

Public Relations Information Sources, edited by Martha B. Lightwood, 1972, 314 pp.

Public Relations Information Sources, edited by Alice Norton, 1970, 153 pp.

Research in Transportation: Legal/Legislative and Economic Sources and Procedure, edited by Kenneth U. Flood, 1970, 126 pp.

Marketing Information Guide

(Garden City, N.Y.: Hoke Communications, Inc.) Cumulative indexes issued quarterly; $10 annually. An annotated bibliography that shows both source and availability for each item listed.

Monthly Catalogue to U.S. Government Documents

Contains documents that are available through the U.S. Government Printing Office, such as bulletins, reports, laws, pamphlets, and other nonclassified material.

New York Times Index

Provides a classification and summarization of the news published in the pages of the *New York Times* newspaper during the previous year. Items are classified alphabetically by subject, person, and organization. Contains a variety of news of both technical importance and human interest. Published annually.

Psychological Abstracts

Provides nonevaluative summaries of scientific literature in psychology and related areas. Abstracts are drawn from over 800 journals, technical reports, monographs, and other documents. Topics are indexed by subject and author and are approximately 30 to 50 words in length. Published bimonthly and arranged under 17 major classification categories such as psychometrics and statistics, personality, social behavior and interpersonal processes, and applied psychology.

Public Affairs Information Service Bulletin

(New York: Public Affairs Information Service, Inc.) A selective list by subject of the latest books, government documents, pamphlets, periodical articles, and other useful library material relating to economics and public affairs. Emphasis is placed on factual and statistical information.

Readers' Guide to Periodical Literature

A cumulative index to periodicals of general interest published in the United States. Listing is by author and subject matter. Periodicals of particular interst to the field of management are *Dun's Review, Business Week, Fortune, Harvard Business Review,* and *Newsweek.*

Science Citation Index

(Philadelphia: Institute for Scientific Information, Inc.) An international index to authors and sources of literature in agriculture, medicine, science, and technology.

Social Sciences Citation Index

(Philadelphia: Institute for Scientific Information, Inc.) An international index to authors and sources of literature in the social and behavioral sciences.

Sociological Abstracts

International in scope, provides abstracts of articles appearing in approximately 100 publications in the field of sociology. Abstracts are listed under 29 separate subject classifications ranging from methodology and research technology to feminist studies. Also included is a section on complex management organizations. Separate lists are maintained in each volume for author, subject, and periodicals included. Published five times per year in April, June, August, October, and December.

Sources of Business Information, 2nd edition, by Edwin T. Coman, Jr.

(Berkeley and Los Angeles, Calif.: University of California Press, 1964.) $11.00. A guide to reference materials in accounting, advertising, finance, insurance, management, marketing, real estate, statistics, etc. For each field, this work lists bibliographies, periodicals, sources of statistics, business or professional associations, handbooks, and the like.

Standard and Poor's Corporation Records

Provides descriptions and recent new items pertaining to particular businesses. Also included are a listing of the major businesses by industry, bond quality rating for each listed business, and information on recent stock and bond offerings, including mutual funds and foreign bonds.

Statistical Abstracts of the United States

(Washington, D.C.: Superintendent of Documents, U.S. Government Printing Office.) Published annually. Includes vital statistics, census data, and additional sources for more detailed statistical information.

Statistical Yearbook

(New York: United Nations, 1975.) Issued annually; $38 cloth or $30 paper. A body of international statistics on population, agriculture, mining, manufacturing, finance, trade, education, etc. The tables cover a number of years; references to the original sources are included.

Statistics Sources, 4th edition

(Detroit: Gale Research Company, 1974.) Edited by Paul Wasserman et al. $45.00. Designed to locate current statistical data, it includes a subject guide to data on business, educational, financial, industrial, social, and other topics for the United States and selected foreign countries.

Survey of Current Business

(Washington, D.C.: U.S. Department of Commerce, Bureau of Economic Analysis.) Issued monthly; $48.30 annually including a weekly statistical supplement; $3.80 per single copy. The official source for gross national product, national income, and international balance of payments. A survey that brings some 2600 different statistical series up to date in each issue under these headings: general business indicators; commodity prices; construction and real estate; domestic trade; labor force, employment, and earnings; finance; foreign trade of the United States; transportation and communications; and several headings on specific raw material industries.

Wall Street Journal Index

Provides a listing of all news items printed in the *Wall Street Journal* newspaper during the preceding year. Items are listed under two headings: corporate news and general news. Included under the corporate news heading are corporate descriptions, news items pertaining to each corporation listed, and profit and dividend reports.

name index

subject index